The Human Spark

THE
Human Spark

The Science of Human Development

Jerome Kagan

BASIC BOOKS

A MEMBER OF THE PERSEUS BOOKS GROUP

New York

Books published by Basic Books are available at special discounts for bulk purchases
in the United States by corporations, institutions, and other organizations. For more
information, please contact the Special Markets Department at the Perseus Books
Group, 2300 Chestnut Street, Suite 200, Philadelphia, PA 19103, or call (800) 810-4145,
ext. 5000, or e-mail special.markets@perseusbooks.com.

Designed by Timm Bryson

Library of Congress Cataloging-in-Publication Data
Kagan, Jerome.
  The human spark : the science of human development / Jerome Kagan.
    pages cm
  Includes bibliographical references and index.
  ISBN 978-0-465-02982-2 (hardcover)—ISBN 978-0-465-03773-5 (e-book) 1. Child
psychology. 2. Child development. 3. Psychology. I. Title.
  BF721.K155 2013
  155—dc23
                                    2012047558

10 9 8 7 6 5 4 3 2 1

CONTENTS

PREFACE

Social scientists who were trained in American universities during the first half of the twentieth century found it hard to escape the assumptions about human nature that history had bestowed on them. As that century began, large numbers of children from impoverished, illiterate immigrant families living in densely populated neighborhoods were doing poorly in school and disrupting civic harmony. The social scientists' preferred explanation of such facts emphasized the power of experience to create these and other profiles. This unquestioned faith in the malleability of the mind, an idea not yet documented by research, sustained the hope that proper rearing within the family and proper instruction by conscientious teachers in the schools could transform all children into productive citizens.

Only a few decades earlier, many experts had assumed that the less-than-adequate adjustment of the children born to poor immigrants was attributable to inherited biological defects. This pessimistic explanation bothered liberal Americans who, believing in the power of experience to conquer all but the most serious deficiencies, hungered for scientific support of their belief. Freud and the behaviorists supplied the reassurance by announcing that variation in experience could account for most of the variation in children's competences and behaviors. By the 1950s, a large majority of developmental psychologists were certain that the events of early childhood, especially in the home, were the primary determinants of adolescent and adult profiles. Each child's biological features, which the psychologists did not deny, could essentially be ignored.

A rash of unexpected scientific discoveries after 1960 challenged this optimistic position. Stella Chess and Alexander Thomas described the contribution of infant temperaments to later personality at the same time that others were finding evidence for genetic contributions to many talents. These discoveries—combined with the failure to provide convincing evidence that experience alone could create an extremely shy, aggressive, or intellectually impaired child—forced the next cohort of psychologists to acknowledge biology's influence.

I entered graduate school in 1950 committed to the older environmental position but sufficiently receptive to the biological perspective to take advantage of a chance event that led to a personal epiphany. This event occurred during the 1960s, when I visited Guatemala as a member of a team of American scientists charged with evaluating a research proposal on the effects of nutritional supplements on the health and cognitive talents of malnourished children living in poor, rural villages. Following our formal meeting, Robert Klein, the American psychologist who would direct the day-to-day operations of the research, took me to Lake Atitlan in the northwest part of the country. This exquisitely beautiful, cobalt-blue lake at the foot of a volcano was rimmed by a number of villages containing the descendants of Mayan Indians, some living under conditions that had not changed much over the previous two hundred years.

This scene provoked my curiosity about the development of children in this non-Western setting, and I spent my sabbatical year in 1972–1973 observing adults and children in one of the poorest, most isolated villages on the lake. It was there, after several months of study, that I was forced to acknowledge biology's substantial contribution to psychological development through its control of brain maturation—an idea supported by evidence from other laboratories as well. Upon returning to Harvard in the fall of 1973, I devoted much of the work of my own laboratory to the pursuit of this idea.

I summarized my revised views of development in 1984 in *The Nature of the Child*. This book (and its 1994 revision) contained three major themes. The first was that the major changes in behavior over the first few years of life depend on stages of brain maturation. This idea implied the second theme—namely, that the habits and emotions established during the first year might be so seriously altered as to have little influence on the psychological profiles of older adolescents. The third theme was that the human capacity to understand the distinction between right and wrong emerges during the second year. All three ideas, which were tentative twenty-eight years ago, are now firm facts thanks to the efforts of many investigators.

As I was searching for a writing project in the spring of 2011, the idea of revising *The Nature of the Child* pierced consciousness and T.J. Kelleher of Basic Books found this proposal attractive. Upon completing the early drafts of each chapter, I was surprised by the need to recast the arguments and to elaborate three questions that had been less clearly articulated in the 1984 book: What is the expected developmental course for the cognitive talents, motor skills, emotions, beliefs, and moral values that are inherent possibilities in all children? How does variation in experience affect the rates at which these properties develop and the forms they assume? And, finally, what factors determine the variation among children and adults within every community? The present book probes the concepts of morality and emotion more deeply than the original and addresses a concern that was less salient in 1984 but is now widespread: mental illness in children and adolescents. Because this book covers a larger territory than the earlier one, it needed a new title.

Chapter 1 considers the influences of culture and history. Each person's experiences in a particular culture during a particular era select one profile from an envelope of possibilities that existed during the first hours after birth. Human behavior is controlled by features in the local setting and the person's motives and beliefs. On the one hand, children must react to events that threaten their survival or mental serenity. They must do something if attacked and maintain relationships with those supporting them. On the other hand, many actions are provoked by ideas, especially representations of the properties one ought to attain—whether good grades, friends, love, money, a higher status, or greater power.

Events during a historical era within a culture often challenge existing values to produce a generation with different ethical premises. The generation of Americans who came to maturity after 1970 were more tolerant, more skeptical of authority, and less prudish about sexuality than their grandparents.

Chapters 2 and 3 document the biologically based progression of cognitive advances during the first three years. Among the most important advances are the nature of the infant's representations of experience, the enhancement of working memory, and the emergence of the first forms of language, inference, a moral sense, and consciousness.

Developmental scientists are engaged in a lively debate over the similarity between the infant's knowledge and what seem to be similar ideas in adolescents. Some psychologists claim that the infant's understanding of the concepts of number and causality shares important features with thirteen-year-olds' understanding of the corresponding conceptions. I consider the evidence and side with the skeptics.

Chapter 4 considers the complementary influences on development of a variety of factors, including parental practices, identifications with family members and social groups, birth order, size of community, and historical era. I award considerable power to the social class of the child's family. Many psychologists regard a child's class of rearing as a nuisance variable that must be controlled statistically in order to prove the critical influence of a particular experience, whether harsh punishment, abuse, bullying, or maternal illness. Unfortunately, statistically controlling for the consequences of class eliminates an important causal condition because the influence of the unpleasant experiences listed above is diluted in children from more advantaged families. The child's social class represents a large collection of correlated experiences that cannot be removed from the total pattern without affecting the outcome.

The child's identifications with parents, family pedigree, class, and ethnicity—based on shared features and vicarious emotions—have a profound effect on moods and expectations that can last a lifetime. Unfortunately, psychologists have not invented methods that measure these identifications accurately. Hence, I was forced to rely on memoirs and autobiographies to document the emotional consequences of being, for example, the grandchild of an eminent writer or Nazi official. This chapter also considers the popular concept of attachment and concludes that John Bowlby's bold assertion that the quality of an infant's attachment to a parent is a sensitive predictor of the person's later adjustment has not been affirmed.

Chapter 5 deals with two critical puzzles: which properties of early childhood are preserved and whether the child's developmental stage affects the degree of preservation. The evidence implies that most public behaviors show minimal long-term preservation until children reach six or seven years of age. This fact motivates a discussion of the stages of psychological development that are accompanied by new cognitive talents that, in turn, have implications for the preservation of habits and moods.

Human morality has always been a source of deep curiosity. I continue to believe, as I did in 1984, that acquisition of the concepts *right, wrong, good,* and *bad* affect many aspects of the child's behavior. Chapter 6 contains an analysis of the varied meanings of morality as well as a description of the phases that precede the establishment of a more permanent moral position during adolescence. I remain skeptical of the Darwinian notion that human morality is a derivative of the sociability of monkeys and apes. Indeed, I argue that the defining feature of human altruism is a person's intention, whereas the comparable feature in animals is the consequence of an agent's action on another animal. Humans help others because they want to regard themselves as good persons and wish to avoid the unpleasant feeling of guilt that can occur when one is indifferent to the suffering of another. Despite the use of the same word by students of animals and humans, the two meanings of *altruism* are seriously discrepant.

The puzzle surrounding the relation between bodily feelings and human emotional states continues to evade satisfying solutions. Chapter 7 begins with an analysis of the many definitions of *emotion* and claims that the popular emotional words in all languages are interpretations of bodily feelings. These words can be used in the absence of a feeling—and when a feeling is present, words often fail to specify the quality and origin of the feeling and the target of any given behavior.

The extraordinary increase in the diagnoses of mental illnesses in children and adults over the past three decades demanded a chapter on this troublesome fact. Chapter 8 questions the usefulness of contemporary illness categories because they are indifferent to the causes of the symptom; it also discusses why a belief in the effectiveness of a therapy, whether a drug or psychotherapy, is the most essential reason for remission or cure.

The final chapter describes four reasons for the slower progress of the social sciences compared with the biological sciences. One barrier is the habit of relying on single causes and single outcome measures rather than on patterns of causes and outcomes. Too many psychologists studying humans rely solely on questionnaires as evidence. This information does not capture the complexity of the feelings, intentions, and thoughts that the informant's answers purport to describe. Even when single behaviors are measured, the accompanying concepts do not have an unambiguous meaning because most behaviors are the result of more than one condition. To understand the theoretical significance or meaning of a particular behavior, we need additional information, including measurements of the brain and/or bodily activity accompanying a behavior.

Many psychologists are exploiting technical advances in brain measurement such as the electroencephalogram, the magnetic resonance scanner, and the magnetoencephalogram. The results of studies using these machines have taught us the homely truth that two sources of evidence are always better than one. When replies to questionnaires are combined with measures of the brain, investigators have a richer understanding of the meaning of both the verbal statements and the biology.

The lack of attention to processes that account for the striking psychological differences between members of divergent social classes is a second barrier to progress in the social sciences. Many reports document disparities in academic achievement, mental illness, and criminal behavior, but few psychologists try to discover the patina of events that create the private perceptions of one's place in society.

A preference for initiating research guided by an intuitively attractive hypothesis, rather than a puzzling phenomenon, is a third obstruction to progress. Natural scientists usually try to understand the causes of a robust fact. Why do cats beget cats? Why does the moon's position in the sky change throughout each month? Why do only some people come down with a fever during an epidemic? Why does milk sour?

By contrast, social scientists more often begin with a big word, such as *regulation, anxiety,* or *stress,* that originates in an intuition and does not specify the agent, setting, or source of evidence for the concept. The temptation to fall in love with an abstract idea and search for proof of its existence in evidence produced by a single procedure administered in a single setting is a major reason for the slow progress of the social sciences. Many significant discoveries in biology were accidental observations that had not been predicted from existing theory. These include the power of experience to silence a gene, the effect of chronic stress on the integrity of the immune system, the neural bases for knowing one's location in an environment, and the role of the amygdala in states of fear.

The inability to explain how a psychological phenomenon emerges from a brain state is a fourth barrier. The reasons for this state of affairs include a reluctance to acknowledge that a brain state can be the foundation for more than one psychological outcome; the problems trailing heavy reliance on magnetic scanners, which provide too crude an index of psychological processes; and neuroscientists' failure to invent a vocabulary that describes brain profiles.

Despite these problems, there are good reasons to celebrate the substantial progress of the last thirty years. Few psychologists today argue, as many did earlier, that children learn to speak or develop a moral sense through conditioning mechanisms alone. We now recognize the contribution of temperament to personality development and the term *emotion,* which had been viewed as too fuzzy to study, now has a journal with that term as its title. The wall that existed between thought and feeling has been breached.

Most important, many members of the younger cohort are willing to learn the complex technologies needed to measure brain activity, genes, and molecular concentrations in order to evaluate the biological influences on development. The scientific study of children is less than 150 years old. Physics has a 400-year history if we assign its birth to Galileo's discoveries in the early seventeenth century. The first cohorts of natural scientists who followed Galileo had no idea that leptons, quarks, and bosons were the foundations of matter. I hope that readers will regard my interpretation of the hard-won victories of talented investigators as reasonable, readable, and an incentive for reflection. I have tried to be honest, occasionally harshly honest, in my interpretations of the available evidence—though such evidence may be uneven, scattered, and insufficiently firm to insulate many tentative conclusions from further questioning. Every author imagines an audience sitting on a shoulder peeking at the prose being cobbled together. As I composed this manuscript, my imaginary readers were those who had not made up their minds about the defining features of human nature and the forces that transform infants into children, children into adolescents, and adolescents into adults. I hope such readers exist.

I thank Marshall Haith, David Kupfer, Jay Schulkin, and Robert Levine for their critical comments on separate chapters. I am also deeply indebted to Thomas Kelleher for his masterful editing of a draft that I thought was fine. I thank Christine Arden for her excellent copyediting and Moira Dillon for preparing figures.

CHAPTER ONE

Setting the Stage

There are two answers to the question "What does it mean to be human?" On the one hand, most members of the species *Homo sapiens* inherit a brain and body that award them the potential to acquire a set of psychological properties that distinguish them from every other animal. On the other hand, most of these properties, especially varied talents, memories, beliefs, moral standards, and emotions, began as vessels that have to be filled. The potential to learn a language is present in the newborn, but that inherent capacity can result in the acquisition of any of six thousand different languages. The child's cultural setting and historical era "fill" these vessels. The beliefs held by medieval French adults concerning family relationships, sex, and life after death were not shared by thirteenth-century Chinese adults, are not held by contemporary Parisians, and would not be present in the minds of infants from all three settings. A satisfying understanding of how children acquire the habits, skills, emotions, values, and ideas that define their culture has so far evaded us. This book weaves a developmental thread into the larger tapestry we lovingly call human nature.

The mystery of the infant's mind makes it easy to construe early behaviors as confirming whatever assumptions an observer would like to believe. Imagine three women watching a sixteen-week-old infant's facial expressions, directions of gaze, limb movements, and vocalizations. After about twenty minutes of simply watching, one woman, standing behind the infant, moves a mobile constructed from attractively colored toys back and forth in front of the infant's face while all three observers note the vigor of the infant's arm and leg movements and any fretting or crying. When the infant has calmed down, the second woman places a drop of sugar water on the infant's tongue, waits a few minutes, and then places a drop of lemon juice on the tongue while all three observers note any change in facial expression. The third woman then looks down at the infant and—in sequence—smiles, frowns, says a few words, and finally gently caresses the infant's forehead. When the three women share what they believe the infant felt, perceived, or thought during the past forty minutes, they discover that they arrived at dissimilar impressions.

The ambiguity of infant behaviors, which we might compare to the facial expression on the Mona Lisa, frustrates those who study development. Are infants born without ideas, or do they possess certain core understandings of the world? Do they have a self? Are they biased toward selfish or caring behavior? Are they consciously aware of events around them? Although the answers to these questions are being debated, one truth seems relatively certain. All children, excluding the small number with serious compromises in brain function, have the potential to acquire a large number of talents, beliefs, habits, values, and emotions. The family and the local culture select for elaboration those properties that are likely to protect the child from harm and allow the adult to enjoy respect and acceptance from a majority in the society.

The practices of Mayan Indian mothers in small, isolated villages in northwest Guatemala provide an example of cultural selection. Mayan parents believe that infants during the first year are vulnerable to being harmed by the stares of strangers. The gaze of a man wet with perspiration from a day's work is exceptionally dangerous. Mothers protect their infants by wrapping them tightly and placing them in a hammock in a dark region at the back of the hut where, except for times when they are nursing, the infants remain for most of the first year. As a result, these one-year-olds are pale, listless, and display a motor and psychological profile that lags behind most of their counterparts elsewhere in the world. After their first birthday, however, mothers no longer consider them vulnerable and they are allowed to leave the hut to play with objects and other children. By their third birthday they have developed the basic motor skills and psychological talents that are inherent in the biology of all three-year-olds.

A tribe residing in an isolated region of New Guinea holds the rarer belief that all male infants are born sterile. Because these boys must eventually become fathers, the society invented a ritual to guarantee their future fertility. When a group of boys is within a few years of puberty, the older men of the village take them to a secluded spot, arrange the boys in a circle, and march around them playing flutes. From that day forward until late adolescence, but before they marry, the boys perform fellatio on the unmarried older adolescent boys in order to acquire the seed they need to become fathers. Once these boys become older adolescents, the fellatio ceases; when they marry and sire children, they affirm the truth of the culture's premise.[1]

Nineteenth-century Americans were convinced that infants were born with an instinct for freedom and individualism that, acting together, facilitated their society's ascent toward a state of perfection. A faith in the inevitability of a progression from less to more mature is present in the writings of the three major Western theorists of development: Freud, Erikson, and Piaget all posited a sequence of developmental stages through which children ascended to more satisfying, creative, or rational states. Adolescents do reason and regulate emotion more effectively than infants, but they are also more often angry, suspicious, deceitful, depressed, and anxious. Psychological development should be seen as a sequence of additions, losses, and transformations in which new traits emerge, no-longer-useful ones are discarded, and some remnants of earlier phases are retained as elements in new patterns. A stairway to paradise is a poor metaphor for development.

Far Eastern cultures, by contrast, regarded nature and society as following cycles in which benevolent eras alternated with intervals of adversity. The cyclical advances and retreats of glaciers throughout Earth's long history provide an example from geology. The creative Greek and Roman societies were replaced by the Dark Ages, which, in turn, were followed by the advances of the medieval era.

Reflection on the societies that gave rise to important inventions during different historical periods supports a cyclical view. China and the Mediterranean basin fostered the most significant inventions during the 5,000 years before the modern era. Europe became dominant over the next 1,800 years, as did the United States during the past two centuries. It is obvious that the features of a cultural setting that make creative ideas and products more probable cycle over time and place. Application of a cyclical conception to human development implies that each stage is marked by specific talents, pleasures, and understandings and that no stage is inherently superior to another.

Although major transformations of beliefs and practices usually occur over long periods of time, important changes can occur in one or two generations. For example, Carl Degler notes that between 1760 and 1820 a majority of Americans adopted three new attitudes: (1) young adults were allowed to use sexual attraction as a basis for choosing a marital partner, (2) wives possessed moral authority in the home, and (3) rearing children was the mother's major responsibility.[2]

The Mayan town of San Pedro, located on the side of a volcano bordering Lake Atitlan in northwest Guatemala, witnessed an equally rapid change in values: today, most youths complete at least twelve years of education, and men whose fathers, grandfathers, and great-grandfathers had been farmers are now plumbers, accountants, dentists, or lawyers using the Internet.[3] I studied the nearby smaller, poorer village of San Marcos in 1972, when it had no foreigners, no running water or electricity, and minimal communication with the outside world. When my wife and I returned in 2008, we were surprised to learn that the village now had a small hotel, an Internet café, a yoga center, and an agency selling tickets to tourists who wanted the delight of a moonlight cruise on the lake.

China experienced three radical transformations during the twentieth century. In 1901, as an autonomous, mainly rural society controlled by an empress, the country suffered the humiliation of defeat and subjugation by European powers who occupied many of its large cities. Fifty years later, Mao Zedong transformed what was then a hierarchical society of peasants exploited by a small group of landlords into a despotic communist state. The third change, accomplished in only forty years, introduced a capitalist economy that celebrated a combination of individualism, materialism, corruption, and cynicism that was a novelty in this ancient society. It took less than half a century to transform China from an economically impoverished society into one of the economic powerhouses of the modern world.

Similarly, Luther's sixteenth-century critique of the Church had a profound effect on the values of succeeding generations. By questioning the sacredness of God's representatives on Earth, the Protestant Reformation legitimized a skeptical posture toward all authority and affirmed the right of a single individual to question the proclamations of those in positions of power. Two centuries later, when industrialization came to England and Scotland, the writings of social philosopher Adam Smith enhanced the primacy of the individual. The declining power of the Church, the rise of the nation-state, discoveries in natural science, industrialization, and democratically elected legislatures coalesced around a question that most cultures had never considered—namely, how much personal freedom is a person entitled to?

Smith thought he saw a harmonious balance in nature and assumed that a similar balance applied to a marketplace model of the economy. This intuition persuaded him that a society would prosper if each person placed his or her welfare and pleasures ahead of the needs of others. Emma Rothschild of Cambridge University invites us to reflect on the fact that Smith's suggestions in *The Wealth of Nations* were motivated primarily by his concern with the large number of poor English families who were superstitious victims of political and economic decisions that led to exorbitantly high food prices they could not afford.[4] Smith assumed that a laissez-faire economy would free these families from the burdens of both poverty and superstition.

The United States has the laissez-faire economy that Smith favored. Nonetheless, more than 40 million poor Americans go to bed hungry each night, an equally large number believe in astrology, and the economic disaster of 2007–2009 was brought on by the self-interest of a small number of Americans who either persuaded poor families to assume mortgage payments they could not meet or sold bundled mortgages they knew were risky investments to individuals who assumed they were safe.

The authors of the Declaration of Independence married the Enlightenment assumption that the individual ought to be the primary beneficiary of personal and governmental decisions with the premise that no person, no matter how elite his or her family, was entitled to more privilege or dignity than any other. The former assumption, which Plato and Hobbes would have rejected, has become a fundamental tenet in a large number of the world's societies.

The changing historical narrative also influences the phenomena that scholars select as important puzzles to resolve. The nature of God and an immaterial soul were the seminal mysteries that European philosophers brooded on during the medieval era. Seven hundred years later, the properties of nature began to compete with the mystery of God and, as a result, uncertainty began to replace a faith in certain truths. A century later, curiosity centered on the essential characteristics of human nature. And by the end of the nineteenth century, the enigma of human psychological development became a target of scientific curiosity for the first time.

The knowledge, talents, traits, and values that children need in order to thrive in their cultural setting require a combination of biology and experience in order to be actualized. Both processes are responsible for the obvious variation in traits and talents among children in any community. The child's biologically based temperaments make a significant contribution to some of this variation. *Temperament* is defined as a proclivity for particular actions and feelings that originate in the chemistry and anatomy of the brain. Adults who have always wakened early and gone to sleep by 10 or 11 in the evening—known as "larks"—have a happier disposition than the "owls" who wake late and go to bed late. These two types were probably born with different temperaments.

Children born in a region of the world that has been reproductively isolated for at least ten thousand years, such as China, Japan, Scandinavia, Southern Europe, India, South America, and Africa, possess unique genomes that can be the foundation of distinctive temperaments. Any two randomly selected pair of humans differ in about 3 million of the bases that are the components of genes. (The sequences of DNA called genes are composed of four molecules called bases.) Although 3 million is a small proportion of the 6.4 billion bases (3.2 billion base pairs), it is large enough to produce a large number of temperamental biases.

The behavioral signs of a temperamental bias in the first year include ease of becoming distressed or active to hunger, cold, pain, or unexpected events; ease of being soothed; ease of alerting to varied events; duration of attention following an initial alerting; and usual mood, often revealed in babbling and smiles or crying and facial frowns. Inherited neurochemical patterns that affect brain activity are likely to be the foundations of most temperamental biases, but scientists do not yet understand the relation between the biology and the behaviors. Hence, behaviors define temperaments at present. One day, however, a child's biological properties will be added to the behaviors.

Rather than guarantee the development of a particular personality, a temperament can only nudge a child in a particular direction. Relaxed four-month-olds who smile frequently and rarely cry inherit a temperament my colleagues and I call *low-reactivity*. Though unlikely to become shy, anxious, vigilant adolescents, these infants can acquire a large number of different personalities. Nathan Fox and his colleagues at the University of Maryland are studying infants they call *exuberant* because they display vigorous motor activity, babbling, and smiling, but no crying, when they encounter unfamiliar events.[5] Infants with this temperament are likely to become sociable and willing to take risks when they are older children. By contrast, infants whose profile is characterized by crying and vigorous motor activity, but little smiling, when exposed to unfamiliar events, are likely to become shy, timid children who are susceptible to high levels of guilt following a misdemeanor. If we assume, hypothetically, that humans have the potential to acquire any of a thousand adult psychological profiles, the possession of a particular temperament lops off a proportion of those possibilities, say two hundred, leaving the child with eight hundred potential personalities.

The child's history of experiences, initially within the family and later with peers and adults, imposes a second set of limitations on the talents, traits, and values an adolescent might possess. Consider two girls—Alice and Mary—born with the same low-reactive temperament favoring a relaxed, minimally irritable mood during the first year followed by a sociable, bold personality during the childhood years. Alice is the first-born child of educated, affectionate parents who encourage their daughter's verbal abilities and have the money to send her to a private school. Mary, born to parents who did not graduate high school, lives with two older brothers in a densely populated neighborhood of a large city with a high crime rate and poor schools. Alice is likely to attend one of America's better colleges and pursue a career in medicine, business, law, science, or politics. Mary has a moderately high probability of dropping out of high school, becoming pregnant before she is seventeen, developing an addiction to drugs or alcohol, and struggling as a single parent in a low-paying job. The two girls in this hypothetical comparison, who began life with the same temperament and behaved similarly during their first few years, grew apart during childhood and adolescence because of their different life circumstances.

This narrative has been less popular than one based on the premise that the traits that emerge during the first two years resist change. The latter view, called infant determinism, received a boost when Charles Darwin—brooding about the history of life forms in the quiet English village of Down in the middle of the nineteenth century—published his thesis on evolution and, a dozen years later, a book defending his belief that humans are only quantitatively different from apes. Darwin wanted to persuade readers that the traits we regard as uniquely human, especially language, reason, and morality, have their origin in similar processes present in higher mammals. This bold idea influenced every discipline in the life sciences but had an especially profound effect on scholars studying psychological development. If the emergence of modern humans was only one chapter in a seamless narrative that began about 3 billion years ago with the first living cell, it was reasonable to assume a comparable continuity in the development of each person's psychological traits. If this were true, then the talents and personalities of twenty-year-olds probably had a partial origin in their biology and the experiences of early childhood.

This intuition motivated scientists to look for early signs of adult traits. One nineteenth-century expert declared that the origin of adult greed could be traced

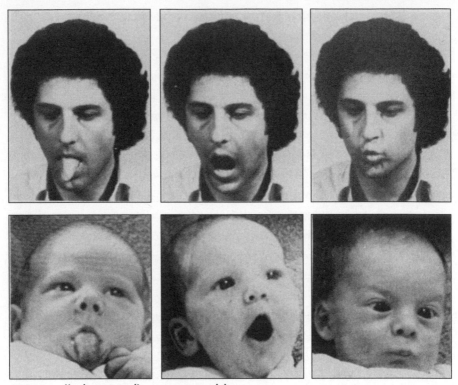

FIGURE 1.1   Newborn protruding tongue to an adult

to the observation that two-week-olds reflexively grasped a pencil placed in their palm. This intuition remains popular. Two contemporary American psychologists announced that two-day-old infants were capable of imitation because they protruded their tongue when an adult, standing close to them, stuck out his tongue.[6] (See Figure 1.1.) Psychologists who were skeptical of this conjecture discovered later that two-day-olds protrude their tongue in response to any small, slim object moving back and forth close to their face (a pencil, for example), because infants use their tongue to explore the environment. Hence, what seemed to be an act of willful imitation was probably a biologically prepared reflex bearing no relation to the imitations seen in ten-month-olds.

The discontinuities in human development are analogous to equally salient discontinuities in evolution. The emergence of the first animal with a backbone, about 530 million years ago, and the appearance of the first mammal, about 200 million years ago, are discontinuous with the life forms that had existed before. These evolutionary changes were due to chance mutations and alterations in the ecology. Psychological discontinuities, by contrast, are the result of maturation of the brain, unpredictable historical events that affect an entire population, or unusual experiences that affect a particular individual.

Unfortunately, the reciprocal influences among each individual's biology, the groups in which he or she participates, and local social conditions are being ignored. The media's frequent references to the extraordinary discoveries in genetics and neuroscience have persuaded the public that biological processes have a greater influence on a child's psychological properties than family practices and local circumstances. Quite by chance, the extraordinary biological discoveries occurred at the same time that inequalities in income and education in America and Europe were widening. Youths growing up in families occupying the bottom 25 percent of the income distribution were finding it harder than their grandparents to ascend in status despite their willingness to work. The gap in academic proficiencies between poor and affluent youths was significantly larger in 2012 than in the decades before World War II. One reason was that the quality of the public schools in urban areas, which had provided a path to status mobility in the mid-twentieth century, began to erode partly because talented women could now choose any vocation they wished. Sex-role stereotypes no longer limited them to a career as a teacher, nurse, or secretary.

At present, Americans and Europeans can select one of two explanations for the thicker barrier to status mobility. They can blame neglectful or uninformed parents and indifferent or poorly trained teachers. Or they may conclude that children who have difficulty learning to read or inhibiting impulsive acts of aggression were born with genes that compromised the brain sites that contribute to language and the regulation of impulsive behavior.

A psychologist who suggests that poor fifth-grade children with deficient reading skills and a disobedient inclination had indifferent parents who neither read to them nor taught them the control of impulses might be accused of holding a prejudiced attitude toward the poor, especially if the parents belonged to a minority group. And a social scientist who argues that the federal government has an obligation to do more to help disadvantaged families might generate resistance among those worried about the federal deficit. In short, blaming defective genes that lowered a child's intelligence or contributed to impulsivity is a more politically correct solution. This explanation has become popular, despite the fact that scientists have not discovered the genes that contribute to variation in intelligence or impulsivity. I suspect that investigators will never discover these genes because concepts like intelligence and impulsivity are simply too broad and heterogeneous to be the kinds of phenomena that are linked to a particular collection of genes. When scientists do discover how nature carved up the domain of human properties, they will find that neither intelligence nor impulsivity are in the collection.

The historical era often has a significant influence on a scientist's answer to the question: "What conditions are responsible for the variation in traits among children and adults?" When Freud's influence was strong, from about 1910 to 1960, psychologists studied the untoward consequences of early weaning, thumb-sucking, and harsh toilet training. When many fathers were serving in the armed forces during World War II, scientists studied the effects of fathers' absence on young children. When divorce rates rose after the war, scholars probed the effects of parental separation. When large numbers of mothers joined the work force and placed their young children in day care centers, psychologists worried about the deleterious effects of surrogate care.

History also affects the kinds of evidence that scientists are likely to use in arriving at conclusions. Readers untrained in the sciences do not appreciate that the meaning, and therefore the validity, of every scientific conclusion depends on the nature and source of the evidence. Scientists cannot separate what they think they know from their reasons for knowing. The age of dogs, for example, varies with the sources of evidence. Fossil data imply that the first dogs evolved from wolves about 12,000 years ago whereas recent studies of the DNA of various species imply that the first dogs appeared about 135,000 years ago. A difference of 123,000 years is not trivial.

Scientists and nonscientists alike rely on three major sources of evidence as the basis for their beliefs. Most inferences originate in perception—for example, seeing an apple fall from a branch. Language—reading that gravity causes an apple to fall—is a second source of evidence. Mathematical statements comprise a third source: the equations of general relativity imply that the mass of an object distorts the shape of space-time to produce the phenomenon of gravity. Many semantic and mathematical concepts—including truth and infinity—cannot be perceived. And some perceptions—say, a richly colored sunset over a mountain—cannot be described with words or equations. The scientist's inability to measure a person's private feelings pleased the poet e. e. cummings, who wrote:

> *Who pays any attention*
> *To the syntax of things*
> *Will never wholly kiss you.*

Psychologists base their conclusions on behaviors, biological reactions, and verbal descriptions. But these sources of evidence do not always invite the same conclusions. When psychologists write that children reared by depressed mothers are more anxious than those growing up with nondepressed mothers, the evidence usually comes from questionnaires or interviews rather than from direct observations of the parents and children. The meaning of the statement "Depressed mothers are likely to have anxious children," when based on direct observations, is not synonymous with the meaning of the same sentence when based on replies to questionnaires. Young children who are described as shy by their mothers are not always shy when observed with a stranger; many adolescents who deny being shy on a questionnaire behave shyly when they are observed interacting with another, and many who say they are shy show no evidence of this trait in their behavior.

Despite these inconsistencies, verbal descriptions of traits dominate research in personality, mental illness, and social psychology. Unfortunately, a person's words provide an incomplete and less-than-faithful index of their knowledge, behaviors, and emotions. One reason is that psychologists often ask individuals to evaluate a trait in ways that might not correspond to the person's style. For example, psychologists ask adults to assess the strength of a feeling or attitude on a continuous scale— say, from 1 to 10, as in "In general, how do you feel about your life these days? Please rate your judgment on a scale from 1, indicating very dissatisfied, to 10, meaning very satisfied." I suspect that many adults do not ask themselves that question and those who do have a two-category answer—either "satisfied" or "dissatisfied." Very few decide that they are six-tenths satisfied. The form of the question forces answers that are not always faithful to the person's private judgment.

Niels Bohr argued in the 1920s that the inference drawn from an observation cannot be separated from the procedure that produced it. Because the source of the observation and the evidence form a seamless whole, different procedures can lead to different conclusions about the presence or absence of a psychological property. This explains why many studies find that a friend's evaluation of a person is often different from, and occasionally more accurate than, the person's own judgment.

White residents of London who forcefully deny any prejudice against Muslims respond more quickly to the word *Muslim* after seeing the word *terrorist* on a monitor than they do to the word *pacifist*. Some psychologists regard this observation as meaning that the Londoners are prejudiced against Muslims, despite their strong verbal denial of bigotry. Bohr's principle is helpful in this example. Psychologists cannot separate a conclusion about a person's attitude toward Muslims from the procedure that produced the evidence. The reaction-time measure is not a more accurate index of prejudice than the verbal reply. Rather, it is simply a different answer to the question of whether the person is prejudiced against Muslims.

A second reason for the disconnect between verbal descriptions and direct observations of behavior is that most respondents want to give logically consistent replies to a series of questions. Behaviors are not bound by a need to be consistent, however. Adolescents who report giving money to a friend in need may be tempted to deny anger toward the friend. Those who feel ambivalent toward a friend to whom they gave money might show that ambivalence in their actions but not in their verbal answers.

A third reason is that most research on human personality, morality, and emotion is conducted in English by American scientists on American participants, usually college students. This is unfortunate because most English words naming psychological states do not specify the origin of the state or the target person to whom a behavior is directed. A parent who reports on a questionnaire that "My son is aggressive" does not reveal the reason for the aggression, the setting in which it occurred, or whether she observed her child hit other children or was told about these actions by a teacher. The words in most languages try to balance a need to be informative with a desire to avoid complexity. The word *aunt,* for example, does not specify whether the woman comes from the husband's or the wife's family. Similarly, the term *anxious* implies an uncomfortable state but does not specify the source or the intensity of the feeling.

Other languages do include words that specify the cause of an emotion—for example, the difference between the anger evoked by a personal mistake and the anger that arises when the same individual is insulted. The ancient Greeks had separate words for each of the five emotions created by: anger over being slighted by another, anger over making a mistake, chronic resentment, justified anger, and the anger of one of the gods. By contrast, the English words *mad, angry, peeved,* and *irritated* are silent on the cause of the emotion or the target of an action.

The desire to describe the self in a desirable light is a fourth reason to question the accuracy of a verbal description. Most descriptions of self are influenced by what individuals regard as good traits. The typical respondent is reluctant to admit to actions, traits, or feelings that might be embarrassing or evoke a critical appraisal from an examiner. This frame of mind leads most respondents to admit to personality traits that reflect their understanding of the desirable traits possessed by the typical person in their region or society. Each respondent possesses a notion of the ideal form of a particular trait, much as a painter has an image of the perfect cloud. Most respondents have difficulty inhibiting a tendency to describe themselves in terms that approach their understanding of the ideal.

Because the regions of the United States vary in income, education, population density, proportion of minority adults, political affiliation, and style of social interaction, it is not surprising that the residents of different regions give slightly different replies to personality questionnaires. For example, many residents of San Francisco think of themselves as extraverted and would describe themselves on questionnaires as more extraverted than residents of Augusta, Maine.

In a study performed at Cambridge University, Peter Rentfrow and his colleagues gathered the self-descriptions of more than 500,000 young adults (most of whom were white and middle class) on the popular personality questionnaire known as the *Big Five* because it measures five personality dimensions: openness to new ideas, conscientiousness, extraversion, agreeableness, and neuroticism.[7] Respondents from the Midwest and Plains states described themselves as high on extraversion and low on openness to new ideas; New England residents were high on neuroticism and openness to new ideas but low on agreeableness and conscientiousness. These findings suggest that individuals are influenced by the ambience of the region in which they live. For example, residents of Massachusetts would find it more difficult than those living in North Dakota to admit to a stranger that they are not open to the idea of gay marriage because opposition to this idea is inconsistent with the values of many who live in New England.

My colleagues and I once studied a small group of boys from several local schools whose classmates and teachers unanimously agreed were unpopular and poor readers. Close to one-half of these boys denied both traits when asked directly, insisting they had many friends and were excellent readers.

In another investigation one of my students presented mothers from different social-class backgrounds a two-minute audio recording of an essay describing the advantages and disadvantages of displaying physical affection toward infants. The student then surprised each woman by asking her to recall everything she remembered from the essay. The college-educated women—many of whom believed that kisses and embraces are required for psychological health—remembered more words describing the benevolent consequences of physical affection. By contrast, many of the working-class women with only a high school diploma believed that children must learn to cope with the difficult challenges of American society and, therefore, did not want to spoil young children by giving them too much affection. These women remembered more words describing the disadvantages of too much kissing and hugging. Yet both groups of women gave the same affirmative answer when asked directly whether physical affection was good for infants because they sensed that this reply was the socially desirable answer.[8]

The disinclination to admit to an undesirable trait explains another phenomenon as well. When a questionnaire asks about a less desirable trait several times, but uses different words to name the trait, many respondents who answered affirmatively on the first question were reluctant to affirm the same trait when it was repeated later. For example, an adolescent who admits that she felt "nervous at parties with strangers" is tempted to deny that she feels "anxious with people she does not know" when this question appears later because she does not want the psychologist to conclude that she is an extremely anxious person.

Even the form of a question can influence the answers. Most people have a natural bias to select the middle value and to avoid the extremes when responding to a question with multiple answers. For example, in a survey investigating the average amount of time spent watching television each day, only one of six adults admitted to watching two and a half hours or more when that was the highest value. However, when two and a half hours or more was the second of six alternatives with four more extreme values, twice as many respondents confessed that they watched television for at least that long.

The language of the questionnaire or interview is always relevant because different languages can contain slightly different semantic networks for the same concept—whether friend, parent, or self. The English term for *self*, for example, is usually understood to refer to personal qualities rather than to relationships with others, whereas the Chinese term for *self* includes this feature. Hong Kong adolescents who were proficient in both English and Chinese described their personalities on two occasions, once in Chinese and once in English. These youths described themselves as autonomous agents when interviewed in English but as interdependent with others when asked the same questions in Chinese.[9]

These problems with verbal evidence explain why the correspondence between what people say about themselves and what they actually do, believe, or feel ranges from negligible to modest. Adults from fifty-five countries filled out the popular Big Five questionnaire. The sex differences in the five personality traits were larger in wealthy, egalitarian societies, such as the United States, than in economically poor traditional societies, such as Indonesia. However, direct observations of the

behaviors of men and women in these two nations would lead to the opposite conclusion. Sex differences in extraversion, agreeableness, and openness to new ideas
are far more obvious in Indonesia than in the United States.

Members of my research group filmed interviews with fifteen-year-old adolescents who had been classified as having either a high- or low-reactive temperament
when they were four months old. I noted that high-reactive infants tend to become
shy, anxious children; low-reactives are likely to become sociable, fearless children.
Several of the high-reactive adolescents told an interviewer that they were neither
shy nor anxious with strangers. However, the same youths often looked away from
the interviewer. Some never looked directly at her at all during the three-hour session. By contrast, not one low-reactive who denied being shy shifted his or her gaze
away from the interviewer's face. The addition of the behavioral observations permitted us to distinguish between two groups of adolescents who gave exactly the
same verbal description of this personality trait.

Scientists cannot even trust the accuracy of a person's statement that he or she
put sunscreen on several hours earlier, upon arriving at a swimming pool. If adults
are inaccurate when providing information about their use of sunscreen, they are
unlikely to be more accurate when describing their personality traits or the traits of
their children. Yet about one-third of the studies of humans published in America's
leading journals between 2007 and 2012 relied on questionnaires as the only source
of evidence.[10]

The denial of the problems trailing sole reliance on verbal reports is not surprising. It took many years for Jean Paul Sartre to recognize the flaw in his belief as
a young man that naming something was equivalent to verifying its existence. A
youthful Sartre had confused what he read in books with what existed in reality. A
story by the French writer Marguerite Yourcenar, which shares elements with the
legend surrounding the experience of the young Buddha, captures Sartre's insight.
The emperor of a kingdom restricted his first-born son to a large apartment whose
walls were covered with the paintings of the kingdom's most acclaimed artist. After
the emperor died, the prince left the apartment for the first time to assume power.
A few months later, he asked one of his attendants to bring the artist to the pal-
ace. When the artist appeared, the new emperor told him he would be shot the
next day. The artist asked why the emperor had arrived at such a harsh decision.
The new ruler explained that for the first twenty years of his life the artist's paintings represented his only knowledge of the outside world. Because these paintings
were so beautiful, the prince had assumed that the world was beautiful as well. After

experiencing the world directly, the young emperor concluded that the artist had lied and so he had to die. Many answers to questionnaires, like the artist's paintings, are insufficiently faithful reflections of a person's knowledge, emotions, or past experiences. The unique features of verbal evidence render it an inadequate foundation on which to construct fully satisfying explanations of human properties and their variation. Yet many psychologists continue to rely on this information and assume that it accurately reflects the respondents' properties. Neuroscientists aren't ashamed to admit that they do not fully understand the meanings of blood flow patterns in the brain, and some are trying to uncover these meanings. Investigators who use questionnaires should be equally concerned with the meanings of verbal descriptions of feelings, beliefs, actions, and past experiences.

The psychologists who gather only verbal information and the neuroscientists who measure the brain often ask similar questions, but because they rely on different evidence they arrive at different conclusions. Missing from the efforts of both groups are observations of behavior that might provide the critical information needed to understand both the verbal and the brain data.

Consider, for example, the fact that the brain activity in individuals who say that they are minimally anxious differs from the brain activity in individuals who, after receiving a dose of oxytocin, report feeling minimally anxious. Observations of the behaviors of the adults who say they are minimally anxious, whether on a questionnaire or after receiving oxytocin, could reveal the different behavioral correlates of the same verbal description.

The phenomena that psychologists wish to understand rest behind a thick curtain containing a large number of tiny holes. The view through a single hole in the curtain, analogous to the information provided by one type of evidence, cannot provide a full comprehension of the events scientists want to understand. This richer understanding requires views through many holes. Unfortunately, about three of every four studies published in the major psychological journals over the past decade have relied on only one source of evidence. There may come a time in the future, after theory is stronger and the web of facts denser, when social scientists, like physicists, will be able to rely on a single source of evidence to affirm or refute a particular idea. No domain in the social sciences is at that level of maturity at the present time.

A majority of psychological concepts, especially those based on verbal reports, fail to specify the contexts in which a behavior, talent, or emotion will be displayed.

This fact poses a problem because the probability that a psychological property will be displayed always depends on the nature of the setting. Adolescents are far more likely to commit an aggressive action if they attend a school where aggression is frequent. Chinese-Americans living in the United States have a lower probability of committing suicide than those who live in the People's Republic of China. And easy access to pornographic websites, a phenomenon that is less than a quarter-century old, has created a historically unique human condition. At this or any other moment at least 28,000 individuals, usually males, are watching one of 4 million porn sites.[11] This behavior was impossible during earlier historical eras, despite no change in the human genome.

Most seven-month-old infants cry when they see an unfamiliar man with a neutral facial expression walk toward them quickly. Few infants cry if the stranger is a woman who smiles as she walks toward them slowly. Six-month-old infants who see their mother and a stranger push a button on a box to produce a sound are likely to imitate the mother if both are in the familiar home setting, but likely to imitate the stranger if the same event occurs in a laboratory.

A detail as seemingly irrelevant as the size of a room affects conclusions regarding the ability of two-year-olds to use a landmark, such as a colored wall, to find a toy hidden in one corner of a room. Children tested in a large room that had windows and three light-colored walls and one dark-blue wall noticed the blue wall and used it as a landmark to find the hidden toy. Children tested in a small, windowless room did not use the blue wall to locate the toy.

Yet despite these and other similar observations, many psychologists persist in assuming that what individuals do or say in one setting is a good predictor of what they will do or say in a different setting. Unfortunately, this optimistic assumption is not affirmed by evidence. Many psychological concepts are valid only in the settings that gave rise to the evidence. This idea can be phrased differently. Most of the time, individuals can display more than one behavior in response to an event—say, a smiling face. Contexts vary in the number of responses they permit to a person who is smiling. Hiking with a partner in an open meadow is maximally permissive; a crowded restaurant is a bit more limiting; a computer screen in a windowless laboratory room instructing an individual to hit a button as quickly as possible when a smiling face appears eliminates most of the behaviors that could occur in reaction to a smiling face.

Not surprisingly, settings affect the information that brains process. A site in the posterior region of the left hemisphere, located between the visual and temporal regions, is active whenever someone sees printed words. The first modern humans possessed this slice of cortex but were not exposed to printed words until relatively late in human history. What events activated this site in those who lived 50,000 years ago? The site is biologically prepared to process simple shapes that have acquired a meaning. Hence, this site was probably activated in early humans when they saw footprints left by the animals they were tracking. When surfaces with hieroglyphs and, later, printed words became more frequent than footprints in the earth, this site became dedicated to processing words rather than footprints.

Social scientists studying cooperation or altruism are tempted to base their conclusions on the reactions of two strangers interacting in brief, game-like procedures in an unfamiliar laboratory. Many of the investigators who conduct this research are indifferent to the fact that each of their participants belongs to a variety of social categories that includes a familial, work, ethnic, religious, or recreational group. The level of cooperation or altruism displayed toward someone who is a member of one of these groups can be very different from the altruism exhibited toward a stranger in a laboratory. Nonetheless, the scientists conducting these experiments make strong claims about human cooperation and altruism that are presumed to apply across many settings.

In one popular game-like procedure, a psychologist gives one participant $10 with the instruction to decide how much to offer to a partner, who is a stranger. The partner, in turn, must decide whether to accept or reject the offer. Most Americans placed in this odd setting as the partner reject an offer of $1. I doubt, however, that these same adults would reject an offer of $1,000 if the participant had been given $10,000. Nor is it likely that the head of a charity requesting a $50,000 donation from a wealthy individual would reject a donation of $5,000. I am certain that a scientist who had requested $1 million from a wealthy philanthropy would not send back a check for $100,000.

Humans enjoy playing games because these activities allow them to cast off the demands of living. But the conclusions about human nature that originate in thirty-minute games between strangers negotiating small amounts of money are often invalidated in life contexts where decisions are governed by a person's social categories, intimate relationships, and concerns about one's reputation under conditions in which the size of the reward that could be gained or lost is large.

Psychologists made an important discovery, called the *attribution error,* in which an individual interprets a behavior as reflecting a firm trait when it is displayed by another person but as reflecting the demands of the setting when displayed by the self. For example, a woman who notices that a man is talking very loudly in a restaurant is prone to assume that the man's inappropriate behavior reflects a stable personality trait, whereas if she noticed herself talking too loudly in a restaurant she would likely attribute her behavior to the idiosyncratic features of the restaurant at that moment. Scientists who announce bold conclusions about human nature based on the behaviors of two strangers who accepted a psychologist's request to play games for small stakes are committing a version of the attribution error.

Psychologists are fond of a strategy in which they try to prove the correctness of a favored hypothesis by placing humans, or animals, in one setting and exposing them to a single procedure in which an agent can make one of two responses. If the evidence supports their hypothesis, they conclude that it is true under all circumstances and are reluctant to disprove their intuition by changing the context in a significant way. Too many psychological assessments resemble the "Have you stopped beating your wife?" query, in which respondents are allowed only a "yes" or "no" reply.

Not surprisingly, the probability of a crime is also affected by the nature of the context. Franklin Zimring, an expert on crime at the University of California, points out in *The City That Became Safe* that adding extra police to crime-ridden New York City neighborhoods led to a dramatic reduction in the crimes committed over the past decade.[12] An analogous phenomenon occurs among elephants. Young male elephants experience periodic surges of testosterone that are accompanied by aggressive rampages that can last as long as six months if no older males are nearby. The presence of older males shortens the duration of these wild displays by a significant amount.

The current rate of imprisonment in the United States is a little over seven out of every one thousand adults. It is believed that only one or two of these seven prisoners possesses a temperament that rendered them vulnerable to low levels of fear, empathy, and guilt. When this biological bias is wedded to a life history of school failure and marginalization, criminal acts become more likely. Such individuals commit at least two-thirds of all crimes. For the remaining prisoners who do not possess these temperaments or life histories, the local context exerts a major influence on the likelihood that they will break the law.

The local context also predicts the likelihood of a successful suicide. The presence of firearms in an American home is an excellent predictor of a suicide. There are more guns per resident in the four states with the highest suicide rates—Alaska, Nevada, Wyoming, and New Mexico—than in the four states with the lowest suicide deaths—New Jersey, New York, Massachusetts, and Rhode Island.

The context in which psychological interventions designed to help children are implemented affects the effectiveness of the intervention. Many social scientists have provided varied educational or therapeutic experiences to needy children. The long-term consequences of most of these efforts have been disappointing. The problem, as Kenneth Dodge notes, is that the interventions were conducted by strangers in a university laboratory or Head Start center for periods lasting from a few weeks to a few months.[13] The children, however, live in settings characterized by crowded schools, unmotivated teachers, playgrounds with bullies, and homes with marital conflict and violence. The majority of African-American and Hispanic youths who drop out of high school come from poor families and are attending schools where the majority of pupils also come from disadvantaged families, often from the same ethnic group. The contexts in which the children live differ significantly from the contexts in which the interventions were implemented. This is one reason for the fragile effects of these well-intentioned efforts.

One notable exception is an unusually extensive educational intervention with poor African-American children from North Carolina that lasted from infancy to five years of age. The thirty-year-olds who had enjoyed the enriched preschool experience, compared with equally poor black adults who did not, had slightly higher incomes and a few more years of education. About one in four children were permanently helped by the program. The remaining 75 percent, by thirty years of age, had lost whatever early advantages the intervention produced because the social contexts in which they lived from age five to thirty were far more powerful than the skills they had acquired when they entered the first grade.[14]

Lisa Barrett and her colleagues have provided a lovely example of the power of context to influence inferences about a person's emotional state.[15] A photograph of the face of Serena Williams without any background reveals closed eyes, mouth wide-open, and tense forehead muscles, which would lead an observer to infer that Serena was in a state of pain. However, this photo was taken on a tennis court the moment Williams won the 2008 US Open championship. A viewer seeing Serena's face in the context in which it was photographed would never infer a state of pain.

Barrett's example has implications for conclusions about the meaning of blood flow patterns in the brain evoked by faces with emotional expressions such as fear, happiness, anger, or disgust. The participants, who usually do not know the kind of picture that will appear on a screen, suddenly see a face with no body and no clue as to the context in which the expression might have occurred. This kind of stimulus never occurs in a natural setting. The brain's reaction to a man's face with a fearful expression will depend on whether the participants did or did not expect to see a face, did or did not expect to see a face without a body, did or did not expect to see a man's face with a fearful expression, or could not determine whether the expression was fear or surprise inasmuch as these two facial patterns are often confused.

Nonetheless, scientists who conduct studies of this type often arrive at bold inferences about the participants' emotional states from their brain profiles. Apparently, they believe that a face with eyes and mouth wide-open, bereft of any background information, has a privileged, automatic link to a biological response independent of the person's expectations. The evidence does not support that premise. A facial expression consisting of eyes and mouth wide-open would be judged as reflecting *fear* if the setting was a jungle trail with a snake curled around a tree, *surprise* if the context was a roomful of people looking at a birthday cake, and *wonder* if the background was a pink sky at dawn over a lagoon. Scientists who base their conclusions on one source of evidence in one setting resemble an observer standing in one place judging the properties of a rainbow; an observer in another location will have a different perception of the rainbow.

Each culture represents a context, albeit a complex one, that affects the life histories of its members. A person's career, for example, is occasionally determined by a society's values during a particular historical era. For a brief interval from 1870 to 1910, the city of Budapest possessed an ambience of tolerance toward Jews and other minorities along with a number of outstanding gymnasia (analogous to high schools in the United States). These social conditions allowed a number of talented youths from minority groups to become unusually eminent in a variety of fields. This group includes the scientists John von Neumann, Eugene Wigner, Edward Teller, and Leo Szilard; the conductors Fritz Reiner and George Szell; and the actress Zsa Zsa Gabor. Had these individuals grown up in Warsaw, they might not have had the opportunity to develop such distinguished careers. In a similar vein, Peter Galison notes that Sigmund Freud's invention of the concept of repression of unacceptable desires may have been aided by the fact that, at the time he was composing his theory, Austria and Russia were severely censoring newspapers and private correspondence sent through the mail. In a letter to a friend he likened the idea of repression to Russian censorship.[16]

This chapter makes three important claims. First, all children, healthy at birth, possess the potential for acquiring a large number of psychological properties that are inherent in their genome. These include the abilities to perceive events, detect bodily feelings, recall the past, anticipate the future, infer the thoughts of others, speak and understand a language, and make moral judgments. It is rare to find a three-year-old in any society, no matter how remotely located, who cannot imitate an adult's action or infer that someone needs help, or a twelve-year-old who cannot remember four unrelated words.

Nevertheless, culture and historical era exert a strong influence on the content of perceptions, beliefs, and values. Megumi Kuwabara and Linda Smith of Indiana University report that Japanese four-year-olds possess a bias toward attending to the spatial relations among a central object and the other elements in a scene.[17] For example, they are likely to note that a bicycle in the foreground is leaning against the door of a house on a city street that ends with three adjoining houses and two stores. The Japanese language has many terms for relationships, and Japanese parents emphasize the obligatory social relationships among individuals. By contrast, American four-year-olds are biased toward focusing on the central object in a scene—in this case, the bicycle—and ignoring its spatial relations to the other objects. Compared with Japanese, the English language has more terms for single objects, fewer words for relationships, and American parents stress the importance of each child's individuality and autonomy rather than his or her relationships to others.

Second, the variation among children that originates in their temperaments, like the clay from different quarries, is molded into different forms by the culture, parental practices, and the family's class position.

Third, members of different cultures hold some beliefs that they regard as universal verities. The premises of Mohandas Gandhi and Winston Churchill provide an example. Gandhi could not understand why Churchill was suspicious of the sincerity of his spirituality and hostile toward his desire for Indian independence. Churchill, in turn, could not understand the sincerity of Gandhi's spirituality and his conviction that Indians could handle independence.

As these themes are elaborated in the chapters that follow, I will return many times to four principles. The first, which I call the *90 percent rule,* is that the initial expression of a trait or talent is usually restricted to a small number of contexts. Brain maturation and experience expand the generality of a trait or ability so that, in time, it will be observed in 90 percent of the settings in which it is appropriate. For example, a four-month-old will grab a rattle close to her body, but she does not possess the adolescent's understanding of all the properties that define a material object. A nine-month-old will display a brain response signifying surprise if his mother says "Look at the duck" when a cat appears on a screen, but he cannot say the word *duck* and will not retrieve a toy duck if asked to do so. A three-year-old knows that a cow is alive but is not sure that the same is true of algae on a pond.

The incompleteness of the child's knowledge leaves psychologists with one of two choices. They can either describe each competence in combination with the settings in which it is displayed or specify the probability that a talent will be expressed in a given context. It is misleading to write that young children possess a competence—say, knowing how to make a noun plural or understanding the concept of number—when the talent is expressed in a limited number of situations. Psychologists are "lumpers" who yearn for generality, whereas nature is a "splitter" preferring particularity. I side with Bohr, who tried—unsuccessfully—to persuade Einstein that the scientist's task is to describe how matter behaves in the settings the scientist creates. Einstein, the idealist, insisted that physicists have a responsibility to discover what nature *is* rather than describe its properties in certain settings.

The second principle, which I call the *tipping point,* is that most relations between phenomena are not linear. The formation of ice is a classic example. Ice will not form in a vessel as the temperature falls until the tipping point of 32 degrees Fahrenheit is reached. Analogously, the probability of a suicide attempt rises to a moderately high value for the small proportion of people who are extremely unhappy with their lives. Those who are only a little unhappy are not at higher risk than those who are not at all unhappy. A parent's occasional spanking of a child is not on a continuum with chronic physical abuse. The former is unlikely to have any important effects on a child's future, whereas the latter is likely to produce an unfavorable outcome. The human mind and brain, like a bridge designed to bear weights up to 5,000 pounds but cracks under heavier loads, can tolerate some stressors without serious cost. Only after the tipping point is passed do particular outcomes, desirable or undesirable, become more probable.

Rare events, such as a suicide or a school massacre carried out by an angry youth are impossible to predict because they require a combination of many conditions acting together to exceed a tipping point. Nassim Taleb refers to these rare events as "black swans."[18]

The third principle is that a *contrast* between anticipated and actual events, feelings, traits, or ideas almost always evokes a brain response, an alert state, and a psychological response. This principle operates even within the retina, for ganglia cells respond to a change in illumination rather than to the intensity of light entering the eye.

Consider some examples of the power of contrast.

1. Many of the events that psychologists call rewards are unexpected experiences that alert the individual and, therefore, are remembered. Fifty-year-olds asked to recall memories of their past typically retrieve experiences that occurred during the decade between ten and twenty years of age—an interval marked by a variety of events that occurred for the first time, including high school graduation, leaving home for college or a job, and the first sexual experience.

2. Children and adults arrive at conclusions regarding their personal traits and skills by comparing their properties with select others, and by noticing a difference between their properties and their conception of the ideal. Children need to know the reading ability of others in order to know if their reading ability is high, moderate, or low. Danes report one of the highest levels of satisfaction with their lives because they compare their high incomes, literacy rates, and good health with citizens of other nations. If Danes were informed that thirty other nations had higher incomes, superior literacy, and better health, they would report feeling less satisfied even if conditions in Danish society remained exactly the same.

3. Later-born children are vulnerable to doubt over their adequacy because they compare their traits and talents with those of the older first-born child and notice their deficiencies. Had they been the first-born they would be more confident and less anxious or resentful, even if their talents had not changed. A similar dynamic can occur between couples when one spouse, after many years, has achieved much more than the other—whether worldly accomplishment, occupational status, or health. Spouses who feel less adequate typically adopt one of two defenses. They either become hostile and argumentative or are driven to prove their contribution to the marital partnership through zealous attention either to the responsibilities of home or work.

4. The power of contrast explains why the introduction of words that name colors follows a universal order across the world's languages.[19] Some languages have only two color words, one for dark and another for light. When a language invents a third name, it is always for red. If a fourth name is introduced it is for green, followed by names for yellow and blue in that order. A team of Italian scientists led by Vittorio Loreto offered an explanation of this phenomenon by noting that the order of color words appears to be influenced

by the magnitude of difference in wavelengths between successive pairs of colors.[20] The wavelength for red, which is the third color name, is maximally different from the wavelength for dark blue (a difference of 180 nanometers). Green takes precedence over yellow because the difference in wavelength between green and red (100 nanometers) is larger than that between yellow and red (60 nanometers). And the term for yellow is introduced before blue because the difference in wavelength between yellow and dark blue is larger than that between light blue and dark blue.

The fourth principle is that *patterns* of conditions, not single events, are the most useful way to think about the causes of behaviors, emotions, and beliefs. For example, the consequences of being a victim of bullying or harsh parental criticism depends on the child's gender, social class, ethnicity, and/or culture. Recall that the boys from the New Guinea tribe required to perform fellatio on older adolescents developed normally because what might be viewed as an experience of victimization in most cultures was for them a culturally approved ritual.

The societies of the world represent distinctive patterns that combine at least nine properties: climate, dominant economy, the ethnic and religious homogeneity of the population, hierarchical versus egalitarian institutions, gender relations, the magnitude of status and income inequality, the balance between favoring the self's interests and those of family and community, primary signs of virtue, and the degree of diversity with respect to primary ethical values. There are many ways to combine these properties and, therefore, a large number of distinct societies. The children growing up in each setting will establish different values, skills, moods, and personalities.

It is also useful to base conclusions on patterns of measurements, rather than on one source of evidence, because almost all behaviors, verbal reports, and brain measures can be the result of more than a single condition. Hence, it is necessary to gather a pattern of measures in order to figure out the most likely cause of a phenomenon. That is why physicians consider blood samples, urine samples, and X-rays when a patient complains of pain in the joints and why parents' descriptions of their children should always be combined with direct observations of the same children. It is especially important to look for patterns of brain measures. A team of German scientists had to examine the pattern of blood flow to nine different sites in order to differentiate pedophiles from normal men when both groups were

looking at pictures of nude children. In another study, a pattern of four features—
being a male, possessing a specific gene, having permissive parents, and socializing
with delinquent peers—was needed to predict which Russian adolescents would
seek the thrill that accompanies committing asocial behavior. The reason for the
ritual killing of a young woman as a sacrifice to a Mayan god is not the reason for
the slaughter of a Tutsi woman by a band of Hutu men. The number of men killed
in duels defending their honor has decreased over the past four hundred years, but
the number of young men killed by soldiers under orders from the state to shoot
protesters in a crowd has probably increased over the same interval. The best predictor of murder in the United States is the number of available firearms. In Sudan
and Iraq it is ethnic conflict, and in Mexico and Columbia it is the amount of illicit
drugs being trafficked.

The suggestion to examine patterns of causes and outcomes was ignored by social scientists who asserted that a nation's average IQ explains a country's wealth.
This claim ignores the fact that the mean IQ of a nation has many causes, including
the prevalence of infectious diseases, availability of health care, number and quality of public schools and universities, and proportion of the population with a high
school diploma. The decision to pluck the average IQ out of this pattern and argue
that it is the cause of a society's wealth is analogous to declaring that the prevalence
of chronic diarrhea in a nation is the cause of famine, premature births, infection
load, poor infrastructure, and a corrupt government.

Readers are urged to remember this quartet of principles as they reflect on what
scientists have learned about the properties that all humans share; the developmental course these properties follow; and the contributions of biology, culture, historical era, and idiosyncratic experiences to the variation among children and adults
that is present in every community.

CHAPTER TWO

The First Year

All beginnings are interesting, but the origins of the talents and traits of children and adults pique a special quality of curiosity. The first chapters in this narrative involve the embryo (the first eight weeks), fetus (the remaining thirty to thirty-two weeks of a typical pregnancy), and the infant during the first postnatal year. Although the genomes of the estimated 140 million infants born last year (about four births every second) vary, the prenatal growth of brain and body is remarkably similar in all infants. Nature attends compulsively to the details when the foundation is being formed and becomes more permissive once the initial scaffolding is in place.

BUILDING A BRAIN AND BODY

The brain has begun its development as early as the fifth week after conception, when the six regions that will become the major areas of the mature central nervous system are established. (See Figure 2.1.) Closest to the forehead is the anterior region, which is destined to become the convoluted cerebral cortex—the brain's outermost layer. The cortex receives initially processed sensory inputs from the environment; mediates voluntary motor movements, memory, language, reasoning, reflection; and coordinates all of these processes. The second area, a few millimeters posterior to (that is, behind) the anterior region, will become the midbrain

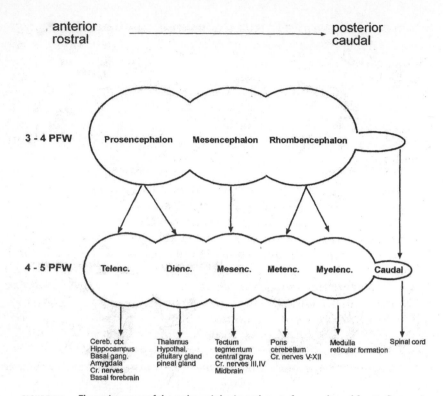

FIGURE 2.1   The major areas of the embryonic brain at three to four weeks and four to five weeks after conception

containing the thalamus, the major relay station between most incoming sensations and the cerebral cortex. The third region will become the colliculi, which process less detailed features of sights and sounds and exert control over the automatic movements of eyes and head when we see or hear events in the environment. The fourth region will become the cerebellum, which is critical for the precise timing of motor actions and movements of the vocal cords and tongue. The fifth region will develop into the sites that modulate breathing and heart rate and receive information from the body. The sixth and most posterior region will become the spinal cord.[1]

No engineer would have designed a brain with this architecture. The most anterior region contains the most recent evolutionary changes as well as the neurons responsible for the sense of smell, which is a capacity possessed by animals that lived many millions of years ago. Regions two and five, which control bodily functions, are separated by regions three and four, and the areas responsible for voluntary motor movements are separated from those that coordinate the timing of those movements. This arrangement means that most psychological functions require the coordination of spatially separated sites that communicate with one another via major hubs. The posterior region of the cortex receives visual sensations; the middle region awards these sensations semantic meaning; and the anterior frontal lobe, functioning as an executive, coordinates this combination of information in the service of activating the most appropriate reaction.

Although development during the early weeks is highly regimented by genes, it is susceptible to particular events that introduce some variability. For example, the month of conception can affect a small number of infant properties. During the eight-week interval from late summer (the end of August in the northern hemisphere and late February in the southern) to the middle of autumn, the hours of daylight decrease from day to day at a faster-than-usual rate. All humans, including pregnant mothers, secrete larger than normal amounts of a molecule called melatonin during this period. Melatonin affects many biological systems, including the brain. Embryos conceived during this interval are a little more likely to be shy as children and more vulnerable, as adults, to alterations in mood when the seasons change. A small proportion are at a higher risk for developing seasonal affective disorder. Melatonin may also play a role in triggering the onset of the more serious mental illness of bipolar disorder. Bipolar individuals who live in regions that are close to the north or south pole have an earlier age of onset of symptoms, perhaps because melatonin production is maximally variable in these regions.[2]

An event that occurs at about eight weeks after fertilization has special significance for male embryos. The developing testes begin secreting the male hormone testosterone, which they will do until about six months after conception, and again for a few months after birth. The rare genetic males who do not secrete testosterone, or who have receptors that are insensitive to this hormone, are usually born with female genitals and given a girl's name.

Some of the testosterone secreted by the male embryo is converted to the female hormone estradiol, and the combination of the two hormones acting on the receptors for each hormone affects brain anatomy. Fetal testosterone slows the growth of the left hemisphere, making it more likely that the right hemisphere will dominate the left. Michael Lombardo and his colleagues at Cambridge University found that preadolescent boys who, as fetuses, had unusually high levels of testosterone in the amniotic fluid that surrounded them (about 25 percent of the children Lombardo studied) had more gray matter—reflecting neurons and glia—in a site within the right hemisphere that contributes to the solving of spatial reasoning problems, but less gray matter in sites within the left hemisphere that contribute to language.[3] This fact, together with the greater connectivity within the right hemisphere of male brains, helps to explain why exceptional performance on difficult spatial reasoning problems, usually scores in the top 1 percent, is typically restricted to males.

The brains of male fetuses contain more neurons in a small region of the hypo-thalamus that is critical for sexual motivation compared with female fetuses. This anatomical fact probably contributes to the more intrusive sexual urges in adoles-cent and adult males. Abnormal concentrations of the sex hormones or atypical re-ceptor densities for these hormones are commonly found in individuals who report having feelings of the opposite sex. This profile, known as gender identity disorder, is under some genetic control.

One extensively studied anatomical feature that is due, in part, to prenatal testos-terone involves the ratio of the lengths of the index and ring fingers. Having a large number of receptors for testosterone, higher levels of prenatal testosterone, low levels of estradiol, or fewer receptors for estradiol—features more characteristic of male fetuses—lengthens the ring finger by a small amount. Hence, most males have a slightly smaller index than ring finger. The lengths of the index and ring fingers of most girls—who have fewer sensitive receptors for testosterone, lower prenatal lev-els of testosterone, higher levels of estradiol, and more receptors for estrogen—are roughly equal. This sex difference is present in human fetuses and other mammals. Gerianne Alexander of Texas A&M University found that the four-month-old in-fant males described by their mothers as becoming extremely upset when anyone imposed limitations on their actions—about 15 percent of the boys studied—had higher levels of testosterone in their saliva than the majority of boys.[4]

The ratio of the length of the index over the ring finger, called the "2D:4D ratio," is under genetic control and has a host of modest correlations with physical and psychological traits. Adult males with masculine ratios of .95 to .97 (the index is slightly shorter than the ring finger) are a little stronger, bolder, aggressive, and more likely to be a member of a varsity athletic team than males with a higher, more feminine ratio. Men with extremely masculine ratios, less than .95, have unusually broad faces, and, if they are portfolio managers, they make more money for their clients than men with less masculine ratios.

Adolescent females with a masculine finger ratio are attracted to occupations that involve working with things rather than with people or ideas. Should these girls have the talent for and interest in a scientific career, they will be biased to select the natural rather than the social sciences. Rita Levi-Montalcini, who shared the 1981

Nobel Prize in Physiology, grew up in a traditional Italian family of the 1920s in which young women were not supposed to pursue professional careers. She opposed her father's wishes by insisting on going to medical school and becoming a scientist. A photograph of Rita as a mature woman reveals the broad face and large chin that is characteristic of men with a masculine 2D:4D ratio. The finger ratio is correlated with comparable differences between species. Chimpanzees, who are far more aggressive than their close relative the bonobos, have a more masculine ratio than the bonobos.[5]

Women who have high concentrations of estrogen and low levels of testosterone are likely to have feminine finger ratios along with a broader mouth and a rounder face than the average man or women with a masculine finger ratio.[6] The average man has thinner lips and a squarer face than the average woman.[7]

Although the embryo and fetus have some protection against a variety of infectious agents and traumata that could disrupt development, the protection is imperfect. The mother's health, diet, illnesses, lifestyle, and stress level can interfere with the fetus's optimal growth. Some stressors contribute to a smaller weight at birth, and this feature in turn is modestly related to a smaller surface area in select cortical sites. Diets with insufficient protein, minerals, or vitamins can also alter normal brain development. Pregnant mothers who take a drug for a medical condition increase by a small amount the odds of altering the normal development of their unborn child. Pregnant women who are depressed or anxious may take a therapeutic drug, called a selective serotonin reuptake inhibitor (SSRI), that affects the level of serotonin in their (and their fetuses') brains. Some infants born to these mothers show small compromises in their ability to cope with stress. Infants who were victims of a serious oxygen deficiency during the birth process are at an enhanced risk for a brain disturbance if their mothers took statins during the pregnancy to keep their cholesterol levels low. Fortunately, such outcomes are unlikely for a majority of children; they become more probable only if the infants possess a genome that renders them especially vulnerable to these abnormal physiological conditions in the mother.[8]

Intense or prolonged periods of anxiety or depression, caused by a natural catastrophe, marital quarrelling, or chronic poverty, also alter the mother's physiology and the chemical environment of the embryo or fetus. The unborn child is especially vulnerable to these events during weeks fourteen to twenty-two, when the corpus callosum, a structure that connects the two hemispheres, is growing.

Pregnant mothers living in Louisiana who were exposed to a severe hurricane during this interval were a little more likely to give birth to an autistic child, compared with pregnant mothers in the same state who lived outside the hurricane area. This result does not mean that maternal stress is a major cause of autism. Rather, it means that fetuses with an uncommon genome that represents a risk for autism are more vulnerable to the biological consequences of maternal stress.

The maternal worry generated by loss of heat and light during a weeks-long blackout following a major ice storm in the Canadian provinces of Quebec and Ontario in January 1998 appeared to affect some fetuses. Although less traumatic than famine, war, or rape, this source of anxiety altered the pregnant mothers' physiology and influenced the growth of their unborn children. Fetuses who were in the second trimester when the storm struck were more likely to be born premature and to possess different ridge patterns on the tips of the corresponding fingers of the right and left hands. Because the skin on the fingers develops at a time when important features in brain growth are occurring, it is possible that the brains of these fetuses were also affected by the mother's physiological reaction to the prolonged absence of light and heat in the middle of the winter.

More generally, slight asymmetries on corresponding sites on the left and right sides of the body can be a sign of a disturbance in fetal development. These asymmetries might appear as small differences in the size of the left and right ears, hands, fingers, wrists, elbows, feet, or ankles. A pregnant mother's immune reaction to a third or fourth male embryo, following pregnancies with two or three prior males, could be one cause of these asymmetries. The mother's immune system generates antibodies against the foreign proteins associated with the Y chromosome in male embryos. Hence, the third and fourth male embryos are vulnerable to an attack by the mother's antibodies that can affect the normal growth of the child's brain and body. Martin Lalumiere and his colleagues at the Center for Mental Health in Toronto found support for this still-controversial idea. They discovered more asymmetries in men who had several older brothers than in men who were first-born or men with no siblings.

The consequences of maternal stress need not be limited to one generation. Severe prenatal stress early in the pregnancy of a female mouse appears to alter the expression of select genes in her male fetuses, as well as in the male offspring of the next generation. These males possessed a feminized brain and a heightened vulnerability to stress. If this result found with mice applies to humans, and it may not, there is some reason to be concerned over the sons and grandsons of mothers whose pregnancies were marked by chronic poverty, serious malnutrition, frequent domestic violence, or homelessness.[9]

Women who have an infectious disease during their pregnancy, including the flu or German measles (rubella), secrete molecules called cytokines that, in susceptible embryos or fetuses, can produce subtle alterations in brain growth that might place the infant at risk for a problem later in development. Maternal infections can also affect physical features—for example, a larger-than-usual distance between the two eyes, large ear lobes, or an abnormally large or small head circumference. School-age boys who possessed several of these subtle deformities were more active and restless in the classroom than a majority of boys.

Maternal abuse of cocaine, heroin, tobacco, marijuana, or alcohol as well as exposure to lead and PCBs can affect the unborn infant. The probability of exposure to these substances is highest among women with lower incomes who live in neighborhoods where these substances are more prevalent. This fact implies that the consequences of exposure could be due partly to the many correlated experiences that are more prevalent among the disadvantaged.

Scientists remain uncertain about the effects of the many pollutants in air, water, and food. In most cases the potential danger posed by these substances depends on the genetic makeup of the fetus. But because a pregnant woman does not know her fetus's genome, she would be wise to honor the advice offered by the elders of many ancient societies and remain vigilant. It is useful to remember that in about one in four identical-twin pairs (who possess exactly the same genes), one twin is right-handed and the other is left-handed.[10]

THE INFANT

Newborn infants come into the world with a number of sensory and motor abilities because the brain areas that mediate these properties developed prenatally. Newborns can see, hear, smell, taste, feel, orient, suck, and grasp, although they are not consciously aware of engaging in these activities and cannot maintain prolonged attention, plan a behavior, or remember most events that happened a few minutes earlier. Nevertheless, infants transform their experiences into mental representations from the first moments after birth and, as a result, alter their brains.

Before describing these representations, we have to consider the conceptual foundations underlying them. Most concepts in physics, chemistry, and biology are based on the material properties of an entity. The concepts *galaxy, atom,* and *protein*

are defined primarily by their physical properties. A large number of biological concepts are defined by what its exemplars do. The concepts *immune system, dopamine
receptor,* and *antidepressant* are defined by their functions rather than by their physical features. Biologists know the physical properties of white blood cells but usually
think about them as structures that fight infection.

Most psychological concepts are defined by their functions. *Intelligence,* for example, refers to a set of processes that aid reasoning and problem solving. A *reward*
is any event that facilitates the establishment of a habit. When the function is un-
clear or controversial, however, a concept is defined by a measurement, which is
the least satisfying strategy. The concept of subjective well-being, for example, is
defined by answers to a particular set of questions.

An important class of functionally defined representations consists of perceptual schemata (the singular form is *schema*). These schemata enable the recognition
of a previously encountered event and are the bases for an alert state when an event
resembles, but is not identical to, one encountered in the past. Hence, moderately
familiar events usually recruit more attention than very familiar or totally unfamiliar events. Psychologists assume that a schema represents only the salient physical
features of an event, omitting many details. An infant acquires a schema merely by
attending to an object or event. No rewarding or subsequent experience is necessary for a process that psychologists call implicit learning.

Psychologists typically infer the possession of a schema by noting whether infants pay more attention to one of two events. If one-day-olds look equally long
at a photograph of their mother's face and the face of an unfamiliar woman, but
three-month-olds look longer at the mother, psychologists conclude that the three-
month-olds, but not the newborns, possess a schema for their mother's face. They
make the same inference if six-month-olds look longer at a photo of an unfamiliar
woman than at one of their mother.

Unfortunately, failure to look longer at one of two events does not always mean
that an infant did not have a schema for one or both events. Our current understanding of the infant brain implies that ten-month-olds can discriminate between
a pair of dark circles enclosed within a larger circle (a stimulus resembling a face)
and a pair of dark circles placed outside a larger circle that is free of any features.
Nonetheless, ten-month olds do not look longer at the latter after establishing a
schema for the former. Failure to look longer at one of two events does not mean
that the infant didn't have a schema for one of them.[11] (See Figure 2.2.) As I noted
in Chapter 1, the validity of a conclusion cannot be separated from the evidence on
which it is based because the procedure and the evidence form an indivisible unit.

FIGURE 2.2   Ten-month-olds look equally long at both stimuli
after being familiarized with the figure on the left.

Psychologists who measure only total time looking at an event can never be certain that the infants who failed to look longer at one of two events did or did not
possess a schema for one of them. Additional measurements are necessary to decide
this question. Some good candidates are the number of times the infant switches
attention between a simultaneously presented pair of stimuli; a facial expression
suggestive of concentration; the appearance of a waveform in an electroencephalogram; or a change in heart rate, skin conductance, muscle tension, or pupil size.
Clay Mash and Marc Bornstein of the National Institutes of Health reported that
five-month-olds displayed a facial expression of intense concentration while looking at an object that was slightly different from one for which a schema was created,
even though the total time looking at that object implied that they did not detect
the difference between their schema and the new form.[12] And Greg Reynolds of
the University of Tennessee has noted that infants sometimes show a distinct brain
response to an event to which they failed to display prolonged looking.[13] Equally
important, infants vary in the way they look at pictures. Some show a number of
brief fixations of a scene; others show one very long, unbroken bout of attention.
The former infants are more likely than the latter to create a schema for the global
pattern, rather than for its detailed features, and, therefore, are likely to display a
brain response to a change in the global pattern.

This and other evidence implies that the popular practice of inferring what an infant knows from differences in total looking time between a pair of events can lead
to questionable conclusions. Karen Wynn, a psychologist at Yale University, made
national headlines when she reported that young infants were capable of the arithmetic operation of addition.[14] Wynn first showed infants a single doll in the center
of a stage. Then, moments after the stage was covered by a curtain, the infants saw
a human hand appear at one edge of the stage adding a second doll to the stage

behind the curtain. Following a brief delay the curtain was raised and the infants saw the test event, consisting of either one doll or two dolls in the center of the stage. Most infants looked longer at the single doll. Wynn's explanation was that the infants had mentally added their schema for the first doll to the schema for the doll added to the stage and, therefore, expected to see two dolls. They looked longer at the single doll because that scene violated their expectation.

There is another way to interpret Wynn's evidence. It is possible that Wynn's infants looked longer at the single doll in the center of the stage because the last thing they saw before the test display was a doll at one edge of the stage (when a hand was placing it behind the curtain). If the schema for that event were dominant when the test event occurred, then seeing one doll in the center of the stage, rather than at the edge, deviated from the infant's schema and therefore recruited attention. Infants are extremely sensitive to the spatial locations of objects and pay attention when these locations are altered. Neurons in the parietal cortex respond to such changes, and this region of the parietal cortex is more mature in the first year than the sites that mediate addition in older children. These facts make it less obvious that Wynn's infants were "adding" dolls. Moreover, developmental psychologists at the University of Milan have discovered that young infants do not automatically relate the third event in a series to the first event. Yet Wynn assumed that her infants related the test event (the third in the series) to the first event consisting of a single doll in the center of a stage.

Wynn should have shown two additional test events to infants who had seen the same pair of earlier events. Specifically, one group of infants sees two dolls located at the edge of the stage opposite from the edge where they saw the hand introduce the second doll and the other group sees only one doll at the opposite edge. If infants devoted more attention to the two dolls at the opposite end of the stage than to both the single doll at the edge or at the center of the stage, it would be reasonable to suggest that Wynn's infants were not performing addition. Rather, they would have been responding to the fact that the single doll in the center of the stage was discrepant from the schema they had created moments earlier of a single doll at the edge of the stage.

This example illustrates the advantage of measuring more than two outcomes. Children prefer the colors red and yellow to brown and black, but consistently prefer red over yellow. Psychologists who showed children only red and yellow objects and asked them which one they preferred would conclude, incorrectly, that they did not like yellow. In the past, pharmaceutical companies evaluated the effectiveness of a drug by comparing it with no treatment. If patients taking a drug felt better than those who had no treatment, the company concluded that the drug was helpful. Scientists discovered later that many patients given a sugar pill, called a *placebo,* also reported feeling better. Hence, companies had to show that a drug was more effective than both a placebo and no treatment. A skipper whose fishing nets had holes that were only two inches in diameter would be tempted to assume that the sea contained no fish with diameters less than two inches.

Species vary in terms of the features that recruit attention and generate schematic representations. Bees, for example, attend preferentially to the visual patterns common to flowers and are relatively insensitive to the linear contours of triangles or checkerboards. Human infants have a bias to attend to a small number of physical features that become the essential elements of their first schemata. One bias in the visual modality is an attraction to the changes in illumination that define a contour or boundary. Newborns shown a single thick black line on a white background automatically move their eyes to the boundary between the black line and the surrounding white space. David Hubel and Torsten Wiesel, working with cats, discovered that contours activate a specific class of neurons in the visual cortex. The attraction to boundaries helps infants create schemata for the shapes of objects (a shape, after all, is a particular contour pattern), and infants as young as eight weeks can detect the differences among triangles, rectangles, circles, and squares.[15]

Young infants are biased to pay more attention to longer rather than shorter contours, but by six months they attend to both. Infants younger than six weeks devote more attention to the longer continuous contour of the head than to the shorter contours of the eyes, nose, ears, and mouth. Older infants are attracted to the contour created by the border between the dark color of the pupil and the surrounding white sclera. Young infants also attend more closely to objects in the upper half of their visual field than to those in the lower half. Newborns look longer at pattern A than at pattern B, but equally long at patterns C and D, even though D resembles a face more than C does.[16] (See Figure 2.3.)

Surfaces vary in luminance, or the amount of light they reflect. The changes in luminance within a particular space define the spatial frequency across that space. Objects with a higher spatial frequency have more changes in luminance within a given region; objects with a lower spatial frequency have fewer. For example, the four-inch space between the outer borders of the two eyes has a higher spatial frequency than the four-inch space filled by exposed teeth in a full smile. The two hemispheres respond to variation in spatial frequency differently. The right

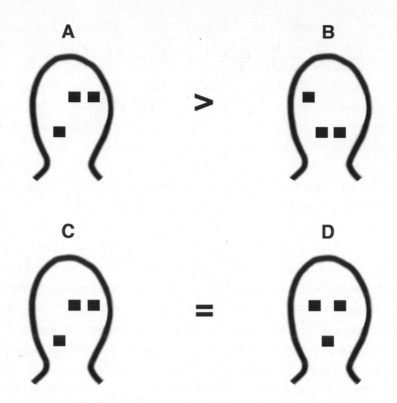

FIGURE 2.3   Infants look longer at stimuli with more elements in the upper part of the figure.

hemisphere is biologically prepared to rapidly process events with a lower spatial frequency; the left hemisphere is prepared to process events with higher spatial frequencies, but a trifle more slowly. Variations in spatial frequency enable young infants to discriminate between a face with a full smile and a face with a frown, even though they do not know the emotion that either face symbolizes.[17]

Infants, like all animals, devote more attention to moving than to still objects. Newly hatched goslings follow the first moving object they see, which most of the time is the mother. Konrad Lorenz—who discovered that young goslings learned to follow him rather than their mother if he happened to be the first moving object they saw—called this phenomenon *imprinting*.[18] Infants only five months old display different brain profiles when observing the movements of people as opposed to the motion of objects.[19]

Curvature is a third biologically privileged feature. Infants look longer at a circular than a straight contour and, after eight weeks of age, stare longer at patterns composed of curved contours than at designs made of straight lines; adult monkeys

FIGURE 2.4   Infants look longer at circular bull's-
eye than at linear figure.

behave the same way. (See Figure 2.4.) Most adults report greater tension to designs that have many angles compared with illustrations containing many curves.
This may help explain why European painters began to insert more angles into their
scenes when the faster pace of life produced by industrialization, automobiles, and
large cities replaced the quieter, slower, gentler pace of the nineteenth century.

Animals and plants have rounded contours, whereas most manufactured objects
have straight contours. This fact—along with the observation that only animals and
people move spontaneously and, unlike small objects, are neither "graspable" nor
linked to one specific function—makes it easy for young children to differentiate
between living and nonliving things. It is not surprising, therefore, that words or
pictures that represent animals or people generate brain profiles that differ from
those evoked by inanimate objects. Apparently, the brain treats the contrasting categories *living* versus *nonliving* as significant.

A fourth bias attracts infants to objects that are symmetrical, especially those
that have vertical symmetry (like a standing human) compared with horizontal
symmetry or no symmetry at all. Blind adults form a firmer schema for objects that
they manipulate with their hands if the objects are symmetrical. Adults judge faces
with near-perfect vertical symmetry as more attractive, and six-month-olds look
longer at such faces. The symbols for Christianity, Judaism, and Buddhism have
vertical symmetry; the symbol for Islam is symmetrical along a horizontal plane.[20]

Color has less salience for infants than contour, motion, and circularity, even
though they can detect the differences among some colors. Newborns look longer
at a blue surface than at one that is green or red, and adults show greater cortical
arousal to blue than to red or green. Blue has a shorter wavelength than red or green
and, therefore, possesses more physical energy. Perhaps that is why blue light has
greater therapeutic value than red for adults suffering from depression. Yet most
adults regard red as more symbolic of a state of arousal than blue.

Human faces contain all the features that naturally recruit an infant's attention.
The two eyes, located in the upper half of the face, possess contour, circularity,

and vertical symmetry, and the tongue and head are in motion when the mother is speaking. Infants are prepared, therefore, to attend to the features that faces contain, much like a newly hatched gull is attracted to the red spot on the beak of an adult gull. Monkeys were raised in a unique environment for the first two years in which they saw many objects but not a single face. The privileged properties of faces was revealed when these animals saw a monkey's face for the first time, for they looked longer at the face than at a variety of objects. No particular face initially has a special potency. Human newborns look equally long at the faces of humans and monkeys. Within a few weeks, however, infants establish an initial schema for the face of their primary caretaker, and by four months they spend more time looking at a normal face of a stranger than at a face in which the eyes, nose, mouth, and eyebrows are arranged randomly.[21]

However, this evidence does not necessarily mean that the patterned features of human faces are inherently the most attractive. Most four-month-old infants look longer at a schematic face, which has black spots for eyes and straight black lines for the nose and mouth, than at a black-and-white photo of a human face. Analogously, Nikolaas Tinbergen found that a newly hatched gull will peck more at a stick with three red stripes than at a beak with a single red spot, as if the former were a super-stimulus. The mother gull does not have three red stripes but her single red spot is sufficient to recruit the young gull's attention. Nature does not always generate the perfect solution, only one that is sufficient. Eric Kandel notes in *The Age of Insight* that artists exploit the attraction to super-stimuli by exaggerating the features most often found in a face, body, object, or scene. The artist makes the eyes a little larger, fingers a bit longer, clouds a trifle whiter, flowers more colorful, and mountains more symmetrical than they appear in nature. The artists who caricature political figures in newspaper cartoons carry this principle to an extreme.

The essential features of the perceptual schemata for sounds are frequency (or pitch), loudness, suddenness of onset, and rhythm. The human brain is especially responsive to the physical features of the human voice. Newborns are alerted by sounds whose patterns of frequency, loudness, and suddenness (called rise time) resemble that of the human voice. Infants only a few days old can discriminate between a person speaking single words and physically similar sounds that were not produced by a human voice. Newborns also display unique brain profiles upon hearing their mother speak, compared with the speech of another woman. This fact implies that the fetus's brain processed some features of the mother's voice and established schemata for this pattern of sounds.[22]

Infants respond differently to consonant and dissonant musical chords. They stare and often smile at a speaker emitting a consonant melody but turn away with a frown when they hear a melody with dissonant chords. Both newly hatched chicks and chimpanzees also display a preference for attending to consonant over dissonant sounds or musical intervals.[23]

Children and adults organize the elements of most patterns in accordance with four principles that were proposed at the end of the nineteenth century. The first principle is to group elements that are close to each other in space or time. The eyes, nose, and mouth are closer to each other than the two ears. The second favors grouping elements that share similar physical features. For example, stimuli from different modalities that have similar levels of physical energy—say, a high-pitched tone and a brightly illuminated object—tend to be grouped. The third principle groups the movements of objects by their outcomes. The varied hand movements a mother uses when feeding her child are secondary to the placement of food in the child's mouth. Finally, a continuous contour or sound is more often perceived as a unit than a contour separated by a small space or a sound separated by a brief period of silence. Hence, infants hearing the mother say "pretty baby" will group the sound "pretty" as a unit separate from the sound "baby" because of the brief pause between the words. These principles, known as the Gestalt laws of perception, operate throughout life.

The ability to exploit the Gestalt principles is enhanced between two and four months of age. Four-month-olds perceive a moving green ball accompanied by a sound tracking the ball and two notes of different pitch occurring in close succession as a unified event. Two-month-olds do not.[24]

An event is most likely to create a schema if it is unexpected. The first year contains two kinds of unexpected events that usually recruit attention. One type alters the existing sensory background. The unexpected sound of a spoon striking the floor of a quiet room is an example. These events are called *sensory deviants*. The second kind, called *discrepant events,* share some, but not all, of the features of perceptual schemata acquired minutes, days, or weeks earlier. Novel events, in contrast to discrepant ones, contain no familiar features, and infants usually devote more attention to discrepant than to novel events. That is why four-month-olds look longer at a face with one eye than at a normal face or an irregularly shaped piece of plastic because the plastic contains no features that match an acquired schema. A blank white screen recruits minimal attention if it is the first thing infants see because it does not engage any schemata. If, however, infants are first familiarized on a white screen containing many objects and are then shown a blank white screen, they will attend to it because they expected to see the screen filled with objects. This early sensitivity to unexpected events is not surprising. The amygdala, a structure in the temporal lobe, is activated by any unexpected experience, and this structure has its greatest growth in the first year of life.[25]

The principle that discrepant events recruit maximal attention operates throughout life. Adults devote more attention to events that are a little different from what they know than to totally unfamiliar ones. That is why most members of a society initially reject radical movements in art or music and revolutionary ideas in science but have an aesthetic response to artistic products or scientific concepts that contain some familiar elements. Monet's impressionist paintings of gardens are more likely than Mondrian's line patterns to evoke an immediate aesthetic reaction in those who have little background in art.

This principle also helps to explain why so many musical compositions contain patterns characterized by one repetition of a sequence of chords (AA) followed by a slight change in the preceding A pattern (called the B pattern). The opening bars of Beethoven's *Fifth Symphony* are an example of an AAB pattern. This pattern is more common than one in which a chord sequence or melody is repeated four times (AAAAB) or is not repeated at all (AB). The occurrence of a B pattern after AA is a moderately discrepant event. It is probably not a coincidence that most jokes follow an AAB pattern in which two reasonable statements are followed by an incongruous one. Many European paintings, before the advent of modern art, contained an AAB pattern. Claude Monet was especially fond of the AAB pattern in his paintings. The rhymes in children's poems usually exploit an AAB pattern, too, as in:

> *Jack and Jill*
> *Went up the hill*
> *To fetch a pail of water.*
> *Jack fell down*
> *And broke his crown*
> *And Jill came tumbling after.*

Schemata that originate in sensations from within the body are called visceral schemata. The sensory events created by the stomach, muscles, heart, tongue, and nose activate brain circuits that differ from the ones activated by sights or sounds.

Nursing infants less than one week old orient more reliably to the odor of the mother's breast than to the odor of her amniotic fluid, implying that visceral schemata can be acquired quickly. Moreover, the odor of the mother's milk is better able to calm a crying two-day-old than the odor of milk taken from another woman. Some visceral schemata are preserved for a relatively long time. One group of nursing mothers placed a balm with a distinctive odor on their nipples; a second group did not use the balm. Infants who nursed for six weeks from the mothers with the balm acquired visceral schemata for the odor and retained that representation for at least eighteen months after they had stopped nursing.[26]

Unlike perceptual schemata, visceral schemata have weaker links to words. Languages have few words that accurately describe the sensations created by tastes, smells, or bodily activity. That is one reason why adults find it more difficult to describe their feelings than to describe what they saw or heard when a feeling occurred. Adolescents can retrieve perceptual schemata for scenes and conversations experienced years earlier but find it much harder to relive the feelings that accompanied those events. Twelve-year-olds can remember the features of the costume on a clown and the shape of the chocolate bar they were eating six years earlier when they were at a circus, but they have difficulty reliving the feelings that the clown evoked and the sweetness of the chocolate bar they were eating when the clown appeared. The visceral schemata may not be lost but are difficult to retrieve and to savor in consciousness.

This difficulty has advantages. The inability to reexperience the pain of a broken leg, the sadness of a lost friendship, or the fear provoked by a large dog with bared teeth is adaptive. Because the feeling components of pain, sadness, and fear are usually more intense than most pleasant feelings, it is reasonable to argue that the barrier to reliving unpleasant events makes life a lot more tolerable. Moreover, if hungry children could reexperience the feeling of being sated after a meal, some might be in danger of not receiving the nutrition they require. If anyone could generate the pleasure of past orgasms with little effort, a central feature of the human narrative would be altered. Novelists and film directors would have to find a new occupation, population sizes would suffer, and the excited pleasure that accompanies one of life's most delightful pursuits would be seriously diluted.

This feature of visceral schemata implies that the use of words like *fear* or *sadness* to describe how one feels now or felt in the past does not mean that the person is experiencing a feeling either at the time or in the past. One year after the events of September 11, 2001, a group of Americans remembered many perceptual schemata they created that day, but they could not retrieve any feelings. Many adults who say they felt anxious or depressed years earlier are often guessing what their feeling state was, or should have been, at that time.

Motor actions directed at a desired object or goal represent a third type of representation that is also difficult to describe with words. These motor representations become especially important between two and four months, when the motor cortex begins to exert more consistent control over motor sites located beneath the cortex called the basal ganglia. Now infants become very proficient in sucking from a breast or bottle and more accurate when grasping small objects.

The acquisition of many, but not all, motor representations requires a particular outcome. Unexpected outcomes facilitate acquisition of the behaviors that produced them. Infants who bang a spoon on a surface are surprised by the sound. That unexpected outcome makes it likely that the infant will repeat the action.

A representation that is an average of the schemata created by many exposures to the same class of events emerges between seven and ten months. This average, called a *perceptual prototype,* is illustrated in the example below. A group of adults heard someone speak the following six-letter sequences:

> a h g l z w
> x h q l z o
> c e b h z m
> a b g l o r
> a h b r f w
> u i b k j w

They then listened to three sequences—*x h q l z o, a b g l o r,* and *a h b l z w*—and indicated which string of letters they had heard seconds earlier. Most of the adults were confident that they heard the third sequence, which was the only one of the three they had not heard. However, *a h b l z w* is the average of the six sequences. The letter *a* occurred three times in position one, the letter *h* three times in position two, the letter *b* three times in position three, the letter *l* three times in position four, the letter *z* three times in position five, and the letter *w* three times in position six.

By the time infants are nine or ten months old, they have established prototypes for the language sounds that are the components of meaningful words. These sounds are called the *phonemes* of a language. Although all three-month-olds can discriminate among the approximately twenty vowels and six hundred consonants that are present in one or more of the world's languages, by the time they are ten months old they behave as if slightly different speech sounds that are not phonemes in their language belong to a prototype and they treat these sounds as if they were identical. For example, *ra* and *la* are distinctive phonemes in English. But Japanese adults treat *ra* and *la* as if they were equivalent sounds. Although three-month-old Japanese infants pay attention when the repeated sound *ra* suddenly becomes *la*, nine-month-old Japanese infants, but not infants from families speaking English, behave as if they were equivalent.[27] This does not mean, however, that the brains of nine-month old Japanese infants do not register the difference.

Research in Patricia Kuhl's laboratory at the University of Washington affirms this suggestion.[28] One-year-old Mexican infants learning Spanish do not orient to the subtle contrast between the English phonemes *ta* and *da,* despite the fact that they display a brain response when one of these phonemes is replaced with the other. Their brains detect a physical difference that they ignore in their behavior. Likewise, residents of rural Maine can detect the difference between their pronunciation of the word *tomorrow* and the pronunciation by rural Texans, but they treat the two phoneme strings as belonging to the same prototype. This principle extends to nonlinguistic prototypes. One-year-olds who have seen ten different dogs do not show prolonged attention to an eleventh dog who differs in shape from the prior ten, even though their visual cortex probably detected the physical differences between the eleventh dog and the ten prior ones.

Infants do not create prototypes for speech sounds that are totally unrelated to any sound in the language they hear each day. For example, the Zulu language contains click sounds that bear no resemblance to any phoneme in English, and one-year-old American infants do orient to click sounds that older Zulu infants would ignore. A similar phenomenon is seen in infants' reactions to faces from different ethnic groups. Caucasian and Chinese four-month-olds can discriminate between two faces belonging to either ethnic group. But by nine months, infants appear to lose this ability. Chinese infants fail to detect the difference between two Caucasian faces and Caucasian infants fail to discriminate between two Chinese faces when duration of attention is the index of discrimination.[29]

Language accelerates the creation of prototypes. Parents who use the same word to name different members of a category help their children establish a prototype for that class of object. One group of mothers of six-month-olds used the word *stroller* as they showed their infants pictures of physically different strollers. Anther group labeled each stroller with a different word. This tutoring went on for three months. When the infants were nine months old they were first familiarized on one stroller and then shown a physically different stroller. The nine-month-olds whose mothers gave each stroller a different name showed increased attention to the novel stroller. The infants who heard the same word for every stroller did not show prolonged attention because hearing the same word applied to slightly different objects helped them create a prototype.[30] Prototypes affirm Immanuel Kant's rebuttal of John Locke's declaration that all knowledge originates in sensory impressions. Human brains and their products, which we call minds, go beyond the sensory information to invent new representations.

The brain growth that permits the creation of perceptual prototypes is also responsible for a major improvement in *working memory*. Working memory refers to two distinct processes. One is the ability to maintain information in an active form for durations up to thirty seconds. Remembering a new telephone number while dialing provides a classic example. The second process involves performing mental work on the information. A driver stuck in traffic in a familiar neighborhood maintains in working memory schemata for the alternate routes he might take, while simultaneously imagining the consequences of taking different routes.

When brain maturation permits the enhancement of both processes, infants remain attentive as they perform mental work on the information contained in their perception of an event and the schemata that are activated by the event. The working memory of infants becomes more robust after seven months of age because of firmer connections between the hippocampus in the temporal lobe, on the one hand, and sites in the frontal lobe, on the other, due to the myelination of fibers connecting these sites. (See Figure 2.5.) Sarah Short and her colleagues at the University of North Carolina first hid a toy in one of two or one of three wells, covered the wells, and had one-year-olds wait for intervals ranging from three to fifteen seconds before allowing them to reach for the toy.[31] The infants who most often reached to the correct location possessed greater myelination of the nerve fibers connecting parietal, temporal, and frontal lobe neurons.

The behaviors of infants who were tested every two weeks from six to fourteen months of age reveal the gradual improvement in working memory during the first year. The infants were given problems that varied in the severity of the demand on the first component of working memory. In the easiest problem, the infants saw an

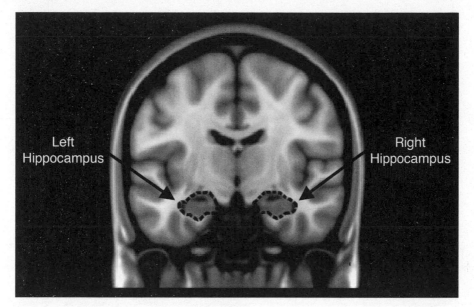

FIGURE 2.5   Location of hippocampus in temporal lobe

adult put a toy under one of three cups and were allowed to reach for the toy after a brief delay of two seconds. The six- and seven-month-olds reached immediately to the correct location, indicating that their working memory could tolerate a delay of two seconds. However, seven-month-olds did not reach to the correct cup when the delay was as long as twelve seconds and the adult put an opaque screen between the infants and the cups so that they could not fix their gaze on the place of hiding and had to maintain the correct location in working memory. Twelve-month-olds solved that problem easily.

It cannot be a coincidence that the improvement in working memory from six to twelve months of age is accompanied by an extraordinary increase in the amount of gray matter in the temporal lobe (an increase of 153 percent from birth to the first birthday) and in the number of neurons across many brain sites that oscillate at the same frequency. Monkeys, whose brains mature at a rate three times that of human infants, display a similar advance in working memory between three and four months of age.[32]

The improvement in working memory explains a number of puzzling phenomena that appear rather suddenly during the last half of the first year. Infants show increasingly shorter bouts of attention to a realistic clay sculpture of a human face during the interval from four to eight months because they find it easier to relate the face to their prototype for human faces. Surprisingly, when they are eight- or nine-months-old they show a prolonged bout of attention to the same realistic face they looked at briefly a month earlier. One explanation is that they are now comparing the face with their prototype for faces in a working-memory circuit and remain attentive while they try to relate the face to their prototype. This process involves both components of working memory.

The sturdier working memory also explains why eight-month-olds, but not four-month-olds, are likely to cry when they see a stranger with a neutral facial expression approach them quickly. The older infants relate the stranger's unfamiliar face and posture with their schematic prototype for the people they know and try to resolve the discrepancy while holding the perception of the stranger and the retrieved prototype in working memory. If they cannot resolve the difference, they become uncertain and cry. Four-month-olds do not cry in reaction to strangers because their less mature working memory prevents them from working at a resolution of the discrepancy between the stranger and their schemata. If, on the other hand, infants can resolve a discrepancy between an event and their schema, they laugh or smile. Eight-month-olds laugh if the mother puts a piece of cloth in her mouth and crawls on the floor like an infant.

Enhanced working memory also explains why infants older than seven or eight months cry when their primary caretaker leaves them unexpectedly, especially if the departure occurs in an unfamiliar place. This phenomenon, called separation anxiety, emerges at the same age as the cry that is displayed to strangers and for the same reason. A mother's unexpected departure from an unfamiliar room is discrepant from the child's schema of being with the mother moments earlier and from the prototype for the many times that the mother told the infant that she planned to leave temporarily. Older infants retrieve these schemata, hold them in a working-memory circuit along with the current perception of her absence, and try to relate the two. If they cannot, they cry.

Infants growing up in four different cultural settings—a rural village in Botswana, an Israeli kibbutz, the Guatemalan city of Antigua, and a small Indian village in northwest Guatemala—behaved like American infants when their mother left them alone in an unfamiliar place. The probability of crying rose sharply after seven months, peaked between ten and fifteen months, and declined during the latter half of the second year because the older children were able to resolve the discrepancy. (See Figure 2.6.) The similarity in the ages of onset, peak, and decline in the probability of crying is remarkable since the infants on the kibbutz saw their mothers only a few hours each day, whereas the Botswana infants were with their

SECOND TRANSITION

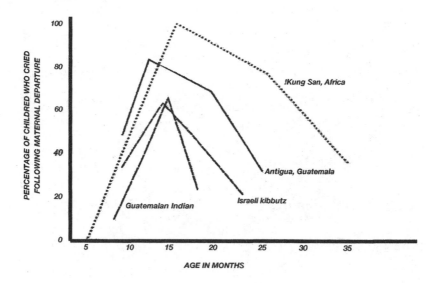

FIGURE 2.6   Percentage of infants from four cultural settings who cried

mothers almost continually. The same phenomenon is seen in infants from rural Bangladesh. Two-month-old rhesus monkeys, comparable to six-month-old human infants, do not become upset when separated from their mothers. But monkeys older than three months, comparable to nine-month-old human infants, do show a stress reaction when separated from their mothers. It cannot be a coincidence that the monkey's amygdala, which is part of a circuit that produces fearful responses to unfamiliar events, grows fastest during the first three postnatal months.[33]

The sturdier working memory also explains infants' behavior on an apparatus called the *visual cliff.* The visual cliff is a glass table with a checkerboard-patterned sheet pasted directly under the glass on one half of the table but resting on the floor on the other half. Infants older than eight months placed in the middle of the table will not cross over the half where the checkerboard pattern is on the floor, even if the mother beckons them to do so, because they perceive a drop-off. (See Figure 2.7.) This visual perception is discrepant from the tactile sensation of solidity in their hands, which are touching the solid glass surface. The infants who maintain these two schemata in working memory and are unable to resolve the discrepancy become uncertain, experience a rise in heart rate, and refuse to crawl over the apparently deep side.[34]

Adults engage in a similar process when they hear an atypical sound coming from a jet engine as the plane taxis for takeoff. They compare the sound with their

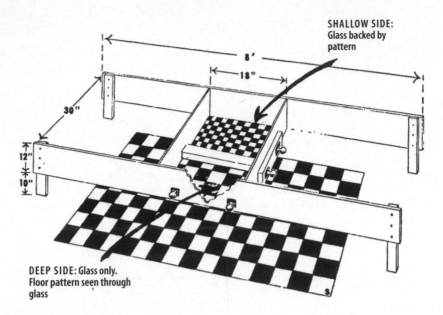

SHALLOW SIDE:
Glass backed by
pattern

DEEP SIDE: Glass only.
Floor pattern seen through
glass

FIGURE 2.7   The visual cliff

schematic prototype for the sounds heard on prior trips and, if they cannot relate the two, might become anxious. Humans live in a narrow corridor surrounded on one side by fear of events that cannot be understood and, on the other, by joy when discrepancies are quickly resolved.

Animals and humans are capable of three different states of uncertainty, each accompanied by a distinct brain profile. Unfamiliar or unexpected events evoke event uncertainty. If, in addition, the person is unable to decide which of several actions to implement, or has no appropriate response to make, response uncertainty emerges. Finally, there are occasions when the individual cannot predict a future event even though no action is required. This state, which we might call "predictive uncertainty," is accompanied by distinct changes at the level of the synapse (the narrow space between adjacent neurons).[35] Event uncertainty emerges early in development, followed by response uncertainty during the second half of the first year and uncertainty of prediction during the second year.

The brain changes that accompany a sturdier working memory also enable infants to extract a feature shared by events from different sensory modalities—for example, vision and touch. An adult placed a small cube in the mouths of one-year-olds, making sure that they could not see the cube. Moments later, when shown a cube alongside a sphere, the infants looked longer at the sphere because its curved contours were discrepant from the linear contours of the cube.[36] Although the phenomena that emerge between six and twelve months are very different, they are probably dependent on the same brain growth and enhanced connectivity that is inherent in the maturational sequences that all infants inherit.

HOW LONG DOES A SCHEMA LAST?

Scientists and parents would like to know how long a schema for an event lasts. Unfortunately, there is no simple answer to that question. The estimate always depends on the nature of the event, the frequency or duration of exposure, the delay between the last exposure and the evaluation, and, especially, the evidence used to decide whether the infant did or did not create a schema. Psychologists rely on six different procedures to decide if a representation was retained; three are used with young infants, and all six with older children. The infant measures are looking times, a conditioned motor response, or a biological measure such as heart rate, skin conductance, blood flow, or a waveform in the electroencephalogram. Psychologists testing older infants and children add to this list the imitation of an action seen in the past, finding an object seen earlier, or a verbal response. These latter procedures reflect the ability to retrieve a schema or semantic form, which is more difficult than recognition. For example, it is easier to recognize that the term *mutation* refers to a change in a person's genes than to retrieve the word *mutation* when asked "What word do biologists use to refer to changes in a gene?" That is why students prefer true-false examinations to essay questions.

Each method of measurement yields a different answer to the question of how long a representation was preserved. Estimates based on duration of looking differ from estimates based on brain activity; estimates based on brain activity differ from those based on imitation.

Rachel Clifton and her colleagues reported an example of a schema that was preserved for two years.[37] Six-and-a-half-month-olds sitting on their mothers' laps in a totally dark room reflexively reached forward upon hearing a sound originating in the space in front of them. When these children returned to the same dark room two years later, most reached forward when they heard a sound. Two-year-olds who had never experienced the earlier event did not do so.

Five-year-olds who had played with a group of children at a nursery school several years earlier, but had not seen them for at least two years, were shown photographs of these children, along with photographs of children they had never seen,

and had to say which photos they recognized as former playmates. Their verbal answers indicated that they had lost the perceptual schemata for their former friends.
However, the psychologists also measured momentary changes in the activity of
the sweat glands on the hands, called the skin conductance response. Many of the
five-year-olds who did not consciously recognize their former playmates showed an
increase in skin conductance when they saw photographs of these children, but not
when they saw photos of children they had never known.

The significance of the source of evidence permeates all the sciences. Estimates
of the ages of human fossils by nineteenth-century scientists were altered when ra-
dioactive tracing techniques became the basis for judging a fossil's age. A respected
cosmologist, when asked about the age of the universe, replied that the method
used to arrive at the estimate was far more important than any number he might
offer: today's estimate of 13. 7 billion years might be altered if and when a more
sophisticated method is discovered. It is useful to remember that Lord Kelvin, ar-
guably the nineteenth century's most eminent physical scientist, rejected Darwin's
theory of evolution because Kelvin's method of estimating the age of the earth implied that our planet was much younger than the age that evolutionary theory required. Kelvin's estimate was wrong because he relied on an insensitive method.

School-age children cannot remember most of the experiences that occurred
during their first two years. One reason is that these events were registered as perceptual schemata without the support of words. Four-year-olds asked to describe
their earliest memories rarely retrieved a memory for any event that occurred before
they were two and a half years old. When asked the same question two years later,
90 percent reported different early memories.[38] Not all representations that appear
to have vanished are lost completely. The behavior of Indian children adopted by
American families implied that they had lost all knowledge of the phonemes of the
language they heard as infants. But the children relearned these phonemes more
quickly than American children who had never heard the Indian phonemes.[39] Because the method used to measure the presence of a representation of an earlier
event cannot be separated from any conclusions about preservation, there is always
the possibility that a new method will reveal the existence of fragments of the past
that no other procedure has detected.

The second half of the first year also marks the age when infants imitate some adult
behaviors more regularly. Mothers from several cultures told an interviewer that
their infants first began to imitate them during the final months of the first year. The
child's sex can affect the specific acts that are imitated. Seven-month-olds saw films

in which an adult either cradled a balloon in the arms or struck it with a fist. Male infants were more likely than females to imitate the more vigorous action.[40] Male monkeys possess a similar bias for displaying vigorous motor actions.

Acts of imitation can be provoked or spontaneous—that is, performed either immediately after the behavior is observed or after delays of hours, days, or months. More important, infants do not imitate every act they have seen. The selection of an action for imitation depends on the person who modeled the act, its degree of discrepancy, and, especially, the infant's ability to perform it. The familiarity of the setting exerts some influence on whom the infant imitates. Sabine Seehagen and Jane Herbert of the University of Sheffield found that six-month-olds are more likely to imitate a novel action performed by their mother if they are at home, but more likely to imitate an action performed by an unfamiliar adult if the infants are in a laboratory.[41]

Infants during the first year are less likely to imitate behaviors they see on television than actions displayed by a familiar person in a natural setting. Actions that are moderately discrepant from what the infant knows, but within their competence, are imitated most often. One-year-olds are unlikely to imitate familiar acts (for example, an adult moving her finger) or totally unfamiliar acts (an adult standing on one foot), but they will imitate a woman who claps her hands three times in succession because that act is relatively uncommon and within the infants' ability.

Michael Posner of the University of Oregon has suggested that the concept of attention, which facilitates the ability to register a schema for an act to be imitated, refers to three different processes.[42] The first two, called alerting and orienting, are present in the first days following birth. The third process, called executive functions, allows infants to regulate and control their actions and feelings, and, like imitation, emerges during the second half of the first year. Indeed, imitation is one of the first signs of this talent. The 90 percent rule applies to all three processes, for infants do not display them in all the settings in which they are appropriate.

Imitation of others serves at least two purposes. It allows infants and children to improve a skill and allows older children to feel they are more similar to a person who displayed an action. Although it is reasonable to assume that imitation contributes to intellectual growth, it may not be necessary for that growth. The small number of children born with no arms but an intact brain show normal intellectual development, even though their ability to imitate is seriously restricted.

We do not understand why ten-month-olds imitate, or whether these actions in the first year contribute in a significant way to later development. Americans and Europeans are friendly to the assumption that a behavior that is universal must serve a useful purpose. But it is instructive to examine another universal behavior that is not required for normal development. Although most infants crawl before they walk, crawling is not necessary for walking. Infants strapped to a cradle board, a practice common on Navajo reservations, cannot crawl but they walk at about the same time as American infants, who are allowed to crawl. It is always fallacious to assume that if A precedes B, A must be necessary for B. Dogwood trees in Massachusetts bloom about a month before the school year ends, but the former event makes no contribution to the latter.

Although psychologists agree that infants acquire perceptual schemata and prototypes, there is disagreement over whether they also possess the more abstract knowledge that is implied by understanding concepts of number, object, and causality. Some eminent scientists argue that infants do possess these concepts, which they call *core knowledge*.[43]

The concept of number provides an excellent example of the controversy. The claim that five-month-olds possess a concept of number is based on the fact that they look longer at two black circles after seeing four black circles, and look longer at four circles after seeing two circles, although they do not look longer at four circles after seeing six circles.[44] This evidence implies that infants can discriminate between the physical features possessed by two compared with four circles. The advocates of core knowledge, however, make the bolder suggestion that such evidence implies that infants possess a concept of number. This conclusion equates a perceptual schema with a semantic concept that has logical properties in older children.

A good reason to question the claim that infants under one year possess a number concept is that arrays of two and four black circles differ in the density, pattern, and spatial frequency of the elements. The retina as well as neurons in select brain sites are sensitive to these physical features and generate different patterns of activation to one, two, or three circles, compared with four or more circles. This fact implies that infants' brains may be responding to the physical differences between two and four dark circles.[45]

The following experiment, which has not yet been implemented, might reveal whether infants have a number concept or are responding to variations in physical features. Five-month-olds first see a pair of dark circles placed side by side in the middle of a white square, after which they see one of two arrays. One group sees three circles side by side in the middle of a white square. A second group sees two circles, but each is placed at an opposite corner of the square. If infants can count, they should look longer at the three circles because this array is discrepant from the two-circle array seen earlier. If they are responding to the physical features of the array, they should look longer at the two circles located in opposite corners. I suspect that most infants will pay more attention to the latter array.

Caitlin Brez of Indiana University, along with her colleagues, affirmed that infants can process both the spatial properties of three cookies on a plate or the shape, size, and color of the cookies.[46] It turns out that nine-month-olds have a preference to attend to the spatial properties of the arrays of three cookies. Older infants—eleven and thirteenth months—preferentially attend to the shape of the cookies rather than to their spatial arrangement.

Number—like time, goodness, and justice—is not an inherent property of a natural event but, rather, a concept humans invented to represent a single, symbolic feature that is shared by different events. A pile composed of playing cards from two decks creates a similar perceptual schema in all observers, but it can be classified, symbolically, as one pile, two decks, or 104 cards. My front lawn has eight trees and my neighbor's lawn has six trees, a fact I was unaware of for forty years until I counted them recently. When I gaze out my study window I perceive the difference between the spatial arrangements of the trees on the two lawns. I do not see eight and six trees. I suggest that infants, too, do not perceive three circles, cookies, or pennies. Rather, they see arrays of well-defined shapes in particular spatial arrangements.

Two-year-olds who have acquired the word *two* do not apply it to pairs of objects, even though they pluralize the word *doll* when they see two dolls. Nor do three-year-olds understand that the word *four* applies to an array of four cups. Four-year-olds who moments earlier told an adult that two rows of four equally spaced buttons had the same number changed their minds when the adult increased the space between each of the buttons so that the row appeared longer. If four-year-olds have not linked the semantic concepts for 2, 3, and 4 to the perception of arrays of two, three, or four objects, the claim that infants possess a concept of number is relying on a special meaning of this concept.[47]

Five-month-olds familiarized on the letter *V* will show increased looking at the letter *L* because their visual cortex is sensitive to the physical differences between these two contours. This does not mean that the infants possess the concept of angle as it is understood in geometry. Nor should we conclude that infants have a concept of grammar if they were alerted by hearing a grammatically incorrect sentence—say, "Ate girl bread the"—after hearing many repetitions of the correct form "The girl ate the bread."

Indeed, we have learned from the study of many species that animals are able to make highly refined discriminations that do not require the assumption that they possess abstract competences. For example, the features of the dance that bees perform when they return to the hive vary with the distance between the hive and a clump of flowers. The form of the dance is determined by the density of contours the bee's small brain registered as it flew from the hive to the flowers. The bee's behavior is based on the texture of the landscape and does not imply possession of a concept of distance. Honeybees can be conditioned to fly toward a location where a red disc rests above a purple one and to avoid flying toward a location where a red disc is below a purple one. This behavior does not require the conclusion that bees possess the symbolic concepts *above* and *below*. Pigeons can be taught to discriminate between the limb movements mammals make when they are moving at a slow pace compared with a rapid one. No scientist would claim that these pigeons possessed the concepts *walking* and *running*. The main point is that the ability to tell the difference between physically distinctive events cannot be used as an argument for the possession of abstract concepts.

The claim that infants have a concept of number, object, or causality is largely based on differences in the duration of time they look at each of two events. Once again we confront the problems trailing reliance on one source of evidence.[48] A pair of scientists at the University of Kansas discovered that although seven-month-olds did not show longer looking times when the number of objects in an array was changed, they did display a change in heart rate. Very few behaviors have only one meaning and invite only one explanation, whether the behavior is an exaggerated startle to a loud sound, a pattern of answers on a questionnaire, or a smile. Put plainly, the meaning of *know* in sentences of the form "Children know . . . " depends on the source of evidence.

Psychologists who believe that infants possess a concept of number—or of objects, causality, or physical impossibility—may be making an error similar to one Konrad Lorenz and Nicholaas Tinbergen made in the 1930s when they claimed that newly hatched goslings were born with an innate fear of hawks. Their evidence was the goslings' avoidance of a moving silhouette of a bird with a short neck and a long tail, resembling a hawk. Later research revealed that goslings avoid *any* event that is discrepant from the schemata created from their limited experience; for example, they also avoid a silhouette of a moving triangle. Hence, the young birds were not born with an unlearned fear of hawks.[49]

The intuition that infants are born with a core understanding of concepts that older children possess is reminiscent of the belief in "preformation" held by seventeenth-century scholars who did not understand how a fertilized egg could develop into an animal with organs and limbs. They eliminated their frustration by declaring that the egg contained miniature versions of the fully formed organs of the newborn. I once suggested that a hypothetical experiment would reveal that infants understood the difference between truth and falsity. After looking at the letter string *T R U E* printed in bold letters for a minute, they subsequently looked longer at the string *F A L S E* and vice versa.

TEMPERAMENTAL BIASES

Until now I have considered the properties possessed by all infants with an intact brain and largely ignored the obvious variation among infants. Although experiences in the home make a major contribution to this variation, a second source originates in each infant's temperamental biases. A *temperament* is a disposition originating in the child's biology that favors particular patterns of actions and feelings to specific events, much as breeds of dogs vary in their behavior. Infants vary in the frequency and intensity of a small number of observable behaviors. The most obvious properties include attentiveness, ease of becoming distressed in reaction to specific events, the form of the distress, the ability to regulate distress, ease of being soothed by another, and the frequency of spontaneous crying, fretting, smiling, babbling, and limb and trunk movements.

My colleagues and I conducted a long-term study of two temperamental biases in healthy, white, middle-class infants born to caring mothers. About 20 percent of the infants showed vigorous movements of the arms and legs, arching of the back, and frequent fretting and crying in reaction to a set of unfamiliar events that include mobiles and recorded speech. We called these infants high-reactive. A second group, representing about 40 percent of the children, usually lay still and rarely cried or arched their back. We called these infants low-reactive.

We assessed these children many times through their eighteenth birthday. High-reactive infants are likely to become shy, timid, fearful two-year-olds and adolescents who worry excessively about improbable events. Low-reactive infants, by contrast, are likely to become relaxed, sociable, fearless toddlers and minimally anxious adolescents. Other psychologists have reported similar results in children, as well as in several animal species. About 20 percent of rhesus monkeys show behavioral profiles that resemble those of children who had been high-reactive infants.[50]

A comparison of two fifteen-year-old girls, one low-reactive and one high-reactive as infants, is instructive. These adolescents were interviewed for three hours in their homes. Jane, the high-reactive, sat stiffly on a hard chair in the living room of her suburban home, wearing a white blouse buttoned to her neck. Her answers to questions about schoolwork and hobbies were typical of girls her age but were terse rather than elaborated, spoken in a soft voice, and accompanied by restless fidgeting with her face, hair, and clothes, infrequent smiles, and frequent blinking of the eyes. Jane said that she has a good relationship with her parents, has a few close friends, and gets good grades but prefers the solitary hobby of swimming over team sports such as soccer.

When the interviewer asked Jane about her worries and moods, her answers revealed that she is not a typical adolescent. Jane cannot sleep before most examinations, has frequent nightmares, and sometimes vomits on evenings when she is excessively worried about her performance the next day. She feels nervous when she meets strangers, is uneasy when touched, and is worried about an imminent class trip to Washington, DC, because she is not sure how she will feel in an unfamiliar city meeting adolescents she does not know. Surprisingly, her teachers as well as her friends are unaware of the intensity of these private worries and regard her as conscientious, quiet, and reserved.

Jennifer, an equally attractive fifteen-year-old who had been a low-reactive infant, was dressed in a loose-fitting sweater and short skirt and sat with her legs crossed under her body on a sofa. Jennifer loves variety, enjoys visiting new cities, is president of her class, and is a member of the school choral group and soccer team. Her answers were often accompanied by a string of anecdotes and bursts of laughter. Jennifer sleeps well, gets excellent grades, and does not worry much about examinations.

At the moment, scientists do not know the total number of human temperaments. It is probably large because 2 to 5 percent of human genes influence the brain in ways that could produce a temperamental bias. Hence, at least fifteen hundred genes could contribute to human temperaments. If each gene had four alleles, there could be as many as six thousand temperamental biases.

It is important to appreciate that no single temperament determines a particular personality. Rather, each temperamental bias limits the outcomes that are most likely to develop. High-reactives, for example, are unlikely to become adolescents who are consistently fearless, exuberant, and highly sociable, but they can acquire any one of a large number of personality profiles. Some will become quiet adults working in solitary vocations. Others may choose to study law. But few will become extremely bold risk takers who love the excitement of new places and people.

Low-reactive children also acquire a variety of personalities, but it is unlikely that anyone with this temperament will become a chronically tense, vigilant adult who worries continually about his or her health, avoids social contacts, and is consistently preoccupied with making a mistake.

The first year is marked by significant psychological changes that are accompanied by the largest increase in brain growth that occurs in any year after birth. This growth results in firmer connections within and among select sites in the visual, parietal, temporal, and frontal cortex. The rate of maturation, however, is dependent on experience. The extraordinary plasticity of the brain is one of the most surprising discoveries of the past few decades. Perceptual and visceral schemata and motor modules are the major products of this initial stage of development. The two most important maturational transitions of the first year occur between two and four months and seven and twelve months. The former is accompanied by increased cortical control over the brain stem. This increased control, in turn, leads to inhibition of reflexes that were present at birth, a firmer representation of the human face, and increased activity of the parasympathetic nervous system. The latter transition is accompanied by an enhancement of working memory that explains infants' distress reactions to strangers and to temporary separation from the mother.

The psychological profiles that infants display as the first year ends are the result of each infant's prenatal environments, inherited temperaments, and history of experiences. These three contributions combine to form a seamless tapestry that is not easily unwound. Scientists would like to have an estimate of their separate contributions to a child's psychological development, but the experiments that would permit such analyses are ethically unacceptable. Thus at present we have to live with the frustration that dessert chefs might feel because they are unable to know the separate contributions of flour, sugar, fruit, and time in the oven to the taste of an apple crisp.

CHAPTER THREE

Early Childhood

———————

Human and chimpanzee infants behave in remarkably similar ways during the first four to six months. It isn't until the second year that these two species begin to diverge in profound ways. Four distinctively human properties emerge in nascent form between twelve and twenty-four months: the ability to understand and speak a symbolic language, to infer feelings and thoughts in others, to understand the meaning of a prohibited action, and to be conscious of one's feelings, intentions, and actions. Because each of these capacities honors the 90 percent rule, their display is restricted to select settings during the early years. Not surprisingly, the emergence of these properties is associated with particular changes in the brain, especially an expanded frontal lobe and a richer connectivity among brain sites. The fact that deaf children exposed to a sign language display their first meaningful gestures at the same age that hearing children speak their first words affirms the influence of lawful brain growth on the readiness to acquire a language.[1]

A SYMBOLIC LANGUAGE

The talents needed to comprehend and speak a language are profoundly cognitive. Some of these skills—especially the ability to hold a sequence of events in working memory, to create prototypes, and to infer others' intentions—are exploited in settings that are minimally related to language. Some capacities, however, appear to be specific to language. The brain's sensitivity to the physical properties of speech is one such feature. The neurons of the temporal lobe are maximally responsive to the frequencies and rates of change in the sounds that humans make when they talk. The ability to produce a variety of sounds, especially the vowels *a*, *i*, and *u*, requires the larynx, which contains the vocal cords, to occupy a lower position in the throat than it does in chimpanzees. This anatomical relocation was a by-product of evolutionary events occurring about 300,000 years ago that reshaped the human head and flattened the face.

The emergence of a symbolic language, however, had to wait at least another 100,000 years. The ability to represent one thing by another is fundamental to every language. Words are symbols because their sounds (or written shapes) usually bear no relation to the events they represent. The physical features of the sound pattern for *dog* share no features with the animal that the word names. A site in the temporal lobe, called *Wernicke's area,* makes a critical contribution to the ability to understand the meanings of words. It is not a coincidence that children begin to play symbolically at the same time they begin to acquire a language. An eighteen-month-old, for example, will use a small stick as a comb to straighten a doll's hair.[2]

The ability to order a series of words that follow particular rules, known as the rules of syntax, is a third competence unique to human language. *Broca's area,* located in the frontal lobe and connected to Wernicke's area, contributes to the ability to articulate words and to speak grammatically correct sentences. (See Figure 3.1.) Sites in the motor cortex that mediate the movements of the tongue and lips during speech are located close to Broca's area. Both Wernicke's and Broca's areas allow children to parse streams of phonemes into word meanings and to acquire the syntactic rules of the language they hear and will eventually speak.

The brain often divides up the responsibility for a complex skill among several sites. This division applies to language. Two fiber tracts that connect Wernicke's area and Broca's area play different roles. One tract, called the arcuate fascicle, processes phoneme strings and the order of words in a sentence. The other, lying beneath the arcuate fascicle and called the extreme capsule, carries information about word meanings as well as some information on word order. The neurons of Broca's area process the information coming from both tracts. Scientists at the Max Planck Institute in Leipzig suggest that the arcuate fascicle may not be fully mature until children are eight to ten years of age. This hypothesis would explain why young children have difficulty understanding sentences with a complex syntax—for example, "The girl holding the knife who was asked by the boy to put it down refused."

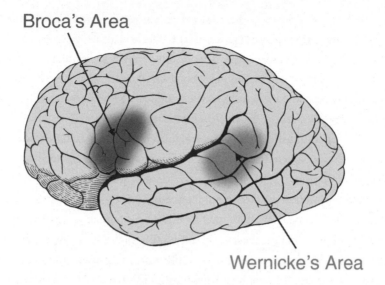

FIGURE 3.1   The location of Broca's and Wernicke's areas

The acquisition of a language requires the blending of several language-specific competences with more general cognitive talents. The same is true for tennis players who combine movements of arms and legs that occur in a variety of contexts with a few motor skills that are unique to tennis, such as the ability to deliver a powerful serve and to adjust the racket so that the ball falls only a few inches over the net.

The scientific study of language is roughly divided into two domains: study of the features that all languages share, called universals, and inquiry into the differences among the world's languages. One difference is that not all languages allow a speaker to ask a question that has only a yes or no answer. In addition, the number of consonants varies from the twenty-four in English to more than a hundred. Because the number of grammars and phoneme sequences in the world's languages is far smaller than the possible number, we are forced to conclude that the human brain imposes serious restrictions on the form a language can assume. For example, no language places two nouns and two verbs next to each other (as in "Mary Paul gave wanted the apple that he") or has words beginning with four consonant sounds (for example, "zbcd").

Despite the considerable variation among the world's languages, the child's mastery of a language proceeds through a number of well-defined stages. First, infants have to learn that the sounds originating in human faces, rather than dogs or telephones, usually refer to things or events they can see, hear, smell, touch, or feel.

Infants look at the eyes of a speaker once they learn that an adult's direction of gaze is a clue to what the speaker is talking about. The area of white sclera surrounding the darker pupil is larger in humans than in any ape species, making it easier to see where another person is looking. David Lewkowicz and Amy Hansen-Tilt of Florida Atlantic University found that most infants do not automatically orient to a speaker's eyes until they are about eleven months old.[3]

"Motherese," the distinctive sing-song vocal style that adults use with infants, plays an important role in the early stages of language learning. Patricia Kuhl of the University of Washington finds that speech sounds are far more salient for infants when adults use motherese as they point to objects or events.[4] Schemata for speech sounds are always acquired more quickly if they are perceptually distinct and can be linked to objects that speakers are manipulating as they talk. Infants find it easier to detect the difference between one-syllable words that vary in the initial or final phoneme—for example, *ball* versus *balls* and *ball* versus *tall*—than to detect the difference between words that differ in an internal phoneme—for example, *tap* versus *top*.

A second task is to detect the regularities in phoneme sequences. I noted that the phoneme sequence *p-r-e* in English is followed by the sequence *t-y* about 80 percent of the time, whereas *p-r-e* is followed by *b-a* less than 1 percent of the time. These facts make it easy for infants to learn that *pretty* is a meaningful word but *preba* is not. When an adult says "Lookatthebigredballoon," the child has to be able to detect the six different words in that phoneme string.

The next assignment is to appreciate that speech sounds belong to different syntactic categories. Some refer to objects, people, or animals (nouns). Others refer to the actions these things display (verbs). Adults reading or hearing these two kinds of words activate different brain sites. Other sounds name the speed and duration of actions (adverbs), features of objects (adjectives), and the spatial relations between objects (prepositions). Each language contains clues that help children create these categories. English, for example, adds the sound *ing* at the end of some verbs to indicate an ongoing action and adds *ly* at the end of some words to describe the speed of an action.[5]

As children master these regularities they acquire the syntactic rules of their language that stipulate the proper ordering of word categories in sentences, as well as the correct way to form verb tenses, plurals, prefixes, and suffixes. The more frequently they hear a sequence, the easier it is to learn the rule. Although most verbs in English form the past tense by adding *ed,* a small number—fewer than two hundred verbs, including *went, sang,* and *saw*—do not follow this rule. When children are learning the rule for the past tense during their second and third years, they often apply the *ed* rule to all verbs and are likely to say *goed* and *singed* rather than *went* and *sang.* The 90 percent rule applies to the mastery of language. One psychologist studying her son's use of the plural found that by the time he was twenty-two months old he was applying the plural correctly 90 percent of the time.

The brain favors certain ways to arrange words in sentences because the world's languages rely on a small number of rules for word order. Most languages use one of three orders for a subject (S), verb (V), and object (O) in simple sentences like "The girl kissed the doll." The most common is S-V-O, which is the order in English. Two other common orders are S-O-V ("The girl doll kissed") and V-S-O ("Kissed girl the doll"). The orders V-O-S, O-V-S, and O-S-V also occur, but they are uncommon. One rare language spoken by a small community in northern Australia permits any word order.[6]

Children also have to learn that the setting can alter the meaning of a word or sentence. A parent who says "Quiet, please" could mean that the child should stop yelling while playing with a friend, turn down the volume on the television set, or make less noise while eating. This ability, called the pragmatics of language, implies that inferring the correct meaning of utterances often depends on the features in the immediate setting. Children use these features to figure out the correct meaning of words—such as *run, fall, tip,* and *hit*—that have more than one meaning. When a mother says to her four-year-old daughter "Don't tip the milk," the child's interpretation depends on whether she is bringing an open carton of milk to a table, holding a glass of milk, or carrying a package containing a carton of milk.

Although many infants understand the meanings of a small number of words before their first birthday, very few speak meaningful words that early. There is a significant improvement in understanding the meanings of words after fourteen months and a comparable rise in speaking short sentences between twenty and twenty-four months. The spurt in spoken words is accompanied by more consistent pointing at objects with the right hand. This action, mediated by the left hemisphere, typically reflects an attempt at communication.[7]

The left hemisphere's special role in symbolic communication is due to a number of anatomical features that are unique to this hemisphere. The left hemisphere has slightly larger neurons, axons with thicker myelin (the insulation that permits faster propagation of the nerve impulse), and more fibers connecting Wernicke's and Broca's areas; it is also especially effective at processing rapidly changing sequences. The right hemisphere, in turn, plays a more important role in processing variations in pitch, loudness, rhythm, and pauses—called the prosody of speech—and is better at processing global patterns. The right hemisphere, for example, is critical for understanding that the sentence "The boy said [brief pause] the girl is tall" implies that the property of being tall belongs to the girl, while the sentence "The boy [pause] said the girl [pause] is tall" implies that tallness describes the boy.

The word receiving vocal emphasis in a sentence usually implies a particular meaning, especially in questions. For example, a child who hears his mother ask "Did you run?" with a vocal emphasis on *run* is apt to interpret the question as asking if he ran or walked. If the vocal emphasis is on the word *you,* the child assumes the mother is asking whether he or another child ran. And if the emphasis is on the word *did,* the child is likely to assume that the mother wants to know if he ran or remained still.

The automatic understanding of speech requires the efficient combination of representations from both hemispheres. The maturational events of the second year facilitate this process. The human cortex consists of six layers, each defined by the properties of the cells in that layer. The neurons in layer three connect the left and right hemispheres through a structure called the corpus callosum, which extends from the frontal lobe to posterior brain regions. The neurons of layer three become larger at the end of the first and beginning of the second year, allowing a more efficient coordination of the processes and representations in both hemispheres.

The perceptual schemata for objects and the timbre and rhythm of speech, which are more fully represented in the right hemisphere, are combined with the phoneme strings of meaningful words, which are more elaborated by the left hemisphere. When a mother points to raindrops falling on the window and says for the first time "Look at the rain," giving vocal emphasis to the word *rain,* the child links the phoneme sequence for the word *rain* with the perception of the raindrops and the prosody of the sentence. Should rain fall several days later, the child is apt to relate her current perception to the mother's comment and the schema of the raindrops established earlier and spontaneously say "Rain."

Some patients suffering from epilepsy are helped if their callosum is severed surgically. The surgical separation of the two hemispheres means that a picture presented very briefly to one hemisphere will be processed only by the other hemisphere. Michael Gazzaniga discovered that when adults with a severed callosum saw a picture in their left visual field (which is processed by the right hemisphere), they recognized the object and might have had an emotional response, but could not name it. For example, a patient who saw a nude adult in her left visual field (processed by the right hemisphere) was unable to name the figure and could not explain why she laughed spontaneously. These observations support the suggestion that the more efficient connectivity between the two hemispheres facilitates the learning of language.[8]

Learning the meanings of words and sentences is more complicated than simply storing schemata and phoneme sequences in memory. Children begin the acquisition of word meanings with three biases that will be modified later. The first leads children to assume that a word for an object—say, a toy car—refers to the whole object rather than to a part. The distinguished philosopher Willard van Quine wrote a famous essay arguing that a visitor to a foreign country who did not know the local language would not understand what a native speaker meant when the latter pointed at a moving rabbit and said "gavagai." This is not true of children. If an adult pointed to a dog and said "Look at the tail," two-year-olds would treat the word *tail* as referring to the whole dog. Fortunately, most mothers do not talk that way. Few parents teach their children the meaning of *tail* before they are certain that the child understands the meaning of *dog*. However, this principle operates best when there is only one object, which is why most picture books for young children contain a single object set against a white background. (If Quine's foreigner saw a scene containing two rabbits, two squirrels, and two deer and the native said "gavagai," the visitor would not understand the meaning of the single word.)

Children also assume that a new word applies to all similar-looking objects and is not restricted to the particular object named. One-year-olds who have been told that *clock* is the name of the drawing of a round alarm clock assume, initially, that all objects with similar shapes, including the moon and cookies, have the same name. However, if young children already know some of the properties of the object, they are likely to use its function as the basis for inferences. Thus, they will call a square wristwatch a clock. Because one- and two-year-olds usually do not know the functional properties of unfamiliar objects whose names they have just learned, they tend to rely on similarity in shape to decide if another object has the same name. By the fourth year this bias is weaker because older children know some of the properties of many objects.

The third bias persuades children that each kind of object has only one name. Most two-year-olds would be confused if on Monday their mother pointed to a cow and said "Look at the cow" but on the next day said "Look at the animal." They will not fully understand that *cow* and *animal* apply to the same object until they are about six years old. Young children do not laugh at puns because they require the child to appreciate that a word can have more than one meaning.

Of course, young children find it easier to learn a word for an object or event if they already possess a related schema. We've seen that events with distinctive features are most likely to become schemata. Distinctiveness is greater for moving objects compared with static ones, large compared with small objects, near compared with far objects, graspable compared with nongraspable objects, objects that produce a sound compared with those that are silent, transient compared with prolonged events, and, finally, events that evoke a feeling compared with those that do not. That is why most children learn the words *fall* and *break* before the words *still* and *rest*.

As is true for schemata, children learn words more quickly if they occur frequently or are moderate deviations from what they expect. A parent who usually says "Time to eat" will alert her child if one day she says "Time for fruit" because the word *fruit* is discrepant from the child's usual experience. Adults who vary the verbs and nouns in their sentences make it easier to learn the meanings of these words. Children who hear the word *jump* linked with different nouns—for example, "Look at the dog jump," "Max jumped yesterday," or "Can you jump?"—extract the essential features of this verb with greater ease.

Children learning English find it easier to learn the meaning of a verb if they hear sentences that follow the sequence noun-verb-object rather than a noun-verb sequence without any object. Toddlers learn the meaning of the verb *hug* earlier if they hear sentences like "The mother hugged the child" compared with "The mother and child are hugging." English-speaking children find it easier to learn noun names for objects than verbs for actions. One reason is that the schemata for most objects are less ambiguous than the schemata for verbs. The contrast between the noun *toaster* and the verb *broke* provides an example. The referent for the verb *broke* is more ambiguous than the referent for *toaster* when a mother says "The toaster broke." Most verbs require a noun to make their meaning clear. The verbs *fall, go, went, move, eat,* and *stop* need a noun that specifies an agent and a target to allow a listener to infer the intended meaning.

In effect, the young child behaves as Sherlock Holmes would when solving a crime. The child gathers the bits and pieces of evidence related to how a word is used, stores the scattered information in memory, and one day has an "aha" moment when he or she understands the meaning of a word or syntactic rule. Children, like all good detectives, attend to the subtlest hints. For example, a parent who pauses in the middle of a sentence to add the sound *um* alerts the child to expect an important new piece of information. Imagine a three-year-old girl watching her mother wash orange-colored potatoes for dinner. The mother who says "These potatoes, [pause] um, I mean, yams" recruits the child's attention to the word *yams* and allows her to add a new word to her vocabulary.

Why do children want to understand the meanings of adult speech and to match their utterances to those of the adult? The biologist's answer is that these two talents are adaptive and the human brain pushes children in this direction, much like the neurobiology of a robin fledgling pushes it to fly. The psychologist's complementary answer is that not knowing what adults intend when they speak evokes an unpleasant feeling of uncertainty whereas the child's ability to match his or her speech to that of adults is satisfying. No one knows whether the young robin has analogous feelings on its initial flight from the nest.

Most of the child's first words refer to frequently named objects or events that can be seen, heard, tasted, felt, or acted upon, such as *mommy, cookie,* or *bottle.* For this reason, children are tempted to assume that all words refer to things or events that are perceptible. Thus, children are willing, at least initially, to believe that the words *ghost, fairy,* and *Santa Claus* refer to things that exist.

Parental reports suggest that by the second birthday the average American child (who, admittedly, is not a fair representative of the world's children) understands between five hundred and six hundred words and speaks between two hundred and three hundred words. Girls and first-born children understand and speak more words than boys and later-borns. Some two-year-olds are not speaking any words, but a delay of five or six months does not necessarily pose a serious risk for emotional or academic problems during later childhood. Albert Einstein was a late talker.[9] Three- and four-year-old children who are not speaking do represent a problem that requires attention.

By the end of the second and beginning of the third year, children have acquired clusters of closely associated words representing the semantic networks that are the bases of concepts. Some three-year-olds possess a semantic network for the concept *food* that contains the words *milk, cookie, bread, cereal,* and *apple.* Each network usually has a prototypic schema and/or word that functions as a best example of the concept. A piece of bread, for example, might be the prototype for the semantic concept *food.*

These networks expand throughout life. Adults across many cultures possess semantic networks for about sixty universal concepts. These include kinds of people (*men, women, boys, girls, infants*); types of family relationships (*mother, father, brother, sister, aunt, uncle*); parts of the body; plants and animals; the sun and moon; the numbers 1 and 2; the time and location of an event; causal relations; the capacities to see, hear, taste, smell, think, and feel; and the evaluative terms *good, bad, right,* and *wrong.* Some networks contain opposite qualities. Four such networks contain the contrast between *good* and *bad* (which includes the contrast between *clean* and *dirty* and *right* and *wrong*); *potent* and *impotent* (which includes the contrast between *large* and *small, strong* and *weak, dangerous* and *safe, male* and *female*); *active* and *passive* (which includes the contrast between *moving* and *still* and *approach* and *avoid*); and *natural* and *artificial* (which includes the contrast between animals, humans, and plants, on the one hand, and all manufactured objects, on the other).

Although shared meaning is the primary basis for membership in a semantic network, similarities in rhyme and in number of syllables add to the likelihood that two words will belong to the same network. When individuals cannot recall a word they know, a state called tip-of-the-tongue, their guesses are usually words that rhyme and have the same number of syllables as the correct term. An adolescent who temporarily cannot remember that *shilling* is the name of a class of British coin might retrieve the words *billing, killing, filling,* or *drilling* as he searches for the correct term.

Somewhat more mysterious is the observation that when English-speaking children or adults have to decide whether a curved or an angular design is the best match for the meaningless words *bouba* or *kiki,* they usually select the curve for *bouba* and the angle for *kiki.* One explanation is that the brain is sensitive to the frequency and duration of sounds. The vowel *i* has a higher frequency than the vowel *u* and the consonant *k* has a briefer duration than *b.* The brain creates one prototype for sounds that combine a high frequency with a brief duration and another for sounds with a lower frequency and a longer duration. Curves are more likely to have a lower spatial frequency and a longer unbroken contour than angles. It is noteworthy that songs whose melodies have a lower frequency (pitch) and whose words have a longer duration—characteristic of lullabies—are more common in pleasant mental states, whereas sounds with a high frequency and short duration— for example, screams—more often characterize unpleasant mental states. The words *love* and *hug* have a lower frequency and a longer duration than *hate* and *bite.*

The consonants *p* and *b* (called plosives) have a shorter duration and a higher frequency than the consonants *m* and *n* (called nasals). It may not be surprising, therefore, that across many languages the word for *mother* begins with *m* or *n,* the word for *father* begins with *p* or *b,* and young children from many cultures associate curved designs with the mother and angular designs with the father.[10]

The important differences between schemata and words lead humans to process experience in three distinctive ways. First, schemata and schematic prototypes represent patterns of the physical features of events. A particular word, however, often names a collection of events that do not share a common physical feature. The words *play* and *recreation* include picnics, athletic events, board games, and movie viewing. The critical feature shared by these events is a state of mind. There is no single schema for the abstract term *play,* only schemata for each of the activities belonging to that concept.

Second, only semantic concepts can be part of a hierarchy of nested concepts or members of an antonym pair. The term *cow* is nested within the category *animal,* which includes concepts for hyenas, elephants, and alligators, and *animals* are nested, in turn, within the concept *living things.* The perceptual prototype for a cow, however, is not usually linked to schemata for hyenas, elephants, and alligators. The schematic prototype for an ice cream cone, which is classified as good, does not evoke a schema for rotted food, which is bad.

Third, most semantic concepts provide no information regarding the contexts in which they might be relevant, whereas many schemata include strong associations to a specific context. The schema for a cow, for example, is often linked to a schema for a barn, meadow, or prairie. The word *cow* is more closely linked to semantic categories for other domesticated animals, such as pigs, sheep, chickens, and goats.

Most of the semantic concepts in children younger than six years are associated with one or more schemata. As children mature, however, some of the links between semantic networks and schemata become diluted and the networks begin to float relatively free of any perceptual structures. The semantic network for *animal* in three-year-olds is probably linked to schemata for the animals they have seen and thus may not include schemata for worms and wasps. The network for *animal* in adolescents includes biological functions that may not have corresponding schemata. Among most adolescents, worms and wasps are members of the semantic network for animals—even if some youth have no schemata for respiration or digestion in wasps and worms.

There are occasions when semantic networks and schemata imply different meanings. Consider a six-year-old girl whose perceptual schemata for her parents include the frequent temper outbursts of her tense professional mother and the soft voice and gentle manner of her father. When this girl acquires her culture's semantic networks for *male* and *female,* which imply that females are kinder and gentler than males, she may begin to regard the mother as gentler and the father as harsher than her schemata imply. Recall that young children shown a curved design alongside a design composed of sharp angles pointed to the latter when asked which one is more like their father. When an adult asked why they chose the angle to represent their father, a typical reply was "These can hurt you." Words have the power to alter the schematic products of experience. Every victim of bigoted verbal attacks understands this truth.

Some ideas can only be represented semantically. The spatial extent of the universe, estimated at 10^{23} miles, is one example. It is difficult to create a schema that represents a size this large. On the other hand, some schemata have no corresponding semantic networks. Words cannot fully describe the schema created by seeing the skyline of a large unfamiliar city from a plane preparing to land or the blend of schemata generated by walking in a dense Vermont forest in early October when the maple leaves are in high color.

The claim by some linguists that language is an autonomous capacity implies that active and passive sentences have identical meanings. For example, "The boy kissed the girl" is regarded as having exactly the same semantic meaning as "The girl was kissed by the boy." If, however, some listeners activate different schemata to these two sentences, which is likely, the sentences would have different meanings. The active form is apt to evoke a schema in which the boy is the central feature. In the passive sentence the girl is the central object of the schema, for she is receiving the kiss. If scientists tracked the eye movements of individuals hearing the active or passive sentence while they were watching a film of this event, most viewers would focus their eyes on the boy in the active sentence but on the girl in the passive sentence. I also suspect that adults would generate different associations to these two sentences.

Caitlin Fausey and Lera Boroditsky of Indiana University point out that assignments of blame for actions that have an ambiguous ethical status can vary with the form the sentence assumes.[11] Observers tend to blame the teacher for initiating an ethically questionable behavior if the sentence reads "The teacher embraced the student." They are less likely to blame the teacher if he or she is the object of the same action in a sentence in the passive voice, as in "The student was embraced by the teacher." These two sentences evoke different schemata and different evaluations of the receptivity of the student to the teacher's action.

A person who did something that harmed another is generally regarded as behaving more amorally than one who, through inaction, caused equivalent harm. The executives who sold derivatives composed of high-risk mortgages to naïve investors are perceived as more responsible for the economic recession than the officials at the Federal Reserve, the Securities and Exchange Commission, or the members of the congressional oversight committees who did nothing to stop this practice. Our society is much more critical of a parent who abuses a child than of one who abandons responsibility for socializing proper habits.

Poets rely on schemata to achieve an aesthetic effect. Consider these two lines from T. S. Eliot's *The Love Song of J. Alfred Prufrock:*

> *For the yellow smoke that slides along the street,*
> *Rubbing its back upon the window pane;*

The aesthetic power of these lines would be diluted if Eliot had made the street and window panes, rather than the yellow smoke, the salient objects and had written

> *The street with its sliding yellow smoke*
> *Rubbing window panes with its back;*

Films are popular because they combine semantic networks with schemata. Few books could create representations of war as rich as those generated by the film *Saving Private Ryan.* The schemata that are part of the semantic network for Earth's orbiting of the sun depend on whether one relies on Newton's description of the gravitational force between the two objects or on Einstein's explanation of a massive sun creating a warp in the fabric of space-time. The former is linked to schemata for the invisible lines of force between the two heavenly bodies, resembling the effect of a magnet on iron filings. The latter engages a schema of a trampoline in which the sun, resting in a sunken spot on the surface, creates a trough around which Earth orbits like a marble in a groove. These different schemata award distinctive meanings to the sentence "Earth orbits the sun." The typical adolescent possesses Newton's understanding; physicists are loyal to Einstein's perspective.

A feeling of uncertainty evoked by inconsistency between two semantic networks is a feature of language that does not apply to schemata. Reading the sentence "A man traveled at 186,000 miles a second" evokes this feeling because there is inconsistency between the semantic network for humans and the semantic network for the speed of light. Everyone knows that no human can move at that velocity. Nonetheless, Albert Einstein's schema of his body traveling alongside a beam of light inspired his development of relativity theory. A 1932 diagram by Sigmund Freud suggests that he may have thought of the id, ego, and superego as located in different places in the brain. The ego occupied the frontal region of the diagram; the id was in the back of the brain; and off to the side, near the temporal lobe, was the superego.

Sentences can be true or false, whereas perceptions can only be accurate or inaccurate. The sentence "The room in which I am writing is moving with respect to the sun" is true, despite the accuracy of my perception that the room in which I am writing is not in motion. Some older adults hear sounds that originate in spontaneous brain activity. Their perception of the sounds is accurate, but they would have uttered a false statement if they said they heard sounds coming from an unlit lamp.

The dissociation of schemata from semantic networks, which increases with age, implies that many adults understand and speak some words that do not have a strong link to schemata. A person who has never seen a photograph of the HIV virus can nonetheless engage in a coherent conversation about the virus. It is because of this dissociation that adults often find it hard to explain some of their preferences. British college students could not say why they preferred a deep blue over seven other colors. When Chloe Taylor and Anna Franklin of the University of Surrey measured the number of associations each student produced in response to each of eight colors, they found that dark blue had the smallest number of associations with undesirable events.[12] This unexpected result suggests that the preference for dark blue may have a partial basis in experiences that few understand or can articulate.

The development of autonomous semantic networks after the sixth or seventh birthday is preceded by an important change in blood flow patterns within the brain. Children younger than six years possess a pattern that favors greater blood flow to the right hemisphere. Those older than seven have a pattern that favors the left hemisphere. This shift is accompanied by a change in a child's immediate associations to nouns. English-speaking five-year-olds reporting the first word they think of in a word association task usually select a word that specifies a perceptible property of the object named by the first word, often a verb. For example, they are likely to say *bark* to *dog, shine* to *sun,* and *break* to *glass.* After age seven, children are more likely to say *cat* to *dog, moon* to *sun,* and *cup* to *glass.* These associations imply that the semantic networks automatically select a single semantic property that was shared by the two words. Dogs and cats are pets; sun and moon are located above the earth; glass and cup receive liquids that people drink.

The increasing dominance of semantic networks is accompanied by errors in recognizing words that were heard or read earlier. Many adults who heard the words *mattress, pillow, bed, night,* and *tired* interspersed with five words for vegetables or fruits, reported later that the word *sleep* was on the list they heard because they possessed a semantic network that contained the term *sleep* along with the other five related words. Younger children are less likely to make this error because their network for *sleep* is less coherent and more closely tied to schemata. Adults do not make this error when they are shown pictures of a pillow, a bed, a mattress, a night sky, and a tired person and are asked later if they saw a picture of a person sleeping.

Semantic networks invite stereotypes of ethnic, religious, national, gender, age, or social-class groups that are based on a single salient property. Europeans hold a stereotype of Americans as extraverts. The selection of this single feature to characterize more than 300 million adults is indifferent to the many other features of Americans that have nothing to do with extraversion.

The elaborate semantic networks for *male* and *female* contain surprising associations that have all the features of stereotypes. Among American children, the words *woman* and *school* belong to the same network because women are the teachers in most classrooms from kindergarten through the fifth grade. As a result, the semantic networks for objects found in classrooms often include a word or words referring to *women.* Six-year-olds who were initially taught to associate one nonsense word (for example, *dep*) with obviously feminine objects and a different nonsense word (*rov*) with masculine objects later classified pictures of a blackboard, a piece of chalk, and a book as feminine and pictures of a ship, a tractor, and an airplane as masculine.[13]

Semantic networks for some concepts can influence society's attitudes toward the objects that belong to the concept. The semantic concepts *female* and *nature* provide an illustration of this dynamic. School-age children know that infants, flowers, trees, lakes, and clouds are part of nature. Because only women conceive and give birth, children regard the concept *female* as part of the network that includes *flower, tree,* and *lake,* with *nature* as the central term. A nursing mother was the dominant schema for the concept *nature* among eighteenth-century Europeans. Contemporary television documentaries on nature have replaced lactating women with lions killing gazelles. Because a culture's semantic network for nature often influences its conception of femaleness, it may not be a coincidence that contemporary American and European women are more competitive, assertive, and aggressive than their counterparts 250 years earlier.

A number of eminent scientists remember being exceptionally curious about nature during their childhood years. They enjoyed collecting insects and rocks or gazing at the night sky. This behavior begs for an explanation inasmuch as many children do not display a persistent curiosity about insects, spiders, lizards, or rocks.

If a child's semantic networks and schemata for nature are linked to the network for *female,* we might speculate that an intense curiosity about the natural world reflects, in part, a deep curiosity about women who, in the average child's mind, are more mysterious than men. Mothers and wives are far more affectionate, trusting, and self-sacrificing than fathers and men, and they hide their mysterious sexuality behind a mound of hair. Perhaps the decline in the proportion of college seniors choosing one of the natural sciences for a career, when we compare the decade 2000–2010 with 1960–1970, is the partial consequence of a more permissive atmosphere surrounding female sexuality and the increased number of women who are as selfish as the average man. If women lose their mystery, there is the possibility that nature might lose some of its attractiveness as a target of childhood curiosity.

Soldiers, robbers, murderers, and school bullies are more often male than female, and the semantic networks for the words *danger, fighting,* and *death* usually contain the words *boy* and *man.* Even in Sweden, which has a low crime rate, the ratio of males to females who commit a violent crime, excluding rape, is 5 to 1. That is one reason why children's semantic network for *good* is more likely to contain the concept *girl* than *boy.* The semantic concepts *life, birth,* and *the left side of the body* (the site of the heart) are more closely associated with the concept *female* than *male.* Perhaps that is why Michelangelo painted Adam receiving the life force with his left hand.[14] One might even speculate that the networks for *male* and *female* influence the features that define heroes and heroines. American high school students asked to nominate several past heroes and heroines from any culture would probably include George Washington, Abraham Lincoln, Princess Diana, and Mother Teresa. If asked why, I suspect they would say that they admired the men for their pragmatism and courage under stress but admired the women for their kind, nurturing attitude toward those in need.

Speculations aside, these facts support the social scientists who argue that the concept of gender, in contrast to the concept of biological sex, consists of culturally constructed networks that contrast aggression, agency, large size, and strength with love, passivity, small size, and weakness. The acquisition of these networks begins early. Many American four-year-olds possess a semantic network for *female* that contains the terms *small, weak, cooking,* and *cleaning* and a second network for male that links the words *large, strong, hunting,* and *fighting.*

If there were a culture in which most men cooked and cared for infants, and most women were soldiers and hunters, the semantic networks for males and females would differ. Because, on average, males are stronger, larger, and less fearful of novelty and dangerous situations than females (a tendency that is also true of many animals), most societies construct a semantic network for each gender that is in partial agreement with the biological facts. Although the semantic networks for the genders are susceptible to change, they are biased by the small number of biological differences between the sexes.

One final point warrants mention. The first five years may be a sensitive period for learning a new language because the ability to learn a language becomes more difficult after seven years of age. A facility with language has become more critical to the attainment of a challenging vocation that offers dignity and a secure financial future than it was in the past. Hence, parents should talk with and read to their children regularly. Social scientists are certain of two robust facts: the size and richness of a child's vocabulary at age five are excellent predictors of the child's grade-point average in high school and college, and college-educated parents stimulate their child's language more consistently than parents who did not graduate high school.

While watching films made in the Boston homes of immigrants from Central America I was surprised by how little verbal communication there was between mothers and their two-year-old children. These mothers love their children but do not appreciate the importance of encouraging language and are unaware of their ability to contribute to this skill in their children. This attitude is one reason why there is a large gap in income and status in most societies, whether an economically developed nation like the United States or an undeveloped one like Madagascar where almost all residents are poor.[15]

INFERENCE

The ability to infer the thoughts, intentions, and feelings of others is a second distinctively human talent that appears at about the same time children speak their first words. This is not a coincidence. Inference facilitates the acquisition of language because one- and two-year-olds guess that when their mother or father speaks to them the parent intends to communicate information. This talent explains why children presented with a cup, whose name they know, alongside an unfamiliar object for which they have no name, and asked, "Give me the zoob," pick up the unfamiliar object.

Similarly, children older than eighteen months infer the correct location of a hidden toy when an adult looks directly at one of three places where it might be hidden. Two-year-olds can even infer whether an adult who is asking them a question is in a serious or a playful mood.[16]

A persuasive example of the capacity for inference was observed in two-year-old children who wore either transparent or opaque ski goggles at home for an hour a day for several days. Several weeks later, in a laboratory playroom, they saw their mother wearing the same ski goggles they had worn at home. The children who had worn the opaque goggles inferred that their mother could not see and assumed a puzzled facial expression when she asked the child to bring her a toy resting in a particular location. The children who wore the transparent goggles did not make that inference.[17]

The ability to infer some of the psychological states of others is essential for *empathy*, a state that can assume three different forms in children who notice that someone needs help: a child can experience a feeling of sympathy that does not resemble the victim's state, recognize that another needs help but experience no feeling, or experience a feeling that resembles the state of the victim. Children might try to help the other in any of these states. Thus, the behavior does not reveal the child's private state. Children older than eighteen months use voice, gesture, or action as a sign of concern when an adult pretends she has hurt her hand by shaking it and displaying a facial expression of pain.[18]

A capacity for empathy toward pain or distress in others facilitates the suppression of aggressive actions. Children have acquired visceral schemata for the pain of a bruise and the distress of being rebuked. As a result, they infer that anyone encountering the same or similar experiences must feel equally unpleasant.

It appears that a pair of adjacent brain sites in the frontal lobe, called the anterior insula and the anterior cingulate, contribute to the ability to experience empathy. These two sites also have the greatest density of a distinctively shaped neuron, which appeared late in evolution, called a von Economo neuron. Human brains not only have more of these neurons than ape brains but they also possess a distinctive biochemistry that might be essential for the uniquely human capacity to infer a variety of mental and emotional states in others.

Michael Tomasello and his colleagues at the Max Planck Institute in Leipzig, Germany, have expanded on observations that my students and I described more than thirty years ago in *The Second Year*.[19] Two- to three-year-old humans, but not chimpanzees, spontaneously join in collaborative behavior requiring coordinated actions, share the spoils of a collaborative effort fairly, reject offers of spoils that are unfair, and are aware of the evaluations others might impose if they violate norms on stealing, disobedience, and selfishness.

Each of these behaviors requires the ability to infer the thoughts and needs of others and to understand aspects of the concepts *fair* and *just*. Early humans stalked large animals for food in ventures that required the collaboration of many adults. This collaboration would have been impossible if the participants did not possess an inferential capacity and a need to believe in fairness when resources are distributed. The adult residents of Catalonia feel that their monetary contribution to Spain's economy is much larger than the amount they receive, and many want to secede from the larger nation. Chimpanzees become uncertain in situations where another animal might take their food or harm them. Humans become uncertain when they do not know what another person is thinking about them.

At least three processes are activated when two-year-olds help an adult in pain, point to a correct location, or look puzzled when a mother with opaque ski goggles asks for an object. First, they retrieve the schemata and semantic networks they acquired when they were agents in similar settings. Second, they attribute this knowledge to another person because they have created a prototypic category that includes themselves and a select group of other living things. And, third, they act as if they understood the private experience of an animal or person. I remember watching a pair of three-year-old boys in a playroom that contained only one attractive Batman costume. When the boy who put on the costume realized that the other boy was envious, he said, "You can hate me if you want."

The ability to infer the thoughts and feelings of those who are not present and to act in response to these inferences has both advantages and disadvantages. On the one hand, this talent often motivates benevolent actions. On the other hand, incorrect inferences can lead to anger, sadness, guilt, or disruptions in personal relationships.

An adolescent's misinterpretation of a parent's thoughts can have tragic consequences. I remember a Harvard freshman who interpreted her father's extreme permissiveness as signifying paternal indifference, and her anger motivated her to sleep with a friend of the father, hoping the parent would learn of the affair. But the father had granted his daughter great freedom because of an affectionate wish to aid her growth. Even middle-aged adults hold incorrect assumptions about a parent's private thoughts. These false inferences are often the cause of quarrels when families get together at Thanksgiving and Christmas. It is also common for parents to misinterpret their child's failure to obtain excellent grades as a sign of hostility to the parent. It is equally common for children to incorrectly assume that the parent is disappointed in a less-than-perfect grade record and to conclude that the parent's love is contingent on the children's school performance.

The emergence of inference is rooted in two features of brain maturation. The first is the same enhanced connectivity between the left and right hemispheres that contributes to the emergence of language. Recall that the right hemisphere contains the visceral and perceptual schemata for past feelings and events. Patients with lesions of the right hemisphere are less empathic than those with lesions in the left hemisphere. Also recall that semantic networks for situations and people are stored primarily in the left hemisphere. The combining of the visceral and perceptual schemata with the semantic networks for situations and people makes inferences of feelings possible.

The second feature is a major spurt in the size of the hippocampus during the second year. (Most brain sites undergo their greatest growth prenatally or during the first year.) The hippocampus makes a critical contribution to the ability to retrieve past experiences that are relevant to the present. Every act of inference requires retrieval of stored knowledge. The two-year-olds who wore the opaque ski goggles at home had to remember that days earlier they were unable to see through them when they saw their mother wear the same goggles in the laboratory.

A MORAL SENSE

The language and inferential capacities are necessary for the acquisition of the concepts *good, bad, right,* and *wrong.* The initial comprehension of these concepts implies the emergence of a moral sense, which I define as a combination of three representations: semantic networks for the words *bad, good,* and their synonyms; visceral schemata for unpleasant feelings; and schematic prototypes for acts that have been punished or praised.

Eight-month-olds who have been rebuked for throwing food on the floor learn to inhibit that behavior because of the conditioned feeling of uncertainty evoked by an urge to commit a prohibited act. A similar mechanism leads puppies to inhibit defecating on the kitchen floor. Two-year-olds, however, inhibit actions that have never been punished because they infer that a parent will disapprove of a behavior that belongs to the prototype for prohibited acts. Most two-year-olds who have never spilled cranberry juice on a clean tablecloth, and have never been punished for that act, are reluctant to obey a mother who says "Pour the cranberry juice on the tablecloth." Some three-year-olds protest if an adult throws away a toy that belonged to another child because they infer that loss of the toy will produce distress in the other.[20]

Children during the second year have an early understanding of the concept of obligation. In one study, an adult displayed three coherent, complex actions with familiar toys in front of children growing up in Boston or on an atoll in the Fiji chain and said "It is your turn to play." The one-year-olds in both cultures displayed a variety of actions with the toys, but none became distressed. Most of the two-year-olds, however, cried because they inferred that the adult wanted them to imitate actions they could not perform and assumed that this failure would provoke adult disapproval. This inference implies that they had an initial understanding of the meaning of *ought,* which is a critical component of morality.

Two-year-olds are also concerned when they see flaws in the usual integrity of objects. Children this age point to a hole in a towel, a missing button on a shirt, or a spot of ink on a chair and, in a serious tone of voice, say, "boo-boo" or "yucky," indicating that they regard the flaw as a deviation from the object's ideal state, presumably caused by a person who acted inappropriately. Two-year-olds generate representations of ideal states and are motivated to attain them. A two-year-old girl holding a small doll and a large toy bed searched for several minutes for a small bed because it was more appropriate for the small doll.

The fairness of rewards is also a matter of concern to two-year-olds. Stephanie Sloane and her colleagues at the University of Illinois reported that toddlers who cooperated in completing a chore believed that each of them was entitled to a just distribution of any reward.[21] Plato would have regarded this belief as an affirmation of his assumption "To know the good, is to do the good."

The emergence of a moral sense as early as the second birthday has advantages. Before humans had access to contraception, most mothers gave birth to the next infant after they stopped nursing the previous child, at about two or three years. Most three-year-olds are jealous of the attention given the new infant and have many opportunities to harm the helpless child. But very few children commit such an act because they understand that harming the infant is wrong and they can empathize with the pain of the potential victim. Whenever a three- or four-year-old injures a younger sibling seriously, the rarity of the event makes headlines in every newspaper. Parents who abuse their infants have lost an emotional response they possessed when they were three years old.

The emergence of a moral sense is also aided by the more effective coordination of the brain's two hemispheres. The visceral schemata that represent the unpleasant feelings produced by parental criticism, or its anticipation, are more fully represented in the right hemisphere; the semantic representations of good and bad acts and their intentions are mediated more fully by the left hemisphere. Thus, the emergence of a moral sense, as with language and inference, is partially due to the growth of neurons in cortical layer three during the second year. Parents living on isolated atolls in the Fijian chain recognize these advances. They believe that once children pass their second birthday they possess *vakayala,* which means good sense.

CONSCIOUSNESS

The first signs of a conscious awareness of one's feelings, thoughts, actions, or traits, combined with the ability to inhibit an action and redirect attention, also appear during the second year. These are the defining properties of *consciousness,* a term that is not synonymous with *sensation.* Infants and animals experience the sensations of pain, sweetness, and touch, but they do not recruit the additional brain circuits that allow older humans to believe that they can examine or manipulate these states at will. The distinctive features of consciousness depend on a special form of connectivity between the frontal lobe and other parts of the brain.

Discovery of the brain events that make consciousness possible remains one of the most important challenges of this century. Unfortunately, scientists are not even close to attaining this goal. The best they can say at present is that consciousness emerges from particular patterns of brain activity that include the frontal lobes, as a blizzard emerges from a pattern of water and air molecules at a particular range of temperatures.[22]

Most neuroscientists attempting to illuminate the material foundations of consciousness have assumed it is a unitary phenomenon, rather than a family of states that originate in various brain profiles. If slightly different brain circuits mediate the awareness of the pain of a burn, reflection on the joys of last year's holiday, and the redirection of a pair of hands trying to catch a ball thrown on a windy day, it is reasonable to posit more than one state of consciousness. Michael Gazzaniga accords special importance to the contribution of the left hemisphere to states of consciousness, as he believes it is this hemisphere that tries to make sense of the blended combination of internal and external sensations.[23]

Consider a scenario in which a mother surreptitiously puts rouge on her child's nose and asks him or her to stand in front of a full-length mirror. The child's behavior in this situation provides one of the classic signs of an awareness of self. Most children older than eighteen months, but very few one-year-olds, automatically touch their nose when they see their reflection in the mirror. This response is

FIGURE 3.2   Two-year-old touching a spot of rouge on his nose

delayed among children growing up in rural, economically impoverished regions. (See Figure 3.2.) The touching of the nose implies that the children inferred that the reflection represents themselves. This action is often preceded by simpler acts; for example, somewhat younger children may touch some part of their body when they see their reflection in the mirror.[24]

The emergence of an awareness of what one is doing can be observed when children play. Two-year-olds play with toys for longer durations than they did twelve months earlier because they are conscious of an action plan they composed and sustain play bouts because they are aware of a goal they are pursuing. For example, they will put a telephone to the ear of a doll, rather than to their own ear, implying that they are playing the role of a director in a script they are composing.

Two-year-olds can pick out a photograph of their face embedded in an array of photos of unfamiliar children, use the personal pronouns *I, me,* and *mine,* and resist giving up a toy they are playing with, even if another child offers them a more attractive one. Apes do not display this sense of ownership as long as the object is not food. Children also describe what they are doing while they are engaging in an action. A two-year-old girl will say "up" as she climbs up on a chair, "open" as she tries to open a box containing a toy, "Mary eat" while munching on a cookie; she will also use the words *feel, hurt,* and *know.* These utterances suggest that children have an awareness of what they are doing and of some of their mental states. Because the feeling of awareness is novel, it is arousing and motivates a verbal description. When the novelty of consciousness wears off, usually by the end of the third year, children stop describing what they are doing.[25]

Awareness of the self's actions renders two-year-olds more sensitive to the relation between an action and its outcome. This awareness makes it likely that they will inhibit behaviors that produce undesirable consequences and work harder on difficult tasks. The ability to remember the location of a prize that was hidden in one of eight locations improves dramatically during the second year, in part because children are aware that an adult is evaluating their ability. Takaaki Kaneko of Kyoto University reported that, unlike humans, chimpanzees do not seem to be aware of what their hands are doing as they manipulate a cursor toward a target.[26] The chimps attend to the target and ignore the subtle feedback coming from their muscles.

Obviously, the two-year-old's states of consciousness are not as complex as the states of twelve-year-olds. The process that begins with recognizing oneself in a mirror will be elaborated over many years. Psychoanalysts had assumed that the sense of self was initially merged with the parent and that children required experience to differentiate their self from that of the adult. But the evidence suggests that there is no self prior to the middle of the second year, just as there is no frog in the tadpole and no blossom in the seed.

The emergence of self-awareness, like that of language, inference, and a moral sense, also has a partial foundation in the enhanced connectivity of the two hemispheres through the callosum. The visceral schemata for feelings, represented mainly in the right hemisphere, are coordinated with the semantic categories for the self's properties and actions, represented mainly in the left hemisphere. Although coordination of the two hemispheres cannot fully explain states of consciousness, it probably contributes to these phenomena. Antonio Damasio once wrote that Descartes should have modified his famous statement "I think, therefore I am" to read "I think and feel, therefore, I am."[27]

A DEEPER UNITY

Language, inference, a moral sense, and consciousness appear on the surface to be distinctly different talents. But because all four emerge at roughly the same time in development, it is tempting to search for a more fundamental process, or processes, that might be necessary for all four capacities. The firmer connectivity between the two hemispheres and the growth of the hippocampus are two of the biological bases for these talents. Consciousness might be the integrator of the other three capacities because inference, language, and a moral sense would operate more effectively if children were aware of their intentions, feelings, and thoughts as well as the possible responses of others. The late Theodosius Dobzhansky, an influential twentieth-century geneticist, suggested that consciousness was the property that best differentiated humans from other animal species.[28]

The capabilities of the second year build on the child's earlier abilities to recognize that an event is familiar or unfamiliar and to retrieve and maintain schemata in a working-memory circuit. Language, inference, a moral sense, and consciousness could not emerge without these prior talents. We do not yet understand all the biological changes and experiences that make the psychological competences of the second year possible. The current evidence, albeit preliminary, implies that a small number of mutations in protein-producing genes—combined with the removal of methyl groups (called demethylation) from the base cytosine in the promoter region of genes that control brain development—were partially responsible for the obvious differences between apes and humans.

Social scientists who knew only the psychological properties of two-year-olds could not imagine the underlying biology, and biologists who knew only the brain evidence could not imagine the psychological phenomena. A deeper knowledge of both the biological and psychological information will help scientists arrive at an explanation of this developmental stage. The twelve-month interval that begins with a smile following the successful completion of a block tower and ends with a child's tearful confession to a parent "I can't do that" contains a pattern of cognitive abilities, feelings, and behaviors that renders humans qualitatively different from every other animal species.

Biologists continue to brood about the traits that made the most significant contribution to the evolution of the remarkably adaptive traits of modern humans. The usual candidates are the abilities to make tools, throw spears, run long distances without overheating, bond to a friend, mate, care for children, cooperate with those who are not family members, anticipate the distant future, remember the deep past, and the four properties described in this chapter. I suspect that these four properties were among the most important.

All of these features required a genome that could be the foundation of a brain anatomy and physiology that rendered humans less fearful, and more trusting of strangers, than chimpanzees. These two traits are seminal features of domesticated mammals, such as horses, pigs, and goats. These tamer forms possess a shorter snout and flatter face than their nondomesticated relatives residing in natural ecologies. It cannot be a coincidence that humans have much flatter faces than chimpanzees. Perhaps some of the genes that were responsible for this anatomical change in the face also contributed to the talents of language, inference, morality, and consciousness. Nature is full of surprises.

CHAPTER FOUR

The Family and Beyond

———

The properties that humans share are the inevitable result of similar brains extracting similar representations from similar encounters with people, plants, animals, and objects. Some of the properties that differentiate one person from another originate in biology, but many are the result of parental practices, experiences with siblings and peers, cultural setting, and historical era. It is to these last four factors, and especially the family, that I now turn.

The family is responsible for the young child's physical survival, first ethical values, and initial belief in his or her value as a person. Survival is the pressing concern for families residing in communities with many infectious agents and inadequate medical care. Families in developed nations (which enjoy chlorinated water, sewers, relatively safe food, and access to doctors and medicines) worry more about four other issues: whether the behaviors and moods of their children are likely predictors of later problems; how to motivate their children to do well in school; how to teach their children to control impulsive displays of anger and sexual urges; and, finally, how to ensure that their children will develop into satisfied adults. These parental concerns match the society's hope that its citizens will obey the law, acquire the skills and motivation needed to support a family, and contribute to civic harmony.

The modern Western family—private, nuclear, child-centered, and based on a sentimental relationship between wife and husband—emerged in Europe during the eighteenth century. But all families affect the child's psychological properties through two basic, though different, mechanisms. One is the pattern of parental rewards and punishments, which are most effective during the years prior to puberty. Identifications—first with the parents and later with the child's family pedigree, gender, class, ethnicity, religion, and nationality—represent the second influential mechanism, which emerges during the early school years. In addition to parental practices and identifications, a child's birth order, size of community, culture, and historical era play a role in shaping beliefs, values, and behaviors. We consider all of these in due course, beginning with the consequences of parental practices.

The power of rewards and punishments to establish the habits and values that parents favor is enhanced when the child wants parental approval but feels a little uncertain about obtaining it. Praise or punishment is most effective when it is unexpected. Parents who always reward their children, no matter what they do, will be less able to socialize the habits and values they prefer than parents who reward only some of the time. The child who is a trifle uncertain about the likelihood of praise or punishment will experience a more intense emotion when either event actually occurs.

The child's *interpretations* of the parent's practices and personality traits permeate both rewards and punishments. Once children pass their third birthday, they consistently evaluate their experiences against a background of assumptions about themselves and others. These assumptions function like filters that permit certain interpretations and reject others. A parent's punishment for spilling food, for example, could be interpreted as reflecting a pervasive hostility toward the child or as a benevolent action designed to build good character. A child who is convinced that the parent does not like him will interpret a punishment as supporting the former belief; the child who assumes he is loved will treat the same punishment as motivated by the parent's wish to socialize him properly.

Frequent punishments that are interpreted as excessive or unjust can prime the child, and later the adult, to overreact to the slightest comment by anyone that might be construed as critical. There is an analogous process in the brain. Some neurons that are exposed to repeated pulses of electrical stimulation become permanently hyper-responsive. Muriel Hagenaars and her colleagues at Leiden University found that adults who had experienced frequent punishments as children were likely to possess a vigilant, defensive personality that was reluctant to take risks and prone to deny responsibility for mistakes.[1]

Children also vary in their interpretations of who is responsible for unhappiness or tension in the home. Not all children assume that their actions contributed to a parent's illness, marital quarrels, or a divorce; some decide that they are not responsible for the parent's psychological state. The child's belief that he or she can or cannot cope with serious challenges is a third interpretive choice that affects the reaction to a stressful event. The variation among children in their interpretations of punishment, family tension, and ability to cope with challenge makes it difficult to predict an older child's personality from observations of particular parental behaviors.

The intrusion of these subjective interpretations raises a serious problem for scientists who want to use research on animals to illuminate the causes of human problems. Those who study animals do not have to worry about interpretive processes. They see their task as discovering relations among observable events. These investigators might want to understand the relation between separating a juvenile monkey from its mother and a later observable behavioral outcome—say, fearful or aggressive behavior. Because this relation in humans is affected by the child's interpretation of a separation, these scientists might arrive at a conclusion that does not apply to children.

PARENTAL VALUES AND CLASS

A family's social class has a pervasive influence on the parents' practices and values. The criteria that define *class* change with time and culture. The current definition of this term, based on income and education, implies that potentially anyone can change his or her status. The probability that an American child born to poor parents who did not graduate high school will ascend in status is much lower in 2012 than it was a hundred years earlier. As a result, a majority of contemporary children will remain in the same class as their parents and encounter similar settings. The sturdier barrier to social mobility implies that current class differences in moral standards, sensitivity to loss or frustration, social interaction patterns, peer loyalties, adult occupation, and sense of agency will be preserved in youths who remain in the same class as their parents.

The belief that one has some control over daily experiences is one of the best predictors of life satisfaction among adults in most societies. This belief is usually firmer among those who belong to an advantaged social class, in part because they have easier access to those in power. Youths and adults who see themselves as marginalized—existing in an orbit far from the halls of power—feel a bit freer to ignore, or in some cases to violate, the ethical standards upheld by the majority in their society.

Contemporary college-educated parents from North America and Europe praise autonomy, a private conscience, and the mastery of intellectual skills and are gentler in their punishments than parents who never attended college. Serious physical abuse of an infant in the United States, estimated at 1 out of every 750 infants in 2006, is more frequent in families in which the parents have less than twelve years of formal education.

The relation between membership in a less advantaged class and parental harshness is not present in all cultures and was not characteristic of European or American families two hundred years ago. Elite British families during the early decades of the nineteenth century could be exceptionally harsh with their children. The morning ritual in one family in which the father was a member of Parliament was to plunge the children into a cold bath, followed by a breakfast of bread and milk. If the children left some food on the plate, they were locked in a dark closet until they conformed. British and American boys from wealthy families were usually sent to schools where harsh discipline was regarded as necessary to produce gentlemen. Whipping children on the bare buttocks for disobedience or suspected masturbation was a common occurrence in these schools. Richard Henry Dana Jr., an elite Bostonian who wrote *Two Years Before the Mast,* described in his personal journal the frequent flogging of students at the private schools he attended.[2]

The family's class has a special effect on the socialization of daughters. Working-class American parents are prone to assume that a girl's opportunity to ascend in status requires marriage to a man with a steady job and a reliable income. They believe this prize is most likely if the girl is sexually attractive. The majority of American mothers who enroll their four- to six-year-old daughters in regional beauty contests have limited incomes. Nonetheless, they often spend several thousand dollars for the costumes their daughters need for these competitions. College-educated mothers with higher incomes enroll their daughters in expensive preschools with the expectation that these schools will teach the skills needed for admission to an elite elementary school, with the ultimate goal of admission to an elite college.

The family's class almost always influences a child's cognitive skills and school performance, a fact confirmed by research on children growing up in Soviet-occupied Warsaw in the years after World War II. The Soviet Union required families from different classes to live in the same apartment buildings and to send their children to the same schools. Nonetheless, the children from college-educated families had better grades than the children from less well-educated parents, despite exposure to the same teachers and curricula. This does not mean that family practices are the only important cause of a child's cognitive talents.

Children born with the genetic potential to develop an exceptional talent in language, mathematics, music, or painting may not actualize their ability if their families and the schools they attend fail to provide the opportunities needed to realize their inherent skill. This fact explains why the IQ scores of children born to poor, less well-educated parents appear to be unrelated to their genetic potential, inasmuch as the daily experiences needed to allow the genes to have an effect are missing. The influence of genes on IQ is substantial in children from middle-class homes because a majority of these children enjoy the benefits of intellectual enrichment and, therefore, the genetic influence is not overpowered by the lack of cognitive stimulation.

A potential competence always requires a set of experiences in order to flower. About one in four American youths drop out of high school before graduation. The vast majority of these adolescents grew up in poor African-American or Hispanic families, many living in southern or southwestern states. When these youths were asked why they quit school, their replies implied low motivation. An education did not seem to have sufficient value to maintain the effort required to master their schools' demands. Because Asian children from poor families are far less likely to drop out, it seems fair to conclude that African-American and Hispanic parents are not communicating to their children the value of an education.[3]

The relation between a family's class and children's verbal talents is present even in countries in which a majority are poor, because relative differences in income and education within a society—not absolute levels—are the critical determinants of parental behavior. Children born in Madagascar to parents whose incomes were in the top 20 percent of that small population performed better on a variety of cognitive tests than children from families whose incomes were in the bottom 20 percent, even though the incomes of the top 20 percent in Madagascar were roughly equivalent to the incomes of the lowest third of contemporary American families.[4]

In 1972, all 850 families in the poor Guatemalan village of San Marcos on the shores of Lake Atitlan lived in small adobe huts with dirt floors and no running water or electricity. Nonetheless, the children born to parents who owned the small plot of land on which their home stood performed better on a variety of cognitive tests than the children from poorer families who rented the land. Despite the fact that the American families living below the poverty line in 2012 have more food, better shelter, and greater access to information than the American families who were poor in 1912, the poorer school performance of children who grow up in relative poverty has not changed.

Har Gobind Khorana, who shared the 1968 Nobel Prize in Medicine, provides a persuasive example of the principle that relative status in a society trumps any absolute index. Khorana lived in a small village in the Punjab region of India with a family whose absolute income was quite modest. But because his parents were the only literate adults in the village, the family enjoyed a level of respect typically awarded to wealthy, high-status families. The behaviors of Khorana's parents were in accord with their elevated position. Had this family lived in Paris, where more than 90 percent were literate, the parents might have regarded themselves as marginalized and treated their son differently.

The feeling of enhanced status enjoyed by adults with many years of education is not limited to India. Many years ago my wife and I were guests at a New Year's Eve party with four other couples. As midnight approached, the hostess, who'd had too much to drink, decided that each of us was to confess our deepest disappointment. The last one to reply was a respected Bostonian who was the wealthiest person in the room. He surprised the group by declaring that his deepest disappointment was not attending college.

Contemporary American society faces a serious problem inasmuch as it combines the praiseworthy commitment to equal dignity for all citizens with the less defensible assumption that graduating from a traditional four-year college with an arts and science curriculum is necessary to command that dignity. The economy of the United States needs more men and women with the technical skills required for working with computers, machines, and patients in health care institutions. Many seventeen-year-olds who could master these domains are not highly motivated to study philosophy, English literature, physics, or world history. They could enjoy a life of economic security and emotional satisfaction if more institutions were devoted primarily to teaching these skills and American society was willing to relinquish the premise that dignity and respect require a degree from a traditional four-year college.

The consequences of class position extend to the body as well as the mind. Gregory Miller of the University of British Columbia reviewed the extensive evidence on the relation between class of rearing and physical health. Adults from developed nations who grow up in a disadvantaged family are more vulnerable to cardiovascular and respiratory problems, diabetes, and an earlier death than adults from the same society whose childhoods are spent in an affluent family.

The chronic state of uncertainty created by financial insecurity, the possibility of crime or violence in the home and neighborhood, and coercion or domination by those in high-status positions can compromise the immune system, leading to an inflammatory state mediated by proteins called cytokines. When youths experiencing these sources of uncertainty reach adulthood, their immune system—which is already in an inflammatory state—overreacts to a physical or psychological stress, rendering them more vulnerable to one of the chronic diseases as well as to the common cold and rarer afflictions such as multiple sclerosis. Similar effects have been observed in monkeys and baboons who belong to groups with unstable hierarchies that create comparable states of uncertainty.

Fortunately, fewer than one-half of the adults who experienced a childhood of uncertainty develop a compromised immune profile. This fact implies that many adults possess one or more protective mechanisms (for example, a genome that blocked the exaggerated immune response, a nurturing parent or relative, or an unusual talent) or have interpreted their experiences as chance events with no implication for their worthiness or future success.[5]

The primary villains in this sequence from an early inflammatory state to a disease are not knowing when an undesirable event might occur and being unsure of what one can do to prevent or cope with a challenge when it does occur. The awake brain, and its heir—the mind—are continually anticipating what might happen in the next few moments and preparing for the most appropriate response. When these predictions or preparations are prevented frequently over a long period of time, physiological changes occur that compromise brain and body. Not knowing whether or when one might be harmed, demeaned, or frustrated can have consequences as profound as those accompanying the actual experience of being hurt, demeaned, or frustrated.

Social scientists study two major classes of human properties. The traits that facilitate or obstruct adaptation to society comprise one type. The other category includes a host of features that have less relevance for adaptation, such as style of social interaction, hobbies, and preference for a solitary versus social life. Although each person's biology, life history, and social class contribute to both properties, class of rearing has a larger influence on the characteristics that facilitate or interfere with adaptation.

Imagine a twelve-year-old boy who is a mediocre student, misbehaves in school, is callous toward those in distress, and has an indifferent father plagued with syphilis and an equally unloving mother who is having an extramarital affair This description fits Winston Churchill, who grew up in an elite British family. If young

Winston had grown up in a poor, uneducated family in Liverpool, he would not have become one of the most important figures of the twentieth century.

The archaeologist Loren Eiseley once wrote that scientists could be divided into big-bone hunters and little-bone hunters. The social scientists looking for a big bone should try to discover why growing up as a member of a privileged or disadvantaged class in a particular community has such a large influence on an individual's academic talents, occupation, income, and physical and mental health. This does not mean that genes make no contribution to the above properties, only that their contribution is often dwarfed by the influence of social class.

IDENTIFICATION

Children are biologically prepared to recognize those who possess the same distinctive physical or psychological features. Although children know little about genes, they sense that they share unique, invisible biological properties with the adults who conceived them. They also know that they and their parents share the same last name. A small number even share a parent's first name—John Adams and his son John Quincy Adams are a famous example. Children are quick to notice that they and a parent have a distinctive bodily feature (perhaps freckles, red hair, or olive-colored skin), especially when the feature is uncommon in the community. Children have many opportunities to recognize that they and one or both parents laugh at and are saddened or angered by similar events.

All of these experiences lead six-year-olds to conclude that they share more properties with one or both parents than with anyone else they know. Once this belief is in place, they entertain the irrational assumption that if they share some distinctive, observable properties, perhaps they also share qualities that have no basis in fact. Amos Oz, a celebrated Israeli writer, had an epiphany when his father, a respected writer, told his six-year-old son he now had permission to put his childhood books on the same shelf that held the father's many volumes. This unexpected sharing of an unusual feature with an admired father who regarded books as sacred objects was probably an important reason why the son, too, chose to become a writer.

A six-year-old girl who notices that her mother becomes frightened when she sees a mouse infers that a fear of mice may be one of her characteristics, too. A girl who perceives her mother as dominant over her father and popular with friends is tempted to assume that she possesses an early form of these qualities. This habit of inferring what is possible but cannot be verified is common. If there are many puddles on the ground in the morning, we infer that it must have rained during the night.

The child's belief that he or she shares distinctive features with another, usually a parent, can be accompanied by a *vicarious emotion,* defined as a feeling that is appropriate for another person. A vicarious emotion resembles, but is not identical to, the one experienced by the other person. Such emotions reflect the child's assumption that members of the community will regard the child and the parent as belonging to the same category. Therefore, both are apt to receive the same evaluation by others for acts committed by the parent.

The writer John Updike confessed that, as an adolescent, he felt vicarious shame because of his father's compromised status as a schoolteacher in a small Pennsylvania city. In his memoir *Self-Consciousness,* Updike wrote: "I would avenge all the slights and abasements visited upon my father—the disrespect of the students, the laughter in the movie house at the name of Updike."

A child is identified with another when he or she believes that both share some distinctive features and, in addition, experiences vicarious emotions. Both phenomena must be present before we say that one person is identified with another. A child can experience an empathic reaction toward a stranger in distress without being identified with the victim. And children can recognize that they share distinctive features with those of the same sex or religion without feeling any vicarious emotions when members of these groups experience a pleasant or unpleasant event.

Children, adolescents, and adults often establish an identification with an ethnic, class, or religious group when the group has distinctive features, often because its members are a minority in the community. Michael MacDonald, born in 1967 to a poor Irish family, recalled feeling intense vicarious pride when the Irish adults in South Boston resisted court-ordered busing of Irish children to schools outside the area. Mersheena Murray of Kent State University describes the strong emotions some African-American youths feel when they or a close friend are accused of "acting white." One boy noted, "It's a judgment against the core of who you are." I suspect that white American youths accused of "acting black" would be less upset because, being in the majority, their identification with their ethnicity is weaker.[6]

The popular concept of identity is not synonymous with my use of the term *identification.* Individuals acquire, over a lifetime, a number of adjectives they use to describe themselves. These words, which define an identity, belong to one of four categories that coexist in every person. One set refers to the features the person shares with a large number of others in their community. The categories for nationality and gender are always on this list. The second set refers to properties that distinguish the individual from others, often religion and ethnicity when these categories are in the minority. The third category involves moral standards that the person believes he or she must honor. These include concepts like *smart, friendly, caring, honest, loyal,* and *dominant.* The features in the fourth set are the least stable because they change with age and their salience depends on the situation. The concepts *mother, father, grandparent, partner, student, scientist, banker, teacher, soldier,* and *retired* are on this list. These properties have the largest influence on a person's daily behaviors but are less likely to be accompanied by vicarious emotions than those in the second set.

When individuals are asked to describe their identity they draw from all four lists, some of which have no power to generate vicarious emotions and, therefore, are unrelated to their identifications. Being a member of the category of retired professors is a central feature of my current identity, but I feel no vicarious emotion when another retired professor wins a prize or does something foolish. The essential point here is that the answers to the question "Please describe who you are" or "Please tell me the words you use when you think about yourself" do not always reveal the person's pattern of identifications.

Identifications with particular family members do not become firm until five to six years of age. An identification with a class, religious, or ethnic group requires a few additional years to become equally strong. Children younger than age five can infer another's psychological state, but they are not yet capable of the cognitive processes required for an identification. Specifically, they do not appreciate that all the members of a family pedigree belong to a common category and they do not assume that strangers will react to them as they do to a member of their family.

Children who view the person or group with whom they are identified as possessing desirable traits—popularity, kindness, talent, courage—will try to increase their level of similarity by adopting more of the values and behaviors that characterize the person or group. If, on the other hand, the model is undesirable—cruel, uneducated, dishonest, irascible, slovenly—children are motivated to differentiate themselves from the model. Many adolescents of illiterate, immigrant parents reject the religious and political beliefs of their family in order to persuade themselves that they are unlike their parents. Although this attempt at psychological separation can lessen the intensity of vicarious emotions, it rarely eliminates them completely. Many adults spend their lives trying to establish an identification with those who have more desirable properties while simultaneously trying to dilute childhood identifications with less desirable models.

The self-doubt possessed by some youths who have identified with an impoverished class or victimized minority group can persist, even if they become accomplished adults. Robert Nozick was a distinguished American philosopher who grew up in a poor family of Jewish immigrants. Nozick's identification with his class and ethnic group led him to question his right to probe profound philosophical themes. In the preface to one of his books he wrote, "Isn't it ludicrous for someone just one generation from the shtetl, a pisher from Brownsville and East Flatbush in Brooklyn, even to touch on the topics of the monumental thinkers?" Michel Montaigne and Bertrand Russell, who grew up in privileged homes, would not have harbored these doubts.[7]

Frank Kermode, born to an extremely poor family on the Isle of Man, became a celebrated literary critic and distinguished faculty member at an elite British university. Nonetheless, Kermode remained haunted by the feeling that he had no business being a participant in these high-status settings. Hence, he titled his memoir *Not Entitled.*[8] Most youths from poor or minority families who are accepted by an elite college adapt well. A small proportion, however, experience the uncomfortable feelings of an outsider who does not belong in this setting. Some of these students manage to get themselves expelled by failing courses or violating a law, although they are unaware of why they behaved in a self-destructive fashion.

Thomas Becket may have done something similar. The position of archbishop of Canterbury in the twelfth century was usually filled by a member of an elite family. In 1162, however, Henry II appointed the commoner Thomas Becket, who had been a close friend, to this prestigious position. Surprisingly, Becket proceeded to defy the man whose generosity made his ascent to power and legitimacy possible, knowing that his rebellion could cost him his life. Some psychologists might argue that Becket may have felt that he did not deserve his elevated position. It is also relevant that, although Becket disagreed with the king's lifestyle, he remained silent for many years before being appointed to archbishop. The feelings he experienced as an outsider, combined with guilt over his earlier hypocritical deference to the king, may have been unconscious causes of the rebellious actions that motivated the king to arrange for Becket's murder in his own cathedral.

The probability of experiencing vicarious pride or shame because of an identification with a class, ethnic, or religious group depends, in part, on the group's reputation in the community. If the group is respected, vicarious pride following a virtuous act by a member of the category is more likely than vicarious shame following an ethical mistake. For example, many Catholic youths in the Boston metropolitan area are identified with their religious category and feel vicarious pride when a Catholic does something admirable. Most of these youths did not experience vicarious shame when they learned about the sexual abuses committed by local priests because the category *Catholic* in New England during the 1990s was free of serious blemishes. Hence, the Catholic youths did not anticipate that their non-Catholic friends would regard them as less worthy owing to the actions of a small number of priests.

By contrast, Christians have for centuries regarded Jews as possessing undesirable features. The traits of the uneducated Jews who prior to 1938 lived in the Baltic countries, Poland, or Russia were prototypic. Not surprisingly, many French Jews in late nineteenth-century France felt vicarious shame when Captain Alfred Dreyfus was convicted of treason in 1894. A fair proportion of American Jews believe that many Christians continue to hold a derogatory attitude toward their ethnic category. I suspect, but cannot prove, that more American Jews felt vicarious shame when they learned of Bernard Madoff's Ponzi scheme than experienced vicarious pride when the media announced that Daniel Shechtman, an Israeli, won the 2011 Nobel Prize in chemistry.

Adults who are identified with their religion, ethnicity, and nation are tempted to unite this trio of identifications into one network. Many Tea Party members regard their membership in the categories *Protestant, white,* and *American* as a source of pride, just as politically liberal citizens from the so-called blue states brood on the blemishes their nation acquired by the wars in Vietnam, Iraq, and Afghanistan, which provoked critical attitudes toward the United States by citizens from other countries. I suspect that many Tea Party members experienced vicarious pride when an American won an Olympic gold medal but felt minimal shame when the media announced that an American soldier tortured an innocent Iraqi civilian. Blue-state liberals, who are more critical of their nation's policies, were more likely to feel vicarious shame over the soldier's behavior and less pride over the gold medal.

Many contemporary white Protestants identify with the men and women who founded the United States and contributed to America's remarkable ascendance. A proportion of this group is bothered by the fact that in 2012 white Protestants lost a great deal of their earlier power. America has an African-American president and attorney general, Catholics and Jews dominate membership on the Supreme Court, and Jewish, Mormon, Muslim, Buddhist, and Sikh places of worship can be found in many cities throughout the country. It is not surprising that large numbers of white Protestants tell pollsters they are angry at the government's encroachment on their freedom. However, I suspect that the more fundamental reason for their frustration, which is probably less conscious, is that the groups with whom they identify have lost some of the status, respect, and power that had been sources of vicarious pride.

Religious, ethnic, and national groups recognize the importance of distinctive rituals in building and maintaining an identification. In *Interesting Times,* the historian Eric Hobsbawm describes the required dress and prayer of grace recited in Latin before each dinner at King's College, Cambridge, in the years before World War II.[9] Such rituals make it easier to identify with a group. The rebellion by contemporary youths against such arbitrary practices, which separate human groups, is motivated by a well-intentioned desire to make all outsiders feel more comfortable. But the absence of all rituals makes it harder for insiders to commit to the mission of their group. Rituals transform ordinary events into special, often sacred, experiences. That is why we still have high school and college commencements and brides in white gowns walking down the aisles of places of worship.

Although the Internet, iPhones, television, and radio have made it possible for adults in the varied sections of a particular country, as well as those living in any of the world's regions, to know the same facts and watch the same films and athletic events, surprisingly this sharing of information has not led to a stronger identification with one's nation. Many British citizens would like England to leave the European Union; Catalans want to secede from Spain; and following Obama's re-election in November 2012, hundreds of thousands of Texans have signed a petition to secede from the United States. Why? I suspect that this sharing of facts has reminded adults belonging to different groups of the sharp differences in opinions and values among them. This knowledge dilutes an identification with nation or region. Although a majority of American adults watch the Super Bowl and see the same popular films each year, the sense of shared similarity that is based on these experiences cannot compete with the acute awareness of the different attitudes toward abortion, gay marriage, taxes, and affirmative action. The differences usually win.

An identification with a member of one's family pedigree does not require direct contact. The vicarious shame or guilt felt by adolescents or young adults whose grandparents carried out Hitler's orders reveals the power of an identification with an individual the adolescents never knew. Rainer Hoess is the grandson of Rudolf

Hoess, the commandant of the concentration camp at Auschwitz from 1941 to 1943 who ordered the murders of over 400,000 Hungarian Jews before Rainer was born. When twelve-year-old Rainer learned about his grandfather's actions, a corrosive guilt provoked two suicide attempts and a confession to a reporter: "My grandfather was a mass murderer—something I can only be ashamed and saddened about." Rainer's emotion was vicarious, as there is no reason to believe that his grandfather experienced any shame or guilt.

Rainer Hoess was not the only German with a vicarious reaction. Ursula Boger, whose grandfather, Wilhelm Boger, beat prisoners on their genitals while they hung upside down, reported: "I felt numb for days after I read about what he did. I felt guilty even though I haven't committed a crime myself, I felt I had to do good things in order to make up for his evil." The grandniece of Hermann Goring, the head of Hitler's Luftwaffe, explained her voluntary sterilization by confessing "I was afraid to bear another such monster."[10]

Vicarious shame for actions by grandparents is not inevitable. The grandchildren of the Japanese soldiers who slaughtered and raped Chinese innocents in Nanking, the American soldiers who killed innocent native Indians, and the Russian officials responsible for the deaths of millions of adults in Ukraine and Poland felt either a diluted shame or no shame at all. One possible reason is that these grandchildren regarded their nation in a more desirable light. German youths were more vulnerable to shame because they knew that a prior generation of Germans was responsible for World War I, was irrationally anti-Semitic, elected Adolf Hitler, and did little to obstruct the Nazi's use of crematoria, toxic gases, and medical experiments to murder men, women, and children. This was the first time in recorded history that state policy legitimized stuffing defenseless people of all ages, none of whom were threats to the society, into oversized ovens. The evocation of vicarious disgust requires more than murder. Cooking pregnant women who had been gassed to death while under the impression that they were taking a shower is not just wrong, it is disgusting.

Several contemporary German films illustrating the callousness of Nazi officers generate shame among contemporary Germans who are identified with their nation. The many films and books on antebellum slavery remind white Americans of the vicarious responsibility they bear. Paul Piff of the University of California describes the shame felt by some American college students over the cruel treatment of Iraqi prisoners by American soldiers.[11] Recent Israeli films portray the unjust actions of their government against Palestinians. The Australian film *The Rabbit Fence* documents the cruel government treatment of Aboriginal families during the last century. The producers of media in nations that are troubled by the actions of past generations obsessively return to the scenes of the crimes in order to help citizens understand how they happened and provide a moment to cleanse the vicarious shame evoked by vivid reminders of the moral errors of their ancestors. The world is so weary of war—more than a dozen major international or civil wars in the last century alone—that men and women who had been portrayed years earlier as courageous heroes are now cast as villains.

Unlike vicarious shame, vicarious pride facilitates confidence and often potentiates vaulting ambition. Youths with a relative who had a reputation for unusual bravery, religiosity, or accomplishment are tempted to believe that they, too, possess a potential for greatness. Jean-Paul Sartre recalled his childhood exhilaration when told that many of the books on a shelf in his home were written by his grandfather. "How proud I felt! I was the grandson of a craftsman who specialized in the making of sacred objects." Sartre's identification was a critical reason for his adult addictions to reading and writing.

George Homans was an eminent Harvard sociologist who, as a child, was homely, friendless, had poor school grades, and was incompetent at baseball and football. He confessed in an autobiography that he often muted his despair by mentally tracing his family pedigree to John Adams, the second president of the United States. Youths who have an identification with a distinguished family member are often motivated to aspire to an equivalent greatness in some domain.

Individuals who have experienced prejudice, bullying, or other forms of deprivation or oppression are biased to identify with others who are or have been victims. Jennifer Stellar of the University of California found that college students who grew up in poor families were more likely than wealthier students to report a feeling of compassion for a child suffering from cancer.[12] The disproportionate number of American Jews who supported the civil rights legislation intended to help African-Americans provides another example.

Some adults who regard themselves as victims feel more vital when they are defending the rights of other victims. These individuals seem to always have their "fists up" ready to support an underdog. A colleague of mine who grew up in a family that was poor and belonged to a minority group enjoyed defending unpopular minority views in intellectual controversies, even if he did not believe the position he advocated. I once asked him why he was supporting an idea that was inconsistent with the evidence and rejected by most psychologists. He replied that someone had to stand up for a position that the majority dismissed.

Individuals who extract vitality from playing the victim role can experience uncertainty if they suddenly become dominant. Hamid Dabashi, an Iranian expert on

Shi'ism, notes that the Shia have traditionally perceived themselves as victims who must maintain a defiant stance. When they are victorious, as they were in Iran in the late 1970s, they become confused because victims are not supposed to be success-ful. I recall a few male Harvard students who identified with the victim role because they had been bullied in high school by boys who held high-status positions in the school. These experiences created the conviction that any high-status person was morally tainted. When these young men attained an outstanding academic record in college, they were suddenly thrust into a position of enhanced status with their peers and the faculty. The unexpected ascent in power was threatening because they now occupied the role they had earlier categorized as tainted. These students reacted to the threat by studying less diligently.

Youths who regard themselves as victims of prejudice feel freer to reject the dominant values of their society. This attitude can lead to great accomplishments or to disruptive actions motivated by anger. On the one hand, the Puritans who escaped victim status in Europe by settling in America established the foundation of a successful society. On the other, the Catholic paramilitary groups in Belfast exploited their victimhood as an excuse to murder innocents. One such youth told Neil Ferguson of Liverpool Hope University how the perception of his victim role unleashed actions that violated his moral beliefs: "They let the genie out of its bot-tle. They turned us into monsters. . . . And now I feel awful that they brought this instinct out in me, the violent part that wasn't me."[13]

Many Hutus used their victim role as a reason for slaughtering Tutsis. Israelis defend the expanded settlements on the West Bank as an acceptable response to their precarious position in the Middle East, their unpopularity in the world, and the victimization of Jews over so many centuries.

An identification is always stronger when the shared features are distinctive or uncommon. African-American six-year-olds are more conscious of their skin color than white children because America has more whites than blacks. The opposite is true in the Congo. Those who belong to a class, ethnic, or religious group that comprises less than 20 percent of a nation's population are likely to identify with that group. African-American, Asian-American, and Hispanic-American children exhibit stronger identifications with their ethnic category than American children whose family pedigree originated in Europe. If current population projections are correct, however, white youths will represent a minority by the turn of the next century. When that time arrives they, like the white citizens of Zimbabwe, will be more strongly identified with their ethnic group than they are today.

An ethnic identification can, in some instances, generate conflict between expressing loyalty to the values of the ethnic group and honoring the values held by the majority in the society. African-American youths from disadvantaged families typically get poorer grades than European-Americans from the same social class. A perception of white prejudice toward African-Americans motivates many black youths to demean the better grades of their white classmates and to classify them as nerds who "suck up" to the teacher. This attitude interferes with their motivation to obtain better grades because, in so doing, they would begin to resemble the white youths they dislike.[14]

Historians who use the layers of the sea as a metaphor for a society argue that the surface features of the society are easily altered, whereas the deepest layers are more stable. A person's public behaviors, like the sea's surface, are affected by local conditions and change when these conditions do. The beliefs about the self that are products of identifications lie at the deepest layers and are more resistant to change. The behaviors and beliefs that are the result of praise and punishment are easier to alter than the emotions created by identifications resting on irrational inferences, such as Rainer Hoess's identification with his grandfather. Neither conditioning principles, cognitive theory, nor evolutionary biology can explain why young Rainer tried to kill himself. This behavior was neither a conditioned response, a rational decision, nor a contribution to his inclusive fitness.

ATTACHMENT

I know of no psychologist who denies that a parent's behaviors affect the infant's emotional relationship with that parent. The popular form of this assumption states that a parent's sensitivity with the infant, especially when the child is distressed, is a critical determinant of the quality of the attachment bond between them. An attachment, the argument goes, is an emotional relationship that emerges through a combination of parental sensitivity and the infant's holding, manipulating, smiling, and vocalizing while interacting with the parent. Because these experiences vary across families, infants vary in the security of their attachment to each parent during the first year. A small group of psychologists have made the stronger claim that the security or insecurity of the attachment bond established during the first year is preserved for an indefinite time and influences adult moods and behaviors. This bolder assumption invites a closer analysis.

Although many young adults blame their current unhappiness on their parents' earlier practices (an accusation that is more common among middle-class than among disadvantaged adults), the assumption that a parent's actions in the first year could exert such an extraordinary effect on the future is uncommon. Thomas More devoted less than a page to the parental treatment of infants or children in his sixteenth-century classic *Utopia*, even though he was describing an ideal community. The Old Testament mentions only one forbidden parental behavior: a father cannot sell his daughter into a life of harlotry.

Most middle-class, white youths born after 1960 grew up in reasonably affectionate, supportive families, never went hungry, did not have to serve in the armed forces, and did not suffer serious stress because of a natural catastrophe or prejudice. Their gentle childhoods left them with few conditions they could nominate as the reason for any bouts of misery. The media helped them select their parents as villains by disseminating the writings of self-appointed experts who declared that children deprived of parental love were susceptible to anxiety or depression.

The popularity of this idea lies less with established evidence than with historical conditions. The broad concern with the long-term significance of a mother's psychological relationship with her infant is less than three hundred years old. Its origins can be traced to Europe in the middle of the eighteenth century, when social mobility became a greater possibility than it had been in previous centuries. Families that had attained middle-class status did not require mothers of young children to leave home to work, so the society gave these women the responsibility of sculpting traits in their children that might lead to enhanced family status. The ideal, and typical, middle-class nineteenth-century American family consisted of a father who left home for work and a mother who remained at home caring for her children while maintaining a haven of gentleness, grace, and love waiting for the return of the harried father who had suffered the pressures of competition, frustration, and occasional coercion. By the 1940s, faith in the psychological power of maternal love was so strong that the American psychiatrist Leo Kanner persuaded almost every physician and psychologist that autistic children, whom a majority had never seen, were products of a mother who was emotionally cool and aloof with her young child. I confess, with embarrassment, that I, too, had never seen an autistic child when, as a graduate student in 1950, I concluded that Kanner had arrived at a profound insight.

The wildlife photographer Jean François Largot released a short film in 2012 depicting an infant lion who had fallen down a steep cliff and was crying for help. Four lionesses, one being the mother, stared down the cliff wall, but only the mother inched her way down to rescue her cub. This film was intended to remind viewers that even in an aggressive species "maternal love" is a biological urge that is difficult to suppress. The film's moral message is clear. A mother who does not love her infant must be a seriously abnormal woman.

It seems a mistake, however, to classify as abnormal the many poor, unmarried women in Lyon, France, during the early decades of the nineteenth century who abandoned their newborns to a charity hospital. Nor should we label as abnormal the working American mothers who, during the same century, paid the owners of homes housing many children about two dollars a week to care for their infants. A few homes in a number of East Coast cities had the reputation of disposing of the infant if the mother's payments were in arrears.[15] Poor mothers, usually unmarried, took their unwanted infants to one of these homes knowing that the baby would be killed or abandoned at midnight in an alley.

History's muse wrote a new chapter in the human narrative to cover the events of the twentieth century. The horrors of two world wars generated a hunger for a gentler conception of human nature that emphasized an infant's need to be loved and to love. Erik Erikson, the author of the 1950 book *Childhood and Society,* replaced Freud's oral stage describing infants as selfish with a stage in which infants established a feeling of trust in their primary caretaker (typically, Erikson thought, the biological mother, because of the premise that women have a greater capacity to love than men).[16]

The demand for a large work force during World War II required many mothers of young children to place them in surrogate care while they worked in defense plants. When women's rights were enhanced following the end of the war, increasing numbers of mothers decided they wanted to work and had to find someone to care for their young child. The disruption of a family structure that had persisted for at least eight generations, combined with images of millions of infants in day care centers, threatened the society's conception of how infants ought to be raised. At the same time, the rise in divorces and juvenile crime motivated a search for the cause of these worrisome social changes. The disruption in the tradition of maternal care for infants in the home became the villain, catapulting the concept of attachment into the consciousness of scientists studying human development.

The reaction to this new hypothesis was swift. The British psychiatrist John Bowlby likened the absence of a mother's love to the lack of a vitamin needed for proper physical development. His 1951 essay on maternal deprivation was followed by a trilogy of books on attachment between 1969 and 1980 that asserted, with insufficient evidence, that an infant's attachment had a lasting effect on the child's future.[17] His intuition that good experiences in early childhood must be followed by good traits in adulthood resembles Copernicus's assumption that because God made only beautiful objects, the earth's orbit had to follow the beautiful trajectory of a circle.

Humans find it hard to believe that something good could be followed by something bad or that a good psychological outcome could have been preceded by an improper upbringing. Seventeenth-century European mothers were told that the quality of their breast milk contributed to their child's future personality—specifically, that the milk from angry or stressed mothers could contain unknown toxins. Mothers who could afford a wet nurse were advised to select a woman who was free of disease, licentiousness, and hostility; possessed a plump body; and had a ruddy complexion without moles and freckles. Nineteenth-century experts on child rearing replaced the quality of breast milk with the quality of the mother's behavior. The evidence for this belief was no better than the evidence for the dangers of improper breast milk. The proposed explanation rested on the twin assumptions that maternal love would produce a secure child and that a secure child would become a happy adult. A good beginning had to be followed by a good ending. Any other sequence would be both unseemly and unaesthetic.[18]

A bold, controversial idea is most likely to become a popular target of scientific study if there is a way to measure it. Psychologists did not know how to measure the emotional relationship between an infant and mother when Bowlby wrote his first volume. Any psychologist who invented a procedure that measured the quality of an infant's attachment was guaranteed immediate fame. Into this void stepped the talented child psychologist Mary Ainsworth, who, after studying with John Bowlby in London, became a professor of psychology at The Johns Hopkins University in Baltimore.

Ainsworth, assisted by a group of conscientious students, believed she had found a laboratory procedure that assessed the quality of the attachment bond. She called her procedure the Strange Situation. The critical evidence was the behavior of one-year-olds in an unfamiliar laboratory when the mother left the room twice for about three minutes. On one occasion she left the child alone with a stranger and on the other she left the child completely alone.

Ainsworth understood that she had to gather observations in the home in order to persuade colleagues that the variation in infant behaviors in the Strange Situation was the product of the continuing interaction between mother and infant in the home during the prior twelve months. Her graduate students visited the mothers of twenty-eight primarily middle-class, white infants many times during the first year. Although this small sample was far from a fair representation of the world's children, Ainsworth and her students made what they thought was a significant discovery.

A majority of the infants, about 60 percent, became mildly upset when the mothers left the infants in the laboratory room, but the infants were easily soothed when the mothers returned. To the students, these mothers appeared to be more sensitive with their infants in the home setting. In this context the term *sensitive* meant that the mother usually came quickly to soothe her crying infant, often displaying physical affection. It seemed intuitively obvious that these infants should have developed a secure attachment to the mother.

The infants of the remaining mothers behaved differently in the Strange Situation. One small group of infants (only 25 percent of the sample) did not cry when the mother left and continued playing when she returned. Because the mothers of these infants were somewhat less attentive to the infant at home, Ainsworth and her students speculated that these children must be insecurely attached. The smallest group (only 10 percent of the sample) became exceedingly upset the moment the mother left and continued to cry after she returned, despite the mother's efforts to calm them. It seemed reasonable to conclude that infants who could not be soothed by their mother must have a less secure attachment. Recent research uncovered a fourth, rare attachment category. These children become seriously disorganized when their mother leaves them and are likely to have been born with a biological deficit or were maltreated at home.[19]

Once these findings were published, their implications spread like wildfire. In less than a decade many psychologists were confident that they could measure the quality of an infant's attachment to a parent and evaluate the validity of Bowlby's claims. Although Ainsworth's conclusions seemed eminently reasonable, there is another way to think about her evidence. Let's behave as Sherlock Holmes might and return to the scene where the Strange Situation was conducted. A one-year-old who has been playing with toys in an unfamiliar room for less than twenty minutes suddenly sees the mother stand up for no obvious reason, say nothing, and leave the room. Mothers do not usually leave their infants in an unfamiliar place without an explanation and no information about when they will return. The unexpected departure, which is a serious violation of the infant's prototypic representation of the mother's usual behavior, alerts the child.

What happens next depends, in part, on the child's past experiences with maternal departures and, in part, on the child's temperament. Infants vary in the intensity of the uncertainty provoked by a deviation from their prototype. The infants who possess the temperament I call low-reactive do not become upset by most deviations. Because they do not become distressed, they have little motivation to return to the mother when she returns to the laboratory room. About 25 percent of Ainsworth's infants behaved that way. Because these infants were minimally irritable in the home and soothed themselves quickly when they were upset, their mothers might have concluded that it was not necessary to comfort them every time they cried. Nonetheless, Ainsworth regarded these mothers as insensitive because they did not rush to their infants every time they cried, and she called the infants insecurely attached because they ignored the mother when she returned. The potential error in that decision was the assumption that all infants should be upset by the mother's absence.

The 10 percent of infants who became extremely upset and were difficult to soothe in the Strange Situation resembled the infants born with the temperamental bias I call high-reactive. Peter Marshall and Nathan Fox confirmed that infants with this temperament behave like insecurely attached one-year-olds in the Strange Situation.[20] The mothers of these infants might have decided that they had given birth to unusually irritable children who were not easily soothed by their attempts to nurture. These mothers might have learned that their infants eventually stopped crying and concluded that it was a waste of time to rush to them every time they cried. The students who observed this type of mother in the home classified them as insensitive. And because these infants were not soothed by the mother when she returned, Ainsworth classified them as insecurely attached. Japanese infants behave similarly but for a different reason. Japanese mothers rarely, if ever, leave their infant alone in a strange place. As a result, Japanese infants become extremely upset by maternal departures and are unusually difficult to soothe. However, observations in the home reveal that most Japanese mothers are extremely sensitive parents.[21]

The largest group of one-year-olds, who were classified as securely attached, cried a little when the mother left but were easily soothed when she returned and picked them up. The mothers of these easy-to-care-for infants learned that they could comfort their infant with minimal effort and did so more regularly in the home setting.

Evidence gathered by many investigators invites an interpretation of the behaviors in the Strange Situation that differs from Ainsworth's account. Many infants classified as securely attached are calm and smile frequently before the mother leaves them for the first time in the Strange Situation. By contrast, insecurely attached infants (also described as insecure-resistant) cry before being left alone with the stranger and are likely to cry to a variety of unexpected events even when their mother is present. This evidence implies the contribution of temperament to Ainsworth's attachment categories.[22]

Many other studies are inconsistent with Ainsworth's conclusions. Almost one-half of a group of children who spent their first eighteen months in a severely depriving Romanian orphanage before being adopted met the criterion for a secure attachment in the Strange Situation when they were forty-two months old.[23]

More critical is the fact that the same proportions of secure and insecure attachments were found among children who remained home with the mother and those who attended a day care center.[24] Loving mothers in some parts of Germany and the Netherlands do not tend to their infants every time they cry because they believe that they must teach their infants to cope with distress. This strategy works, and the children do not cry when the mother leaves them alone in the Strange Situation. But they do not develop the psychological problems that are supposed to be the consequences of an insecure attachment.

Alan Sroufe of the University of Minnesota is a respected scientist who had been a strong advocate of Bowlby's ideas and Ainsworth's original conclusions. The evidence he and his colleagues gathered over the past thirty years led him to soften his earlier views, for he discovered that some securely attached children developed psychological problems whereas some insecurely attached children have satisfactory adjustments as adults. These data prompted Sroufe to acknowledge, first, that parental behaviors in the first year do not exert a strong influence on the future and, second, that infants' temperaments make a contribution to their behavior in the Strange Situation as well as to their later social adjustment.[25]

The complete collection of evidence implies that Ainsworth's original observations were products of each child's temperamental biases, past experiences with maternal departures, and the behaviors that mothers had learned as accommodations to their infant's temperament.[26] Scientists do not yet possess a sensitive index of the quality of an infant's attachment to each caretaker. Therefore, no firm conclusions regarding the long-term consequences of the early attachment relationship are possible at the present time.

This statement bothers those who do not want to relinquish Bowlby's assumptions. In an attempt to save the concept of attachment, a group of psychologists invented a protocol known as the Adult Attachment Interview that presumably evaluates a person's early attachment relationship. The measure of attachment, however, was the semantic coherence of an adult's narrative while talking about their childhood. There are two serious problems with this assumption. First, few persons can remember what happened before their third birthday. Second, and more important, adults who gave coherent or incoherent narratives when recalling their childhoods would have been equally coherent or incoherent if they had discussed Obama's presidency, their last holiday, or reasons for the recession of 2008. The coherence of a verbal narrative is influenced by variation in verbal skills, quality of schools attended, and time spent reading. There is no reason to expect that these factors should have any relation to the sensitivity of a narrator's attachment bond to his or her parents during the first year. This interview should have been called the Adult Semantic Coherence Interview, not the Adult Attachment Interview.

I suspect that scientists born after 1950 who were attracted to Bowlby's intuition that "uncertainty over the accessibility of an attachment figure is a principal condition for the development of an unstable, anxious personality"[27] were projecting their personal wish for more trusting relationships with lovers, friends, and colleagues onto young infants. It is easy for adults to assume that infants deal with some of the same problems they confront and to assign these problems to young children.

The assumption that the care of an infant by anyone other than the mother cannot be good does not die easily. Aric Sigman, a Fellow of Britain's Royal Society of Medicine, wrote an essay in 2011 reminiscent of nineteenth-century sermons and magazine articles declaring that the biological mother was always the best caretaker and, therefore, day care for young children was dangerous. A small proportion of contemporary American mothers are loyal to a protocol called "attachment parenting," which requires them to be ready to nurse their infants whenever they are hungry.

Future research will have to resolve these intriguing questions. I suspect that when the evidence is gathered, it will prove that the attachment bond of the first year is a less important determinant of children's futures than their social class, gender, culture, and experiences after the first year.[28] The psychologists who continue to believe in the persistence of a secure or insecure attachment bond at the end of the first year, based on the child's behavior in the Strange Situation, should reflect on lines written in 1947 by W. H. Auden in *The Age of Anxiety:* "We would rather die in our dread than climb the cross of the moment and let our illusions die."

BIRTH ORDER

A child's birth order, especially when the child is first- or later-born, exerts a small, but nonetheless reliable, influence on a few select traits—albeit less significant than parental practices or identifications. The effects of birth order are strongest when the difference in age between a particular child and the next oldest or youngest sibling is less than five years and both siblings are of the same sex. I suspect that the effects of birth order were stronger before schooling was mandatory and a child's evaluation of his or her skills and traits was based largely on comparisons with siblings. Today, children also compare their qualities with those of classmates as well as siblings. The existence of two sources of comparison should dilute the power of the comparison with an older brother or sister.[29]

The attitude toward legitimate authority is the most consistent outcome of birth order. First-borns, who represent about 45 percent of contemporary Americans, are more likely than later-borns to respect authority figures and conform to their requests, as long as the parents have been sufficiently nurturing. The arrival of the next child, which generates uncertainty over the loss of parental attention, enhances the first-born's motivation to obey parents' requests and adopt their values. The first-born's attitude toward parents—and, later, to legitimate authorities—seems to be "What is it you wish me to do?" This attitude, the result of the many experiences in the home that created an expectation of adult benevolence as long as one conformed to adult demands, biases first-borns to favor a less rebellious posture than later-borns because they want to avoid offending those in positions of authority.

If the parents' values match those of the majority culture, first-borns will be loyal to their society's dominant values. American parents value academic success and a profession with prestige and a respectable income. It is not surprising, therefore, that first-borns from middle-class American homes, compared with their later-born siblings, are more often valedictorians of their high school and college and more likely to attend an elite university, to enter the professions of law, medicine, or business, and to be listed in *Who's Who in America*. In cases where two brothers were both major-league baseball players, the first-born usually had a higher batting average.[30]

Later-borns establish a different set of expectations because the older sibling dominates them and they are forced to defend against the adoption of a passive posture. Later-borns want to be different from and better than their first-born sibling in some domain and often perfect a talent other than the one selected by the first-born. If the first-born is curious about science, the later-born might become interested in business. If the first-born is proficient in baseball, the later-born might master a musical instrument.[31]

Of course, later-borns need to have an opportunity to compete successfully with an older sibling. If the opportunities to develop a talent are restricted, later-borns are at some risk for violating the law. Among economically disadvantaged families, more later- than first-borns are incarcerated in American prisons. An example is provided by John Wideman and his younger brother, who grew up in the impoverished African-American neighborhood of Homewood in Pittsburgh. John, the first-born, became a popular writer and university professor. His younger brother is serving life for a murder committed during a robbery.

Imagine two brothers, aged six and ten, living with well-educated, affectionate parents. The first-born perceives his parents as authority figures who possess a number of desirable characteristics, especially the power the child would like to command. His younger brother experiences a family environment in which the parents seem to favor the first-born by awarding him privileges denied to the younger brother, including greater freedom, a later bedtime, and more expensive birthday gifts. In addition, the older brother teases his younger sibling and reminds him of his relative inferiority. These experiences, day after day, can create a chronic, low-level resentment toward the older sibling and the parents. Such feelings, in turn, weaken the motivation to conform to parental requests and create the foundation for a rebellious attitude toward all authority figures during adolescence. Later-borns resemble the Shia Muslims, mentioned above, who regard themselves as victims of injustice.

These ideas find persuasive support in the fact that more men who were elected world leaders between 1960 and 1970 were first- rather than later-borns. The leaders who were later-born males—for example, Qaddafi, Castro, Mugabe, and Nasser—usually seized power from traditional authority in an aggressive coup. A similar difference favoring first-borns was found among women who were prime ministers, presidents, or American governors during the 1980s.[32]

First- and later-born scientists hold distinctively different attitudes toward novel ideas that have social implications. Among the small number of families in which both first- and later-born brothers became scientists, the latter more often agreed with a serious challenge to a popular theoretical position whereas their first-born brothers resisted the novel idea. The historian Frank Sulloway examined the views of a large number of first- and later-born scientists (born to different families) toward twenty-eight ideas that had revolutionary implications for premises held by the broader society. Sulloway excluded the large number of brilliant inventions, ideas, or discoveries, such as the transistor and antibiotics, that did not challenge a community's basic values or assumptions. Later-borns were twice as likely as first-borns to support the radical idea and reject the status quo. Three such revolutionary ideas were those proposed by Copernicus, Freud, and Pasteur.[33]

A fourth revolutionary idea was Darwin's evolutionary theory. Most first-born natural scientists who commented on Darwin's theory between 1860 and 1875 rejected his ideas because they challenged popular biblical explanations of the origin of humans. Later-borns were three times more likely than first-borns to endorse Darwin's theory. Both Charles Darwin and Alfred Russell Wallace, who arrived independently at the idea of natural selection, were later-borns. The ideological independence of the later-born is apparent in this sentence from Darwin's autobiography: "As far as I can judge, I am not apt to follow blindly the lead of other men."

Lyndon Johnson had appointed Earl Warren to head a commission charged with deciding whether Lee Harvey Oswald acted alone when he assassinated John Kennedy in November 1963 or was a member of a conspiratorial group. On the day the commission issued its final report declaring that Oswald acted alone, I was discussing birth order in a seminar with Harvard undergraduates. This was a perfect opportunity to test the idea that later-borns do not trust authority. I asked the students to locate as many fellow students as they could and find out whether they had heard about the commission's decision, whether they agreed or disagreed with it, and whether they were first- or later-born. The replies of several hundred Harvard students revealed that most first-borns agreed with the decision by the Warren commission; most later-borns disagreed. A few later-borns insisted there was a conspiracy. I am a first-born with one younger brother. I accepted the commission's conclusion. My brother did not.

Members of minority groups who are subject to prejudice by the majority share some of the feelings and attitudes of later-borns because they, too, regard themselves as victims unjustly placed outside the halls of power. Hence, they feel freer to question popular beliefs. This frame of mind helps to explain why a disproportionate number of Nobel Laureates in science (close to one in four) were Jews who grew up in societies holding anti-Semitic views. Albert Einstein is a classic example, for he repeated in conversations and writings a mantra that demanded the same skeptical view of received wisdom that Darwin held.

Indeed, if Max Planck, a respected member of an elite German family, had been willing to reject the popular understanding of light as a wave, he—not Einstein—might have written the paper arguing that light consisted of discrete packets of energy. Five years before Einstein made that suggestion, Max Planck had discovered that a heated vessel emitted its energy in discrete packets, which he called quanta. But Planck regarded quanta as a convenient way to describe what was observed. He was not ready to question the consensual belief held by respected physicists and claim that quanta were natural phenomena.

Radical writing styles that break with tradition have a higher probability of emerging in societies that are geographically close to a more successful society—in a position analogous to being a later-born. Ireland's chronically subordinate position in relation to England provides an example. The former country, which was invaded or dominated by England for more than a thousand years, was the childhood home of George Bernard Shaw, James Joyce, Dylan Thomas, and Samuel Beckett. All four rejected the dominant style of their generation. Shaw scoffed at the superficiality of those who possessed elite status in his play *Pygmalion,* which became the basis of the popular film *My Fair Lady.* An uneducated flower girl from an ordinary family could attain elite status simply by changing her dialect. The airs of superiority held by patrician families rested on nothing more than how one spoke at a party.

Those in a subordinate position, whether later-borns or members of an oppressed religious, ethnic, national, or social-class group, are biased toward perceiving themselves as outsiders who enjoy challenging those in power by demonstrating that the latter have clay feet. The same is true for younger institutions. The faculty at the University of Chicago in 1945 wanted, but did not have, the prestige of Yale, Princeton, or Harvard. Under Robert Hutchins's leadership, the undergraduate school adopted a curriculum so different from the Ivy League colleges that its faculty and students could regard their university as unique, making it impossible to compare the University of Chicago with other universities. Hutchins's action was an example of a popular later-born strategy: if you can't beat them, take a different path.

SIZE OF COMMUNITY

A child's evaluations of his or her abilities and personality traits are affected, to some degree, by the size of the community, especially during childhood and early adolescence. Children cannot know how smart, popular, or brave they are without comparing themselves with others of the same age. (This is an example of the principle of contrast described in Chapter 1.) Hence, their private judgments are colored by the comparisons they choose.

More than 130,000 eighth-grade students from twenty-seven countries across the world took the same test of mathematics achievement. The students with the greatest confidence in their mathematical ability had only moderately high scores but were attending schools that had many students with very low ability. Hence, they were among the best students in their school. Students with exactly the same test scores attending schools in which many children earned high scores had the poorest opinion of their mathematical ability.[34]

For the same reason, moderately talented children living in a small town find it easier to conclude that they are exceptional in some domain. Equally talented children living in large cities are reminded every day of many peers who are more accomplished. More than one of every three Americans live in a large metropolitan area with access to art and science museums, libraries, a university, and diverse opportunities for self-improvement. Yet more adults listed in *Who's Who in America* spent their childhoods in towns or small cities than in large urban centers. More than two-thirds of the most respected twentieth-century cosmologists grew up in small towns, as did America's most famous astronaut, John Glenn, and presidents Jimmy Carter, Ronald Reagan, and Bill Clinton. Because small towns are often located far from a metropolis, these communities create an ambience that is less cynical, impersonal, and competitive than the one that permeates the modern city. Moreover, youths in small towns are better behaved because they know that misbehaviors or violations of local mores will generate criticism among the several hundred adults who know them or their family. Those who want anonymity prefer the city.   .

CULTURE AND HISTORICAL ERA

The institutions, values, technology, and crises of a culture during a particular historical interval represent a final set of influences on development. History alters sources of worry, opportunities for social mobility, the magnitude of status inequality, ethical values, the economy, and the institutions of a society. For example, during the interval from 1812 to 2012, Americans became more tolerant, better educated, and healthier, and women not only were empowered to work with their minds rather than their hands but also felt less guilt surrounding sexuality.

On the other hand, the same two centuries were characterized by greater income inequality; less opportunity for the average youth to do better than his or her parents; more single-parent families, youth gangs, and drug addicts; the loss of moral authority among elites; greater confusion over ethical values that demand loyalty; and a more permissive sexuality among youths. A national survey of more than 14,000 American adolescents revealed that the average age of the first sexual experience is now less than sixteen years. This historical trend has removed some of the mystery from the sexual intimacies of newly married adults. A new iPhone holds more excitement than sex for many contemporary youths, who treat their sexual appetite as they do a desire for lunch. A rise in the instability of and dissatisfaction with marriage among American couples with a high school diploma is one of the consequences of this new frame of mind. Six decades ago, this group of Americans had the most stable marriages.

The fact that homicide became the second leading cause of death among Americans under age twenty-five in 2011 is one reason why contemporary psychologists are conferring significance to the control of impulses, which they assign to the executive functions of emotional regulation, effortful control, and mindfulness. A century earlier, psychologists—following Freud—were far more concerned with youths who regulated their urges excessively.

A child's birth cohort (that is, year of birth) can influence his or her future. American and European men born between 1914 and 1924 had a high probability of being wounded, killed, or held as a prisoner of war in World War II. The cohort born between 1925 and 1935 missed these dangers. Close to 90 percent of contemporary American youths spend their spare time playing video games, many of which are violent or erotic, while sitting alone in a room in their home. Fifty years earlier they would have been engaged in a recreational activity with friends. It is not known whether the solitary quality of contemporary recreation has contributed to the increase in self-interest and loneliness among today's youths.

Adults who became scientists before 1960 had a far easier time obtaining grants and advancing their careers than equally talented individuals who began their careers after 1980, because there was a larger increase in the number of scientists than in the amount of research funds during the later years. This asymmetry has created a level of tense competitiveness among today's young scientists that was palpably less in my generation.

The extraordinary rise in the number of natural scientist faculty over the course of the past half-century has made the supply larger than the demand. Young scientists were advised by an editorial in *Science* magazine dated September 7, 2012, to prepare an individual development plan that articulated their career goals and the steps needed to attain them. (The teachers of children with learning disabilities, and many of the children themselves, also constructed individual learning plans.) Thus, in less than three generations, the advice given to twenty-five-year-olds with an advanced degree in science to "make an important discovery" was replaced with "consult with your mentor and write out the steps you must take to obtain a tenure position." I wonder what Newton, Darwin, Pasteur, Bohr, Curie, Einstein, McClintock, Crick, or Watson would say if they learned of this historical alteration in the nature of a career in science. I can't imagine any of these scientists at age twenty-five listing the concrete things they had to do to gain a secure position in a university or research institution but omitting any reference to the phenomena that captured their curiosity and attracted them to science.

When a society passes the tipping point for the amount of diversity in ethical values, the average citizen in that society no longer assumes that most of his acquaintances will share his values. This realization sensitizes the majority to the potentially fragile harmony of their society and motivates a heightened concern with maintaining social order. American journalists and political commentators today worry a great deal over offending a particular group. This concern was less intense during the first half of the last century. H. L. Mencken, a popular journalist and essayist who died in 1956, regularly published politically incorrect columns that offended large numbers of Americans. For example, he once wrote: "A poet more than thirty years old is simply an overgrown child" and "Democracy is the theory that the common people know what they want and deserve to get it good and hard." I cannot imagine *New York Times* columnists David Brooks or Thomas Friedman being that blunt with an unpopular belief they held because the subsequent letters of protest might cost them their jobs. The suppression of unpopular beliefs is a new feature in the American ethos that is discrepant from the long-standing admiration for those who "speak their mind."

The information technology that has permitted the residents of every world region to be aware of the resources, beliefs, and values of the individuals from every other region represents one of the most important historical changes of the last century. The advantages are obvious and need not be listed. There is, however, a downside to this technology that is often ignored. Adults living in poor or coercive countries have become more acutely conscious of their deprivations because they compare themselves with citizens of developed nations rather than with other members of their small community. This new knowledge, not unlike the insights of Adam and Eve after eating the apple, replaces a mild dissatisfaction with one's modest deprivation within a community with a more corrosive envy of or anger at strangers living with high privilege thousands of miles away.

The values of a cultural setting are always potent. Traditional Chinese parents are more accepting of a quiet, timid child than American or European parents. Most Japanese adults viewing a scene attend to the relations among the objects, whereas Americans habitually focus on the single, most dominant element. If the scene were Francisco de Goya's famous painting *The Third of May,* Japanese viewers would distribute their attention broadly and register the spatial relations among the row of soldiers aiming their rifles at the visually dominant figure of the man with arms raised about to be shot, the dead bodies to the right of the man, the onlookers to his left, and the men in back of him with hands over their eyes. Americans, on the other hand, would focus most of their attention on the single man with arms raised; few would register the relations among all the elements in the scene. Megumi Kuwabara and Linda Smith of Indiana University found that this cultural difference in distribution of attention can be detected as early as four years of age.[35] Northern Thailand has a large number of poor families, many child prostitutes, and residents who are loyal to a philosophy declaring that daughters have a moral obligation to help their parents. If a life of prostitution is the only way a girl can meet her obligation to assist her impoverished family, the Thai community regards the girl's behavior as ethically acceptable.[36]

When corporations, laboratories, government agencies, and universities began to grow in size and political influence during the last half of the past century, teams of adults with different talents were required for the advances that new technologies made possible. It is more difficult today than it was a hundred years ago for a solitary scientist to achieve a significant advance without being a member of a large research team that has access to an expensive apparatus. Einstein, by contrast, was working alone in a small patent office in Bern when he wrote his famous paper on special relativity. At present, prize-winning discoveries in particle physics often require a scientist to be part of a large team of investigators and to have access to an accelerator. The discovery of the Higgs boson in 2012 required the talents of thousands of scientists and a machine that cost more than $9 billion.

Medieval Europeans could enjoy a brief feeling of virtue simply by imposing restraints on the temptations of pride, anger, envy, avarice, gluttony, lust, and sloth. They did not need the help of others. These sins have been replaced with failure to attain a career with a respectable status and a high salary, to be part of a marriage replete with sexual pleasures, or to enjoy many close, loyal friends. In short, contemporary adults require the cooperation of others in order to avoid committing the sin of failing to attain one of these goals. Young Swedish adults complain about an absence of intimate relationships and a membership in groups that generate a feeling of vitality. Their grandparents would not have nominated these frustrations as major sources of unhappiness.[37]

TOUGH CHILDHOODS

I have concentrated on children growing up in the typical families of a culture rather than in a depriving institution, abusive family, or no home at all. It is estimated that about 140 million children across the world do not have a parent caring for them. Some were placed in institutions soon after birth and remained there unless or until they were adopted. Although many institutionalized children continue to have psychological problems, even when their environments become more benevolent, a fair number are protected from serious problems either because they enjoyed emotional support and cognitive enrichment in their adoptive families or because they inherited a resilient temperament.[38]

The consequences of early institutional rearing differ from the consequences of physical abuse, sexual abuse, or neglect within a family setting. Because the child's interpretation of his or her experiences affects later outcomes, institutionalization, physical abuse, and chronic neglect must be distinguished from strict discipline on the part of a parent who is perceived as caring about the child. Eighteenth-century American parents were exceptionally harsh with children when they disobeyed, but most grew up to become well-adapted adults. Although Japanese fathers before World War II were excessively strict with their sons, many became accomplished, productive adults. A president of a successful automobile company recalled his father: "Once his anger was over, he did not nag or complain, but when he was angry, I was really afraid of him." These fathers did not believe they were maltreating their children, and their sons did not feel unloved. The belief that one is loved or rejected is a private interpretation that cannot always be inferred from the parent's behavior.

Charles Nelson, Nathan Fox, and Charles Zeanah are studying the development of a large number of children who spent varying amounts of time in one of several depriving Romanian orphanages before being adopted by Romanian families.[39] Most of the children who were adopted before their second birthday gradually attained the cognitive talents and social behaviors of the average family-reared child by the time they were eight years old. However, a large number of these adopted children who had developed normative cognitive skills continued to show an indiscriminate friendliness with strangers. It remains a possibility that human infants require a minimal amount of unpredictability in interactions with adults and objects during the first year in order to develop a normal posture of cautiousness when they encounter unfamiliar persons. In the absence of such experiences, there might be less pruning of synapses in the amygdala and a subsequent failure to acquire the initial wariness that most young children display toward strangers. Nim Tottenham of the University of California reported that institutionalized children possessed larger amygdalae than normal children.[40]

An examination of all the evidence on the effects of institutional rearing of infants led Robert McCall and his colleagues to three major conclusions.[41] First, most institutionalized children exhibit delays in both physical and cognitive development while in the institution and during the initial months after adoption, but their intellectual talents and social behaviors improve gradually with age in both the home and the institution. Second, many children adopted by nurturing families before age two eventually attain the values for physical growth and cognitive abilities possessed by family-reared children. Finally, children adopted before six months of age have the best chance of a full recovery, whereas those adopted after their second birthday have the greatest difficulty attaining expected milestones.[42]

Parental abuse or neglect have consequences that differ from those associated with institutionalization. Because abuse and neglect are more frequent in disadvantaged families, it is often difficult to separate the effects of class of rearing from the effects of the abuse. Furthermore, abused children do not constitute a random sample of all the children in a society. Girls are more frequent victims of sexual abuse than boys, and infants or young children with a serious intellectual deficit or physical defect are most likely to be physically abused. Thus, abnormal moods or intellectual deficits in adulthood could be a partial consequence of the earlier compromise rather than attributable only to the abuse.

That said, the evidence does indicate that any form of abuse renders a majority of children vulnerable to a psychological problem, independent of their social class and early traits. According to a research team at Columbia University, about one in ten American adults reported being sexually abused as children. These individuals are at a higher risk for later depression, suicide attempts, or one or more anxiety disorders because they are likely to interpret the sexual abuse as implying either that the perpetrator, often a parent or relative, did not care about their welfare or that they allowed themselves to participate in a seriously amoral act. Either interpretation renders the child and, later, the adult vulnerable to guilt, shame, anger, anxiety, or all four emotions.

Fortunately, the vast majority of the world's children are not reared in depriving institutions or abusive homes. Most family-reared children who experience physical punishments, a natural disaster, loss of a parent, or war eventually recover normal functioning. Resilience, not permanent impairment, is the expected outcome for most children exposed to a serious but temporary stress.

It is not uncommon for children with a chronic illness to fight back. H. Robert Horvitz, a biologist who shared the 2002 Nobel Prize in Physiology, could not engage in any prolonged physical activity during his childhood because of a severe case of asthma. Horvitz decided to confront his burden. "Instead of becoming afraid of life," he wrote, "I became more and more determined to ... conquer it. ... I became determined to persevere even when my shortness of breath made my physical suffering so great I could barely force myself to move."[43]

THE SUM OF OUR EXPERIENCES

Psychologists do not understand why some children react to a disability, poverty, prejudice, or trauma by attempting to overcome their disadvantage whereas others become passively impotent. Experts asked to predict the exact place where a hundred-pound boulder that has begun to roll down a thousand-foot mountain will eventually land can eliminate a large number of possible resting places simply by knowing the rock's weight, shape, and position at the top. But prediction of the final resting place is impossible because the experts cannot know how many gullies, trees, or old logs the boulder will strike on its long descent.

Who would have predicted George Washington's ascent to become America's first president based on knowledge of his traits as a young adult? At least four relatively independent and unpredictable events had to occur to allow this heroic outcome. His older stepbrother Lawrence had to die prematurely, leaving large land holdings to the young Washington. He had to have the good fortune of meeting the wealthy head of the elite Fairfax family, who was instrumental in advancing his career. He had to marry the wealthy Martha Custis. And, finally, the French had to help the bedraggled Americans defeat the British. Without this quartet of events, it is unlikely that a shy, reserved, cautious, self-educated twenty-year-old Virginian—who had lost his father and had a shrew for a mother, limited financial resources, an intense fear of failure, and a reluctance to offend those who enjoyed higher status—would attain a celebrated position in America's history.

Equally low was the probability in January 1933 that a fourth-born eighteen-year-old from a lower-middle-class, undistinguished Jewish family, whose initial articles and multiple requests for a Guggenheim fellowship were rejected, would win the 1976 Nobel Prize in Literature. The fact that Saul Bellow did so affirms the impossibility of predicting the future of a single person, even from his properties as an adolescent, because later events and the person's interpretations of them are unknown.

Stephen Joseph's book *What Doesn't Kill Us* wisely notes that contemporary Americans and Europeans emphasize the harmful effects of stressful experiences and ignore the many individuals who responded to similar experiences with a desire to prove their competence and virtue and dilute their earlier feelings of insecurity.[44] Put plainly, a conception of children as frail, helpless, passive pawns errs by disregarding their coping capacities and the power of a loss or frustration to provoke a thoughtful analysis and attempts to carve out a satisfying, productive life. Experts who write that all stressors permanently impair children run the risk of persuading victims of their impotence—which, in turn, tempts some to fulfill this pessimistic prophecy. Abraham Lincoln was fortunate to have been born before these simplistic ideas became popular.

The personality and cognitive profiles of a large group of twenty-year-olds are the result of complex interactions among so many different conditions it is unreasonable for anyone to claim that knowledge of only one condition—whether a secure or insecure attachment, being first- or later-born, growing up with a loving or neglectful family, or living in a small town or large city—can eliminate the uncertainty that is an inherent feature of human development. There are simply too many unexpected, improbable events that can have a profound effect on a child, including an especially supportive teacher, an affectionate grandparent, an experience that violates one of the child's premises, and, especially, the possibility of a trauma. The physicist Niels Bohr understood that "prediction is very difficult, especially if it's about the future."

Although this book was not intended as a source of advice for parents, I feel some obligation to state a few personal opinions. Obviously, these suggestions apply to parents rearing children in contemporary, economically developed societies that require children to acquire particular values, skills, and habits. I do not claim that all of these suggestions are supported by firm evidence or that a majority of psychologists would agree with all of them. They are simply my personal views. Caveat emptor.

The most important requirement during the first year is to provide infants with affectionate care that is predictable and to engage them in reciprocal play that involves physical contact, conversation, laughter, and modest surprises in all the sensory modalities. Unexpected events that infants can understand with effort are major sources of brain growth and, therefore, the foundation of cognitive and emotional development. In cases where surrogate care is necessary, parents should spend a few hours observing a few day care centers or homes and pick the one in which most of the infants seem lively and happy.

Parents during the second and third years should encourage language development and be clear and consistent about the rules they want the child to follow. If the child violates one of these rules, verbal rebukes, frowns, or withdrawal of desired privileges are effective. Physical punishment is not necessary, but it is not damning as long as children understand the reason for the spanking and accept it as appropriate. Parents should make clear that they are criticizing the action and not implying that the child is inherently bad.

I remember interviewing some twenty-year-olds in 1958 who were members of a group of normal Ohio children who had been studied from infancy to their third decade. The evidence gathered in the home when these adults were children indicated that the parents were unusually strict and exceptionally harsh in their punishment of violations. When I asked the twenty-year-olds about their parents' socialization practices, they acknowledged a strict atmosphere in the home. But they quickly added that they felt gratitude toward their parents for implementing a regimen they believe helped them become happy, successful adults.

It is critical that preschool children believe their parents value them as persons. Once children pass their third birthday, they possess the concepts *good* and *bad* and need to believe that the former adjective applies to them. One basis for this assignment is evidence that someone, preferably the parents, values them. When families were large and had modest incomes, children were given responsibilities that helped the family and persuaded them of their intrinsic value. This condition is rarer in 2012.

If the symbolic communication of value does not come from the family, school-age children will seek it from the peer group. Parents can communicate this message with a variety of strategies. Many Chinese mothers cook a child's favorite food.

Pick the message that fits your personality and circumstances. The perception that the parents enjoy being with the child is especially persuasive.

In addition, parents should display in their daily behavior the values they encourage verbally. Children are extremely sensitive to inconsistencies between the values the parents declare and those they adopt for themselves, and such inconsistencies affect the identification process. School-age children should be given more autonomy, although parents should still insist that the child cannot set all the rules.

Parents can further loosen the reigns during adolescence. Award more freedom, while letting adolescents know that you are there if needed. Most important, parents should not allow adolescents to infer that their well-being depends on their achievements. Let youths' victories belong to them. Do not be afraid of criticizing or rebuking youths when they violate an ethical norm you value. If parents disapprove of an adolescent's decision, they should say so. Indeed, most young adolescents are counting on a parent to impose restrictions when they are about to make a serious error.

On the other hand, parents have to be willing to let adolescents make a few choices they sense might be modest mistakes. Parents have now become friends as well as protectors and mentors. The Japanese concept *amae* captures the ideal relationship during this stage. This term refers to the beliefs shared by the members of a dyad. The adolescent knows he or she can rely on the parents to be supportive no matter what the circumstances, and parents accept this implicit obligation.

These suggestions, even if valid, cannot guarantee a happy outcome because the child's temperament, new and lost friendships, envy or admiration of a talented sibling, quality of schools attended, and identifications with an advantaged or disadvantaged class or ethnic group have the power to generate moods of shame or pride over which parents have little control. Death and taxes are the only certainties.

CHAPTER FIVE

What Is Preserved— for How Long?

Somewhere in America today a pregnant mother is holding an iPod playing a recording of a Beethoven sonata close to her abdomen in the hope that her unborn child will become sensitized to good music. Another mother reading a Keats poem assumes that her fetus will hear enough words to put him ahead of his peers when it is time to enter kindergarten. These parents, who take the writings of Sigmund Freud and John Bowlby seriously, are certain that their infant's future is controlled in a nontrivial way by the events of the earliest developmental phases.

The preservation of the properties that comprise the first phase of a prolonged sequence intrigues scientists and the public. Physicists are certain that the background energy permeating our universe at this moment is a remnant of the extraordinary burst of energy released by the Big Bang more than 13 billion years ago. Psychologists and parents entertain a more modest curiosity. They wish to know whether some adolescent or adult feelings, beliefs, or habits are remnants of those that were present during the first few years of development. If so, which ones were preserved and why?

This curiosity rests on the popular, but unproven, assumption that some infant experiences must contribute to the psyche of the young adult. An adult plunged into a depression after losing a loved one might want to know at what stage in his or her development did the probability of this corrosive mood approach a high value?

Two kinds of properties are candidates for long-term preservation. The first includes the sensory capacities and motor modules all humans possess, given the nature of the human brain and the fact that all human environments contain objects, people, and dynamic events. The capacities to see, hear, touch, smell, and taste are preserved from infancy to old age, even though their sensitivity may be compromised in older adults.

Parents and the general public care more about the preservation of habits, feelings, beliefs, and ethical values that vary among members of a society and affect adaptation. The present chapter deals mainly with these properties, many of which are called *personality traits*.

Until recently few psychologists questioned the popular assumption that some psychological products of early experiences were preserved and exerted an influence on the moods and habits of adults. This premise, called infant determinism, was held as dogmatically as the nineteenth-century physicist's belief in an ether that was the medium through which light waves traveled. The advocates of infant determinism assumed that the primary responsibility for establishing the proper habits, values, and intentions in children rested with mothers. Listen to the eighteenth-century philosopher Rousseau: "When mothers deign to nurse their own children, then will be a reform in morals. . . . When women become good mothers, men will become good husbands and fathers." One self-appointed expert repeated Rousseau's proclamation during the early decades of the last century: "The powerful significance of the intellectual processes have their first roots in the specifically human mental structures of the 3-month-old child. . . . Historically, all phenomena of adult mental life must be traceable to birth."[1]

Another warned that even the movies posed a danger to young brains: "The baby may show no signs of restlessness and be as good as you please or make up for lost sleep by an extra nap the next day, and yet be harmed thereby. . . . Someday the accounting must come—it may be in 20 or 40 years later before it is paid-in-full, but paid-in-full it will be."[2]

Why have so many commentators attributed such extraordinary power to the experiences of the opening years? One reason rests with the change in women's roles in Europe during the eighteenth century. When middle-class women were freed of the responsibility of gathering wood, picking berries, and weeding vegetable plots, society gave them the responsibility of shaping their infant's future. At the same time, the children of the bourgeoisie had lost much of their economic value to the family and had become psychological investments whose dividends were the enhancement of family pride. Children who for centuries had been workhorses had now become show horses.

Most middle-class children in contemporary, economically developed nations make little or no material contribution to their family. They do not earn money, care for younger siblings, prepare meals, or wash clothes. In effect, they are guests at a comfortable hotel. This parasitic role renders them needy for a symbolic sign of their value. Parents provide that sign by communicating a sentiment of love. Most societies assume that mothers are better able than fathers to send this message.

When historical events made it possible for the child of a bank clerk to rise or fall in the social hierarchy, change in social status became a source of hope and worry for families occupying the middle rungs of the class ladder. When a mood of uncertainty pierces the consciousness of a large segment of society, self-appointed experts announce that they have discovered rituals that will mute the uncomfortable anxiety. Chief among the recommendations offered by eighteenth-century commentators was that proper parental actions would guarantee acquisition of the traits needed for a successful future. The dark side of this advice contained a warning to mothers who did not care for their infant properly. They would bear the responsibility for rearing a child burdened with a dull mind and a wild spirit.

Many contemporary scientists share this pair of assumptions. A team of Japanese investigators reported that newborns placed on their mother's skin within the first two minutes after birth showed better regulation of "stress" during the next hour than infants placed on the mother twenty-six minutes after being born. The authors then suggested that the former group might show better regulation in the future. This bold speculation assumes that on the first postnatal day a difference of twenty-four minutes before experiencing skin contact could have significant future consequences. Apparently, these scientists regard the infant's brain as a hard disc that preserves all messages with fidelity for an indefinite time.

A journalist wrote in *Time* magazine on February 3, 1997: "Experience in the first year of life lays the basis for networks of neurons that enable us to be smart, creative, and adaptable in all the years that follow." More than eighty years earlier, a United States government pamphlet written for expectant mothers contained the same warning with even less evidence: "The first nervous impulses which pass through the baby's eyes, ears, fingers, and mouth to the tender brain make a pathway for itself; the next time another impulse travels over the same path, it deepens the impression of the first."

This advice, whether offered in 1914 or 1997, was well-intentioned. Infants who are played with and talked to regularly are cognitively ahead of those who are ignored. It is a bit dishonest, however, to suggest to poor, uneducated parents living in a crime-infested neighborhood that playing with and talking to their infants regularly will protect their child from future academic failure, drug addiction, or imprisonment and guarantee a professional career with a high salary. I make this claim because the quality of schools attended, the values of the child's friends, and the coherence of the neighborhood, together with the older child's identification with a disadvantaged class category—which occur after the fifth birthday—exert significant influences on development. Put plainly, a trusting expectation of kindness from adults established during the first year might not be adaptive for adolescents living in settings replete with deceit, betrayals, and violence.

The traditional belief is inconsistent with the many studies showing that the products of early experience often undergo serious changes over time. Children who were orphaned during World War II or the Korean conflict had fragile bonds to all adult caretakers during their early years. Nonetheless, most of these children developed an adequate adjustment after being adopted by affectionate foster parents.

Some psychological representations established in the early years, like old photos lying in the attic, might exist somewhere in the brain but they have lost all relevance to the present.

Of course, parents should be affectionate, playful, and engage in conversations with their young children. What is less certain is the degree to which these experiences guarantee a satisfactory adaptation to their society. Every American infant born in 2012 will be compared with more than 4 million others on a variety of abilities and personality traits when that cohort enters the first grade. From first grade through high school graduation, each child's academic performances will be compared with the other children in the community, and each community will be compared with thousands of other communities. The child's absolute level of talent in any of these skills is irrelevant. All that matters is where each child's performances rank in relation to those of other children of the same age.

Contemporary adolescents growing up in economically disadvantaged families in 2012 know much more about the world than the adolescents who grew up in privileged families in the same communities in the eighteenth century. Nonetheless, the former are at a disadvantage because so many other children possess superior skills and more knowledge. If every person in the world was infected with a virus that reduced their working memory and verbal ability by 10 percent, little would change. The same youths would be admitted to the same colleges and occupy the same status positions a dozen years later. The average IQ of American children has increased substantially over the past fifty years due, in part, to television and the Internet. But in both 1962 and 2012, the children whose IQ scores were in the top third of the distribution are receiving the highest school grades and those whose IQs were in the bottom third are getting the poorest grades. There is an anecdote about an older professor and a student running from a bear. The student, a few feet in back of the professor, yelled, "The bear is going to catch us and we will be killed unless we run faster." The professor replied, "It is not necessary for me to run faster than the bear, only faster than you."

Reflect on the following hypothetical experiment. A group of 5,000 impoverished American mothers without a high school diploma talk and play with their young children at least four hours each day for the first two years of life, and a group of 5,000 professional mothers with an annual family income greater than $100,000 talk and play with their infant for only two minutes a day. All other differences between the two groups remain unchanged. I am relatively certain that more children from the former group will fail to graduate high school and, as adults, will work as clerks or unskilled laborers. More children of the professional parents will graduate college and enter a professional career. This does not mean that parental behaviors have no effect on children, only that these other conditions also matter.

Why, then, do many psychologists, psychiatrists, and parents continue to believe in a strong connection between the experiences of early childhood and the young adult's psychological profile? The immaturity of our understanding of development, which rests on weak theory, insensitive methods, and the absence of a tapestry of firm facts, is one reason. This unfortunate state of affairs allows the scientists who believe in connectivity to maintain their faith in a strong predictive relation between early childhood and adulthood. No contemporary fact requires the committed advocates of infant determinism to relinquish their favorite premise.

The most convincing evidence for preservation of properties shaped by experiences during infancy comes from experiments with laboratory animals. If a newborn rat is taken from its mother for a few minutes a day over the first few weeks of life, the hippocampus is altered and the adult animal is less stressed in novel surroundings than rats left undisturbed with their mother. In this and similar experiments, however, the rats lived in cages with a regular supply of food and water as well as protection from the predators and unpredictable events that occur in natural habitats. If the rats had been returned to their natural environments, the products of their early experience might not have been preserved. Artificial conditions can create artificial facts.

The extraordinary malleability of the brain was revealed in a study of rats who were transferred from their austere cages to larger spaces containing rope bridges and objects. Exposure to this enriched environment was accompanied by an increase in the number of tiny spines that grow on the dendrites of neurons; in other words, the more stimulating environment changed the animals' brains. But these material alterations were impermanent. When the rats who enjoyed the enriched environment were placed back in their small cages, the extra spines disappeared and their brains came to resemble the brains of animals deprived of the enriched environment. The visual cortex of the ferret is equally malleable.[3] If material changes in rat and ferret brains created by experience are not preserved indefinitely, it is unlikely that the changes created by parental behaviors during the child's first two years have a special quality that awards them a resistance to being altered.

The infants born today across the world will encounter dramatically different environments during their opening years. Some will be reared by hired caretakers, others by grandmothers or older sisters; some will remain at home with their mothers. Some will play with many toys in brightly lit rooms full of picture books and television images; some will spend their first year in a dark hut with no toys. Yet despite the extraordinary variation in early experience, excluding the small proportion born with serious brain damage or a genetic defect, the majority will speak a few words by their second birthday, infer the feelings of others by their third birthday, and be ready to assume family responsibilities by seven or eight years of age. The differences among the world's children and adolescents are trivial when compared with the similarities.

I noted in the preceding chapter that the child's interpretations of experience, which assume significance after the second birthday, exert considerable influence on future outcomes. Many millions of young children growing up during Mao Zedong's reign attended state-run day care centers twelve hours a day, seven days a week. Most of the children interpreted this experience as normative rather than as a sign of parental indifference, and many grew up to become successful entrepreneurs, brilliant scientists, or powerful members of the political elite.

More than fifty years ago I observed and tested a two-year-old girl a few days after the police had removed her from a bedroom in the home where she and her older sister had been imprisoned since infancy. The girl was mute, without emotion, and profoundly retarded. The sisters were adopted by the same affectionate family and were living with them when I returned eleven years later to interview the formerly mute girl. She was attending high school, had adequate grades, was socially appropriate, and had the interests and values of a typical Ohio adolescent in 1970. When I asked her why she thought her mother locked her in the bedroom, she replied that her mother had to care for several older children and locking her in the room with the sister made the mother's life easier. I detected no anger in her voice and even sensed some sympathy for her mentally disturbed parent.

Puritan parents in seventeenth-century New England used extremely harsh socialization methods, but most of their children developed adaptive personalities because they interpreted their severe upbringing as signs of parental concern with building their character. The philosopher John Stuart Mill, who described his father as aloof, stern, and lacking in affection, did not interpret his father's behavior as a sign of rejection: "I was loyally devoted to him. . . . I hesitate to announce whether I was more a loser or a gainer by his severity." None of this evidence is intended to claim that objectively traumatic events rarely have undesirable consequences. Rather, I am suggesting that children, like skilled actors and actresses, interpret the scripts they are given.

It is easy to be persuaded that parental behaviors have long-term consequences. We see a child cry after a punishment or smile after a kiss and automatically assume a fixity to the psychological products of those experiences. In this frame, the parents' actions are the buoy around which the child's mind moves. However, this frame neglects the many times that parents punish children but they do not obey, as well as the many instances in which parents who reward civility have children who are rude. In this latter frame, the child's mind is the buoy around which the world moves. If children's interpretations of events have the influential power I am granting them, a hard disc is a misleading metaphor for a brain.

TWO MEANINGS OF PRESERVATION

Parents and psychologists hold different understandings of the meaning of preservation of a trait. Most parents think of preservation as the persistence of a particular behavior or mood. A mother who notices that her eight-year-old son disobeys most of her requests, but remembers that he had been obedient when he was two, would conclude that her child did not preserve his earlier obedient posture.

Psychologists rely on a very different definition of preservation. They measure the frequency of a particular behavior (or the frequency of several related behaviors) in a large group of children on two or more occasions separated by several years and note changes in each child's rank within the group. Consider this hypothetical illustration. A psychologist measures the frequency of obeying or disobeying maternal requests at home during a three-hour interval among a hundred children residing in the same city. The children are observed first at age two and again at age eight. If some children are more disobedient than their peers at both ages, and others are more obedient than others, the psychologist would conclude that the tendency to be disobedient, or obedient, is a stable trait even if all the eight-year-olds are far more obedient than they were six years earlier. In fact, disobedience declines in almost all children across this age interval. So, although many parents might say that their child has become less disobedient over the past six years, psychologists might say that many children preserve a disobedient posture. The majority of studies on the preservation of personality traits rely on the psychologist's rank-order definition, not on the parent's definition, which is based on the stable frequency of a behavior or mood. (See Figure 5.1.)

One problem with the psychologist's definition is that a person's rank on a trait always depends on the individuals with whom he or she is being compared. American children are more talkative with strangers than Asian children. A moderately quiet American boy who ranked very low on talkativeness when compared with one hundred American children might receive a much higher rank if he were compared with one hundred Asian children. Most studies of trait preservation are conducted with white children from middle-class American families. Hence, the published conclusions on the preservation of traits might be valid only for this category of children. It is useful to remember that Americans comprise only 5 percent, and white Americans about 3 percent, of the world's population.

Two more issues warrant mention. First, psychologists who discover preservation of a particular habit, mood, or talent usually conclude that the trait was inherent in the child's biology or early history. They typically ignore the contribution of the stable environmental settings that contributed to the preservation. If a child's environment changed in a dramatic way between age two and adolescence, the preservation of the trait might also change.

Four-year-olds from economically disadvantaged families have smaller vocabularies than children from affluent families and, not surprisingly, adolescents from disadvantaged families have less extensive vocabularies than adolescents from advantaged homes. The preservation of a large or a small vocabulary from four to fourteen years is due, in part, to the stability of environmental experiences—including the presence or absence of frequent conversations between parents and children,

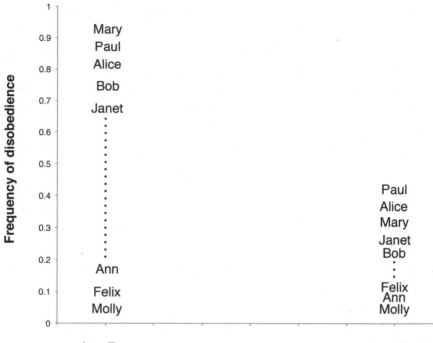

FIGURE 5.1   Illustration of preservation of rank order

the quality of schools attended, the nature of peer interactions, and a host of other experiences—and does not just reflect each child's inherent language talent. If four-year-olds with a sparse vocabulary, because their parents did not talk to them, were transferred to homes where the adults spoke frequently, their vocabularies would improve considerably. Several studies find that infants who can process subtle features in speech have better language skills two years later. The investigators imply that these infants preserved an inherent "language competence." But they failed to consider the possibility that the parents' continuing linguistic stimulation of the infant and later the older child might be a major reason for the superior language talent at both ages. Infants who inherited a special talent, but had parents who did not talk to them, might not show advanced language skills during the toddler years. Preservation of a trait requires both the child's inherent properties and the stability of his or her surroundings.[4]

A marble placed in a straight groove preserves its direction of motion. The marble does not have an inherent disposition to move in a straight line. A child's social class is analogous to a groove because a majority of children remain in the same social class in which they were born, at least until the late adolescent years. Hence, if a preserved trait is correlated with the family's social class, we have to entertain the possibility that the preservation is partly attributable to the sameness of the contexts the child encountered. A shrub planted in northern Canada attains a shorter height than the same shrub planted in Brazil because of stable differences in temperature and rainfall, rather than because of a defect in the seeds planted in Canada or more loving care in Brazil.

Children often find themselves placed in a groove. Some peer groups, for example, cast a youth with a particular personality trait into a well-defined role. If one adolescent in a group of six friends possesses the largest number of leadership traits, he or she will be placed in that position. Another member of the group may take on the role of intellectual, comic, risk taker, optimist, nurturer, adventurer, or pragmatist. This can occur among adults as well. Three middle-aged men and I who were collaborating on a scientific project in the 1970s formed a network of mutually reciprocal friendships. Each man had a salient, admired trait that made it easy for the others to assign him a distinctive role, which he accepted. One of the men was physically courageous, one a sexual adventurer, one a pragmatist, and one an intellectual.

My adolescent daughter found herself in a high school peer group in which she was cast as Miss Sunshine because she was the only girl who maintained an optimistic mood free of cynicism. Had my daughter been a member of a different clique, she might not have preserved this trait, for she was aware of her obligation to always present this persona within the group. Most individuals who are unhappy with their assigned role do not try to change it; the costs of withdrawing from or being excluded from a group of friends that provides emotional support and companionship are too heavy. Members of contemporary societies are more likely than those born centuries earlier to change their residence and work setting over the first twenty years of life. Hence, I suspect that the preservation of personality traits and cognitive talents from childhood to maturity is weaker in this century than it was before the industrial revolution.

The second issue deserving discussion is the fact that most research on the preservation of children's traits relies on parental verbal descriptions or descriptions by teachers or peers. Although this evidence can be gathered easily at a modest cost, its accuracy is open to question. David Funder of the University of California points out that the validity of verbal evaluations of an individual's traits requires not only that the traits in question are easy to evaluate but also that that the person making the judgment has the ability to evaluate the traits and has access to extensive observations of the individual being judged. All three criteria are not always met when parents describe their children in studies of preservation.[5] In Chapter 1, I described some of the problems with this class of evidence. First, most parents are reluctant to ascribe to their child traits that they regard as undesirable—for example, extreme shyness, laziness, or aggression. Second, the parents' personality and level of education affects their descriptions. Mothers who are extreme perfectionists describe their infants as fussier than do neutral observers, and parents who have less than twelve years of formal education are less accurate than college graduates.

A parent's experience with children is a third reason for disparities between parental descriptions and direct observations of the child. Parents who have only one child are prone to exaggerate the seriousness of mild disobedience or occasional timidity. Fourth, parents' conception of the ideal child tempts them to deny traits that deviate from the ideal. The ideal among many American mothers combines fearlessness, sociability, and verbal skills. Hence, many mothers deny or minimize extreme levels of timidity, shyness, or language delay in their children.

I was associated with a study of shyness and timidity among a large number of twins being studied at the University of Colorado. Direct observations of the children from fourteen to thirty-six months revealed that about 15 percent of the twin girls were extremely timid. But the parents' descriptions indicated that only 3 percent were very timid.

Even the order in which questions are presented can affect the replies. A study by Virginia Kwan of Arizona State University and her colleagues has troubling implications.[6] A questionnaire designed to measure children's personalities listed several common, related traits in succession (for example, "My child often disobeys, occasionally yells, and refuses to eat vegetables"). This format tempted parents who endorsed one of these traits to endorse all three. When the questionnaire separated the traits and alternated each with questions about less frequent properties (for example, "hears voices," "sleeps most of the morning," "is not toilet trained"), parents were less likely to endorse all three traits.

Verbal descriptions of personality traits are useful information, but they should not be equated with the traits that direct observations would reveal. A comparison of the autobiographies of past presidents with their biographies reveals that the latter often present a personality quite different from the one reflected in the autobiography.

Unfortunately, most conclusions regarding the preservation of traits created by family experience rely solely on parents' verbal descriptions of their practices, their personality, and their child's traits. Although the parent, usually the mother, supplies all the information, some investigators conclude that a maternal trait or practice contributed to a particular behavior in the child. This conclusion ignores the real possibility that the mother's personality and values had a profound influence on her verbal descriptions of herself and her child. If, for example, mothers who say they are affectionate describe their children as happy, some psychologists are tempted to conclude that maternal affection generates a happy mood in children, even though there is no external check on the validity of the maternal statements.

This strategy reminds me of a story about a boy living in a village with a church, a man who rang the church bells each day at noon, and a watchmaker. One afternoon the boy climbed the hill to the church to ask the man who rang the bells how he knew when it was noon. The man said that he used the time on his watch to make that determination. The boy asked how he could be certain that his watch was accurate. The man replied that every morning after breakfast he walked by the watchmaker's shop and set his watch to match the time on the clock in the shop window. The boy walked down the hill to the watchmaker and asked him how he knew that the time on the clock in the window was correct. The watchmaker said that he set the clock each morning by the ringing of the church bells the prior day.

Our current understanding of the preservation of children's habits and moods might be substantially different if investigators had observed parents and children in a variety of settings over many years and did not rely only on parental reports. Nonetheless, it is useful to ask what the evidence from parental reports and behavioral observations reveals.

WHAT HAVE WE LEARNED?

In Chapter 1, which introduced the concept of temperamental biases, I noted that a temperament can be preserved over time, even though the specific behaviors that are products of the bias change with development. About 5 percent of Dutch mothers reported that their two-year-olds cried frequently for no obvious reason. These highly irritable children were more likely to be described as anxious and timid when they were seven years old. I suspect that most of these children were born with the temperamental bias my colleagues and I call high-reactivity. High-reactive four-month-old infants cry and thrash their limbs in reaction to unexpected events. This temperament assumes a different behavioral form in older children. At fourteen months it takes the form of a reticence with strangers and timidity or outright fear in response to novel events. At fifteen years the bias is expressed through unrealistic fears, very high standards for performance, and feelings of tension with strangers. By contrast, low-reactive infants, who display minimal motor activity and crying at four months, are likely to become fearless two-year-olds and talkative, sociable, and minimally anxious adolescents. The temperamental bias is preserved, but its behavioral expressions change over time.[7]

The available evidence regarding preservation of traits over long time intervals suggests three major conclusions. First, as noted in Chapter 4, many children who suffered chronic abuse or neglect during the early years preserve some remnants of their earlier traumata, even if they enjoy a more benevolent environment later. The smaller number who do not show signs of their earlier stress probably possess a resilient temperament. The implication is that children vary in their susceptibility to preserving or altering early habits or emotions. However, it is important to appreciate that most of the world's children are not victims of such stressful experiences.

The second conclusion applies to the majority of children who escape serious deprivation or abuse. Those who preserve a trait across many years typically have extremely high or low values on that particular trait. Usually, only the 10 to 15 percent of children who have high or low values on a trait retain a form of that behavior for ten or more years. Only 5 percent of boys preserved frequent display of physical aggression, misconduct, and a callous personality from seven to thirteen years. These children are qualitatively different from those who occasionally fight or skip school. Youths who massacre classmates are not just a little more aggressive than those who tease their peers.[8]

The majority of correlations between measures of the same traits at two points in time are modest (between .20 and .30), implying that a majority of children change their rank on a personality trait between the first and later assessments. Only 15 percent of preschool children preserved extremely shy, timid behavior across three assessments conducted during the preschool years.[9]

The third conclusion is that the degree of preservation of a behavior improves after age six or seven, although it is still restricted to those whose behaviors are extreme. One reason is that seven-year-olds identify with their gender, class, or ethnic group and, as a result, feel an obligation to honor the group's standards in order to avoid feelings of shame or guilt.[10]

Another reason for the more substantial preservation of behaviors after age six or seven is that these children are attending school and a majority of the children in any particular school come from the same social-class background. The values associated with a family's social class act like a groove channeling a marble, making it easier for children to retain the traits they possessed prior to school attendance.[11]

The absence of several longitudinal studies of children from different social-class and ethnic backgrounds that gathered evidence on behaviors, temperaments, and patterns of identification makes it impossible, at present, to arrive at firm conclusions about the long-term preservation of many psychological properties. There is one exception to this unsatisfying state of affairs. The usual style of social interaction that emerges at puberty is usually preserved for many years. Adults who are not happy with the way they talk and interact with others outside the family find it difficult to alter their style. Mitt Romney knows that strangers find him emotionally distant, and Barack Obama is aware that he sounds like a professor when he gives a political speech. But neither man is able to change habits he would like to alter.

One reason for the ambiguity surrounding the persistence of early traits is that psychologists do not present older children or adults with the incentives that might reveal the preservation of a trait because they do not know which incentives are best for each person they study. Consider a seven-year-old boy who was bullied by a large boy with red hair and freckles during the first six months of the second grade but experienced no additional bullying for the remainder of his school years. As an adult he had forgotten about the bullying that occurred thirty years earlier. A psychologist would have no way of knowing whether the schemata and semantic networks generated by the bullying, which might still be present, are affecting his adult functioning. I suspect they have little or no influence as long as they remain unprovoked. However, these early representations might suddenly intrude into consciousness and alter the man's mood for a few moments if he saw a film in which a red-haired man with freckles behaved aggressively toward a weaker person.

Sixty-year-olds who have forgotten the lyrics to the songs Peter, Paul, and Mary sang in the 1960s, and whose daily behaviors are unaffected by the content of those songs, spontaneously shed tears when they hear this trio, also aging, sing those songs again. In another study, Erika Skoe and Nina Kraus of Northwestern University found that the brains of adults who had played a musical instrument for several years during childhood and then gave it up were more responsive to auditory stimuli than those with no musical training.[12] Many early representations that are not available to consciousness require activation by some event in order to affect contemporary functioning. But, as noted, psychologists usually do not know which events have that power for the individuals they study. Hence, the events they present are often ineffective in activating emotionally significant implicit memories. I had a frightening experience in a rowboat on a lake when I was five years old. No psychologist who had recruited me for a study when I was an undergraduate could have known that fact and would not have presented me with a similar scene that would have been arousing.

It remains possible that some experiences during the first two or three years created representations that were preserved for a decade or longer, even though behavioral profiles did not reveal them. I have less confidence in this possibility than many colleagues who are studying this question. However, given the inadequacy of the evidence, the jury must remain deadlocked on this intriguing question.

DEVELOPMENTAL STAGES IN LATER CHILDHOOD

The more obvious preservation of traits after age six is due, in part, to the fact that this age marks a new developmental stage accompanied by important changes in the brain. This suggestion invites a discussion of developmental stages, a concept that implies sensitive periods during which new properties are added and old ones are either lost or reorganized into patterns that might resist alteration.

A small number of phenomena observed in animals fit the definition of a sensitive period. Recall that soon after a duckling or gosling hatches it follows the first moving object it sees, which is normally the mother. Several days later, following brain maturation, the young bird will not follow any other object. Scientists say that it is *imprinted* on its mother—or on Konrad Lorenz, if he happened to be the first moving object the bird saw. A few hours after the fertilization of an ovum, any cell in a cluster of cells called embryonic stem cells can become any tissue in the body. But with each passing hour these cells lose this potency, until a time arrives when each cell can become only one type of tissue. It has been difficult to find sensitive periods in psychological development that are as robust as imprinting or stem cells. Studies of language development reveal a sensitive period that occurs later in development. Adolescents who learn a second language after puberty usually retain the distinctive dialect of their first language, implying that the brain structures that mediate speech resist change, albeit late in development. Musical ability also shows evidence of a sensitive period. Adult musicians who began their training before age nine come closer to having perfect pitch than those whose training began after their ninth birthday.[13]

It is useful to think about sensitive periods as setting limits on optimal levels of functioning. For example, infants born with cataracts that were not removed until the end of the first year recovered the ability to perceive most events, but their visual acuity was not quite as good as it would have been had they been born without cataracts. The demands on most children across the world do not require a consistently high level of competence. As a result, many children who experienced a period of neglect or a trauma eventually attain normal functioning in their community as long as the demands are not excessive. Remnants of their earlier stress would appear, however, if they faced serious challenges. The obstetrician who brought me into this world had to use an instrument that damaged the cornea of my left eye. As a result, I have relied only on my right eye all my life. This vulnerability in visual perception compromised my ability to play squash when I was younger, because it was difficult to keep track of the small rubber ball when it bounced off the corner between two back walls. Otherwise, my visual abilities have been as good as those of any person with the use of both eyes.

The remainder of this chapter summarizes the psychological changes that accompany three developmental stages that cover the interval from three to fifteen years. Readers may recall that I have already described the transitions that occur between two and four months, when the ability to attend selectively to different physical features of an event is improved; between seven and ten months, when working memory is enhanced; and between seventeen and twenty-four months, when language, inference, a moral sense, and self-awareness emerge.

A fourth transition occurs between three and four years, when children integrate the past and the present more consistently and are able to recall the temporal, spatial, and physical features of a prior event more reliably. The latter phenomenon is called episodic memory. The ability of many adults to recall exactly where they were on the November day in 1963 when they first learned of the assassination of John Kennedy is a classic example of an episodic memory. Episodic memory—which is distinguished from procedural memory, declarative memory, and implicit memory—involves the retrieval of perceptual schemata for the contextual details of a past experience.

Eric Loken conducted a study in my laboratory that illustrates the emergent ability to integrate the past with a present demand. Eric presented parts of a coherent narrative to three- and four-year-olds on three separate days. On the first day, he showed the child a puppet in the shape of a clam whose name was Clem. Eric told the child that Clem liked to eat frogs, showed the child a bright-orange frog, and asked the toddler to feed the frog to Clem. On the second day, Eric took the child to a corner of the room where there was a toy house with three brightly colored locked doors, showed the child how to use a red key to open one of the doors to find the orange frog seen on the previous day, replaced the orange frog in the toy house, and locked the door. On the third day, Eric led the child to another part of the room containing the red key that was used the day before to unlock the door.

Eric returned five days later, showed the child the puppet, said "Clem is hungry, can you give Clem something to eat?" and waited to see whether the child remembered the location of the red key needed to open the door of the house, retrieve the frog from the house, and feed it to the puppet. Two-thirds of the four-year-olds, but only one-fourth of the three-year-olds, retrieved their memory of the events experienced days earlier and retrieved the key, unlocked the house, and grabbed the frog. When the same narrative was presented in a single five-minute session, all of the three-year-olds performed as well as the four-year-olds.[14]

This cognitive advance is fragile, however, and does not protect four-year-olds from serious memory errors. My former colleague Michelle Leichtman demonstrated children's susceptibility to believing in the occurrence of an event that never happened.[15] The teacher at a preschool introduced a stranger named Sam Stone to her class. The man walked around the room, greeted the teacher, commented about a story the teacher was reading, and after two minutes left. Some time later, a woman discussing Sam's visit with each child purposely asked misleading questions that referred to actions Sam Stone never committed. For example, the woman asked, "Remember the time Sam Stone visited your classroom and spilled chocolate on that white teddy bear? Did he do it on purpose, or was it an accident?" When the children were interviewed ten weeks later, more than half said they were certain that Sam Stone had committed many acts the woman had mentioned that had not occurred. This study and others indicate that young children are susceptible to believing in the reality of events never experienced simply because adults talked about them.

The ability to relate the past and present implies that children older than four years think more regularly about the cause of an event that originated minutes, hours, or days earlier. Children in this age range ask, "Where did I come from?" or "Why is water wet?" Three-year-olds might say, "My shoe fell off because the ties are loose," but causal thought is less frequent in children under four years of age.

The ability to relate the immediate past to a present situation is required for the moments of self-blame following an action that violated a family standard. Children older than age four appreciate that if they had not run carelessly through the living room, they would not have bumped into a table holding a vase that fell to the floor and broke. Self-blame is not possible for two-year-olds because they fail to rerun the sequence of actions that led to the violation of a standard. This ability is also involved when children have to use the location of an object in a small area—say, an egg in the upper-left corner of a small rectangle—to place the object in the corresponding location on a large rectangle. (This is the talent needed to read a map.) The largest improvement in solving this task occurs between three and four years of age.[16]

The next transition occurs between five and seven years in most American children, but later in children from less modern societies who do not attend a school. Children this age possess the initial forms of eight seminal talents that, in combination, allow performances that are not observed in apes. Specifically, they now appreciate that an object can belong to more than one semantic category (a dog can be a pet or animal), understand that two people in different locations looking at a scene have different perceptions, can inhibit an incorrect response based on what is perceived, can reflect on mistakes and correct themselves on the next occasion, can construct representations of ideal states and traits, are more accurate in predicting future events, can detect a shared relation among events, and can award some semantic concepts an autonomy that is not closely tied to schemata.

The Swiss philosopher-psychologist Jean Piaget devoted many years of his productive career to studying the advances of this stage. Two such advances—conservation of mass and conservation of number—require the ability to inhibit an incorrect response and to separate the semantic meaning of quantity from perceptual schemata. To test for conservation of mass, an adult shows a child two balls of clay that appear identical in volume and shape and says, "This ball is your candy and this ball is my candy. Do I have more candy than you, do you have more candy than I, or do we have the same amount of candy?" Most children of any age acknowledge that the two balls of clay have the same amount of candy. The adult then molds her clay into the shape of a long, thin sausage and repeats the question. Four- and five-year-olds stare a few seconds at the longer sausage and reply that the adult has more candy. By contrast, seven-year-olds automatically say that there is the same amount of candy in each piece of clay. (See Figure 5.2.)

In the procedure for conservation of number, the adult places one row of five objects—say, buttons—in front of the child and another row of five equally spaced buttons in front of herself. Children acknowledge that the two rows have the same number of buttons. The adult then spreads out her buttons so that her row appears

FIGURE 5.2   **Four-year-old pointing to an elongated piece of clay in Piaget's demonstration**

longer than the child's row and asks again which array has more buttons. Children younger than five years say that the adult has more buttons than they do, whereas older children acknowledge that the number of buttons remains the same.

At least four processes contribute to the older child's correct answers. The first two involve integrating past with present and holding both in a working-memory circuit—two talents that emerged several years earlier. In the procedure using balls of clay, children maintain in working memory their schemata of the two identical balls, the examiner's question, and the remolding of the ball as they reflect on the reason for the new shape. Because no clay was added or taken away, the older child concludes that the two balls have the same amount of candy. A similar sequence occurs in the number task.

A third contribution is the enhanced capacity to inhibit an incorrect answer based on immediate perception. The elaboration of this ability over the next decade involves a family of processes called executive control. French scientists measured blood flow profiles in the brains of five- and ten-year-olds as they were being administered the conservation-of-number problem.[17] The older children, who answered correctly, displayed activation of a circuit that connects sites in the parietal lobe with sites in the frontal cortex that are active when individuals inhibit incorrect responses.

The final contribution is attributable to the ascendance of semantic concepts for quantity over perception. The word *more,* for example, takes on a new meaning during this stage. Younger children assume that *more* refers to the perceptual appearance of one object or array compared with another. The long, thin sausage appears to have more clay and the widely spaced array of buttons appears to have more buttons. Older children, by contrast, recognize that the examiner's use of the word *more* in her question refers to the abstract semantic meaning of quantity, which can be independent of perceptual appearance. That is, older children infer that what the examiner intended when she asked "Which ball has more candy"? was "Ignoring the possibility that tiny pieces of clay might have been lost when I transformed the ball into the sausage, does one of these pieces of clay have more mass than the other, or do they have the same amount because no clay was removed from the altered ball?" The ability to understand the perspective of another person is a critical property of this stage.[18] The young child's apparently "incorrect" answers to a psychologist's questions are often due to a misinterpretation of the query the adult had in mind rather than to a fundamental flaw in knowledge or reasoning. I remember an afternoon watching an African-American child from a disadvantaged home who answered "I don't know" when the examiner asked "What do you have to do to make water boil?" I guessed that the child had never heard the grammatical form "What do you have to do . . . " and suggested that the examiner rephrase the question as "How do you make water boil?" When she did so, the child answered correctly.

The improved ability to think about the future was revealed when children were asked to indicate on a time line how long it would be before each of a number of familiar events would occur—for example, their next birthday, Christmas, and Thanksgiving. Most of the seven-year-olds differentiated between events that were close in time from those that were distant, whereas the four-year-olds did not.[19]

Seven-year-olds are also better able to anticipate the difficulty of a task and activate strategies to aid performance. Second-grade children asked to remember a series of five numbers silently rehearse each number as it is being read, because they recall prior occasions when rehearsal helped them remember information. Younger children fail to rehearse the numbers because they neither anticipate the difficulty of a task nor reflect on relevant past experiences that might be helpful.

The silent rehearsal of a string of numbers to be remembered is one of several mental operations. If children are asked to add 2 to each number in the string

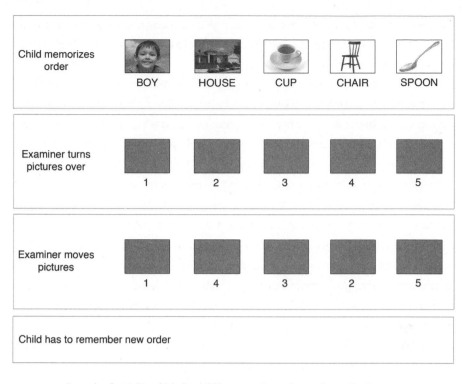

FIGURE 5.3   Example of a trial in which the child has to perform an operation on five items

4-9-7-2-1 before recalling all five numbers, they must perform an operation on the information in working memory and answer 6-11-9-4-3. Several of my students administered a variety of different tasks requiring mental operations to middle-class children in Cambridge, Massachusetts, as well as to Mayan Indian children from the town of San Pedro and the nearby, smaller village of San Marcos on Lake Atitlan in northwest Guatemala. One task required the children to memorize the order of a series of pictures of familiar objects lying on a table; for example, they had to remember that the order was "boy, house, cup, chair, spoon." After the child had memorized the correct sequence of these five pictures, the examiner turned the pictures over and changed the location of one or more pictures while the child watched. The child's task was to remember the new order, which might be "boy, chair, cup, house, spoon." The longest sequence required the oldest children to memorize the order of twelve pictures and perform the operations needed to remember the new locations of the pictures. (See Figure 5.3.)

The middle-class American children showed their greatest improvement in performance on these problems between six and eight years of age. The San Pedro children, who attended a well-run school, displayed their largest gain between eight and eleven years. The San Marcos children, who lived in the least modern setting with an inadequate school that few attended, did not display a major gain in performance until they were ten to twelve years old. The ability to perform mental operations on information in working memory matured in all of the children, but the circumstances of the local culture influenced the age at which this ability emerged.

Readers may recall from Chapter 3 that the ability to understand sentences with a complex syntax is not complete until seven to ten years. Consider the sentence "The puppy lying asleep on a mat beside a boy on a rug woke up when he accidentally rolled over." The ability to figure out that it was the puppy who woke up and the boy who rolled over requires holding twenty words in working memory and performing mental operations on the sequence of words.

The ability to reflect on past mistakes and alter one's behavior accordingly is another important property of this stage. Four- and seven-year-olds were asked to find the one picture in a set of six that was exactly like a standard. The older children took longer to make a decision on a trial that followed one in which they made an error. (See Figure 5.4.) Most of the children younger than five years did not display this reflective strategy because they did not appreciate that their error on a problem was due to their failure to examine all the alternatives carefully.

Parents across the world use the emergence of a more reflective attitude to assign their children more serious responsibilities, perhaps tending the family cow or caring for a younger sibling for an entire day. The children's behaviors inform the parents that they now understand the advantages of reflection before making a decision. Most societies wait until age six or seven before sending children to school or holding them responsible for violating ethical norms. The Catholic Church does not require confession before age seven.

The ability to recognize that two or more events share the same observable feature is present in infancy. But the ability to recognize that different events share the same relation does not emerge until the sixth or seventh birthday. The relation could be based on similar patterns of features. For example, older children shown a picture of one large apple between two small apples recognize that this array is similar to one in which one tall girl is standing between two short girls.

The relation can be linguistic. Seven-year-olds recognize that the number terms *one, two,* and *three* share the property *ascending in magnitude* with the terms *big, bigger,* and *biggest.* School-age children regularly compare themselves with peers and adults to arrive at conclusions about their talents and personality traits in relation

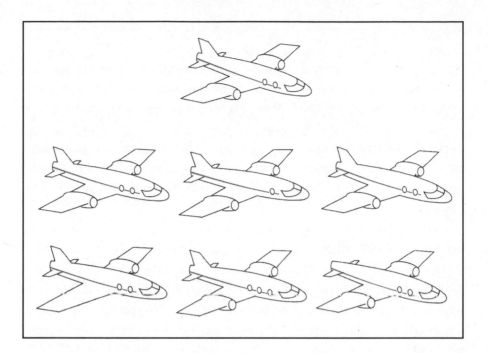

FIGURE 5.4   Item from Matching Familiar Figures Test

to others. And many of the absolute judgments of three-year-olds are now replaced with relative ones. Children appreciate that skill in reading is relative; they may read better than a friend but not as well as their mother.

When two events share the same function—for example, both a chair and an old log are places to sit—the child must infer a fact that is not observable. Apes, by contrast, find it hard to imagine novel functions for familiar objects and have to be taught new functions or discover them by trial and error. The capacity to spontaneously generate a function that was never previously experienced is a major element in human creativity. The first person who imagined that the hard point of a bird's feather, when properly carved, could be dipped into a dark liquid and used to make marks on a smooth surface displayed this talent. This new ability requires the person to perceive an object or event in different ways or as belonging to different categories. A woman can be a wife, a mother, a grandmother, a doctor, or even an angel. A six-year-old boy being tucked into bed surprised his mother by asking, "How long does it take after a person dies before they turn into an angel?" The mother's reply, "About twenty minutes," satisfied the boy, and he went to sleep. The absolutism of the younger child is being replaced with a recognition of multiple perspectives on the same event. The maturational processes in the brain that made this transition possible remain mysterious.

An expanded reliance on semantic networks that can, on occasion, operate free of schemata is a critical property of this stage. Most adults can remember events that occurred after their fourth birthday, but few can describe any experiences that occurred prior to age three. One reason for this amnesia of events that occurred during the first three years is that young children rely mainly on schemata to register their experiences, whereas older children rely more on words. Seven-year-olds asked to describe events that occurred several years earlier have to use words for events that had been represented as schemata.[20]

I once unwittingly bought a ticket for the Ingmar Bergman film *Shame*, forgetting that I had seen this film seven or eight years earlier. Although I quickly recognized that the film was familiar, I decided to stay in the theater to test my ability to predict particular scenes before they appeared on the screen. At one point I was certain that a future scene contained an argument between a couple. But I could not retrieve the schemata representing the particular people and the context in which the quarrel occurred. I was able to remember only the semantic concept of a quarrel.

College students who have never seen an autistic child or schematic illustrations of the strings of bases that define a gene read about autistic children who possess rare genetic mutations. These students acquire many semantic networks for concepts that are devoid of schemata. Adolescents and adults are acquiring an increasing number of ideas through reading sentences that have few schemata attached to the words or the settings in which the presumed events occurred. These experiences bias them to think in terms of abstract categories, such as Arabs, autistics, and carbon dioxide levels, that transcend particular places and ignore the variation among the members of a category.

The balance between schemata and semantic forms in the registration of experience changes with age. Julia Badger and Laura Shapiro of Aston University note that, after age six, children rely more often on an object's semantic category than on its physical similarity to another object.[21] They treat a small round cookie as more similar to a plate of vegetables than to a coin because the former pair belong to the semantic category *food*. The right hemisphere is the more important foundation of perceptual schemata; the left hemisphere is more critical for semantic representations, and it dominates the right more consistently after the sixth birthday. The left hemisphere is biased toward assigning experiences to discrete categories, whereas the right hemisphere preserves the physical variation among events belonging to the same category.[22] The left hemisphere of a ten-year-old gazing at a field of six grazing cows is likely to represent the scene as a herd of cows; the right hemisphere is likely to process the size and coloring of each of the animals. When the left hemisphere begins to dominate the right after the fifth or sixth birthday, children more consistently classify similarly appearing events into discrete semantic categories and award secondary importance to the physical variation among the events.

The English language makes it difficult to link schemata for contexts to words for objects because most words contain no information about the setting. The word *crowded* in the spoken sentence "It was very crowded" could refer to a city street, a gallery in a museum, a queue outside a movie theatre, a stadium, or a department store. A listener has to infer the setting when she hears a friend say "It was very crowded."[23]

As children mature, the bodily sensations that created the visceral schemata that are essential elements of feelings can, like perceptual schemata, become dissociated from the emotional words selected to describe an experience. Older children and adults often use emotional words, such as *afraid, sad,* or *happy,* without experiencing any feeling. I remember visiting a psychiatrist at the University of California who had persuaded some patients to allow their therapy sessions to be filmed while electrodes on numerous bodily sites recorded changes in their heart rate, blood pressure, sweating, breathing, skin temperature, and muscle tension. There were many instances in which a patient was talking about a highly emotional theme but showed no change in any bodily measure. One memory is particularly clear. As a middle-aged man was telling his therapist how guilty he felt when he masturbated, I gazed up at the bank of machines recording his bodily reactions and was surprised to see no change in any physiological target. I suspect that he was not experiencing any change in feeling as he spoke.

The ascendance of semantic concepts helps children think about relations between objects that have nothing to do with their physical features. Four- and seven-year-olds shown a large and a small toy dog and asked which one was smaller answered correctly. But four-year-olds became confused when shown the small dog seen previously alongside a new, smaller dog and asked the same question. Seven-year-olds answered correctly because they understood that the semantic concepts *smaller* and *bigger* refer to a relation between two objects and not to their physical properties. They also appreciate that the largest of six dogs, the smartest of six children, and the tastiest of six apples belong to the semantic network *most.* School-age children do not possess a schema for this semantic concept. Chimpanzees can be taught to pick the largest of two objects but it takes many, many trials, and this ability has a restricted generality.[24]

Once semantic networks gain a degree of autonomy from schemata that award them a particular meaning, it becomes easy to misinterpret the meanings of sentences written centuries earlier that described conditions that no longer exist. Scholars continue to debate the meaning of the concept *dukkha* in ancient Buddhist texts. It is not clear whether the Buddha intended this term to refer to pain, sorrow, desperation, or any other form of suffering. The phrase *ivory tower* was linked to a schema of the Virgin Mary among early Christians. Today the schema most often associated with this phrase is a classics professor at a university. And in 1776, when Adam Smith wrote in *The Wealth of Nations* that humans are self-interested, he intended that thought to apply to the relationships between the owners of modest-sized businesses and their small number of employees in an early capitalist economy. He did not intend those sentences to apply to friends or relatives. But some contemporary economists interpret Smith's words as applicable to all economic interactions, including a brother selling an old car to his sister.

Supreme Court justices who argue that the meanings of the sentences in our Constitution have not changed over the past two and a half centuries (Antonin Scalia is an example) fail to acknowledge that the men who authored that document possessed schemata that awarded particular, often unique, meanings to the words in some of those sentences. Many eighteenth-century contexts have vanished and been replaced with conditions the founders could not have imagined. The Internet and the abolition of slaves are two examples. As a result, sentences written today that contain the word *freedom* are linked to schemata that Americans in 1776 did not possess. Hence, the earlier meaning of *freedom* is not synonymous with the meaning understood by modern citizens.

It is difficult to be certain of the meaning Shakespeare intended when he had Polonius tell his son Laertes in *Hamlet:* "To thy own self be true." I suspect that the schemata Shakespeare relied on as he wrote those words were not the schemata of a contemporary Taliban soldier carrying a bomb on a suicide mission against an ideological enemy.

The new talents of this fifth developmental stage between five and seven years are accompanied by a number of brain changes. Among the most important is the firmer control the frontal lobe imposes on the rest of the brain. This control results in fewer careless mistakes because frontal lobe activity contributes to suppression of potential errors before they occur. Four other important changes also occur during this stage. The difference in size between Broca's area in the left and right hemispheres reaches a maximum, blood flow to the left hemisphere exceeds blood flow to the right hemisphere for the first time, many abstract words no longer activate sites in the visual cortex, and sites in different parts of the brain become connected more efficiently. The trails in a forest provide a metaphor for the more mature connectivity. A newly discovered forest contains few clearly marked trails. Over time the trails that are used frequently become broader and easier to traverse while the unused trails become narrower or disappear.

A sixth stage accompanying the onset of puberty adds a quartet of new or elaborated capacities. Youths can now think logically about hypothetical events never experienced, appreciate a variety of metaphors, feel certain that all the possible solutions to a problem have been considered, and detect semantic inconsistencies among a set of related beliefs. Ruben Gur and his colleagues at the University of Pennsylvania assessed fourteen cognitive abilities, some requiring the above-mentioned talents, in children of different ages.[25] The largest improvement in performance on most of the tests occurred between eleven and fourteen years of age.

Adolescents are able to reason correctly about hypothetical events and accept the truth of a conclusion that violates their understanding of the world. For example, they acknowledge the correctness of the conclusion in the following syllogism: "All objects with wings can fly; watermelons have wings; therefore, watermelons can fly." Seven-year-olds insist that watermelons don't have wings or that the conclusion is incorrect. The ability to think about hypothetical possibilities requires suppression of schematic knowledge and sole reliance on semantic networks. We do not teach algebra to seven-year-olds because they have difficulty ignoring what is true about the world and are not ready to accept the premise that the letter x in an equation can stand for anything.

The ability to compare the primary features of one concept with the secondary features of another allows adolescents to understand a variety of metaphors that younger children do not appreciate. In the metaphor "Boys are the school's gorillas," the potential to harm another is a primary property of gorillas but a secondary feature of boys. The sentence "Gorillas are the school's male students" is an unaesthetic metaphor. In order to comprehend metaphors, adolescents have to know the primary and secondary properties of two concepts, detect the relation between them, and ignore the literal meaning of the sentence. Seven-year-old children find this task difficult because it requires them to balance the salient properties of one concept with the less salient features of another. This is harder than recognizing that a large apple placed between two small apples resembles a scene depicting one tall girl between two short ones.

Nathan Kogan and his colleagues invented a test that measures an appreciation of metaphorical relations in pictures rather than sentences.[26] Children saw trios of pictures illustrating three objects and had to select the two objects that belonged together. One trio featured a person who appeared drowsy, a house that drooped, and a living room. The first two pictures represented a metaphorical relation. A consistent preference for the metaphorically related pair did not emerge until twelve or thirteen years. This may explain why young children do not experience a strong aesthetic reaction to paintings that require the viewer to recognize the symbolic idea intended by the artist. A viewer must understand the horrors of war to appreciate Goya's painting *The Third of May* or Picasso's *Guernica*. Physicists often rely on visual metaphors to explain their mathematical concepts. Niels Bohr, for example, used the solar system as a metaphor for electrons orbiting the nucleus of an atom.

An important aspect of adolescent thought is the ability to integrate three sources of information when evaluating a comment: the context, the speaker's intention, and past knowledge. A twelve-year-old evaluating a comment by her friend Mary who described a mutual friend Paula as "fresh as week-old bread" is able to integrate her benevolent evaluation of Paula with her knowledge that Paula and Mary are rivals and week-old bread is unattractive. Seven-year-olds would find this integration difficult.

The ability to think about the hypothetical and appreciate metaphors is an insufficient foundation for understanding most technical concepts. Youths also need facts. A majority of Massachusetts adolescents do not understand how a vaccine works or why the evaluation of a new drug requires the use of two groups: one that receives the drug and one that receives a placebo.

The recent hiring practices of investment firms reveal the danger of an indifference to mastering the facts that are relevant to the solution of a problem in a particular domain of knowledge. The heads of investment banks in the 1990s hired physicists and mathematicians whose assignment was to invent mathematical models that could guide investment decisions. These men and women were experts in working with mathematical equations for probabilities, but they knew next to nothing about finance or economics. Their models awarded too low a probability to the risk that subprime mortgages and derivatives would default, thereby contributing to the economic crisis of 2008. I know several statisticians who are terrible poker players, whereas most championship poker players never took a course in statistics.

Each cognitive domain contains a set of facts and rules that have to be mastered before anyone can be creative in that domain. There is no fundamental set of abstract rules or skills that transcends all disciplines.

A feeling of certainty that one has exhausted all the possible solutions to a problem is a third talent appearing at puberty. Consider an adult posing the following problem to eight- and thirteen-year-olds: "A policeman finds a car slammed against a tree with an unconscious adult lying in the backseat. What events might have led to this scene?" Most eight-year-olds will say that the driver was thrown into the backseat after the car hit the tree. If asked whether any other scenario is possible, they are likely to shrug their shoulders or say they don't know.

Adolescents are likely to offer several scenarios. Either the driver was thrown into the backseat or the driver went to find help and left the passenger in the backseat, or a robber stopped the car, stole the driver's money, knocked him unconscious, put him in the backseat, and then drove the car into the tree to create the appearance of an accident. Asked if there are any other ways this event might have occurred, adolescents will say "no" with certainty and feel confident that they have considered all of the possible sequences that could have produced this event. The feeling of certainty regarding a conclusion is the critical feature of this stage.

This new feature has the disadvantage of rendering adolescents vulnerable to a hopelessness that can bring on depression or suicidal thoughts if they are certain they have exhausted the solutions to a personal problem. An adolescent girl who learns she is pregnant reviews the possible actions she can take. She could tell her parents, but she knows they will become angry and refuse to help. She could try to get an abortion, but she has no money. Or she could ask the boy who impregnated her to pay for the abortion, but she does not know where he is or how to reach him. Because the girl is convinced she has considered all the possible solutions to her problem, and none is feasible, she may slip into a depression and consider killing herself. Five-year-old children are protected from this form of hopelessness.

The automatic detection of semantic inconsistency in a set of related premises, combined with a desire to resolve the inconsistency, is a fourth process enhanced during this stage. Most seven-year-olds are not bothered by the inconsistency between the thought that their father is a good person because he reads to them at bedtime and is a bad person because he occasionally comes home drunk and is cruel to his wife. Adolescents faced with this pair of semantically inconsistent evaluations of the father experience *cognitive dissonance* and are motivated to select a single evaluation of the father in order to achieve consistency.

The desire to hold consistent beliefs leads high school students, but few fourth graders, to try to decide, once and for all, whether masturbation is good or bad, whether loyalty to family or friends should or should not assume precedence over one's desires, whether postponing a hedonic pleasure in order to achieve a better adult life is a wise strategy, and whether God does or does not exist. The guilt that follows a failure to honor an obligation to a close friend is more intense in adolescence because youths who fail to help a friend when they believe they ought to do so confront a semantic inconsistency. They want to believe they are good individuals, but they recognize that if they did not help they would have committed a bad action.

The desire for semantic consistency can be the basis for an uncomfortable conflict among adolescents who wonder why they are investing effort in trying to master difficult academic skills that they do not believe are necessary for their future well-being. Six-year-olds do not regularly ask themselves why they go to school. The adolescent's private explanation for regular school attendance, studying for exams, and preparing for college is that these activities will eventually lead to many highly valued goals. Youths who question the value of the prizes that academic achievement promises experience the dissonance of inconsistency. Those who find mastery of academic subject matter difficult, or extract too little pleasure from good grades, become vulnerable to this inconsistency and might spend less time studying and more time with friends.

Adolescent girls pressured to engage in sexual behavior face a more excruciating conflict. On the one hand, they can persuade themselves that oral sex or one-night stands are pleasurable. If this rationale fails, however, they must choose between engaging in actions they do not like or refusing their boyfriend's requests and risking rejection. Adolescent girls who have been sexually molested by a father experience a conflict that has no happy outcome. If they decide that they should have resisted, they are vulnerable to shame over their passivity. If they conclude that they experienced some pleasure, they are vulnerable to guilt.

An apt analogy for this new cognitive ability is a pair of surfaces, representing a pair of inconsistent beliefs, separated by a thin membrane. The brain changes that occur prior to puberty remove the membrane and allow the two surfaces to touch. (These changes include a slowing in the rate of pruning of synapses; the attainment of peak cortical thicknesses across many sites; and the myelination of long-distance axons, which facilitates communication between sites.)[27]

This sixth stage is also accompanied by increased secretion of the molecule dopamine, which makes a small contribution to the display of high-risk behaviors. The anticipation of an uncertain but desired event is accompanied by the secretion of dopamine and a brief, pleasant feeling. The consequences of most risky actions—drag racing, smoking pot, getting drunk, or engaging in one-night stands with new acquaintances—are inherently unpredictable. When a person anticipates a desirable outcome that accompanies or follows an action, the resulting surge of dopamine enhances the pleasure that accompanies the attainment of the goal. This sequence helps to explain why on a typical day more than 250,000 Americans visit a gambling casino and close to 90 percent of male adolescents play a video game (many of which involve violence or sex). The popularity of athletic events and mysteries on television rests, in part, on the same mechanism. The brief state created by this form of unpredictability is inherently pleasurable, especially if the desired outcome occurs in a setting in which there is no possibility of personal harm or loss.

One reason males find risky behavior attractive is that most male brains contain a larger number of receptors for dopamine that are prepared to be activated. More receptors in female brains are already occupied with dopamine and, therefore, unprepared. As a result, most boys and men experience a slightly larger jolt of dopamine-generated excitement, compared with girls and women, when they engage in behaviors with unpredictable outcomes.

Parents and policy makers are concerned about the many high-risk behaviors of contemporary adolescents. One possible reason for the apparent increase in the frequency of these acts is that biological puberty in 2012 occurs at least five to six years earlier than it did during the medieval era because of the better health enjoyed by today's youths. Eight centuries earlier (say, in 1200 c.e.), puberty occurred at age sixteen or seventeen, an age when most adolescents had acquired the cognitive abilities needed to regulate risky urges. In addition, most seventeen-year-olds during that early period had lost one or both parents to disease, lived in small villages, had serious responsibilities, and had no access to cars, guns, arcades, bars, gangs, video games, and cell phones. The essential point is that the "wild" behavior of today's youths is not an inevitable feature of being between twelve and twenty years of age. Indeed, the current prolonged interval between reproductive maturity and the responsibilities of adulthood is a recent feature of the human narrative.

The six developmental transitions—two to four months, seven to nine months, one to two years, three to four years, five to seven years, and eleven to fourteen years—are preceded by changes in brain anatomy and physiology that make a host of new cognitive skills and emotions possible. But a critical question remains unresolved: Which representations possessed by one- and two-year-olds are lost, which are seriously transformed, and which are preserved and affect the adolescent? It is easy to prove that some representations are lost. In one study, a group of ten-year-olds who had seen some distinctive, unfamiliar pictures when they were twenty-seven months old were shown these pictures, together with pictures they had never seen, and asked whether they recognized any of the pictures. No child did better than chance. However, the early experience was brief and not a very important event in their lives.[28]

Parents and psychologists want to know if emotionally charged experiences that had personal relevance are preserved and affect current behavior. Some early representations might resemble old e-mail messages that were not erased from a hard disk but have lost all relevance to the present. The possibility that the representations of the emotional experiences of the first two years no longer exert any influence on adolescents is as reasonable as the assumption that they do.

Genes mutate, brain cells die, species become extinct, and societies disappear. Hence, it is likely that many of the emotionally charged representations of infancy are lost or transformed. Life forms, unlike inanimate matter, change continually. The evidence gathered over the past thirty years, albeit inconclusive, has shifted the burden of proof from those who had been skeptical of strong preservation to those who continue to believe in the indefinite preservation of the products of early experiences. That is progress!

No psychologist would deny that some happy two-year-olds growing up in secure, affectionate homes without any serious traumata can become depressed or anxious as adults or that some unhappy two-year-olds growing up in rejecting homes can become happy, productive adults. These observations force us to entertain the idea that some early representations that were linked to strong emotions at the time have vanished or are no longer relevant and many new ones are acquired.

A giant pinball machine provides a metaphor for the varied life journeys of members of a community because it is impossible to predict the path each ball will take as it traverses the machine. The obstacles in the machine represent the different circumstances each child will encounter on his or her itinerary, the variation in size and weight among the balls represents each child's temperamental biases, and each ball's distinctive location at the top of the machine represents the social class and cultural background of each child. The task for the future, which is formidable, is to discover the conditions within the child and in the environment that favor continuity or discontinuity of particular traits and talents. Until then, both advocates and critics of a strong connection between past and present should honor Ludwig Wittgenstein's admonition to refrain from announcing their opinions in a loud voice. He would have preferred complete silence.

CHAPTER SIX

The Development
of Moralities

Previous chapters have considered human properties—for example, schemata, semantic networks, working memory, and inference—whose definitions enjoy a reasonable consensus. However, a comparable level of agreement is missing for the concepts of morality, emotion, and mental illness, which I consider in that order in the next three chapters.

Commentators on human nature, past and present, agree that a symbolic language and a moral sense are two psychological properties that clearly distinguish our species from all others. Although scholars achieved consensus on the essential features of a symbolic language, they have failed to do so for morality, even though social scientists, philosophers, biologists, television talk-show hosts, writers, politicians, and everyday citizens use the words *moral* and *morality* freely. Some clarity might be gained by reflecting on four facts that form the foundation of the concept *moral*.

The first fact is that the terms synonymous with the English words *good* and *bad* are present in all languages. Adults from diverse cultures rated a list of familiar words (such as *food, foot, mother,* and *heart*) on twenty scales, each defined by a pair of antonyms (for example, *fast-slow, large-small, high-low, pretty-ugly,* and *good-bad*).

The ratings were influenced primarily by the raters' judgment of the goodness or badness of the object named. This bias is based, in part, on the pleasantness or unpleasantness of the experiences associated with the object in question. Because pleasant experiences are good and unpleasant ones bad, the semantic networks for *good* and *bad* are inextricably linked to the meanings of *moral* and *amoral*. The terms *moral, good,* and *pleasant* (and their opposites) are as close in meaning as any three terms in any language. Although the adjectives *good* and *bad* can apply to almost anything, the terms *moral* and *amoral* are usually restricted to persons, their intentions, or their actions.

The second fact is that most adults in a society agree on the intentions and actions that are good or bad during a particular historical era. Although societies often disagree with respect to the judgment of particular actions, they generally agree that behaviors that harm another without a reasonable provocation are typically bad and behaviors that help a person in need are usually good. Some cultures and religions emphasize the bad acts that must be suppressed; others award significance to the good ones that should be practiced. The Bible's Ten Commandments allude to many actions that should be suppressed, whereas Theravada Buddhism is more concerned with the good qualities each person ought to perfect.

The third fact is that all individuals wish to live in a society in which dishonesty, betrayal, stealing, greed, aggression, and destruction are recognized as bad and those who suppress these behaviors are considered more moral than those who do not. Although four-year-olds do not know that their society condemns unprovoked aggression, they are certain this type of action is bad.[1]

The fourth fact is that all humans are capable of the emotions that English calls *shame* and *guilt*. Guilt was among the most frequently named psychological states when informants from forty-seven language communities nominated the most common emotions in their society.[2] Individuals who anticipate feeling shame or guilt when they contemplate an action, or experience these emotions when they commit an action, are regarded as more moral than those who fail to experience either state.

Here is where agreement ends and the meaning of a moral intention, action, or person becomes controversial. An important reason for the disagreement is that some want the word *moral* to apply primarily to those who honor the standards for behavior that a majority in a community regard as the most reasonable response to a given situation. Thomas Scanlon in *What We Owe Each Other* favors this definition of a *moral* agent. Others insist that the adjective *moral* should apply to those who honor their personally constructed understanding of right and wrong, even if their community disagrees with an agent's judgment. Most cultures favor the former definition of *moral* that awards priority to the actions the majority in a community endorse. Many contemporary Europeans and North Americans advocate a minority position that defines a moral person as one who is loyal to his or her private conscience.

Anthropologists believe that the first humans lived in small bands holding homogeneous values. Hence, these early groups would be attracted to the notion that a moral person was one who obeyed the majority's ethical code. This criterion is harder to apply in large societies with citizens holding diverse values. Because the United States historically has been a haven for immigrants holding a variety of ethical codes, many Americans are willing to praise those who are loyal to their private moral beliefs.

Cornelius Vanderbilt and Thorstein Veblen, both grandsons of immigrants to the United States, provide an example of contrasting private consciences. Vanderbilt, who accumulated an immense fortune in shipping and railroads during the nineteenth century, was certain that living in mansions and wearing expensive clothes were morally proper. Veblen, born in rural Wisconsin and the author of the 1899 book *The Theory of the Leisure Class,* had little praise for Vanderbilt's conspicuous consumption and died relatively poor. I suspect each man believed he had lived a morally praiseworthy life.

Citizens living in societies with a great deal of religious and ethnic diversity are forced to question the absolute truth of any ethical value, making reliance on private conscience more attractive. The ascendance of science in the eighteenth century facilitated this attitude, inasmuch as scientists are supposed to be skeptical of all received truths. The celebration of private conscience became a more public position in the United States as the twentieth century progressed. Markella Rutherford of Wellesley College analyzed 171 commencement speeches given between 1900 and 1980 to American college graduates and their families.[3] Only 11 percent of the addresses between 1900 and 1910 mentioned the moral integrity of those who adhered to their private values. By contrast, 86 percent of the addresses between 1960 and 1980 reminded the graduates that each of them had to decide what was morally right. The message in the popular 1979 American film *The Electric Horseman,* starring Robert Redford and Jane Fonda, is that the most admired heroes remain true to their values, even if this stance means they will lose their source of income or go to prison for breaking the law.[4] American audiences liked this film so much they made it the eleventh most lucrative movie of that year.

Each of these criteria for defining *morality* has problems. If those who conform to the majority ethics of their society are considered moral, Americans will have to acknowledge the moral integrity of the men from a Gusii tribe in Kenya who murdered their mothers because they were certain they were witches. Neither these men nor their community believed this action violated a local moral standard. Indebted sixth-century Italian fathers often sold a child into servitude without suffering community criticism. More difficult to accept is a thirteenth-century Spanish law that permitted a desperately hungry man charged with defending a besieged castle to eat his child rather than surrender the castle he was morally obligated to defend, unless he received permission from the noble he served.

If loyalty to private conscience defines a moral agent, then Palestinian suicide bombers and eleventh-century Crusaders who slaughtered innocent Muslims acted morally. Scholars brooding on the meaning of *morality* resemble the Greek hero Odysseus who had to avoid both Scylla's sea monsters and the whirlpools of Charybdis. Odysseus was more successful than philosophers and social scientists.

Most Americans disapproved of the behaviors of the men and women who, in the years leading up to the recession of 2008, sold expensive mortgages to individuals who could not afford the monthly payments. But a majority of these sales agents believed they were acting as one ought to in a capitalist society. Tyler Cowen, an economist at George Mason University, seems to side with the morality of these sales agents, for he approves of the ethics of scientists who seek fame, money, and prizes. Cowen believes that these goals motivate scientists to make discoveries that contribute to material progress. I am not sure that the men who invented the transistor, who at the time did not believe their discovery had any pragmatic value, would agree with Cowen's dismissal of character as irrelevant when evaluating an investigator. Gregor Mendel, the monk whose discoveries became the origin of genetics, and I. I. Rabi, whose research was crucial for the later development of the magnetic scanner, would also have disagreed.

Failure to specify the historical, cultural, and social context of an action is an important reason for the lack of agreement on the meaning of *morality*. The context often provides a person with a persuasive rationale for an action that in other settings would be prohibited. Most Americans would say that the American who killed Osama bin Laden in the spring of 2012 behaved morally. If the same person walked up to an innocent adult in Karachi and shot him in the head, they would change their judgment. It is worth remembering that Abraham was willing to carry out God's command to kill his son in order to remain a moral man.

A definition of *morality* that requires an action to be combined with a context and an agent's intention bothers those, such as the British philosopher Derek Parfit, who want to believe in a few imperatives that every human would recognize as binding under all circumstances. One pair of social scientists nominated five obligations they claimed formed the foundation of morality in every culture, present and past: moral persons should care for those in need, treat others fairly, remain loyal to their in-group, respect authority, and avoid experiences that would taint their purity. The problem with these imperatives is that they fail to specify the roles and demands of those that a moral agent is obliged to help or respect, on the one hand, and the sources of impurity, on the other. Shalom Schwartz of Hebrew University found that these five, presumably universal, standards are not the ones celebrated by a majority of young adults in economically developed Western societies in the twenty-first century.[5] These individuals say that hedonic pleasure, excitement, personal achievement, power over others, and the freedom to decide what to think and do are the praiseworthy goals.[6]

Europeans and Americans celebrate Thomas More as a prototypic example of a moral hero because he refused to carry out an order from his king requiring him to violate his private ethical beliefs. All who praise More, and in so doing endorse the importance of loyalty to personally constructed values (the advice Polonius gave to his son Laertes in *Hamlet*), are free to ignore all five of the so-called universal moral obligations. Most Americans smile when they hear Frank Sinatra sing "I did it my way."

A deeper appreciation of how ideas of right and wrong develop might remove some of the ambiguity surrounding the concept of morality, although it cannot eradicate it. A young child's suppression of actions that were punished, such as spilling a glass of milk, could be treated as the first sign of morality. It is probably impossible for parents to avoid rebuking children on some occasions. The parent's unexpected command and excited facial expression alert the two-year-old, create a state of uncertainty, and evoke visceral schemata for past unpleasant experiences of cold, pain, and hunger. Children quickly learn that spilling food is followed by a feeling of uncertainty, and they suppress this act. This first stage of morality resembles the conditioning processes involved in teaching a puppy not to urinate on a rug.

Older children and adults, however, do not act properly simply because they are punished or given a reward. The city of New York spent 35 million privately donated dollars as rewards for disadvantaged families if one of their children attended school regularly or passed the state's Regent's exam or a parent held down a job. This project was abandoned in 2010 because the monetary rewards proved to be ineffective.

The more critical stage of moral development occurs during the second and third years, when children begin to suppress behaviors that have never been punished. Most children hesitate, or do nothing, if a parent or stranger asks them to act in ways that violate their representation of a family norm—say, pouring a glass of cranberry juice on a clean, white tablecloth. The refusal to commit this action implies the possession of a prototypic representation of prohibited acts.

Michael Tomasello and his colleagues at the Max Planck Institute in Leipzig note that by their third birthday children enforce on others a prohibition they had learned earlier. Three-year-olds will inform a playmate who spills milk that such behavior is not permitted. They will even object to violations that occur in playful contexts. When an adult told three-year-olds that the nonsense word *daxing* named a particular action by a cloth puppet, they protested if someone used the same word to name a different action. Young children are absolutists who live in a black-and-white world. Words have one meaning, acts are right or wrong, answers are true or false.

The capacity for empathy that emerges in the second year motivates suppression of behaviors that might cause harm or psychic discomfort to another. The Utku Eskimo of Hudson Bay call this state *ihuma*, translated as reason. The universal capacity for empathy toward someone in obvious need of help has a biological foundation in the human genome. It is difficult, however, to find equally persuasive evidence that points to the early appearance in all children of a favorable evaluation of courage, honesty, or freedom.

Children during the third year display signs of embarrassment—a lowered head and silence—when they violate a family standard on prohibited actions because they are able to infer the private evaluations of others. Adolescents and adults who are ashamed of their appearance, family pedigree, or behavior either become quiet or, if they believe that another person or group is responsible for their shame, become aggressive.[7]

A fourth stage of moral development, usually observed between ages four and seven, requires the cognitive advances described in Chapter 5—especially the ability to rerun mentally a sequence of acts that violated a standard and to recognize that the behavior could have been avoided. This realization often provokes self-blame and guilt. Shame requires only the inference that another person might be criticizing the child privately for an action that, most of the time, he or she believed was unavoidable. Pascal's comment in *Pensées* captures the feature that distinguishes guilt from shame: "We know that truth not only by reason but also by the heart. It is from this last source that we know the first principles and it is in vain that reason, which has no part in it, attempts to combat it."[8]

Some parents notice that their four-year-olds occasionally misbehave purposely in order to be punished. The misbehavior is often prompted by guilt over a thought or action that went unpunished. One four-year-old confessed to her mother that she had done something bad because she had a dream the previous night in which her infant brother died after being stung by a bee. A mother in one of our studies found her three-year-old pinching himself with force. When she asked why, the boy replied, "I don't like myself." The boy was aggressive toward other children in the neighborhood and was aware that these children and their parents disapproved of him.

Chronic sexual abuse can persuade some children that they are irredeemably bad because they were participants in an amoral action, albeit as passive victims. A small proportion of abused children behave aggressively in order to invite a punishment that would confirm their self-imposed category. Others interpret the abuse as awarding them the right to violate societal rules. Mary Bell, an eleven-year-old British girl who had been sexually abused at an early age by her mother's male clients, murdered two preschool boys without anger or a desire for material gain.[9]

I noted earlier that many middle-class children in economically developed democracies make no material contribution to their family. One way to reduce their feelings of indebtedness is to achieve a goal the parents value, such as the perfection of an academic, musical, or athletic talent. Children who fail to meet a parent's demand for exceptional achievement, or believe they contributed to marital quarrels or a divorce, are vulnerable to a chronic guilt that in some children motivates acts of disobedience intended to provoke a parent's anger. If the parent cooperates by inflicting a punishment, the child can treat the punishment as a reason to regard the parent as unfair or cruel and, in so doing, reduce the intensity of the guilt.

This dynamic operates in some marriages marked by frequent quarrels. One spouse feels guilty over not meeting an obligation that is presumed to be held by the partner. The obligation, real or imagined, might refer to sexual ardor, earning a lot of money, effectiveness as a parent, interest in the partner's hobbies, or failure to achieve a high-status position. Some spouses feel guilty even if they imagine an obligation that the partner never held. The guilty spouse often adopts a hyper-critical or demanding posture in order to provoke a retaliation from the other that, in turn, will reduce the hostile partner's guilt.

Children between six and ten years of age are better able to control actions that would have violated their moral standards and possess a firm understanding of the concepts *fair* and *just* that take the context of an action into account. They now assume that the severity of a punishment should match the seriousness of the crime; that the amount of praise should be proportional to the quality of a performance; that the sharing of resources with a collaborator should match the amount of effort the partner expended; and that the difficulty of a task assignment should match the competence of the person. Danish eight-year-olds told an adult that it was unfair for a teacher to exclude a child from a desired activity simply because he or she belonged to an ethnic minority.[10] Hitler exploited the sense of fairness in German citizens in order to provoke anger at Jews, who in 1938 comprised just 1 percent of the German population but more than 50 percent of the country's doctors, lawyers, bankers, and other professional positions. (See Figure 6.1.)

Children during this stage acquire a new set of moral obligations requiring loyalty to the values of the social categories to which they belong. Children believe they ought to behave in ways that are consistent with the defining features of their gender category. American boys now appreciate that they ought to appear to others to be tough and strong, whereas girls understand that they ought to appear friendly. This difference in perspective may explain why it is not until the fourth grade—age nine to ten—that American girls are more likely than boys to be smiling in yearbook photographs.[11]

The anthropologist David Gilmore speculated that males in most societies must do something unusually difficult in order to meet the standards for their gender. They have to show extreme courage by coping with a painful or stressful experience, cleverness by accumulating wealth, brilliance by making an original discovery, or sexual potency by bedding many women. Girls and women must also do something to meet the local standards for femaleness, but the requirements in many societies—marry, have children, sexually satisfy a husband—are somewhat easier to fulfill.[12]

Some of the standards for gender are vulnerable to alteration. Richard Stott's *Male Milieus in Nineteenth-Century America* describes the sex-role standards for white American males from about 1710 to 1820, when more than 90 percent of the population lived in small towns that almost always had a tavern and a general store

1. Conditioned fear of punishment in infancy
2. Prototypes for punished acts and empathy in second year
3. Shame in the third year
4. Guilt in years four to five

FIGURE 6.1 **Developmental sequence for morality**

where men gathered for conversation.[13] Men from all social classes understood that they had an obligation to be capable of fighting, drinking large amounts of alcohol, enjoying gambling, taking risks, engaging in cruel pranks, and playing the role of a "jolly fellow" who did not feel squeamish about hurting animals or humans. American males celebrated the courageous, autonomous, disciplined, self-made man who preferred the wildness of nature over the civility of dinner parties—Daniel Boone, not the effeminate features of European nobility.

These values began to disappear in the eastern states after cities grew in size, and wives—troubled by the consequences of their husband's behavior on family life—initiated a reform movement that included restrictions on drinking and increased religiosity. The combination of empowered women, the need to perfect a skill rather than possess brute strength, businesses and institutions requiring conformity and sedentary work—all of which occurred between 1812 and 1912—created a lingering worry that American men were being psychologically castrated by working with pencils during the day and doing their wives' bidding in the evening and on weekends. The sociologist Michael Kimmel suggested that the three male characters in L. Frank Baum's *The Wizard of Oz*, published in 1900, were intended to symbolize the three categories of American men who had lost their masculinity in the vortex of social changes.[14] The tin man was symbolic of the oppressed factory worker, the scarecrow represented the farmer who had been robbed of his independence, and the cowardly lion was the hapless William Jennings Bryan who tried but never became president. The popularity of reruns of John Wayne and Humphrey Bogart movies implies a lingering nostalgia for the older definition of a man.

Cultures vary in the obligations they assign to the varied social categories. A Muslim group in western Sumatra believes that the obligation to someone who had been kind on only one occasion lasts a lifetime. Mao Zedong persuaded a generation of Chinese adolescents that their obligation to the nation had precedence over obligations to their family. Adolescent members of the Red Guard often reported to authorities a parent who held capitalist values, creating an ambience in which parents were afraid of their children. Wu Fei, a scholar at Peking University, suggests that the very high suicide rate among Chinese women, the highest in the world, is attributable to the fact that maintaining harmony within the family has always been a powerful moral value. Hence, many women who believe they were the cause of a serious quarrel or a disruption in the family's ambience feel guilty and attempt suicide.

A child's social categories are linked to two kinds of moral values: nominal and relational. The obligations implied by the nominal categories of religion, ethnicity, social class, and nationality are applicable in all settings and are not restricted to specific persons or contexts. A nominal category can lose its moral persuasiveness when historical events dilute the feeling of virtue that accompanies loyalty to its obligations. The more consistently the members of a category honor its standards, the stronger is the urge to be loyal to the category, and the more intense the feeling of virtue that is the reward for conformity to its standards. When members of a category violate some of its rules, everyone finds it easier to ignore the standards—and those who continue to adhere to them extract a diluted virtue. The frequent use of contraception by American and European Catholics makes it more difficult for the Catholics who obey the pope's prohibition on contraception to feel a strong sense of virtue for their behavior.

The second type of social category applies to a relationship between a particular agent and a particular other. The relational categories of son, daughter, sibling, father, mother, grandparent, friend, spouse, lover, citizen, and employer carry the obligations of loyalty, honesty, respect, and kindness that are restricted to particular others. A survey asked one thousand randomly chosen Americans in 2008 to rate the differential importance of eight properties that define an American. The majority regarded the relational ethic of "treating others equally" as far more significant than the nominal properties of being born in the United States or being Christian. The obligations to a parent differ from the obligations to a friend, and the obligations to one friend may differ from those appropriate for another. If one friend is anxious, an adolescent might feel obligated to be gentle with and nurturing toward that peer. But if another friend is dominating, the youth might feel obliged to be more passive and follow that friend's suggestions.

Some older women feel an obligation to care for an aging, feeble parent even if the parent had been unloving years earlier. One such woman said, "If she died I'd have it on my conscience." Another confessed, "I wanted a chance to know she loved me before she died." The nineteenth-century artist Eugene Delacroix, who was aware that the persona he presented to others depended on the person with whom he was interacting, confessed in his diary: "I have two or three friends . . . but I am forced to be a different man with each of them, or rather to show to each the side of my nature which he understands."[15]

The media regularly remind local, national, and international audiences of the adults who violate nominal or relational standards. Some men and women change their gender or religion, mothers abandon their children, fathers desert their families, physicians and teachers go on strike, scientists fabricate evidence, healthy workers call in sick, corporate executives lie, priests abuse children, and sixty-year-old husbands wearing sneakers and blue jeans divorce their wives after thirty years of marriage to live with nubile twenty-five-year-old women. The broadcast of such facts weakens the moral force of the values linked to these categories.

Americans have always promoted an ethic that treats the self's needs as a legitimate competitor to the needs of a parent, spouse, relative, employer, or friend. A twenty-one-year-old with an opportunity to advance her career by leaving the family and settling two thousand miles away is encouraged to do so, even if the family would benefit from the young adult's presence.

The American approval of an ethical standard that awards priority to the self's interests is not characteristic of all societies. A celebrated pianist in Kazuo Ishiguro's novel *The Unconsoled* chats with an older porter who is carrying his luggage to the hotel room where the artist will stay for a few days. The porter, who knows that the pianist is scheduled to give a public lecture in a few days, asks if he might insert into the speech some words of praise for the porters of the city. The pianist agrees to do so and, during the next two days, broods on how he can keep his promise. This theme would occur to a Japanese writer, but very few American authors would compose a scene in which a guest at a hotel worries about a casual promise made to a porter in an elevator.

Ishiguro, who was born in Japan but resides in England, also wrote *Remains of the Day*, which portrays the chief butler in a large manor house in England in the years leading up to World War II. The butler's unquestioning loyalty to his employer renders him incapable of doubting the integrity of a man with pro-Nazi sentiments. Ishiguro wants readers to reflect on the dangers of an unquestioned loyalty to anyone. Americans and Europeans enjoy some protection against this temptation. The moral message in the Nuremburg trials of former Nazi officials was that each individual must always award precedence to what he or she personally believes is morally right. The central characters in some recent Hollywood films, reflecting the acts of some investment advisers during the 1990s, violate this standard. The main character in the 2011 film *Margin Call*, who wants to keep his high-paying job at an investment firm, violates one of his deepest moral values by telling the employees to sell securities he knows are worthless to trusting clients.

This discussion makes cognitive processes and the emotions of shame and guilt central to the development of morality. Evolutionary biologists, following Darwin, prefer to locate the origins of morality in social relationships rather than in uniquely human cognitive abilities and moral emotions. Darwin recognized that he had to use arguments consistent with the principle of natural selection in order to explain why humans helped those with whom they had no genetic relationship. Darwin thought he accomplished this task when he decided that all humans, like many primates, inherited a social instinct.

Darwin arrived at this solution by borrowing from David Hume the concept of a human capacity for sympathy toward another and from Adam Smith the premise that all humans want to avoid being ostracized by their community. Both ideas award a person's social relationships the power to restrain antisocial behaviors. However, a younger, twenty-seven-year-old Darwin wrote in one of his notebooks that humans possessed three instincts: social, conjugal, and a sense of right and wrong. Four years later, when he was a father, Darwin awarded the moral sense I described in Chapter 3 to his thirteenth-month-old son. But when he wrote about human morality decades later in *Descent of Man,* he relied on the social instincts of animals and humans and ignored the uniquely human moral sense he had believed in years earlier. This change in perspective enabled him to maintain his belief in a seamless transition from apes to humans. The world's most influential biologist was not immune from the temptation to disregard certain observations in order to maintain consistency in a theoretical argument.

Patricia Churchland, a philosopher who has read broadly in evolution and neurobiology, tweaked Darwin's position in *Brain Trust* by arguing that human morality is a derivative of emotional attachments and sociability. Humans are moral, Churchland writes, because they develop attachments to others.[16] A few examples reveal the flaws in this argument. Alfred Kazin, an acclaimed literary critic and prolific writer who never killed or maimed anyone, confessed in a private journal that he lived with a corrosive guilt over an inability to feel emotionally bound to anyone.[17]

I could, while walking late at night, scratch the paint on a new car sitting in front of a house owned by a neighbor I do not like and know I would not be discovered.

But I am unable to commit that act because I regard it as morally wrong and would feel guilty if I did so. While walking on a deserted beach one summer I spotted a small sand crab inches from the sea struggling to right itself. I picked it up, placed it upright closer to the water, and walked on. I do not believe that this action required the establishment of affectionate bonds with my parents and friends. Rather, this behavior was the inevitable consequence of my belief that it is morally wrong to harm and morally right to help a living being in distress. Even five-year-olds who grew up in institutions without a strong attachment to anyone hold that belief.

Many children who were orphans in Nazi concentration camps, with no strong attachments to anyone, became adults with a deep moral sense and an ethical code requiring kindness to those in need. To my knowledge, no primatologist has ever observed a chimpanzee stop to help another creature, other than a familiar chimp, who was in distress. It is relevant that the small proportion of individuals who hear voices speaking to them, usually but not always schizophrenics, report that the voices either criticize the person for a moral flaw or tell the person to commit an amoral action. They rarely praise the person or talk about neutral themes. This robust fact implies that the mind is preoccupied with the moral status of its host and biased toward assuming that it has moral imperfections.

An important reason why biologists prefer to base human morality on sociability and cooperation is that they do not like theorizing about concepts that cannot be measured objectively. Sociable and cooperative behaviors can be observed in animals and humans, but no one knows how to measure an animal's intentions, feelings, or sense of right and wrong. Churchland, like most biologists, wants to base morality on the traits that are preserved across many species because they are likely to contribute to an individual's inclusive fitness, defined as the reproductive potential of the animal and all genetically related kin.

This issue bears directly on the concept of altruism. Biologists define an altruistic act as any behavior that benefits another animal while not benefiting the actor. Altruism in animals is defined only by the consequences of an agent's behavior on another. The animal's intention is irrelevant because it cannot be known. Altruism in humans, however, always makes the agent's intention the central feature. The biologist's definition implies that a woman is altruistic if she regularly throws uneaten but edible food in a rubbish can and a homeless person gathers it up for nourishment. Even children understand the difference between an intentional act of kindness and an accidental act with the same outcome. A man trying to save a child from drowning who kills both himself and the struggling child committed an altruistic act because of his intention.

Some critics of Alfred Kinsey's 1948 volume on sexual behavior among American males pointed to Kinsey's dogmatic emphasis on what was observed and his indifference to hidden intentions, motives, and feelings. Kinsey answered his critics by declaring that he was interested only in what could be measured objectively. A reported copulation between a man and a woman was an objective event. Kinsey did not care why the sexual act occurred or whether any of the participants enjoyed the experience. This logic implies that an American soldier who shoots an Afghan terrorist and a bank robber who shoots a teller have committed equally amoral actions. No behavior, whether committed by an animal or a human, permits an observer to be certain of the internal states that preceded its display!

Inasmuch as humans and animals expend energy when they help another, altruism seems to be inconsistent with the basic premise of evolutionary theory—namely, that animals award priority to acts that maximize their inclusive fitness. Biologists insist that no animal, and therefore no human, should act to benefit a stranger if they gain nothing, either at the moment or at some later date. This assumption bumps up against the robust observation that many humans do help total strangers on many occasions. Some biologists wiggle out of this uncomfortable fact by suggesting that humans behave altruistically toward strangers because they either expect a reciprocal kindness in return or wish to retain a praiseworthy reputation in their community. But the fact remains that many adults help total strangers when they anonymously send money to a charity, implying that they know their action will bear neither on their reputation nor on the expectation of a reciprocal benevolence.

The anthropologist Christopher Boehm favors a different explanation of altruism. He speculates in *Moral Origins* that early humans may have killed or ostracized the free-loading members of their group.[18] The continuation of this practice, over many generations, should have weeded out those with biological predispositions to selfish behavior and left most contemporary humans with a genome that favors cooperation and altruism.

A serious problem with Boehm's account is his assumption that the biological bases for altruism among early humans who lived in small, egalitarian bands have not changed, despite the very different conditions in which modern humans live. Community sizes, economies, causes of illness and death, sources of knowledge, mechanics of obtaining food, reasons for marriage, kinds of care for children, implementation of justice, and awarding of political power among the small bands of early humans who roamed Africa have been seriously altered over the past 150 millennia. Hunter-gatherer groups worried about being ostracized or becoming a topic of malicious gossip if they failed to be generous. Close to one-half of contemporary humans live in large urban areas where most acts of selfishness are undetected, and worry over a neighbor's gossip has become as rare as worry over a witch's curse. Many properties that were adaptive in early humans—for example, the ability to run long distances to hunt down an animal without overheating—are irrelevant for most contemporary populations. There is no reason to assume that the conditions favoring altruism have not undergone equally dramatic changes.

I suggest that the reciprocal altruism argument—"I'll help you now because I expect that I might need your help later"—cannot explain why in the spring of 2011 the adult residents of Tokyo voluntarily reduced their consumption of electricity to demonstrate their emotional support of the victims of the tsunami living hundreds of miles to the north; they committed an altruistic act knowing it was highly unlikely that the strangers would ever have an opportunity to reciprocate. During the past five years, more Europeans donated blood to strangers than committed rape, murder, or robbery. A woman in her fifth month of volunteer work in an understaffed hospital caring for wounded soldiers in a battle zone secretes inflammatory proteins that compromise her fitness, but she is unable to suppress the urge to engage in these acts of care. There is no comparable phenomenon in any other animal species.

Biologists' reluctance to acknowledge that humans possess a small number of unique psychological properties is hard to understand, given that the human brain possesses features, circuits, and patterns of gene expression that are not found in any other animal. One reason for the difference between humans and apes, as noted by Todd Preuss and his colleagues at Emory University, is that the DNA in the promoter region of genes that control the development of the prefrontal cortex is less methylated in humans than in chimpanzees.[19] As a result, genes affecting brain development and function are more fully expressed in humans. Humans are the only species, for example, that can suppress the powerful biological urge to reproduce offspring and decide not to have any children.

These observations confirm what natural scientists have known for a long time—namely, that many life forms have one or more qualitatively distinctive properties. The DNA of bacteria, for example, are not enclosed in a nucleus and fish do not have lungs. Michael Tomasello and his colleagues at the Max Planck Institute in Leipzig found that adult chimpanzees show no interest in punishing a "thief" who has stolen food from another chimp.[20] Children, however, would do so because they possess concepts of right and wrong. Nor has any primatologist seen a low-ranking male chimpanzee—one who was continually dominated by other members of his troop—harm himself. I know of no biologist who is trying to discover a property in male reptiles that might be an early form of the imprinting of newly hatched goslings on the first moving object they see.

For reasons that are hard to understand, biologists draw a line in the sand when it comes to altruism. They are unwilling to entertain the possibility that humans and animals act benevolently toward others for different reasons. Well-fed hawks soar in the sky because this action is part of their biological repertoire. The unique biology of the human brain motivates children and adults to act in ways that will allow them to arrive at the judgment that they are good persons. This is not the reason why a monkey gives a piece of food to another animal. The uncritical acceptance of Darwin's assumption in *The Descent of Man* that altruism is a derivative of social instincts that enhance greater fitness is sustaining a dogmatic view of human altruism that is uncharacteristic of natural scientists.

The ascendance of self-interest to an undisputed alpha position in the hierarchy of human motives over the past half-century has allowed economics to displace psychology as the central discipline in the social sciences. The enhanced status of economics has been accompanied by an extraordinary expansion of its earlier mission. No longer concerned only with the balance among taxes, investments, the supply and demand of goods, and the circulation of money, the author of one popular textbook defines *economics* as the study of individuals interacting with one another as they go about their lives. This is psychology's mandate. But unlike the psychologists who believe that these interactions are modulated by a variety of factors—brain maturation, learning, conflict, ideals, and identifications—economists assume that most human encounters, including selecting a spouse and having a child, are controlled primarily by incentives for gaining or losing desired resources. Everything else is chaff. This narrow conception of the reasons for human behaviors should invite a smile. It does not, because most adults are susceptible to believing the claims of presumed experts and subsequently behaving in ways that prove the experts right. That is why generations of boys from the isolated New Guinea tribe described in Chapter 1 performed fellatio on older adolescents in order to become fertile.

When physicists discover evidence that does not match the predictions based on their equations, they usually change the equations to fit the observations. When evidence is inconsistent with the semantic networks of evolutionary biologists, however, many ignore the annoying observations in order to retain the assumptions of their theories. The dogmatic insistence that human actions intended to help strangers must share some properties possessed by bees, birds, rats, monkeys, and apes is preventing these scientists from attaining a fuller understanding of the human moral sense.

This resistance to acknowledging the unique meaning of human altruism resembles the resistance that Stanley Prusiner encountered in 1982, when he argued that a deformed protein, called a prion, could infect healthy proteins and thereby cause mad cow disease. Barry Marshall and J. Robin Warren met an equally stubborn resistance from colleagues when they wrote that ulcers were caused by the bacterium *H. pylori* rather than by emotional stress.

Every scientific discipline can point to a small number of rare phenomena that, according to theory, should be highly unlikely. These events, known as "black swans," are common in biology. Among the bird species that produce songs, it is almost always the male who sings. But among plain-tailed wrens, common to Ecuador, both sexes sing, often in duets. It may be true that the primary biological urge in all animals is to maximize inclusive fitness through acts that increase the fecundity of the individual and genetically related kin. But this principle, which the biologist E. O. Wilson has questioned recently in *The Social Conquest of Earth,* has a black swan. Humans are the only species whose members need regular assurance of their virtue because evolutionary events have awarded them a conscious awareness of their psychological properties and a symbolic language in which the concepts *good* and *bad* permeate most decisions.[21] Humans try to avoid committing actions that would cause them to question their membership in the category of good persons. They use the views of others as partial evidence, but the final judgment is private. That is why the distinguished humanist Frank Kermode always felt like an outsider, the celebrated writer John Updike occasionally stammered in front of Boston Brahmins, and the respected Boston businessman whom we met in Chapter 4 confessed at a New Year's Eve party that he regretted not going to college.

Human morality has both advantages and disadvantages. Loyalty to an ethical code facilitates adaptation because moral values help individuals make choices that reduce response uncertainty. Adherence to a moral code also creates a feeling of virtue that makes it easier for the person to love and to accept the love of another. On the other hand, an ethical code can provoke intense guilt, or even a depression or a suicide when the individual violates one of its obligations.

The human need to believe that the self is virtuous helps to explain the dramatic rise over the past twenty years in the number of Chinese affiliated with a religion.

Buddhism, Daoism, Islam, and Christianity are attracting new converts each day. More Chinese attended a place of worship on Sundays during 2011 than the sum of all the church attendees in Western Europe during the same year. It took only one generation of coarse, unrelenting materialism—following a cynicism generated by Mao Zedong's cruel, irrational policies—to create a hunger for an ethical ideal that transcended a sole preoccupation with the accumulation of money and settings in which social encounters were emotionally supportive rather than ruthlessly competitive.

Humans are malleable, but there is a limit to their plasticity. Like a metal spring whose elasticity has been overextended, humans who have been pushed to an extreme psychological state try to return to a position that is in greater harmony with their inherent nature. One component of this nature is the need to believe that they are good. The accumulation of wealth permits this evaluation among some adults. John D. Rockefeller once told a reporter that God wanted him to make money. Rockefeller may have read a sermon by the Boston minister Cotton Mather, delivered in the early 1700s, in which he told the congregation: "If the Lord Jesus Christ might find thee in thy storehouse, in thy shop, in thy ship, or in thy field, or where thy business lies, who knows what blessings He might bestow on thee?" Adam Smith made this obligation for work the cornerstone of his famous 1776 book *The Wealth of Nations.*

The unproven hypothesis that human altruism contributes to fitness resembles the physicists' belief that particles with mass—for example, the W boson—originally had no mass in the first moments after the Big Bang. The Higgs field was invented as a way to add mass to these particles. This concept was necessary because the physicist's equations, collectively known as the Standard Model, could satisfy an a priori demand for symmetry only if these particles had no mass initially. No scientist had ever measured a W boson free of a Higgs field and found that it had no mass. Rather, the mathematical equations were the basis for this premise. Analogously, no scientist has demonstrated that most human altruistic actions add to the fitness of the individual. This idea gains its attractiveness from the evolutionary biologists' premise that if a class of behaviors survives across hundreds of generations, it must contribute to fitness.

Two important and related questions remain unresolved: Should the essential features of the concept *moral* be an action, intention, the consequences of an action, or a combination of two or all three of these properties? And are all humans biologically prepared to regard any particular action, intention, or consequence as moral or amoral?[22]

We could classify all behaviors motivated by an intention to contribute to the welfare of another as the most essential feature of morality. There are occasions, however, when the recipient of an act of kindness experiences a loss of dignity because he or she interprets the charitable behavior as reflecting a condescending attitude on the part of the giver. Luis Buñuel's 1961 film *Viridiana* captures this idea.

If consequences are the primary feature of morality, we confront the paradox of classifying Medea, the mother in the Greek tragedy who killed her children out of anger, in the same category as the mother in Toni Morrison's novel *Beloved,* who killed her child out of love. A tolerant, pacifist cohort of German youths was a benevolent consequence of World War II but few would argue that this outcome makes that war a morally defensible event. On reflection, neither criterion is completely satisfying.

This conclusion makes it reasonable to argue that classifying an act as moral requires specifying a particular person with a particular intention acting in a particular context in a particular culture during a particular era. French law, which had protected the freedom of expression of all religions for more than two hundred years, found an exception when it banned the wearing of the burqa in public. Seventeenth-century Japanese believed that each person was morally obligated to accept the role assigned them. Modern-day Americans would reject such an imperative as preventing unskilled laborers from trying to ascend in social status. The current dean and many of the faculty at Guangzhou Medical University in China regard paying a faculty member a bonus of $47,000 for publishing an article in one of the small number of high-prestige journals in Europe or America as perfectly ethical. I suspect that the deans and faculty at most American medical schools would view this practice as immoral.[23]

I was bothered by reading that my alma mater, Rutgers University, paid the popular author Toni Morrison $30,000 in 2011 for coming to the campus to receive an honorary degree and to give the major commencement speech. I conveyed my feelings in a letter to the president stating that if Ms. Morrison accepted a paid gig at the university, the students were guests at an expensive hotel. His reply indicated that neither he nor his advisers interpreted this action as violating any ethical standard he or the university community held.

Making money has ascended from a lower position in the hierarchy of morally praiseworthy acts to a position of prominence because other values have descended, making the pursuit of wealth one of few goals that still has the power to excite.

When I was chairman of the psychology department at Harvard, a middle-class, white graduate student who needed the money he would be paid for teaching an extra section of a large undergraduate course put up signs on the main campus promising to pay a student $50 if he or she enrolled in the course he was assigned. The Harvard officials viewed this behavior as violating the community's ethical code and asked him to leave the university. The young man came to my office the day he left campus and complained that he still did not understand why his action was morally wrong. "We live in a market economy," he said. "What I did was in perfect accord with the moral premises of a market economy."

Scholars have debated whether loyalty to a moral standard rests on a person's emotions or on reason. Most of the time, individuals act morally automatically, with neither a strong feeling nor a reasoned argument. However, there are occasions when intense feelings, whether lust, anger, or a desire for fame or money, can trump moral standards that would be honored when these feelings are absent. The historian Emmanuel Le Roy Ladourie described a woman from a medieval French village who explained the reason for her sexual affair with a local priest: "In those days it pleased me and it pleased the priest, that he should know me carnally and be known by me; and so I did not think I was sinning and neither did he. But now, with him it does not please me anymore. And so, if he knew me carnally, I should think it is a sin."

Baruch Spinoza, the famous seventeenth-century Dutch philosopher, was among the first Europeans to suggest that scientific facts should inform our conception of morality. A century later, some philosophers elaborated this idea by declaring that morality should be based on what is true in nature. Because private feelings of pleasure or displeasure are quintessentially natural, these scholars argued that feelings should be the essential features of good and bad and, by inference, moral and amoral. Inasmuch as animals are parts of nature, and obviously self-interested, perhaps self-interest should be a moral imperative deserving loyalty.[24]

The assumption that humans are naturally selfish provoked conflict between an emerging group of eighteenth-century libertarians who prized the freedom to pursue their self-interests and scholars who favored a traditional ethic demanding restriction of excessive desires for power, sexual pleasures, and wealth. By the end of that century, this issue had polarized scientists against humanists, the middle class against the working class, and agnostics against Christians.

Some nineteenth-century philosophers responded to this dilemma by abandoning an attempt to defend any particular act as absolutely amoral and adopting a pragmatic criterion declaring that morality should be based on the consequences of an action. If an action or decision made many persons happy, it was moral. But this pragmatic criterion has disadvantages. For example, a majority of Americans would like to believe in the ethically pleasing idea that the biological differences among the major ethnic groups, especially Asians, Hispanics, Africans, and Europeans, are trivial and play little or no role in psychological outcomes. The popularity of this egalitarian premise motivated Congress to pressure the National Institutes of Health to require psychologists and psychiatrists to include representatives from the major ethnic groups in their research, unless they had a good reason for not doing so. This demand flies in the face of robust evidence of nontrivial variation in the genomes and behaviors of individuals from the major ethnic groups. This genetic variation implies that a gene representing a vulnerability for a mental illness in Asians might not pose the same risk for Hispanics, Europeans, or Africans. By requiring scientists to study members of all ethnic groups, the NIH officials made it harder to discover a relation between a particular gene and a symptom that happened to be restricted to one ethnic group.

It took almost 150 years for a small group of American and European scholars to offer a solution that was based on two kinds of moral standards: conventional and principled. Conventional standards apply to the many behaviors that a majority in a society practice but recognize as arbitrary and not binding. Placing a napkin on one's lap when in a restaurant is an example. Violations of conventional standards do not lead to shame or guilt. Principled standards, however, should be honored by everyone and their violation is usually followed by guilt. Parental neglect of an infant is a violation of a principled standard in our society.

Children gain an early appreciation of the difference between these two kinds of standards by four years of age. Most four-year-olds will say that harming another is a principled standard that must be honored even if no adult is present to witness such an action. But it is not until the transition at five to seven years that children understand that a conventional standard for some people might be a principled one for others. Recall that this is the age when children recognize the possibility of two perspectives on the same event. Children say that only violations of principled standards should be reported to an authority; violations of conventional standards do not warrant the same action.[25]

The Russian physicist Andrei Sakharov was "unable to imagine the universe and human life without some guiding principles, without a source of spiritual warmth that is nonmaterial and not bounded by physical laws."[26] The current generation of twenty-year-olds, however, has to cope with an increasing number of standards that had been principled in the past but are becoming, or already are, conventional.

These include marital infidelity, cheating on examinations, and a gay lifestyle. The Brahman's principled standard regarding avoidance of contact with untouchables is also becoming conventional in contemporary Indian society.

Some of the sexual behaviors of unmarried women that had violated a principled standard in the past are slowly becoming conventional as well. Increasing numbers of college-age, American women say they do not believe they are violating a principled standard when they sell sexual services to strangers in order to pay their tuition.[27] These women do not regard themselves as prostitutes because their motives do not match their conception of the psyches of prostitutes. This explanation is not surprising. A survey of undergraduates at a mainly white Midwestern university revealed that one of four women had consensual sex with three or more partners, some of whom were men they knew only briefly, but they did not feel they were disloyal to any personal moral position.

Most nineteenth-century Americans would have regarded these women as violating a principled standard regarding sexual behavior. Richard Dana Jr. described a summer evening in 1842 when he gave a moral lecture to a prostitute who had accosted him, urging her to go to confession the next day. She told Dana the next evening that she had taken his advice. One sign of the change in the average American's judgment of the moral status of female sexuality over the past hundred years is Naomi Wolf's book *Vagina: A New Biography,* which was reviewed in the September 27, 2012, issue of *The New York Review of Books* along with a print of Gustave Courbet's 1866 ultra-realistic painting of the female genital. I suspect that this book would not have been written in 1912, and had this magazine existed at the time it would not have published that print.

As the roll of history rendered some principled standards conventional and formerly conventional standards principled, many youths became confused over the moral values that should be obligatory under all conditions. Youths do not like an ethically flat territory. Many remain uncommitted to any ideology because the failures of the absolute catechisms represented by communism, national socialism, and an unregulated capitalism render them suspicious of all utopias and, therefore, reluctant to sign on to any ethical mission that requires unquestioning loyalty.

When North American and European societies became less willing to award moral authority to those who tended the sick, made scientific discoveries, wrote just legal decisions, loaned money to a small business, or inspired a congregation, the men and women in these roles were less able to enjoy the feeling of virtue they anticipated when they chose those vocations. One sign of the loss of moral authority by life scientists was a 2010 ruling by a European commission requiring investigators to limit their reliance on animals in research, despite strong complaints from the scientific community that this action would slow the discovery of cures for many diseases.

As each of these roles lost the high level of respect they had enjoyed, aggrandizing the self and making money rose to alpha positions. The ascent of this value to the position of a moral imperative was aided by the assumption that accumulating wealth required only hard work and a little luck. These criteria were in perfect accord with an egalitarian ethos demanding that everyone should be eligible for the primary pleasures of life. Not everyone has the talent to become a physicist or a cellist, the spirituality to become a member of the clergy, or the connections needed for an appointment to the Supreme Court. But everyone can persevere, and each person is entitled to a lucky break. One reason why the fantasy figure of Superman became more popular than Buck Rogers, Flash Gordon, or Dick Tracy—other figures that dominated the comic books in the 1930s—was that Superman in everyday life was a shy journalist without exceptional talent. Hence, his fans could entertain the wish that they, too, might become better than they were. This idea captures the root premise of contemporary American society.

Although contemporary films and books depict the men and women working in the financial sector as dishonest, disloyal, selfish, greedy, and caring little about the larger society, business is the most popular undergraduate concentration in American colleges. It attracts more than twice the number of students majoring in education, the second most popular field. A reasonable interpretation of this fact is that contemporary American youths do not regard a career devoted exclusively to making money as violating any standard—whether conventional or principled. Almost all of my college friends in 1946, only six and a half decades ago, viewed students whose choice of career was based solely on the desire to make money as violating a principled standard.

Economically developed democracies became friendly during the past century to four premises that make it harder to defend any particular standard as principled under all circumstances: No action is absolutely wrong; all humans have a right to freedom and dignity; human will is weak and, on occasion, yields to strong temptation; and, finally, all individuals should be true to their private consciences, even if some of their actions provoke critical evaluations from a majority. This quartet of premises permits almost any behavior under certain conditions. (See Figure 6.2.)

1. No action is always evil.
2. All humans have a right to freedom and dignity.
3. Human will is weak.
4. All individuals ought to be true to their private
   consciences.

FIGURE 6.2   Four contemporary moral values in democratic
              societies

The second premise renders soldiers who kill an enemy combatant vulnerable
to guilt. Soldiers who can label the enemy as evil, or less than human, find it easier to kill them. This was possible when American troops were fighting the Nazis.
However, today's nineteen-year-olds who have been socialized to believe that all
humans, no matter what their skin color, religion, or nationality, are entitled to dignity will be more reluctant to murder an enemy unless doing so is necessary for
their survival. This dynamic may explain why the prevalence of serious emotional
problems among the American combatants in Vietnam, Iraq, and Afghanistan is
higher than it was among the troops who fought in World War II.

A person who accepts an imperative to be honest under all circumstances has
to acknowledge that the Japanese regard this imperative as inconsistent with the
demand of *omoiyari,* which requires each person to be continually sensitive to the
feelings of others. This standard allows one to lie if that action will make another
feel better. Children under age six do not understand that a kind statement need
not be honest.[28] The Japanese are more concerned with each individual's concrete,
messy relationships with other people than with an idealistic, spiritual relation to a
supremely omniscient entity.

The Civil Rights Movement of the 1960s, demanding tolerance toward all values
and the people who hold them, meant that fourth-generation white Protestants in
America could no longer use their skin color, social class, education, religion, or the
accomplishments of their relatives as ways to assure themselves that they were morally praiseworthy agents. Hence, they invented other properties. Humans demand
some way to prove that they are good. They refuse to believe that it makes no difference what one believes or does. The Swedish writer Per Lagerkvist describes a conversation in which a dead soul asks God what His purpose was in creating humans.
God's reply: "I only intended that humans would never be satisfied with nothing."

Critics of American society cite the excessive concern with the accumulation
of material wealth. Michael Sandel in *What Money Can't Buy* is bothered by a

contemporary ethic based on the premise that everything, including one's body, is potentially for sale.[29] This preoccupation with accumulating wealth has begun to seep into obituaries. The September 21, 2012, issue of the *New York Times* contains an obituary for Jerome Horwitz, a chemist who invented the drug AZT with the hope that it would cure some cancers. Although the drug was ineffective with cancer, other scientists discovered years later that AZT was helpful with AIDS. Before describing Horwitz's life history or the details of his scientific discovery, which are usually the salient features of an obituary, the author of the essay comes close to demeaning the man he is supposed to praise by writing: "Dr. Horwitz never achieved much fame and did not earn a penny for making the AZT compound."

This commercial perspective on the purpose of a life becomes understandable once we recognize that everyone needs to believe in some goal that is worth pursuing. The accumulation of wealth remains one of the few properties that a majority believe any American can obtain as a way to reassure the self of its virtue. The crass materialism of American society is the price to be paid for diluting or eliminating the older signs of virtue that not everyone could attain. There are no free lunches. At least American cities are not being burned and college students are not occupying university buildings or living with a dozen friends in unheated homes exchanging sex partners each evening. A society composed of individuals with different educational backgrounds, ethnicities, and religions cannot pursue a philosophy of equal dignity for all without compromising some traditional values. No person or society can have it all.

When the moral authority of the traditional eighteenth-century imperatives for humility, charity, restraint, frugality, honesty, and loyalty was weakened, some scientists raised their hands, announcing that they could be of help. The judicial decisions ordering the busing of minority children to white schools in the service of desegregation were presumably based on scientific evidence pointing to the differences in quality of instruction and academic achievement between minority youths in segregated schools and the majority youths in middle-class neighborhoods. However, this factual information would be persuasive to judges and a majority in the society only if both were prepared to accept that ethical decision. Circumcision of an infant boy, which has been a religious issue for millennia, has become a legal one in several countries, and the courts are looking to scientists to tell them if this practice has health benefits. The current debate on abortion centers on whether a woman is free to make decisions about her own body. This dilemma pits the mother's autonomy against the fetus's right to life, a question that cannot be decided by scientific evidence. Although the Supreme Court's last ruling on abortion sided with the mother, future courts might defend the fetus. In all these cases, the scientific facts are less relevant than the sentiment of the majority in a community.

Science confessed at the end of the nineteenth-century that nature had no values and citizens would have to look elsewhere for ethical guidance. Scientific evidence can explain why a person selects one action over another and can even point to an invalid basis for a particular ethical view. But scientific facts cannot supply the foundations for any moral standard. In 2012, about 60 million Americans were living in chronic poverty, which, as we have seen, leads to a host of serious medical problems. Indeed, over the twenty-year interval from 1990 to 2010, the life expectancy of Americans who did not graduate high school was four years less than it had been during the prior twenty years. But voting records and survey data suggest that a large number of Americans do not regard these facts as implying an ethical obligation on government, or the advantaged members of the society, to do something to correct this problem.

My claim that scientific facts cannot be the foundation of a moral code does not appeal to those who demand that all decisions affecting a majority in the society rest on rational arguments that use objective evidence rather than community sentiment. The demand for objective bases for decisions affecting a society is relevant to a current controversy over same-sex classrooms. Even though a fair number of American girls are more comfortable in such classrooms, some social scientists claim that this arrangement should be prohibited because there is no evidence proving that girls in all-female classrooms have higher academic achievement scores. Moreover, they argue that this practice violates an ethical demand for gender equality. This rationale ignores the emotional advantages that some girls enjoy in all-female classes. Because "feeling more comfortable" is harder to measure than scores on achievement tests, those opposing same-sex classrooms dismiss this psychological state as a legitimate rationale. These social scientists have an automatic phobic response to any claim that is based only on an ethical or emotionally based preference that is not supported by a reasoned argument based on hard facts.

The traditional value placed on direct contacts between students and their teachers has come under attack following advances in computer technology that have made it possible for college students to learn the factual content of a field by sitting alone, often in their pajamas, in front of a laptop. This curricular reform serves an egalitarian ethic because it dilutes the prestige of graduating from an elite college or university. The major assumption behind this movement is that the primary purpose of a college education is to acquire a body of facts needed for a job—just the facts and only the facts. A mind full of facts, however, is a quiet place because facts require synthesis.

The facts taught in a majority of college courses are irrelevant to the responsibilities assigned to most workers who learn relevant skills on the job. This new movement ignores the fact that youths who are unsure of a career path can be inspired by contact with an enthusiastic teacher. I decided to become a psychologist rather than a biochemist because a professor of psychology walking with me across campus one day said that I would be a good psychologist. I recognize my view is old-fashioned. Richard De Millo of the Georgia Institute of Technology argues in *Abelard to Apple* that online courses will, and should, be a major force in higher education.[30] Harvard University and the Massachusetts Institute of Technology joined forces in 2012 to initiate such an effort.

The current Zeitgeist minimizes the influence of the psychological relationship between a specific teacher and a particular student. If students learning biology over the Internet acquire the same knowledge as those in regular classrooms, there is no reason to differentiate among them. This premise serves egalitarianism but strays from the facts. A course in genetics, history, or computers taught over the Internet is not equivalent to a course with the same title taught by an enthusiastic teacher interacting with a student audience.

There is an obvious counterargument to my nostalgia for the traditional undergraduate education that includes the humanities, the sciences, and contact with live faculty members. The economies in many nations have altered the purposes of a college degree for many, but not all, students. The primary advantage of a college degree during the centuries before the technological advances and anti-elitism that burgeoned over the past sixty years was to persuade the recipients of a college diploma, and the public, that these adults had demonstrated a level of intelligence and responsibility that earned them the right to lead a platoon in battle, prescribe a medicine, defend a client in court, run a bank, invest a widow's inheritance, apply for and wisely implement a million-dollar grant, or raise the spirits of a congregation. This is the message Frank Baum intended when the wizard gave the straw man a diploma in the *Wizard of Oz*.

Today, computer programs make investment decisions, physicians have access to technology and online information that make their decisions easier, infantry battles between two large armies are less frequent as drone attacks increase, most congregations gather in a place of worship to dilute a feeling of social isolation, and most secure well-paying jobs require workers to have a set of technical skills that earlier generations did not have to master.

Under these conditions it is reasonable to argue that colleges have a responsibility to make sure that a majority of their graduates possess the talents the economy needs. The minority of students at elite institutions who can rely on family affluence to survive can afford the pleasure of courses in history, literature, and philosophy and perhaps a smattering of science and mathematics. I happen to think that all undergraduates ought to be exposed to the literature, history, and philosophy of their own and other cultures, along with courses in computing, biology, physics, and mathematics. Literature, history, and philosophy help students appreciate the values that define their historical moment. But history continually alters the priorities assigned to the domains of understanding. Students at the University of Paris in 1600 had to study the Bible and the history of Greece and Rome. It was less urgent that they understand how the printing press worked or how glass was manufactured. Contemporary students must know how to operate a computer and need not be familiar with the age of Pericles. Sadly, no domain of knowledge, save the ability to read, write, and execute the rules of elementary mathematics, enjoys an unquestioned position in the contemporary curriculum. The muse of history decides which knowledge is privileged, much like the local ecology selects the most adaptive biological traits.

Ethical choices must be made because it is rare that a particular outcome benefits all potential beneficiaries. Very few decisions, actions, or laws simultaneously benefit a person, the person's family, and the society in which that person lives. One courageous commentator even questioned the assumption that public support of medical research directed toward saving two-pound newborns or prolonging the life of eighty-year-olds has an inherent priority. He suggested that our society might benefit more if those funds were used to reduce poverty and improve urban schools.[31]

The decision by rich governments to spend more tax dollars on scientific research designed to understand a puzzling feature of the universe than on studies aimed at discovering better ways to teach poor children academic skills rests on the premise that gaining certain knowledge about the material world ought to be favored over generating less certain understanding of the immaterial phenomena of the mind. I suspect that this ethical preference rests on the tacit belief that human behavior is under the control of events that are less easily altered, understood, or predicted than material phenomena. Scientists find it more satisfying to study puzzling phenomena that are potentially knowable. The aesthetic gratification that accompanies a deep understanding and confident prediction of how photons and cells will behave is a reasonable rationale for supporting research that, on occasion, has pragmatic consequences for the economy, health, and winning a war. The decision by schools and colleges to emphasize science and mathematics in their curricula—rather than an appreciation of history, cultural variation, and philosophical debates on human nature—communicates two messages to the young. It announces, first, that the certain, technical knowledge needed to get a job in the new economy is more valuable than the tentative knowledge generated by historians, social scientists, and humanists and, second, that mastering a body of facts is more useful to youth unsure of what path to follow than the lower probability of being inspired by a teacher or arriving at a deep insight as a result of conversations with an understanding mentor in a quiet room.

Although scientific facts can disconfirm the factual basis of a moral premise, they cannot supply the foundation of any moral proposition. Facts prune the tree of morality; they can never be the seedbed. But if not from science, where can the foundation for the morality of a society or a person originate? The source in democratic societies rests with majority sentiment in the community. This sentiment changes over time because it is the product of historical conditions that generate consensus, often tied to a feeling, that a particular action is right or wrong. Mathematicians also rely on sentiment, for they insist that the beauty of a set of equations should be the primary criterion when choosing one proof from a set of alternatives.

The historical changes of the past three hundred years have created a planet that, by 2100, will house 10 billion humans who will generate tons of nonbiodegradable garbage; pollute the earth, water, and air; and reduce the sea's food supply, the earth's fossil fuels, and the forest's arbors of trees. Only about 100 million humans existed when the Athenians were building the Parthenon. The current conditions could eventually threaten the survival of hundreds of millions of adults and children. It is reasonable, therefore, to promote a value in which the integrity of the planet assumes, for the first time in human history, priority over the welfare of any individual, family, or nation. There is no reason why a majority of adults could not enjoy a feeling of virtue by acting in ways that minimize their contribution to environmental degradation. This standard might fill the gap in the current moral vacuum of many contemporary youths. But the imperative to slow the degradation of our planet also derives its persuasive power from the sentiment of a part of the society. After all, we cannot prevent our sun from eventually becoming a red giant with a temperature so high it will evaporate all of the earth's water, after which all life on earth will disappear.

All of these facts contribute to a profound uncertainty over the moral values that demand an unquestioned loyalty among those who reflect on our current circumstances. A group of American college students was asked in 1998 to list what they thought were the most important moral premises. Most nominated "holding clear values." These students did not name any particular value as mandatory because, I suspect, they could not think of an ethical standard that they believed everyone must honor. The fantasy heroes of my childhood in the 1930s—Flash Gordon, Superman, and Dick Tracy—were not confused over the difference between right and wrong and understood the need to destroy all who are bad.[32]

Large numbers of privileged American youths and young adults who were angry at the racism, sexism, and conduct of the Vietnam War in 1969 marched in cities across the country demanding that those in authority make decisions that would satisfy what the youths regarded as moral imperatives. It is a bit surprising that equally large protests are not occurring now, despite good reasons for moral outrage. More nations are building atomic weapons, increasing the probability of a nuclear accident; thousands of Washington lobbyists representing special interests have enormous power over legislation; many members of Congress are unwilling to compromise with members of the other party; and at least 20 million Americans go to sleep each night hungry. That number swells to more than 1 billion across the world. Yet the only protests are the Occupy Wall Street movements in which small numbers participate. I interpret this passivity as a sign that the current generation of young adults is less sure than the generation of the 1960s about which actions and conditions violate a principled moral standard.

The messages in many of the celebrated novels, plays, poems, and essays composed by respected writers over the past four decades imply that a large proportion of educated, moderately affluent North Americans and Europeans are unhappy. Close to 20 percent of British adolescents admit to harming themselves on at least one occasion, one in twenty confess that they want to die, and essays in psychiatric journals in Britain and the United States bemoan the prevalence of binge drinking, date rape, and suicidal attempts among college students.

The themes in the novels, plays, and poems that won the Nobel Prize in Literature from 1901 to the 1950s celebrated human idealism and the quest for freedom and truth. Beginning in the 1960s, however, the themes of the Laureates were marked by a loss of idealism and a recognition of the impossible human predicament created by the barbaric arbitrariness of historical events that defeated all who sought justice and reason in a cruel, callous world. Compare, for example, the depressing views of the human condition described by Samuel Beckett and Mario Vargas Llosa, who were awarded the Nobel Prize in Literature in 1969 and 2010 respectively, with the more inspiring message in the writings of Romain Rolland, who was a Laureate in 1915, and Hermann Hesse and William Faulkner, who received the award in the 1940s. Some of the reasons for the change in mood are easy to list: the wars in Vietnam, the civil unrest created by the demand for freedom by citizens of former colonial nations, a rash of assassinations, a sexual permissiveness that the contraceptive pill made possible, the threat of nuclear war or a dirty bomb, and Timothy Leary's famous plea to the youth of the 1960s who were experimenting with LSD and marijuana: "Turn on, tune in, and drop out."

But all that was more than four decades ago, and one would have thought that the current generation would have adjusted to those disruptions. Moreover, the current mood of despondency seems odd in light of the gentle life conditions that today's privileged young adults enjoy, compared with the material conditions of their great-grandparents. The members of the contemporary generation are expected to live into their eighties or nineties; are protected from a variety of infectious illnesses; have electrical appliances, computers, cell phones, iPads, supermarkets, insurance against property loss and medical expenses, police protection, and access to travel to exotic places; and can choose what to believe and do. Why, then, are they not joyous? I suspect that six conditions came together to create a low-level but persistent malaise despite a surfeit of material comforts.

First is the reduction or elimination of a prior period of intense pain or deprivation, which usually brings a moment of joy. Too many members of the current generation cannot enjoy this feeling because they have not suffered any prolonged deprivations. Reciprocally gratifying social relationships are a second source of happiness. Sadly, contemporary youths and adults are suspicious of being betrayed and must cope with the self-doubt that betrayal brings. Niobe Way's interviews with adolescents reveal that youths during the senior year of high school replace earlier trusting friendships with emotionally distant relationships because of an expectation of betrayal. One boy summarized this mood by telling the psychologist, "Can't trust nobody these days."

Opportunities to feel useful to another or to society are a third way to generate well-being. However, many youths do not seek these opportunities because they are not sure they can "make a difference." In one study, older parents who had accepted their unemployed twenty-five year-old sons and daughters into their childhood homes reported feeling useful once again.[33] The recognition that everyone is expendable can provoke a sadness penetrated with the thought that one is irrelevant. The historical events of the last hundred years have made it harder for the average adult to feel that only he or she can meet the needs of a particular other. Fathers and day care centers can care for young children, and frozen foods and take-out meals make wives feel less necessary. Several lovers of either sex are always available to satisfy sexual needs that are not being fully gratified by a familiar partner. And there is usually more than one lawyer, doctor, dentist, scientist, accountant, banker, butcher, baker, plumber, carpenter, or mechanic to choose from when a problem arises. This horn of plenty deprives each person of the good feeling that accompanies the conviction that he or she is the only one who can satisfy the needs of a particular other. Too many North Americans and Europeans have become replaceable parts in the machinery of their societies.

A fourth source of pleasure is the attainment of a goal following sustained effort. If a digital device is available, however, one can find the answer to almost any question in a few seconds. About a year ago I needed to learn about the plant Achillae. Twenty years earlier I would have gone to the library, searched for the right volume, and looked for the correct entry to find the answer. This effort would have required several hours and I would have experienced a moment of joy upon finding the information. On this more recent occasion, I went to Google and found the answer quickly but did not experience the buzz of victory—because it was too easy. Many writers, ancient and modern, have recognized that the joy accompanying the effort expended during the pursuit of a goal is greater than the joy felt when the goal is reached. The smiles on the faces of students on commencement day or of Nobel Laureates at the December ceremony reflect the effort that led to the prize.

A fifth obstruction is generated by the conditions in contemporary society that deprive the current generation of a way to assure themselves of their virtue without the help of others. This feeling used to be possible through the imposition of restraints on temptations. Nineteenth-century adults could self-administer a dose of virtue by inhibiting the urge to engage in a casual sexual affair, lie to a client, steal from an employer, or get drunk. These acts of suppression did not require anyone's help. Today's goals, which include gaining more friends, ascending in status, acquiring a promotion, and accumulating wealth, require the cooperation of others. Most groundbreaking research in the natural sciences relies on the talents of many colleagues because of the complex technologies involved. Einstein was the sole author of his seminal papers on relativity. An article in a contemporary physics journal may have more than fifty authors.

As history made it harder for young adults to feel virtuous because they were certain of the values that guided each day's decisions, many compensated for this loss by turning to friendships. I suspect that when most adolescents or adults complain of loneliness it is because they are uncertain about the values they should treat as absolutely binding. They are lonely for the reassurance that an ethical code provides. The fortunate ones who find an ethical value rarely complain of loneliness, even if they are friendless. The attainment of this prize requires a solitary journey. The anthropologist Loren Eiseley recalled an encounter with a black girl on the island of Bimini who told him: "Those as hunts treasures must go alone, at night, and when they find it they have to leave a little of their blood behind them."[34]

Fred Guterl, executive editor of the magazine *Scientific American,* described the final condition that blocks a feeling of sustained joy: humans find it easier to remain happy if the future appears brighter than the present.[35] This attitude is difficult to generate in light of four serious threats facing humanity. The increase in the number of nations that will possess nuclear weapons makes a nuclear accident more likely. A pandemic caused by a natural mutation or a synthetically made virus is a second danger. The climate changes that are melting the ice caps and glaciers promise a rise in sea levels and floods or droughts in new locations. And, finally, a cyber-attack on electric grids or financial institutions would bring chaos to entire populations. The recognition that one of these events has a modest probability of occurring within the next fifty years renders a confidently sanguine outlook for one's children or grandchildren impossible.

There are many villains in this narrative, which, in less than three generations, created an ethical ambience in much of the developed world that made winning—whether the prize was money, celebrity, an election, promotion, a medal, or admission to an elite institution—the only value deserving loyalty. Societal conditions have bred investment advisers who lie to their clients, doctors who request payment from Medicare for diagnostic tests they did not administer, teachers who alter student test scores to meet expected performance levels for their school, scientists who publish fraudulent data, Olympic athletes who purposely lose a match so that they will have an easier opponent in the next contest, and armed forces personnel pressured to meet enlistment quotas hiring educated young men to take the required cognitive tests using the names of young recruits who could not pass the tests. Some readers might excuse these behaviors by claiming that the status, jobs, or incomes of these individuals were at risk if they did not violate their own or their community's ethical rules.

This rationale does not explain why smart, white high school youths from affluent families charged less confident students up to several thousand dollars to take the SAT for them. The College Board, which administers the SAT, estimates that each year about three thousand tests are fraudulent (probably an underestimate). On January 1, 2012, a *60 Minutes* interviewer asked one of the young men who took the test at least fifteen times why he committed an act he knew was wrong. The best rationale the student could muster was to say in a soft voice that he could have used the money. Because some parents of the less-prepared students provided the money for an action they knew was amoral, there are three sets of culprits— the test taker, the students who allowed him to represent them, and the parents of those students.

But before readers weep, we have to add a fourth group that also seems unsure of which behaviors are serious moral errors. Officials at the college that the test taker was attending must have known of his arrest and conviction because this information made headlines in several papers. Yet the college did not reprimand him for violating an ethical standard that even first-grade children view as binding. About thirty years ago, a professor at an Ivy League university allowed his name to be listed as the author of a textbook he did not write. After a federal judge ruled that the book that bore his authorship had plagiarized an existing, successful book, the university asked for his resignation. But, soon after, another Ivy League university, aware of the court's ruling and his forced resignation, hired him. Now readers have permission to cry.

Three crises in American history provoked debate over the definition of a moral person. The first centered on whether those who possessed slaves were moral. The second, which peaked during the early years of the last century, hinged on whether a person who legally exploited a laissez-faire capitalistic economy with the sole purpose of accumulating great wealth was acting morally. And the third, most recent crisis occurred during the 1960s, when the society had to decide whether a young man who avoided serving in the Vietnam War by leaving the country or tearing up his draft card was a traitor or a moral hero. In all these cases, a majority believed that a moral question was involved.

Today's crisis has a different flavor because many adults under fifty are not certain there are any moral imperatives that demand loyalty under all conditions.

Ferris Fang and his colleagues at the University of Washington found that as of May 2012 more than two thousand scientific papers in the biological sciences had to be retracted from high-prestige journals because of investigator misconduct, usually the reporting of fraudulent results.[36] An unknown number of other fraudulent papers have gone undetected.

It appears that the extraordinary material progress of the last century exacted a cost. By eliminating many sources of distress, it has reduced the moments of joy that occur when pain or anxiety is conquered. By minimizing the need for sustained effort to gain an important goal, it has diluted the pleasure that accompanies the pursuit. By rendering each person expendable, it has made it more difficult to experience the warm feeling that accompanies the belief that one is needed by another. By relying on machines that have made sustained perseverance less necessary, it has diluted the pride that accompanies an accomplishment requiring prolonged effort. The ethical demands for material success and many friendships require the cooperation of others; hence, individuals can no longer assure themselves of their virtue simply by practicing restraint. The laws intended to bring more happiness to all by making equality of outcome more important than merit have deprived a proportion of the population of the pleasure that accompanies the understanding that their prize was earned because of a developed talent and sustained effort. And the products of brilliant minds working to make things better for all have increased the probability of a nuclear accident, a pandemic, a serious drought, or a cyber-attack.

Even the easy availability of antibiotics and the chlorination of water supplies have their small downside. Thomas McDade of Northwestern University found, to his surprise, that impoverished adults living under extremely unhygienic conditions in the Philippines or lowland Ecuador had lower blood concentrations of the proteins that are signs of the inflammatory states that can lead to cancer, diabetes, and cardiac problems.[37] Apparently, childhood exposure to microbes that are common in the natural environment tunes the immune system in healthy ways, especially when this exposure is combined with a normal birth weight, lowered intake of fats and sugars, and a less sedentary life style. Loving American and European mothers with the best intentions who do not let their children play with dirt and who give antibiotics at the first sign of a cold may unwittingly be making their children more rather than less susceptible to a compromised immune system later in life.

How cruel of history to turn our most certain premises against us and to taunt us with accusations of arrogance for harboring the illusion that we knew what humans needed. These lines from a popular song are fitting:

But where are the clowns?
There ought to be clowns.
Quick, send in the clowns. . . .
Don't bother—they're here.

The ancient Greeks understood that a feeling of well-being, which they called *eudaimonia,* was based on a judgment that bubbled up in those who remained loyal to their principled moral standards. Without a commitment to at least one such standard, it is not possible to attain a persistently happy mood. The Greek philosopher Epicurus wrote that fear, which disturbs a quiet mind, is the major obstacle to happiness. I suspect that the greater enemy of happiness is the absence of any moral imperatives and too little regret over abandoning adolescent vows.

The current malaise will be lifted, eventually. History reveals that dark eras are replaced with enlightened ones. Sometime in the future, I don't know when, history's muse will change the script and make it possible for the heirs of today's apathetic youths to experience the refreshing vitality that a feeling of worthiness brings. I am not suggesting that the many material advantages enjoyed by the current generation are unimportant or unappreciated, only that they are not free gifts. The progress of the last century has been accompanied by an erosion in the private judgment that psychologists call "well-being." The citizens of developed nations have been participants in an exchange. They were given a longer life, better health, and a host of technologies that eased the demand for physical work and provided more variation during each day. In return, they had to relinquish the illusion that there was a spiritual entity concerned with their welfare, the human condition was steadily progressing toward a more perfect state, and there was an inherent justice in human affairs.

Finally, we have to ask why all societies invent a moral code. Evolutionary theory insists that a trait preserved for close to seven thousand generations must serve fitness; otherwise, it would have been discarded. Religious commentators believed that morality served God's purpose. Chinese philosophers were certain that an ethical life was necessary for civic harmony. Freud tweaked the Chinese view when he wrote that the superego was needed to keep the id in check and, in so doing, protect the person from actions that would lead to isolation by the community. Plato claimed that by knowing what was right, one would do the good. The contemporary biologist Francisco Ayala believes that human morality is a derivative of the superior cognitive capacities of our species.

It is odd that the Roman poet Lucretius, who translated Epicurus's philosophy into Latin in the poem *On the Nature of Things*, dwelled more on happiness than on morality. Happiness, he argued, was attained by understanding the stochastic nature of a world without an ulterior meaning or purpose and removing oneself from the delusions of the masses. Lucretius did not mention that those who met these criteria were at risk for a depressed mood unless they honored some ethical beliefs.

My answer to the question of why societies invent moral codes, which the earlier discussion anticipates, is that the human moral sense was selected as a biologically adaptive property because humans can harbor jealousy, envy, and anger at another for a very long time and have the strength, prowess, and opportunity to harm those they dislike in a variety of ways. If children did not have the biologically prepared moral sense that the young Darwin posited, many more toddlers would harm their infant siblings and would become adults who regularly stole from their neighbors. We are fortunate that humans cannot help but evaluate themselves on a continuum defined by the worthiness of their intentions and actions. As each person's evaluation moves closer to their understanding of a virtuous person, a state of happiness emerges as spontaneously as an embryo emerges from a fertilized egg. The privilege of basking in the precious state of *eudaimonia* is awarded to those who, with effort, attain some of the goals they selected years earlier as ethically worthy. Only these individuals can assume the special smile generated by the recognition of a journey that was truly a good run.

CHAPTER SEVEN

Emotions and
Their Development

———

Scientists trying to understand the phenomena we call *emotions* face a number of daunting problems. The most frustrating is arriving at a consensus on the properties that define an emotion. Until that problem is resolved there will continue to be sharp disagreements over whether a person (or an animal) is in an emotional state. An awareness of a change in bodily feeling has been regarded for centuries as the most essential feature of a human emotion. Unfortunately, a person's verbal descriptions, which at the present time are the most frequent measure of an emotion, are flawed because the words that people use are interpretations of their feelings rather than descriptions of the bodily sensations being experienced. The world's languages have many more words for interpretations of feelings than for the sensations. These interpretive words comprise a culture's collection of emotional terms. In the pages that follow, I describe the controversies surrounding the concept of emotion, suggest a possible resolution, and offer a way to think about the development of emotional states from infancy to adolescence.

Most adults correctly interpret the relaxed feeling that follows the drinking of a glass of wine at the end of a hard day. But there is more than one reasonable interpretation of an unexpected, unpleasant feeling of tension centered in the stomach.

Many contemporary Americans and Europeans are likely to interpret this feeling as anxiety if they cannot attribute it to a microbe or something they ate. Members of other cultures might interpret the same feeling as meaning that they offended God or have been bewitched. The feelings produced by an undiagnosed illness are often misinterpreted as an emotion brought on by a psychological event. Adults who do not know they have mononucleosis, for example, are prone to interpret their low energy level as meaning that they are sad, lonely, or guilty.

I recall a morning years ago when I awoke with a feeling that blended low energy with muscle tension. I could not decide if I was tired because I'd had only five hours sleep, worried because my income tax return was due in two days, or sad because I'd just learned of the death of a friend. It was also possible that the feeling was brought on by all three conditions. If that were true, no word in my vocabulary could name my emotional state. The prevalence of these and other misattributions is one reason for the controversies surrounding the definition and measurement of the emotional concepts that in English have the names *happy, excited, surprised, disgusted, ashamed, guilty, sad, angry, anxious, fearful,* and *depressed.*

On some occasions a feeling can become a conditioned stimulus for an interpretation that varies with the context. Consider an adolescent girl who feels apathetic on a Saturday evening when she has no plans. If the girl decides that the absence of an activity with friends is the reason for her apathy, she will be tempted to conclude that she is lonely. Several repetitions of this sequence can transform feelings of apathy into conditioned stimuli that automatically evoke an interpretation of loneliness. A second adolescent who felt apathetic soon after she stole some money from her mother's purse might acquire an association between apathy and guilt.

Even the psychological state evoked by being touched depends on a person's interpretation of the source of the touch. A team of Dutch scientists at the University of Groningen found that young men who believed their leg was being caressed by a woman reported more pleasure and showed greater activation of the neurons that are responsive to touch than did young men who thought that a man was applying the caress, even though all of the caresses were applied by the same person.

A large slice of cortex extending from the temporal to the frontal lobe, called the insula, receives an initially processed version of every sensation—from touch to taste. The output of the insula forms the basis for all conscious feelings. Individuals use this information, along with the output of activity in sites representing the context and past experience, to construct semantic interpretations that are their best guess as to the cause of a feeling. That guess determines the emotional term selected.

However, scientists and clinicians do not have direct access to a person's feelings; hence they have to decide which measures might be sensitive signs of these feelings. For example, clinicians often rely on a woman's speech and posture to decide that she is experiencing the feelings that define depression. But the same woman might deny this emotional label and insist that she is fatigued.

The distinction between a person's interpretation of a feeling and an investigator's inference based on objective measures bedevils the study of emotion. Joseph LeDoux, one of the most influential scientists studying emotions in animals, asked rhetorically: "If we don't have an agreed-upon definition of emotion that allows us to say what an emotion is, . . . how can we study emotions in animals or humans?" Ledoux's refreshingly honest answer was "We fake it."

That candid assessment leaves scientists in an uncomfortable position. They are certain that humans and animals have emotions, but because they are unable to agree on a definition of these states they are not sure how to measure them. Biologists were in a similar position in 1900 because they believed there were genes, but they had no clue as to their molecular structure.

DEFINING (AND DETECTING) EMOTIONS

An important reason for the current controversy is that neuroscientists changed the traditional definition of a human emotion without acknowledging that they had done so. When natural scientists borrow a popular word but change its essential features, they usually inform the community about the new meaning. Particle physicists explained that when they used the term *charm* they intended to describe a property of a quark. Scientists in 1983 replaced the old definition of a meter, which was the length of a platinum-iridium bar lying under glass in a Paris building, with the length of the path that light traveled in a vacuum during that tiny fraction of a second that is the result of dividing 1 by 299,792,458.

The scientists who replaced a person's subjective interpretation of a feeling with a brain profile or other biological measure did not recognize that they had altered the meaning of *emotion* held by social scientists and by the broader community. A distinguished team of Swedish scientists at Uppsala University, for example, assumed that increased activity in the human sweat glands (called the skin conductance response or SCR) to a stimulus that signaled electric shock was a sensitive index of fear. They did not ask the adults they studied if they were afraid or examine their faces or posture, and they ignored the robust fact that increases in skin conductance occur in response to any unexpected event, whether it signals an unpleasant or a pleasant experience. This contrast between a person's subjective interpretation of a feeling and the scientist's objective measure is reminiscent of the contrast between basing morality on a person's private conscience or abiding by the ethical standards held by a majority in the community.

The distinguished neuroscientist Edmund Rolls tries to combine both points of view in his book *Neuroculture*.[1] Rolls defines an emotion as a brain state generated by any event that the agent, animal or human, treats as a reward or a punishment. The key word here is *treats*. If two persons do not regard an experience as rewarding or punishing, they will have different brain states. This means that the scientist cannot know ahead of time whether an event will create an emotion. Rolls's position is most appropriate for animals who do not impose symbolic interpretations on the receipt of food or electric shock, both of which create distinctive brain states and often lead to a particular behavior.

Scientists rely on three kinds of phenomena when deciding whether an emotion is present in an animal or human. They measure reactions in the brain or body, observe behaviors, and, in humans, record the words people use to describe their feelings in situations that are presumed to generate a feeling. The problem is that these three sources of evidence are usually uncorrelated and, therefore, do not lead to the same conclusion.

A consequence of this discouraging state of affairs is that scientists who study animals decided to ignore feelings and interpretations and rely only on biological or behavioral reactions. Their position of authority in the academy persuaded many psychologists and psychiatrists who study humans to adopt the same point of view. The assumption that a change in any biological measure reflects an emotion, independent of what a person felt, said, or did, would have been defensible if these investigators had invented new words for the biological state that accompanied a waveform in an electroencephalogram, a surge of blood flow to a brain site, a skin conductance response, or a change in heart rate. Unfortunately, these scientists continued to use the same popular emotional words adults use when they interpret their feelings and report the interpretation to another person.

In light of the honest debates over the definition of *emotion,* it seems wise to avoid quarreling over what an emotion is, or should be, and instead consider the phenomena that scientists point to when they say that a person or animal is in an emotional state. The heart of the debate centers on the phenomena that provide the most fruitful definition of this semantic concept. Should they be changes in the brain or

1. Profile of activity in brain, body, or facial muscles
2. A detected feeling
3. The interpretation of a feeling
4. Verbal description
5. Behavior

FIGURE 7.1   The bases for inferring an emotional state

body, feelings, verbal descriptions of feelings, public behaviors, or combinations of these phenomena? Rarely do all these measures cohere in a meaningful pattern. Coherence usually occurs when a person encounters very dangerous threats or extremely salient pleasures. (See Figure 7.1.)

Emotions therefore resemble the weather. Most of the time, individuals do not notice a slight change in wind velocity, temperature, or cloud cover, but they do pay attention to blizzards, hurricanes, and thunderstorms. Feelings are most often noticed, interpreted, and acted upon when they are so intrusive that they interfere with ongoing behavior or thought. These states usually generate the interpretations that have the names *fear, depression, anger, guilt, shame, disgust,* and *joy.* The seminal claim in this chapter is that the interpretation selected is not completely determined by the brain profile or the quality of the feeling because the context and the person's past history are influential.

Research on the molecule oxytocin provides a good example of the influence of interpretation on a feeling generated by a brain state. Most scientists assume that oxytocin activates brain sites whose outputs automatically induce closer, more trusting relationships, whether between friends, lovers, spouses, or a parent and infant. However, Patricia Churchland and Piotr Winkielman of the University of California suggest that the relation between oxytocin and bonding to another does not mean that this outcome is the primary function of the molecule.[2] This molecule evolved to serve physiological functions, such as the "let-down reflex," which occurs when mothers nurse, and the contractions of the uterus during labor.

Oxytocin influences neuronal activity in many brain sites. Its primary effects include a lower and more variable heart rate; less intense smooth muscle contractions in the stomach, colon, and heart; greater secretion of serotonin; and a feeling of satiety. Oxytocin also enhances the expression of a gene that results in a reduced responsivity of receptors lying on the surface of neurons in the amygdala. A less aroused amygdala, which should lead to a feeling of relaxation, would increase the pleasure derived from many experiences. Orgasm, for example, is accompanied by a surge of oxytocin and a feeling of extreme relaxation.

A person's interpretation of a relaxed feeling, however, depends on the context. The feeling is likely to be interpreted as love or affection if one is interacting with a child, friend, spouse, or romantic partner. If the same feeling were to bubble up during a conversation with a stockbroker, the person might interpret the state as one of increased confidence and purchase a riskier security. If it occurred during dinner at a restaurant, the person might feel sated early in the meal and not order dessert. And if it occurred during a solitary hike in a flowering meadow on a lovely spring afternoon, the person might interpret the state as a oneness with nature. I suspect that if oxytocin were given to tennis players before a match, they would be more likely to lose the match, and, if given to individuals preparing to pray alone, they would report a more spiritual experience.

Oxytocin is first and foremost a relaxing molecule and secondarily a bonding molecule. That is why it facilitates labor and the let-down reflex in nursing mothers. Young adults given oxytocin describe themselves as more open to new ideas and display larger, not smaller, surges of blood flow to the amygdala when shown threatening scenes. Men administered oxytocin have a poorer memory for pictures of faces and houses because their relaxed state reduces their motivation to perform at a high level. Surprisingly, emotionally labile adults who are normally distrustful of others become even less trusting after given oxytocin. Put plainly, an increase in oxytocin can create a variety of emotional states. The one that emerges depends on the interpretation the person imposes on the relaxed feeling that the oxytocin generated. That interpretation, in turn, is influenced by the individual's prior history and always by the immediate setting, which could be a mother caring for her infant, a laboratory in which a college student must decide how generous to be with a stranger, or an empty beach at midnight as an adolescent looks up at a star-filled, moonless sky.[3]

Neuroscientists' assumption that a particular brain state provides a useful definition of an emotion has a partial origin in Darwin's writings. In *Expression of the Emotions in Man and Animals,* Darwin suggested that a small number of emotional states were automatically expressed in distinct arrangements of facial muscles—a claim that implied that these emotions were produced by patterns of brain activity responsible for the facial expressions. As Lisa Barrett of Northeastern University points out, Darwin also considered the possibility that some human facial expressions were vestigial and no longer sensitive indexes of an emotional state.[4]

Most changes in brain state do not generate a conscious feeling, and the small number that do are accompanied by a variety of interpretations. Hence, the brain state, considered alone, is an incomplete measure of an emotion. Studies of the excitability of the amygdala in humans, usually based on the amount of blood flow to this site, support this claim. Many scientists believe that activation of the amygdala in response to an event they classified as threatening implies the presence of fear. However, many adults who display a larger surge of blood flow to the amygdala when they see pictures of guns and snakes compared with pictures of smiling children and ice cream neither report a change in feeling nor show a fearful facial expression. The reason is that the amygdala responds to any unexpected event, especially if it is experienced infrequently. Because guns and snakes are encountered less often than smiling children and plates of ice cream, pictures of the former are more likely to activate the amygdala. This activation is apt to be a sign of surprise rather than fear—a suggestion supported by the fact that individuals usually show a decrease in heart rate to such pictures and not the increase in heart rate that typically accompanies fear.

A second problem is that many conditions unrelated to the person's feeling can activate the amygdala. A team of Italian scientists led by Barbara Basile produced automatic activation of the amygdala simply by stimulating the parasympathetic nervous system. I noted that most humans display a decrease in heart rate, a sign of parasympathetic activity, in reaction to unexpected or unfamiliar events, including snakes, guns, and faces with fearful or angry expressions.[5] The amygdala is also part of a circuit that mediates the movements of the eyes when individuals scan the different parts of a scene. These eye movements are usually more frequent in response to unexpected or unfamiliar events than to expected or familiar ones.

All adults, including those with a phobia of snakes, show decreasing activation of the amygdala when the same snakes, or other unpleasant scenes, are shown repeatedly. But the quieter amygdala does not necessarily mean that the adults had become less fearful, because if different snakes or unpleasant objects appear, the amygdala becomes active again.

Some individuals inherit a brain chemistry that constricts the brain's blood vessels. This condition is accompanied by smaller surges of blood flow to brain sites. Scientists who are unaware of this fact will interpret the reduced blood flow as meaning that these adults experience a less intense emotion in response to the stimulus presented.

Other problems confound the inferences about emotion based on blood flow evidence. A team of Japanese scientists led by Tsutomu Nakada found that the brain's response to an event involves at least two stages that occur within a half-second.[6] The brain reacts first to the meaningfulness of the event, defined by the number of representations recruited, and milliseconds later to its unexpectedness. Because neurons are usually more reactive to unexpected events than to expected ones, scientists measuring blood flow in reaction to pictures of snakes cannot know whether those who showed a large surge of blood flow to the amygdala found the snakes to be more meaningful, did not expect to see snakes, or experienced a state of fear. It is also possible that all three processes contributed to the greater blood flow in reaction to snakes than to smiling infants.

Another problem is that many events evoke a brief feeling that lasts about a second and then disappears. But there is little change in blood flow to a brain site during the initial second. The peak in the blood flow signal occurs about six seconds after the event occurred and, therefore, five seconds after a feeling may have vanished. The blood flow measure reflects a cascade of phenomena that include associations to the event, a possible feeling, and perhaps a private query as to why the scientist presented that particular stimulus.

Emile Bruneau and his colleagues at the Massachusetts Institute of Technology gathered evidence that supports this last conclusion.[7] Arabs and Israelis reading vignettes about fictitious Arabs or Israelis suffering pain or loss said they felt more compassion toward an adult from their own ethnic group than to one from the other group. But their blood flow to brain sites believed to be active when humans feel empathic were similar, whether they were reading about the suffering of someone from their group or about someone from the disliked group. This evidence implies that activation of these sites reflected the meaningfulness of the vignette rather than feelings of empathy.

Blood flow profiles are also affected by the person's genome, state of health, past history, posture, breathing pattern, idiosyncratic thoughts, and even social class. College students from different social-class backgrounds displayed different blood flow profiles to the amygdala and frontal lobe while looking at the same angry faces. Unfortunately, many investigators are indifferent to the social class of those on whom they gather brain measures.

The initial brain response is also influenced by physical features of the event that have nothing to do with its meaning. These features include its color, shape, angularity, and contrast in reflected light, as well as the properties of the laboratory setting. A pleasant odor in the scanning room, for example, affects the pattern of blood flow, as do the typical shapes, colors, and symmetries in pictures of guns and knives compared with the patterns in flowers and cakes. The former pictures have darker colors and more linear contours; the latter possess lighter colors and more curved contours. Moreover, human forms in paintings evoke blood flow patterns that differ from those evoked by photographs of humans because the visual cortex and amygdala respond to the physical differences between these two types of representations.

The supine posture that participants typically assume in the scanner is accompanied by a blood flow pattern to the brain that can be different from the pattern generated when the same individuals are sitting up or standing. An especially troubling issue is that scientists' inferences are based on the difference in the amount of blood flow to an emotional event compared with the blood flow to a baseline state or an emotionally neutral event. This strategy can lead to results that are difficult to interpret. In one study, women saw words intended to provoke past experiences marked by guilt, shame, or sadness and were asked to relive the emotion that had occurred earlier. The sites uniquely activated by reliving the emotion of guilt depended on whether the scientists subtracted the pattern of blood flow to shame plus sadness from the blood flow to guilt, or subtracted the blood flow to shame from the flow to guilt. Surprisingly, no brain site showed a unique pattern of activation to the reliving of shame.[8]

The problem with inferences based on subtraction of one blood flow magnitude from another is illustrated in the following scenario. Suppose that scientists could determine the relative but not the absolute weight of a typical Valencia orange by subtracting the weights of oranges from the weights of other fruits. If the average weight of ten oranges was compared with the weight of ten limes, the scientists would conclude that the oranges have substantial weight. If, however, they compared the weight of ten oranges with the weight of ten grapefruit, or the weight of a hundred limes, they would infer that oranges had relatively little weight.

This example is not unfair. Investigators interested in measuring fear typically subtract a person's blood flow to the amygdala while looking at happy faces from the flow when they are looking at fearful faces. They infer the presence of a fear state if the blood flow is greater to the fear faces. But a face with eyes and mouth wide-open, which are the critical features of a fearful face, is encountered less frequently than smiling faces. Hence, most adults are more surprised by faces with a fearful expression than by smiling faces. In addition, fear faces are more ambiguous than happy faces because the former are often interpreted as reflecting a state of surprise. Thus, the proper comparison for a fear face is not a happy face but another infrequent, ambiguous face—perhaps the face of a newborn infant with only the slightest suggestion of a smile. If this infant face produced the same level of blood flow as the fearful adult face, scientists would have to reconsider their past inference that fearful faces induce a fear state in observers.

This list does not exhaust the problems that trail the interpretations of blood flow. When a person is at rest, doing nothing (a condition known as a baseline, default state), there are usually large surges of blood flow to a circuit consisting of several brain sites because it is difficult to prevent a person from thinking. If one site in this circuit—for example, a location in the frontal lobe—was also activated by an emotional picture, the practice of subtracting the small increase in blood flow to this site while a person is looking at an emotional picture from the larger response during the baseline state would imply that this site made little or no contribution to the person's reaction to the emotional event. This situation poses a problem for investigators who attribute psychological states to individuals based on the differences between blood flow profiles.

Also relevant is the fact that the magnitude of blood flow to a site is a more accurate index of the amount of input to the neurons at that location than of the firing rate of those neurons when they send information to other sites. But the sending of information from one neuronal cluster to another is also critical for an emotion. For example, the output of neurons in the central nucleus of the amygdala is responsible for the bodily changes in heart rate and muscle tension that give rise to feelings that are often interpreted as anxiety. But the central nucleus receives fewer inputs than some brain sites that make a smaller contribution to the emotion of fear as well as other emotions.

Although I have written thus far that the amount of blood flow to a site is an index of neuronal activity, it is time for readers to appreciate what this measure reflects. Specifically, investigators are measuring changes in the amount of hemoglobin in the blood that lost its oxygen as a result of being used by the neurons at a particular site. Because the neural activity accompanying psychological processes usually generates far more oxygenated blood than the neurons require, the index of brain activity called the BOLD signal (standing for "blood oxygen level dependent signal") is a change in the proportion of venous blood containing hemoglobin shorn of its oxygen (following a stimulus or task) compared with the baseline value for this class of hemoglobin. A team at the University of Pittsburgh claims that the magnitude of the BOLD measure at a particular site happens to correlate with the amount of blood in the veins at a particular site before any stimulus is ever

1. The effect of unexpected events
2. Variation due to genome and history of the person
3. Physical features of the event
4. Use of difference scores with blood flow
5. Input measured more accurately by bloodflow than output
6. Artificiality of the scanner setting
7. Many brain sites activated
8. Blood supply not equal to all sites

FIGURE 7.2   **Problems accompanying reliance on blood flow as a basis for emotion**

presented. This important fact implies that individuals who ordinarily have more blood flowing in the veins at a site will display larger BOLD signals at that site, independent of any emotional reaction to the event presented.

Still another annoyance is that accurate inferences from the BOLD measure require participants to hold their head perfectly still and breathe at a regular rate while ignoring the noise created by the scanner. If they move their head by even a tiny amount, or begin to breathe at a rapid rate, the resulting blood flow patterns will imply reduced connectivity between frontal and parietal sites. Children and mentally ill patients find it difficult to maintain a perfectly still posture for the duration of an experiment, leading scientists to conclude, incorrectly, that their brains have a compromised connectivity. This difficulty is especially likely among children who have attention deficit hyperactivity disorder (ADHD) or autism. Finally, the loud noise the scanner makes creates a brain state that usually occurs when a person is trying to control an unpleasant stimulus. This defensive state differs from the person's usual state in most natural settings. (See Figure 7.2.)

All of these problems frustrate investigators trying to infer the presence of an emotion from the BOLD signals to varied sites. Investigators at Heidelberg University measured blood flow in healthy adults who possessed the alleles of a gene that either increases or decreases the excitability of the amygdala. Those with the allele that excite the amygdala showed a larger BOLD signal from the amygdala when a conditioned stimulus signaled an imminent electric shock. But neither the allele nor the BOLD signal bore any relation to participants' reports of feeling anxious or their skin conductance reactions to the conditioned stimulus. This dissociation between the brain state and a person's conscious emotional state is not surprising because, as I noted, the BOLD measure is a rough approximation of the amount of neuronal activity at a location—and the amount of neuronal activity, in turn, is an equally rough index of a person's thoughts and feelings. Hence, it is impossible to know a person's emotional state by examining only BOLD signals. Yet several respected neuroscientists wrote essays in 2012 claiming that the psychological states named by the popular emotional words—*anxiety, fear, anger, happiness*—could be inferred from BOLD signals.

Before assuming that the BOLD signal accompanying the presentation of angry or fearful faces reflects an emotion, scientists should perform the following experiment. Show adults a series of faces with fearful, angry, disgusted, happy, and neutral expressions and ask each person to indicate, using a key, the moment he or she experiences any change in feeling to a face and how long the feeling lasted. Obviously, there will be considerable variation in the frequency and duration of these feelings. The scientist's task is to examine the BOLD signals and determine who experienced a feeling in reaction to a particular type of face and what the quality of that feeling was. If the investigators were correct about 70 percent of the time, I would be persuaded that the BOLD signal is a useful index of an emotion. To my knowledge no investigator has performed such a study and met the 70 percent criterion.

Natural scientists studying the relation between two phenomena usually have a good understanding of one of them and exploit that knowledge to illuminate the more mysterious one. For example, biologists know that genes are composed of strings of DNA molecules, and they use that knowledge as a scaffold to further their understanding of a disease they believe is inherited. The scientists who use BOLD signals to understand an emotion do not work with this advantage. They have an incomplete understanding of how the brain works, are unsure of the degree to which blood flow to a site reflects the degree of neuronal activity in that site, and are unable to specify the intrinsic features that clearly distinguish emotions from other psychological processes. It is chastening to remember that nineteenth-century scientists interpreted the decreased blood flow to the finger when a person saw the word *serpent* as a sign of fear. We now know that this response reflects the deceleration in heart rate that accompanies attention.

For all these reasons, it is not possible, at least at present, to rely only on a profile of brain activity in reaction to pictures, words, or tasks to infer the presence of an emotional state. This judgment is shared with several neuroscientists, who would probably agree with the following comment by the mathematician Frank Ramsey: "What we can't say, we can't say, and we can't whistle it either."

DESCRIBING EMOTIONS

Ramsey's statement applies to an equally critical evaluation of the assumption that the words people use to describe how they feel, in the present or past, are faithful reflections of their psychological state. One obvious problem is that infants and animals cannot talk and young children have a limited vocabulary. Additionally, adults often use emotional words in the absence of any feeling and fail to use emotional language when they do have a feeling. Americans habitually say "I love you" to a spouse, lover, or child without any feeling at all. On the other hand, hundreds of text messages sent by Manhattan residents on September 11, 2001, contained no emotional words.

Simone Kuhn and Jurgen Gallinat of Ghent University found that verbal reports of pleasant feelings were accompanied by activation of the same seven brain areas, whether the brain was measured at a time when the individuals said they were experiencing a pleasant state or at another time when no incentive for pleasure was present.[9] This implies that the brain measure was reflecting the person's cognitive judgment of how they believed they felt rather than the feeling that occurred the moment they were exposed to the pleasure-producing event.

Some languages have no words for certain feelings. Indeed, many languages have no words for the emotions that in English are called *awe, wonder,* or *alienated,* even though the individuals in these communities might experience these psychological states. The Yucatec language, spoken by some Mayan Indians, does not have separate words for anger and disgust. Nonetheless, these Indians can distinguish between the feelings evoked by being insulted and those evoked by the sight of rotting food, and they can distinguish between the facial expressions evoked by these events. Other examples abound. Residents of Sumatra use the word *malu* to describe the feeling accompanying the commission of a mistake made in front of others, as well as the feeling that pierces consciousness when a person is in the presence of someone with much higher status. Americans would use the word *shame* for the former but not for the latter.

Orhan Pamuk, the Turkish writer who won a Nobel Prize, notes that residents of Istanbul experience an emotion they call *huzun,* which is the mood evoked when one reflects on the glory their city lost after the fall of the Ottoman Empire.[10] I suspect that most Americans have not experienced a similar emotion because few Americans who live in large cities—for example, New York, Boston, Chicago, San Francisco, and Los Angeles—have such a strong identification with their community.

Most languages have more distinctive words for unpleasant states, objects, and people than for pleasant ones. For example, English has fewer words for the desired trait of honesty than for its opposite, a category that includes *dishonest, deceitful, shrewd, sly,* and *cunning.* English also has more words for unpleasant than for pleasant emotions. One reason for this asymmetry is that distinctly unpleasant feelings are typically less frequent and more salient than pleasant ones. Hence, the former are more likely to recruit attention and the invention of a verbal label.

This asymmetry among emotional words is an instance of a more general principle: infrequent variations on what is familiar recruit more names than frequent variations on the familiar. English has fewer words for good weather, despite the frequent variations in the temperature, wind velocity, and pattern of cloud cover, than for the less frequent variations on bad weather that include the terms *shower, rain storm, blizzard, ice storm, hurricane,* and *tornado.* English has no adjective that describes how most people move, but it invented the terms *graceful* and *clumsy* to describe individuals who move in unusual ways.

It is always difficult to know whether a feeling accompanies the use of an emotional word. Adults who are versatile in two languages—say, English acquired as a child and Italian learned as a second language in college—experience a feeling and show a brain response only when they swear in English, because there are no visceral schemata linked to the Italian swear words.[11] No emotional word is linked to only one brain or psychological state. Six different states associated with the word *guilt* are possible if we distinguish, first, between inappropriate actions for which an agent accepts responsibility and actions for which the agent feels no responsibility. Within each of these two categories, the agent can be concerned with a critical evaluation by others; an evaluation that the self imposes, excluding self-blame; or an evaluation accompanied by self-blame. This combination yields six emotions, each requiring a different name. Figure 7.3 contains a suggested set of terms that English-speaking adults might apply to these six states of mind. Other languages may use different words, but the specific words are less important than the distinctive feelings and likely actions provoked by the varied interpretations of the feelings.

	Self Responsible	**Self Not Responsible**
Concern with others' judgment	Blend of shame and guilt	Shame
Concern with the self's evaluation, no self-blame	Regret	Survivor guilt
Concern with the self's evaluation, with self-blame	Guilt	Sad

FIGURE 7.3   Six emotional states derived from the evaluation of personal responsibility

There are two reasons why a few psychologists regard the unpleasant feeling following social rejection as resembling the brain state produced by physical pain. English speakers often use the word *painful* to describe both states, and the same two brain sites are activated by both experiences. Those who describe a friend's rejection as painful, however, are employing a metaphor, as T. S. Eliot did when he called April cruel. The sensory components of physical pain are not shared by social rejection, and the evaluation of both states as unpleasant applies to a variety of experiences that are unrelated to pain or rejection—for example, hearing the telephone ring at 2:00 A.M., biting into a cold hamburger, or losing one's car keys. Sites in my motor and visual cortex are activated when I tie my shoes, pick up food with a fork, pet a whining puppy, feed an infant, take a pill for a headache, and hammer a nail. But these acts are not the products of the same psychological state and are not accompanied by the same brain circuits, even though they share a small number of activated brain sites.

A serious disadvantage of treating words as faithful reflections of feelings is the fact that most languages have very few words that name blends of feelings—for example, the state of an adolescent who, as he swears at a stranger who pushed him, simultaneously anticipates the stranger's retaliation. The failure of most languages to capture the quality and intensity of blends of feelings may be due to the fact that the brain and mind favor a single perception over an average of two events that occur at the same time. If the right eye sees one-half of the face of Bill Clinton and one-half of a house while the left eye sees the other half of the face and house, most participants would report seeing alternating perceptions of Clinton's face and the house rather than a blend of the two objects. The brain is biased toward representing a single coherent object.

Analogously, humans, who dislike ambiguity, want to know the best name for a blend of feelings. English contains mainly single words for feelings, but no term that describes a blend of the feelings that usually are interpreted as anxiety and shame. The individual, demanding resolution of the ambiguity, selects one of these words as the best interpretation of the state generated when, for example, one accidentally spills coffee on a table while being interviewed for a job.

The popular English words for emotions, therefore, resemble the abstract botanical concept *plant.* If someone says "I saw a plant yesterday," the listener cannot know if the speaker is referring to a tree in a forest, a flower in a garden, a lily pad on a pond, or algae on an old log. Unlike scientists who study emotion, physicists and chemists do not rely on words that the members of a community use in everyday conversation as bases for fruitful concepts. They invent new words, such as *black hole* and *oxidation,* that accommodate the evidence.

Scientists interested in the biological foundations of an emotion often invest many hours measuring a neurotransmitter or brain profile and then, surprisingly, invest only a few minutes in evaluating the emotion by asking individuals how they feel. The asymmetry in effort is analogous to using an atomic clock to determine whether a person is walking rapidly, at a normal pace, or slowly. Put simply, the popular words for emotions eliminate too many important features to be adequate bases for understanding. An emotional word, like a still photo of a dancer, transforms a dynamic event that changes with time into an event that is frozen in time and space.

Psychologists who continue to rely only on informants' words to understand human emotions are making as serious an error as the early astrophysicists who relied only on what they could see to make inferences about the cosmos. Francis Bacon understood that words are free agents that can assume different meanings across cultures and historical eras. Samuel Beckett captured this mischievous property of words when he urged readers to "bore one hole after another" into every statement "until what lurks behind it—be it something or nothing—begins to seep through."

BEHAVIORAL INDEXES OF EMOTIONS

The measurement of behaviors, including facial expressions, as the criteria for an emotion suffers as many problems as measures of the brain or verbal descriptions. One problem is that individuals who display an altered brain state and simultaneously experience a feeling do not always display a change in behavior or facial expression. In addition, individuals vary in their susceptibility to changes in facial expression. Chinese infants are less likely than Japanese or Caucasian infants to show a distinctive facial expression in reaction to an event that should have pro-voked a feeling in all infants.[12]

Adults often greet a passerby with a reflex smile that is unaccompanied by any feeling. Moreover, the correct interpretation of a facial expression is not always obvious. Brain profiles and facial expressions imply different psychological states in young men trying to enhance their emotional state as they look at unpleasant scenes.[13] Psychologists could not rely on facial expressions to decide which adults in an audience watching an erotic film were sexually aroused. It is even difficult to tell the difference between the faces of adults having an orgasm and the faces of adults in pain. In both states the eyes are closed, the eyebrows are lowered, and the mouth is open.

Nonetheless, many psychologists continue to follow Darwin in claiming that the face reflects six universal emotions: fear, surprise, anger, happy, sad, and disgust. Darwin seemed to think about these states as if they were anatomical features, like a bird's beak or a tortoise's carapace. On reflection, Darwin's exclusive focus on the face as a sensitive index of an emotion is surprising. In his earlier, magisterial thesis on evolution, he did not rely on only one source of evidence as the basis for an important concept.

It is also difficult to understand why Darwin posited a small set of universal emo-tions, for he did not suggest in *The Origin of Species* that nature was populated with a small number of basic species. Darwin began writing the book on emotions soon after *The Origin* was completed. Perhaps his worry over the public's reception to the book on evolution, which contained many speculative sections unsupported by evidence, motivated him to base his claims on objective observations that anyone could make by looking at faces. The claim that fear is a universal emotion that can be verified by examining the muscles of the face was less controversial than the sug-gestion that humans evolved from apes.

A POSSIBLE RESOLUTION

The evidence implies that neither brain states, words, nor behaviors, when consid-ered alone, provide a satisfactory measure of an emotional state. That is probably why the two authors of a review of research on emotion in an issue of the *Annual Re-view of Psychology* never defined this term.[14] They let readers decide on the meaning they preferred. This semantic permissiveness leaves scientists with two alternative strategies in the study of emotions.

One action plan calls for combining a class of provocative events with biological or behavioral measures. This strategy requires investigators to nominate the major types of provocative events that evoke particular brain profiles or actions among members of a culture. An initial collection of provocations would include the following: events that interrupt an ongoing activity or plan for action, unexpected events that are immediately understood, unexpected events that are not immediately understood, gentle physical contact, violations of a moral standard, the completion of an activity requiring effort, praise, loss of property, loss of social relationships, actions by another that violate a person's moral standard, events warning of possible harm, events implying possible distress, events promising sensory pleasure, and events implying contamination. However, until scientists measure the biological and/or behavioral reactions to each of these provocations, the validity of this suggestion remains uncertain.

The second strategy, which I favor, is to first gather evidence on the relations among the elements of a cascade that begins with a provocative event that generates a brain state and is followed by a feeling, an interpretation, and, on some occasions, a behavior. After these data are gathered, which will take some time, scientists can look for meaningful clusters and invent the best names for them. I suspect that this evidence will require new concepts that take into account the nature of the provocative event and the setting, the brain profile, the subsequent feeling, and the imposed interpretation. It is unlikely that the popular words *fear, sad, angry, disgust,* and *happy* will be able to explain the new evidence. Although humans find these words useful in everyday conversation, they are, like the terms *good* and *beautiful,* too ambiguous for scientific inquiry.

One issue warrants attention before we turn to the development of emotions. Scientists favor explanations that require the smallest number of concepts—a style of argument called parsimony. Loyalty to the principle of parsimony has led some psychologists to posit a small number of basic emotions and a large number of less basic states. Membership in the former, privileged category is usually based on seven features. Basic emotions occur in all societies, contribute to survival, are accompanied by a salient feeling, are associated with a biologically prepared brain profile, have a pleasant or unpleasant valence, affect social relationships, and are accompanied by a facial or postural response. These criteria explain why fear, sadness, shame, anger, joy, and disgust are nominated as basic emotions. There are many universal feeling states that do not meet all seven of the criteria for a basic emotion. The states that accompany a feeling of obligation to a friend, an unexpected sound that is not understood, seeing a blood-red sunset, and the prospect of a rainy day with nothing to do evoke similar feelings in members of all societies. The decision to exclude these states from the category of basic emotions has no sound basis in theory or fact.

I suspect that the absence of a distinctive facial expression is one reason why an emotion is not regarded as basic. The facial expressions confer a material reality to a semantic concept and, in so doing, persuade scholars of its significance. The authors of the biblical Genesis seemed to share this bias. They wrote that God gave life to Adam by transferring His breath to what was inert matter. Apparently, these religious scholars did not feel comfortable declaring that an omnipotent God was able to give life to the first human without the help of any material substance. The states we call *serenity, nostalgia, guilt, lust,* and *ambivalence,* which have no specific facial profile, seem to be immaterial products of mind and for that reason are presumably less important.

The attractiveness of a tidy list of basic emotions resembles the belief held by the sixteenth-century physician Paracelsus that the properties of all natural phenomena could be derived from three substances: sulfur, mercury, and salt. The hope of finding a small set of basic emotions that transcends time and culture is the product of a misplaced admiration for physics. Although physicists believe in the possibility of discovering the small number of concepts that represent the foundations of all matter, life scientists view nature from the opposite direction and continue to posit more, rather than fewer, categories for natural phenomena. The original concept of a gene, invented in 1900, has been supplemented with concepts like exon, intron, enhancer, promoter, transposon, and microRNA. The features of matter, such as photons and electrons, are fixed. Biological entities are continually changing. Emotions are biological phenomena!

Rather than assume a small set of basic emotions, it will be more fruitful to regard all emotional states as subject to historical change, analogous to the origin, burgeoning, and extinction of a species. The emotion that a naked Greek youth in 400 B.C.E. experienced when he failed to suppress his sexual feelings when his tutor embraced him has been transformed by history into the emotion of a contemporary Greek youth who is teased by peers for being gay. The competence required to pick up a stone is not more basic than the ability to prune a tree. But some cultures do not have pruning shears.

Many Americans reflecting on the events of the past six decades experience an emotion that combines a recognition of life's unpredictability, the need to be suspicious of strangers, an inability to understand the meaning of their existence, and a fraying moral certainty over values that demand an unquestioned commitment. This emotional state, for which there is not yet a name, is the product of a sequence of historical events that began with the industrial revolution and was followed by bureaucratic economies, densely populated cities, geographic mobility, value diversity in a community, and a demand for tolerance toward all ethical positions—facilitated, in part, by the disseminating power of the Internet and television.

A large number of modern films, novels, and plays depict life as a series of disconnected experiences impinging on individuals without a compass as they sail alone in a small boat on a choppy sea trying to get to a safe port, unaware of the many events that can disrupt their plans. Words like *confused, uncertain,* and *spiritually empty* come close to describing, but do not fully capture, a common contemporary emotion that is not considered basic.

The cartoons in *The New Yorker* date the origin of this emotion to the early 1950s, when cartoonists began to satirize the boredom of work and the spiritual vacuum of modern life. One cartoon depicted an older man telling another: "I did my job and grabbed my pile but no voice at eventide has cried 'Well done.'" Another illustrated a group of men in business suits enclosed in a cattle corral and a man outside the corral saying to a colleague: "In 6 months these MBAs will be ready for market." Although many Americans who experience this feeling do not understand it, they are adjusting to it.

The ancient Chinese wanted to understand the changing properties of phenomena as they were perceived. They decided that these properties reflected a balance between the forces of yang and yin. As one force waxed, the other waned. By contrast, the Greeks, who assumed that surface phenomena were deceptive, invented concepts for the unchanging, invisible elements that were the important foundation of what was perceived. Psychologists who persist in searching for the defining features of fear, anger, and joy are carrying on the Greek tradition. The Chinese scholars would have treated these states as the product of a balance among feelings. Neuroscientists recognize that every brain state is the outcome of a competition between excitatory and inhibitory forces. This fact implies that many emotions are the final product of a cascade of events that generates two or three feelings competing for the privilege of being the one selected as the basis for an interpretation.

THE DEVELOPMENT OF EMOTIONS

The emotional states of infants have to differ from those of adolescents and adults inasmuch as infants are not conscious of their psychological states, do not possess the abilities needed to interpret bodily feelings, and neither reflect on the past nor anticipate the future. Hence, they cannot experience the states implied by the popular English words *anxiety, shame, guilt, disgust, nostalgia, pride,* and *hopelessness.* They do, however, experience sensations and behave in response to those feelings.

Infants less than three months old feel warmth, cold, hunger, and pain; are alerted by and detect changes in all sensory modalities; and display a limited number of facial expressions. However, they do not consistently relate these sensations to acquired schemata and do not impose interpretations on them. Their facial and behavioral reactions are, most of the time, biologically prepared reflexes to particular events. A facial grimace in reaction to a drop of lemon juice placed on the tongue, a smile to sugar water, a startle to an unexpected sound, and a cry to a sudden change in temperature are the outcomes of brain circuits established prenatally and should not be equated with the adult emotions of disgust, happiness, fear, or anger.

Young infants distinguish between pleasant and unpleasant sensations and create visceral schemata that will contribute later to the meaning of the semantic concepts *good* and *bad.* Unexpected sights or sounds evoke an orienting response that is a component of the emotion of surprise that occurs in older children.

Between three and seven months of age, infants relate an event to an acquired schema more regularly and experience a feeling that resembles the state of understanding present in older children. The four-month-old's spontaneous smile upon seeing a face is one sign of this state. Infants occasionally cry in reaction to unfamiliar events they cannot relate to a schema—for example, hearing a human voice speaking sentences but not seeing a human nearby. These infants seem to be asking "What is that?" This state of event uncertainty shares features with the older child's emotion of fear, but it does not contain anticipations of harm or inferences about the origin of the feeling—yet another instance of the 90 percent rule.

Infants during the second half of the first year not only relate an event to a relevant schema but also maintain both representations in a working-memory circuit for intervals up to thirty seconds. Their enhanced working memory allows them to anticipate what might happen in the next few seconds or minutes. Infants are now capable of a state of excitement when their mother plays peek-a-boo with them. This new cognitive competence expands the state of event uncertainty to a larger number of events, including an approaching stranger and separation from the mother.

Eight-month-olds are capable of a response uncertainty that originates in an inability to retrieve or implement an action needed to deal with an event. Both event and response uncertainty share features with the emotion of fear in older children.

The element missing from the fear that ten-year-olds experience is a representation of the harmful consequences of the event. The state that accompanies an inability to do something as a stranger approaches is not equivalent to the state of older children who anticipate that the approaching stranger might harm them. Hence, uncertainty and fear are not synonyms.

The completion of a difficult action sequence directed at a desired goal creates a feeling psychologists call pride or the pleasure of mastery. Eight-month-olds who finish building a tower of four blocks after several minutes of effort recognize that their behavior matches a self-generated goal. The resulting feeling resembles the feeling older children interpret as pride. Finally, once infants have passed the transition at seven to nine months, they become better able to regulate bouts of distress because of the enhanced influence of the frontal lobe on states of arousal.

Once inference, language, a moral sense, and consciousness have emerged during the second or third years, children are capable of a number of new feelings. Two-year-olds now impose interpretations on some feelings that contain the same words their parents use. Two-year-olds may say "I not cry now, I happy," "It's dark, I'm scared," or "I feel bad." The emotions of empathy and shame are possible at this age because of the capacity to infer the thoughts and feelings of others.

Preschool children, aged three to six years, experience many, but still not all, of the adult's emotional repertoire. They integrate past with present and can experience the feeling of self-blame that English calls guilt. They compare some of their personal characteristics with those of others and are vulnerable to feelings they interpret as jealousy, envy, or pride. A distinct feeling is generated when events violate children's understanding of their personal properties. Six-year-old boys who have learned that they usually dominate peers become aroused if they encounter a boy they cannot dominate because this experience is inconsistent with the semantic networks for their personality traits. The resulting feelings are interpreted as anger, disappointment, frustration, or shame.

The emotion that English calls disgust represents two quite different states that emerge at different times. The most common, which appears first, is evoked by events with particular visual, olfactory, or gustatory features. Rotting food, vomit, and feces are the usual causes of this category of disgust. The reaction to these objects is universal, appears first during the preschool years, and is accompanied by a distinct facial expression, occasionally with a feeling of nausea.

The distinctive facial expression that accompanies disgust is mediated by the insula, which also contributes to facial grimaces and frowns. A small proportion of young infants spontaneously display grimaces and frowns for no obvious reason. My colleagues and I found that these unusual infants are more vulnerable than others to extremely labile emotions during later childhood. Because some four-month-olds wrinkle their nose to dissonant musical chords, but not to feces or rotten food, it appears that the emotion of disgust in reaction to bodily products and rotted food requires experience and, perhaps, some of the cognitive abilities that are the result of brain maturation.

Preadolescents, from six to twelve years of age, speak many adult emotional words. For example, they will use the word *regret* when they think about desirable events that did not happen because of a failure to act. Equally important, school-age children evaluate the moral status of their feelings and interpretations. Some children feel guilty over their anger toward an affectionate mother who had a good reason to punish them or to make a demand. On some occasions this guilt can lead to serious symptoms.

A father once asked me for help in understanding why his ten-year-old daughter had suddenly developed a fear of dying. After interviewing the girl I learned that both parents were physicians who left the home early each day to work at their respective hospitals. They had no choice but to give their older daughter the responsibility of feeding and dressing her younger sister and getting her ready for school. The ten-year-old girl began to resent this burden but felt guilty over her anger toward loving parents, who were engaged in benevolent work. The guilt became sufficiently intense to provoke a need for punishment, which assumed the form of a fear of dying.

The emotion generated by failure to honor the standards appropriate to one's gender differs from the state that accompanies willful violation of a moral standard on lying, cheating, or harming another. In the latter states, children realize they could have avoided the violation. In the former, they believe they had no choice. A twelve-year-old boy who does not possess the muscular build he believes is expected for males knows that this condition is not his fault. Hence, he is likely to experience shame rather than guilt.

The second form of disgust emerges during this later stage. Children can experience disgust when an object violates a moral standard because it is in an inappropriate setting—for example, a dead fly on a dish of ice cream. This form of disgust is less often accompanied by the facial reaction displayed in response to rotted food or feces, even though English speakers use the same word. In one study, children ranging in age from three to twelve years told an adult they liked apple juice. The adult then put a sterilized dead grasshopper in a glass of apple juice, drank some of the juice, and asked each child if he or she would drink some of the juice. Most children older than age six refused, whereas close to one-half of the younger children agreed to drink the juice. Neither a glass of apple juice nor a sterilized dead grasshopper on a piece of cloth evokes disgust. But a sterilized dead grasshopper that has touched a glass of apple juice alters the glass and can evoke an avoidance response that is presumably based on a feeling interpreted as disgust.[15]

The central point is that objects that do not provoke disgust when they are in an appropriate setting can do so if their placement in an inappropriate setting violates a moral standard. Few children experience disgust when they see a pile of dirt in a backyard. A pile of dirt on a dinner plate, however, evokes this emotion because a dinner plate is an inappropriate context for dirt and dirty plates are a violation of a moral standard. If an object in an inappropriate setting does not violate a moral code—for example, someone slipped on a banana peel and is sprawled on the floor—disgust does not occur.

The evocation of this later form of disgust requires an evaluation of the appropriateness of an action by a specific actor in a specific setting. A fifteen-year-old girl who is fondled by a boy in a school hall is more likely to become angry than disgusted because she knows that boys often behave this way in this context. The same girl fondled by her father at home is apt to experience disgust because this action is inappropriate and a serious violation of proper paternal behavior. This type of disgust evokes ideas of contamination and pollution. A surgeon covered in a patient's blood does not feel contaminated; a woman covered with the blood of the man who raped her does. History alters the appropriateness—and, therefore, the probability of experiencing—the emotion of disgust due to a feeling of contamination. The reduction, over the past century, in the intensity of disgust felt by adolescent girls performing oral sex on a boyfriend is an example.

The two meanings of the English word *disgust* share one feature: both involve acts that are extremely inappropriate in the settings in which they occur. Members of most societies believe that a person's bodily products ought not to be observed by others. Hence, secretions from the nose, mouth, genitals, anus, or stomach that can be seen, smelled, or touched by another are inappropriate, except when one is ill and being tended by a nurse at a hospital or a relative at home. The two kinds of disgust are likely to be accompanied by different brain states, feelings, and behaviors. A man who is ill and vomits on his shirt at a cocktail party is likely to evoke a brain state, feeling, and action in observers that are unlike the reactions generated in the same observers who see the same man unshaven and dressed in a bathing suit at a funeral.

1. Infancy: Feelings of warmth, cold, pain, hunger, excitement, and uncertainty in reaction to unexpected events.
2. The second year: Empathy, some forms of anxiety, and initial interpretations of some feelings
3. Two to six years: Shame, guilt, jealousy, sadness, happiness
4. Six to ten years: Most adult emotions possible, including disgust
5. Adolescence: Add the emotions of cognitive dissonance, hopelessness, and romantic love

FIGURE 7.4   The stages in development of emotion

Early adolescents between twelve and fifteen years of age are capable of most of the emotional repertoire of adults. As noted in Chapter 5, adolescents who detect semantic inconsistencies in a set of related beliefs are vulnerable to the emotion that psychologists call cognitive dissonance. The ability to appreciate that uncontrollable events can interfere with the self's plans renders adolescents susceptible to the emotions English calls *helpless, despairing,* or *impotent* if the individual believes he has no way to cope with the situation.

The increase at puberty in the brain's secretion of dopamine helps to explain the heady, often unrealistic optimism that many youth display. This emotion could be due, in part, to the increased muscle tone generated by this molecule. Even some older adults temporarily feel that they can conquer the world after an hour of strenuous exercise. The increased secretion of sex hormones at the same age evokes more intense feelings of sexual arousal—feelings that, when directed at certain others, become the emotions known in English as *horny, infatuated,* or *love.* (For a summary of the stages of emotional development, see Figure 7.4.)

This discussion of emotional development contains three seminal suggestions. The first and most important is that new interpretations of feelings, as well as new feelings, emerge as novel cognitive competences, which are dependent on brain growth, appear during the first fifteen years. Freud reversed this cause-effect sequence by assuming that emotions were the causes of the cognitive advances.

Second, the unexpectedness of an experience potentiates its power to evoke strong feeling. Artists, composers, writers, and film producers exploit this principle. The events that are unexpected change over the course of development. Young infants do not expect to see strangers; loss of an affectionate relationship with another is more of a surprise to children than to adolescents; being a victim of bullying or rape is unexpected during the early school years. The "sophomore slump" that is common in college students is fueled, in part, by a reduction in the novelty of the setting.

Third, the same event can produce different feelings and interpretations during different developmental stages. A mother's frown of disapproval alerts a four-month-old, creates event uncertainty in an eight-month-old, shame in a three-year-old, and anger in an adolescent who believes he is too old to be criticized by a parent. That is why we cannot use the same words to name the emotional states of infants, children, and adolescents exposed to the same objective incentive.

Scientists are far from possessing a satisfying understanding of the nature and measurement of emotional states. Hopefully, the discovery of the patterns of provocative events and biological reactions that generate particular feelings and interpretations will provide more fruitful ways to think about emotion. The words for many of these to-be-discovered patterns are missing from the vocabularies of existing languages. That should not be surprising. The vocabularies of experienced hunters and farmers do not contain the concepts that biologists need to explain evolution. Similarly, there is no good reason to assume that the words people use each day to describe their feelings to friends contain all the important concepts needed to construct a better understanding of emotional phenomena.

Finally, it is useful to recognize that historical events both add and eliminate emotional states. The events of the past seven hundred years have made it difficult for contemporary Europeans to experience the emotion created by believing that the Devil has occupied the soul, while making it much easier to experience the emotion of anomie.

A richer understanding of emotions will require the gathering of a great deal of new evidence. The currently popular English words for emotions are inadequate for research because they fail to specify the origin of each state and too few words name blends of feelings. Seminal concepts in physics, chemistry, and biology—for example, *quark, methylation,* and *codon*—were not dictionary entries when they were invented. I am certain that future scientists will discover evidence requiring the invention of emotional terms that are more faithful reflections of the complexity of this domain than the current collection of contextually naked words.

CHAPTER EIGHT

Mental Illness:
A Modern Epidemic

The concept of mental illness joins morality and emotion as a third human property whose uncertain definition isn't simply an arcane debate among academics. Four of every ten American adolescents between ages thirteen and seventeen in 2010 described moods or actions that met the psychiatric criteria for a mental disorder. Although most of the symptoms were mild in severity, the media's hyping of the large number of troubled adolescents worries parents, professionals, and the broader society. Defusing that worry when possible—and dealing with it when necessary—requires a clear definition of mental illness and a better understanding of its many causes.[1]

The number of children, adolescents, and adults diagnosed with a mental illness increased substantially over the past thirty years. The introduction of new genes cannot explain this fact because mutations do not occur that quickly. This leaves us with several complementary explanations.

AN EPIDEMIC'S ROOTS

At least a half-dozen societal conditions have contributed to the high frequency of professional diagnoses of mental illness. We shall see that these diagnoses are judgments influenced by the values of the professionals making the diagnosis and the patients who seek help with a problem. One collection of conditions involves the increased number of children who live with a divorced or unmarried working mother, attend poor-quality public schools, or receive electronic messages from troubled friends describing their anxieties, drug use, acts of self-injury, depressed moods, or suicide attempts. It is easy to imagine how any of these circumstances, alone or in combination, could contribute to anxiety, depression, restlessness and inattentiveness in school, or abuse of alcohol and drugs. The German psychiatrist Emil Kraepelin offered a similar suggestion in 1908 following a sharp rise in mental illness brought on, he believed, by growth in the size of cities, increased rates of urban poverty, and a faster pace of life.

Changes in the economies of developed nations represent a second set of conditions. In particular, the workplace has become more dependent on complex technologies than it was a hundred years earlier. Many young adults with less than twelve years of formal education in 1900 found secure jobs and lived a life of dignity. The current generation needs the knowledge expected of a graduate of a high-performing high school in order to possess the technical skills that a modern economy requires. Youths who appear to be inattentive and restless in the classroom are often referred to a physician, psychologist, or psychiatrist who diagnoses them with ADHD and prescribes the drug Ritalin. Their grandparents, many of whom did not have to remain in school for twelve years, lacked the opportunity to display restless, inattentive behavior and were able to avoid this diagnosis.

A third contribution lies with the more permissive criteria that clinicians are using when they diagnose a mental illness. When physicians believe there is a way to treat an illness, the diagnosis of that illness rises in frequency. Pharmaceutical companies are manufacturing an increasing number of drugs advertised as effective ways to alleviate adult anxiety or depression. The psychiatrists who assume that bouts of anxiety or depression in children are essentially similar to the adult symptoms find it easy to arrive at the same judgment and give shy or depressed children the same drugs they prescribe for adult patients.

Advances in biology and medicine, as well as better diets, have reduced the incidence of—or, in some cases, eliminated—the childhood diseases of measles, mumps, chicken pox, small pox, polio, whooping cough, diphtheria, worms, and rickets. As a result, pediatricians spend more of their time with parents who are worried about their child's disobedience, aggression, or shyness. A century earlier most parents would have been concerned with their child's physical illness and would not have worried about shyness or disobedience if the child had a life-threatening infectious disease.

State and federal laws represent a fifth contribution. If anxiety, depression, restlessness, and awkward social behavior were diseases with a biological foundation, the families of children with these symptoms would be entitled to the same resources given to parents who have a child with diabetes or cancer. Many physicians cooperate with parental requests by diagnosing shy children with social anxiety disorder, restless children with ADHD, and children with unusual styles of social interaction as autistic. Because many psychiatrists assume that these conditions have a partial origin in abnormal genes or brains, their families can request public funds for treatment.

A final contribution is the need for a reliable diagnosis of a mental illness, which insurance companies require before they pay a physician. Sixty years ago, the psychiatrist's guess regarding the cause of a symptom was intrinsic to the diagnosis. Clinicians included past history and family circumstances, along with the patient's posture, voice, facial expression, and verbal complaints, before arriving at a diagnosis. An adolescent girl who complained of insomnia and nightmares was diagnosed as suffering from a hysterical neurosis only if she was anxious over her sexual feelings and motives.

Unfortunately, psychiatrists often disagreed about the causes of a symptom. This poor reliability of diagnoses was embarrassing enough that the professional organization representing psychiatrists asked a committee of experts in the late 1970s to invent definitions of illness that were based primarily on patients' verbal descriptions of their symptoms. The causes became irrelevant. Before the publication of these definitions, only 4 percent of Americans were classified as suffering from an anxiety disorder. Twenty years later the proportion had risen to 30 percent.

The sharp rise in the diagnosis of autism, from one in a thousand early in the last century to one in a hundred in 2012, illustrates one of the unfortunate consequences of relying only on symptoms. The book that contains the current list of illnesses—the fourth edition of the *Diagnostic and Statistical Manual of Mental Disorders* (DSM-IV)—describes 201 mental disorders.

The new strategy worked: diagnoses did become more reliable. However, because psychiatrists ignored the causes of a symptom, the prescribed therapy was based only on symptoms, independent of their etiology. Cardiologists, by contrast, understand that there are many reasons why patients might complain of chest pain, and they treat each cause differently.

1. Changes in social and economic conditions
2. Permissive criteria in diagnoses
3. Availability of many drugs
4. Reduction in the infectious diseases of childhood
5. Treating anxiety and sadness as abnormal
6. Laws requiring public funds to aid families with a child who has a psychological disorder
7. Sole reliance on symptoms in making a diagnosis

FIGURE 8.1   Reasons for the increased prevalence of mental illness

All of these factors came together like a perfect storm to create what appears to be an epidemic of mental illness among children and adults. (See Figure 8.1.) Alice was asked in Lewis Carroll's *Through the Looking Glass,* "What's the use of their having names if they don't answer to them?" "No use to them," Alice answered. "But it is useful to the people who name them." My criticism of the exclusive reliance on symptoms in defining disorders is less harsh than the one written in 2012 by Allen Frances and Thomas Widiger, who suggested that the current hodge-podge of illness categories is hampering research because each illness can be the result of different causes. They defined mental illness as the phenomena clinicians treat, scientists investigate, faculty teach, and insurance companies pay for. Their definition reminded me of an earlier, equally unsatisfactory definition of intelligence as "whatever the IQ test measures."

A serious compromise in the ability to handle the responsibilities a society assigns to its members is one of the features clinicians use when deciding if a patient has a mental illness. Because children less than six years of age have no important responsibilities, strictly speaking they cannot have a mental illness. That is why the concept of childhood mental disorders was absent in texts written before 1800. However, when scientists discovered that extreme shyness or chronic disobedience during the childhood years was moderately predictive of later symptoms that did interfere with the adult's ability to carry out their responsibilities, childhood traits that had been ignored a hundred years earlier were now viewed as signs of a vulnerability to a later mental illness.

A vulnerability can be likened to a wooden bridge that can bear weights up to one thousand pounds but collapses under heavier loads. Genes, prenatal environments, and/or postnatal experiences can render a person vulnerable, but a symptom does not develop until an excessive burden is placed upon the individual. The responsibilities given to most children born before 1850 were well within their capacities, even if they possessed a vulnerability. They were required to do family chores, care for a younger child, or help a parent plant and care for crops and domestic animals. Almost every child could carry out these tasks. However, when twelve years of education became compulsory for many of the world's children, a proportion of those with one or more vulnerabilities found this challenge too burdensome and reacted with asocial behaviors, restless inattention, anxiety, or a depression that interfered with their adaptation.

Twentieth-century scholars emphasized two kinds of vulnerabilities. Experts writing between 1920 and 1970 nominated environmental conditions, especially chronic poverty, frequent changes of residence, and overly permissive or excessively harsh child rearing, because it was easy to invent an explanation of how these experiences might produce a disorder. This narrative was interrupted, rather abruptly, by a confident cohort of investigators armed with novel ways to study genes, molecules, and brains who asserted, prematurely, that inherited biological conditions, called diatheses, represented the more critical vulnerabilities.

There are two reasons why the genetic argument found a receptive audience. First, the social scientists who had advocated the influence of social experiences failed to confirm their prediction that experience alone could create the symptoms of a mental illness. Equally important, as the Nobel Laureate Jacques Monod recognized, natural scientists prefer explanations relying on objective facts that are based on mechanical processes free of ethical or sentimental values. Genes meet those criteria; feeling unloved by a parent does not.

Ultimately, neither position is completely satisfactory. Although genes do influence many symptoms, disabling psychological states require the contribution of many genes, some quite rare, together with a host of life experiences. At least 266 genes contribute to the variation in aggressive behavior among genetically different strains of fruit flies. Identical twins are born with the same genes. Nonetheless, as twin pairs mature they grow increasingly dissimilar in dominant mood because each sibling has unique life experiences. Both Kenneth Kendler, a psychiatric geneticist at Virginia Commonwealth University, and Evan Charney of Duke University urge colleagues to reject the traditionally sharp dichotomy between biological and experiential causes of illness and to acknowledge the blended contribution of both conditions. The correctness of this plea is affirmed by the surprising discovery that many, if not most, of the serious chronic human diseases are influenced by epigenetic changes in DNA caused by environmental events.[2]

CONCEPTUAL ISSUES

Sorting out all the conditions that contribute to mental illness requires grappling with three conceptual issues: the evidence used to define an illness, the vulnerabilities that place a person at risk, and the best ways to categorize the symptoms of mental illnesses. All three are controversial.

Most patients have to meet two criteria before a clinician diagnoses a mental illness. The first requires that the symptom be present in a minority of the community. Anger at a spouse is a frequent emotion, and psychiatrists do not regard this state as a sign of a disorder. A large number of contemporary adolescents and young adults engage in sexual behavior with many partners and participate in weekend binges with alcohol and drugs. Although these behaviors do not meet the criteria for a mental illness in contemporary America, the physicians in seventeenth-century Geneva and colonial New England would have regarded these behaviors as signs of a serious psychological disturbance.

The more important criterion requires that the symptoms be accompanied by subjective distress, a reduced capacity for pleasure, or a serious compromise in the ability to meet assigned responsibilities. Australian adolescents and young adults receive or send, on average, about eighteen text messages each day. Because they enjoy this activity, they are not classified as having a compulsive disorder. A woman who cleans her home daily, washes her hands every hour, and hoards string might not be diagnosed as having obsessive-compulsive disorder if she enjoys engaging in these rituals and meets her responsibilities effectively. A woman with the same symptoms who is unhappy about her inability to control the same behaviors would be diagnosed with obsessive-compulsive disorder.

Most psychiatrists assume, despite inadequate evidence, that the biological and psychological states that define a mental illness are products of abnormal biological conditions, analogous to having malarial parasites in the blood. This premise invites a closer examination of the meaning of *abnormal*. Because many individuals experience at least one serious bout of depression or anxiety during their lifetimes, it is not obvious that these moods require an abnormal biology produced by atypical genes.

Most humans become despondent after losing a cherished prize, whether a lover, spouse, friendship, child, parent, money, or position of high status. It is necessary, therefore, to differentiate between a temporary state of depression brought on by loss and persistent depressive moods that are more often due to an abnormal biology. Some psychiatrists treat the two forms of depression as the same illness. A similar argument applies to anxiety. It is not obvious that the American adolescents who worry daily about grades, friendships, admission to college, or violence in their neighborhood are mentally ill. Samuel Beckett had one of the characters in his play, *Endgame,* remark: "You're on earth, there is no cure for that."[3]

This chapter makes three major points. The most important is that all the current psychiatric categories for mental illness have more than one origin in a particular pattern of biology, experience, and current social circumstances. An unemployed adult who gambles every other day could be mentally ill or simply trying to keep his mind occupied. Some adolescents who willfully injure themselves do so in order to experience some bodily feeling. Others commit the same act to punish the self for a past deed.[4]

The second point, recognized by many ancient scholars but largely ignored during the twentieth century, is that mind and body are a unity. That is why a physical illness or inflammatory state is often associated with a mental disorder. David Kupfer and his colleagues point out that patients with bipolar disorder are more likely than others to be overweight and suffering from diabetes or a compromise in the cardiovascular system.[5] Ronald Kessler of Harvard Medical School, an expert on the prevalence of mental illnesses around the world, notes that three of every four American adults reported at least one problem with their physical or mental health during the past twelve months and a majority had more than one illness.[6] These new facts imply that some mental symptoms are part of a larger pattern of abnormalities that include compromises in the body's physiology.

The final point harkens back to the previous chapter. Verbal reports of anxiety, guilt, anger, or depression are interpretations of bodily feelings by a person functioning in a particular context. None is a direct consequence of genes or experience. A friend of mine who smoked cigarettes for more than fifty years developed insomnia the same week that he stopped smoking and lost a lot of money following a bad investment decision. He interpreted the insomnia as caused by his guilt over the impulsive decision to purchase an unsound equity. When he learned from his physician that insomnia usually occurs among those who stop smoking, he became unsure of the "reason" for his inability to sleep. Patients' complaints of depression or anxiety are interpretations of bodily states that vary with history and across cultures.

David Schuster's book *Neurasthenia Nation* makes this last point crystal clear.[7] In any community a small proportion of adults suffer from combinations of fatigue, insomnia, irritability, and tension. An interpretation of these uncomfortable states could range from fear of God's punishment for blasphemous thoughts to a depression attributed to earlier parental abuse. Nineteenth-century American farmers who suffered frequent bouts of fatigue, insomnia, and tension thought they understood why. The work was physically burdensome, and too little rainfall or too many pests could threaten a harvest and their livelihood.

The industrial revolution brought more sedentary jobs and more secure incomes, but also intense competition and a faster pace of life. As a result, the reason for insomnia, fatigue, and tension in the 1860s was less obvious, since many individuals were not engaged in hard physical labor and did not have to worry about a lost crop. Charles Beard, who promoted the new diagnosis of neurasthenia for these symptoms, suggested that patients were overtaxing their brains and losing vital bodily energy. The therapy was a change in diet, tonics, electrical pulses to the skin, and, if possible, a different job. Some well-known physicians in the 1870s told patients to refrain from masturbation on the assumption that this habit led to a loss of vital energy. American magazines during the 1890s announced that adults whose vocations required mental work—usually white, middle-class men—were victims of a new illness that was the price for the material progress of the great American civilization. When psychiatrists created the DSM-IV categories for anxiety and depressive disorders a century later, Americans had become receptive to the premise that defective genes were the villainous cause of symptoms that had not changed for millennia. Only the gender, class, and ethnicity of the patients and the presumed causal conditions had changed.

Clinical psychiatrists and psychologists treating patients must use the current set of illness categories in DSM-IV if they want to be paid. I've noted that these categories are obstructing scientific discovery of the varied causes of the symptoms. The concept of accidents furnishes an analogy. Scientists would be unable to discover the conditions responsible for plane crashes if they pooled all accidents—plane, automobile, train, ship, bicycle, ladder-related, and skiing—into one category.

The strategy needed for the scientific study of mental illness calls for selecting a set of vulnerabilities, which include biological features, experiences, and life settings, and then finding the proportion of individuals with particular vulnerabilities who developed particular symptoms. For example, what proportion of very shy two-year-olds with an excitable sympathetic nervous system who were reared by

1. Serious compromise in logic, affect, and social behavior
2. Serious or chronic bouts of a form of anxiety or depression that has a partial origin in the person's genes
3. Serious inability to control impulsive actions or inattentiveness due in part to the inherited biology
4. The symptoms of family 2 or 3 due primarily to life history and current circumstances

FIGURE 8.2   McHugh's four families of mental illness

middle-class, white families in urban settings developed social anxiety, depression, panic attacks, alcoholism, or no symptoms at all? Knowing the right question to ask is essential to solving puzzling phenomena. The right question in this case is: "What is the distribution of symptoms for individuals with a particular pattern of vulnerabilities?" The wrong question is: "What properties define social anxiety disorder (or any other diagnosis in the DSM catalogue)?"

Paul McHugh, a distinguished psychiatrist at The Johns Hopkins University, proposed four families of mental illness, each defined by the nature of the symptoms and their presumed origins. (A summary is provided in Figure 8.2.) Although each family contains illnesses with distinctive causes, the disorders in each family share both a small number of symptoms as well as the conditions that gave rise to them. The symptoms of each family reflect unique combinations of biological vulnerabilities, past histories, and current living circumstances. Anxiety or depression can be present in any of the four families. In some patients these states are the result of an inherited susceptibility to tension or apathy, called temperamental biases, combined with a stressful life history and current circumstances. In others, the same emotions are due primarily to childhood history and an adverse life setting without the biological vulnerabilities of the first group.[8]

I add four ideas to McHugh's trio of assumptions. First, a precipitating event is needed to transform a vulnerability into a symptom. Shy children who feel tense with strangers are at a higher risk for social anxiety if their family moves from the small town where they knew everyone in the school to an urban area where they know no one. Equally shy children with the same biology who remained in the small town might not develop social anxiety disorder. Likewise, the commission of a crime often requires settings that are more frequent in the disadvantaged neighborhoods of large cities. The youth of my generation, born during the second and third decades of the last century, did not have access to cocaine or guns and there were few cases of drug addiction or school massacres. Even the rare event called sudden infant death is more likely if the infant is sleeping with an adult rather than in a crib.[9]

Second, the private interpretations of stressful events and the accompanying feelings are more significant causes of symptoms than the events a camera records. A stressor can refer to an event that can be observed—poverty, storms, assaults, rapes, or the loss of a parent—or to an interpretation that the self is threatened accompanied by a biological reaction. These are different definitions of stress. Not everyone finds a hurricane threatening, and only some individuals interpret loss of house keys as a threat. Equally important, the nature of the stress is relevant. Illness, loss of a job, marital quarrels, divorce, loss of property, rape, and failure to attain a desired goal vary in their threat potential and generate different physiological consequences. Hence, scientists should stop the common practice of pooling all unwanted events into a single undifferentiated category called stress.

Many satisfied professionals who work in small offices eight or more hours a day do not interpret their confining physical space as stressful. A team of German scientists asked patients diagnosed with panic disorder to sit alone in a very small, dark room (only four by six feet) for ten minutes. One-third either refused or would not stay the full ten minutes, one-third remained the full time but reported feeling anxious, and another third stayed the full ten minutes without feeling any anxiety. Apparently, these adults imposed different interpretations on the same experience. Not all youths living in the vicinity of Nagasaki, Japan, in 1945, when the United States dropped an atomic bomb, were exposed to dangerous radiation levels. The members of this group who reported the highest levels of anxiety sixty years later believed that exposure to any level of radiation affected mental health. The youths who did not impose that interpretation on the 1945 explosion reported less anxiety in their later years.

Whether the victims of bullying, rape, or a hurricane develop the insomnia and anxiety that define posttraumatic stress disorder (PTSD) depends on their interpretation of these events. If they decide that they are partially responsible for their plight, are vulnerable to another catastrophe, or regard the trauma as having implications for their personal identity, they are at higher risk for this diagnosis. Vietnam veterans who felt guilty over the acts they witnessed or committed were at the highest risk for PTSD. Veterans who experienced the same violence, but regarded it as a chance event with no implications for their virtue, were usually protected from the symptoms of PTSD.[10]

Adolescent girls who had been sexually abused by their biological father are more likely to develop debilitating symptoms than girls who had been abused by another male in the household. This fact implies that the girl's interpretation of the sexual experience, not the abusive act itself, increases the probability of a corrosive guilt that generates symptoms.[11]

Dutch adolescents of both sexes who had frequent sexual relations with strangers in return for clothes, computers, or money insisted they were not prostitutes by arguing that they voluntarily entered into brief sexual relationships that took place far from the red-light districts of Amsterdam where the professional prostitutes lived. Humans have an extraordinary ability to interpret the same experiences and actions in different ways.

The third premise is that unexpected events enhance the intensity of an emotional reaction. Children find a marital quarrel more distressing if the parents rarely quarrel. Quarrels are less upsetting once children have become accustomed to them.[12] Finally, the belief that the individual can do something to alleviate distressing symptoms is always relevant. A bout of anxiety or depression is more upsetting if the individual believes he or she is unable to deal with the crisis or cope with the intrusive feelings. The increased number of American and Chinese adults who affiliated with a religious group during the past three decades, compared with the interval from 1950 to 1980, reflects an attempt among those in less privileged circumstances to cope with the rise in income inequality, dishonesty, materialism, and selfishness in both societies.

MCHUGH'S FOUR FAMILIES

Family 1 is defined by serious compromises in the quality of thought, attention, social behavior, and emotion—due, in part, to uncommon genes and/or a traumatic event or infection that damaged the brain before or soon after birth. Family 1 illnesses are the least common, are more prevalent among males, last the longest time, and are the most difficult to treat. This category contains the diagnoses of schizophrenia, autism, and bipolar disorder. None is a unitary illness with only one origin. Some of the family 1 adults diagnosed with schizophrenia functioned well until late adolescence, when their symptoms appeared suddenly. Others displayed disabling symptoms when they were young children. Still others developed their symptoms after chronic abuse of the drug methamphetamine. A team from the University of Alberta who followed a large group of schizophrenics for thirty-four years found that only one in four patients eventually attained a satisfactory social adjustment.

The family 1 patients diagnosed as schizophrenic possess different genes and life histories. For example, some experience auditory hallucinations that assume the form of voices criticizing them or giving commands. A fair proportion of such patients have one or more abnormalities in the temporal lobe, which is the location of Wernicke's area (described in Chapter 3). One possibility is that these structural abnormalities render the person vulnerable to the random occurrence of a greater-than-normal discharge of neurons in the temporal lobe that is interpreted as voices giving commands.

Although the symptoms of schizophrenia run in families, implying a genetic basis, all who are diagnosed as schizophrenics do not share the same risk genes. This puzzle led a trio of scientists to suggest that the symptoms of schizophrenia may have an unusual biological origin. What schizophrenics inherit, they suggest, is a vulnerability to one or more novel genetic mutations that occurred after fertilization when the fetal brain was developing. It is estimated that, on average, every infant is born with thirty-six mutations that neither parent possessed (thirty-six changes in a genome consisting of 6 billion nucleotides). Each of these mutations could compromise the developing brain, but the exact form of the compromise will differ across patients because the mutations vary.[13]

Jonathan Ting of the Massachusetts Institute of Technology suggests that one such mutation might involve the structure of the proteins on the surface of neurons.[14] The probability of a rare genetic feature increases as the size of a population grows. Because there has been a major increase in the number of humans over the past five centuries, it is possible that more individuals are born with a rare allele that places them or their children at a higher risk for a family 1 illness.

One reason for the sex difference in family 1 disorders is that these profiles are usually accompanied by serious compromises in intellectual functioning due, as noted, to abnormal development of the brain during the prenatal period. The genes on the two X chromosomes are overexpressed during brain development. Because males have only one X chromosome, any mutation on this chromosome that compromised cognitive abilities would be fully expressed. Females have two X chromosomes, and most of the genes on one of them are inactive in one-half of the cells of the brain and body. Hence, a mutation that caused a problem in a male might not affect a girl's intellectual abilities.

The popular intuition that some adults with a family 1 disorder possess the potential for an unusual level of creativity may have a grain of truth. Contemporary Swedish adults with a family 1 disorder, as well as their healthy first-degree relatives, were more likely than the average Swede to be engaged in a creative profession, usually the arts. Perhaps the genes that contribute to family 1 illnesses have survived because they confer some advantages in societies that award respect to those with unusual talents, despite their deviant behaviors.[15] After reading James Joyce's *Ulysses*, Carl Jung thought that the author was probably schizophrenic.

The symptoms that define a diagnosis of autism—more generally known as the autistic spectrum—include the three categories of patients: autism, Asperger's syndrome, and pervasive developmental disorder. Seventy years ago most of these impaired children would have received the coarser diagnosis of "brain damaged." The autistic spectrum in DSM-IV lumps symptoms with very different causes into one catch-all diagnostic category.

For example, fragile X syndrome, which is part of the spectrum, is defined by an alteration in a gene on the X chromosome that is responsible for a molecule that regulates protein synthesis in neurons. During a single year, about one in every five thousand boys and one in every ten thousand girls will be born with fragile X. Another distinctive cause of autistic symptoms, called Rett syndrome, is a mutation in a gene called MECP2. Other members of the autistic spectrum include children born without a corpus callosum, boys who show a large increase in the size of the right amygdala over the course of the first year, children with a microanatomy deficient in long-range connections, and those with a disease of the gastrointestinal system. A small proportion of autistic children were conceived by older fathers or born to mothers who, during the pregnancy, contracted an infection, experienced chronic stress, took medicines, drank excessively, or used illicit drugs.[16]

The extraordinary variety in the conditions that can create a child who falls within the autistic spectrum implies that scientists and clinicians should distinguish among children who have different biological causes, rather than pool all these children into one category called the autistic spectrum—a conclusion shared with Luke Tsai, a psychiatrist at the University of Michigan.[17] The autistic spectrum may contain almost as many disorders as cancer, and oncologists never advocated the concept of a cancer spectrum.

McHugh's family 2 is defined by frequent feelings of tension, vigilance, and irritability (often interpreted as anxiety) as well as fatigue, apathy, sleeplessness, and lack of pleasure (often interpreted as depression). More females than males possess one or more of these states, which psychiatrists call phobias, panic, posttraumatic stress, social anxiety, general anxiety, obsessive-compulsive disorder, anorexia, bulimia, or depression. There are many possible reasons for the sex difference in family 2 illnesses. The different effects of male and female sex hormones on the brain represent one important reason. Another possible contribution, albeit small, comes from an allele of the gene for a molecule called monoamine oxidase A, which degrades the serotonin released into the synapses. A team from the University of South Florida found that American women with a European-Caucasian ancestry were more likely than men to possess an allele that removes the serotonin more quickly. This condition would render the women with this gene more vulnerable to family 2 symptoms.

A second, more speculative reason is based on the fact that females have a slightly larger corpus callosum than males (controlling for the fact that males have larger brains than females). This property might make it easier for females to link semantic networks, elaborated in the left hemisphere, with the feelings mediated by the right hemisphere.

An important cause of the increased prevalence of family 2 illnesses during the past fifty years is the failure to distinguish between individuals who have only one serious, often brief, episode and those who suffer repeated bouts of anxiety or depression. These two types of patients have distinctive biological features and life histories, and they respond differently to therapy. Most adolescents or adults who develop anxiety after a psychological trauma (loss of a parent, social rejection, an earthquake, or a serious accident) eventually recover. Close to one-half of Americans who had a temporary bout of depression after age thirty-five never again have a serious depression.

Individuals with recurrent depressions typically developed this mood first during adolescence or early adulthood and often had a relative who also suffered from depression. These patients are likely to possess an underaroused right hemisphere, which implies a more profound apathy. Kathleen Merikangas and her colleagues at the National Institute of Mental Health found that the 10 percent of American adolescents suffering from a bout of depression, about 2.5 million youths, belong to two different groups.[18] Forty percent of the 2.5 million exhibit a mild apathy, have no relatives with a depressive disorder, and are more likely to be male than female. The remaining 60 percent exhibit a more severe melancholy, have one or more depressed relatives, and are more likely to be female than male.

Although many family 2 disorders have a partial origin in a specific imbalance in brain chemistry, there is considerable variation in the genomes, neurochemical profiles, and experiences that characterize any one disorder. That is why it has proven difficult to discover the neurochemical contribution to any of these illnesses. A symptom with a partial basis in a neurochemical abnormality could be due to deficient or excessive secretion of any of a large number of molecules, an abnormally high or low density of the receptors for a molecule, or receptors that were insensitive to the molecule.

One popular hypothesis holds that a combination of the short allele of the serotonin transporter molecule together with serious maltreatment, neglect, or abuse during childhood represent a serious risk for repeated bouts of depression. The short allele contains fewer repeats of DNA sequences in the promoter region of the gene for the serotonin transporter molecule. As a result, there is reduced expression of the gene that, in turn, results in slower absorption of serotonin from synapses.

Scientists suspect that the longer presence of serotonin could, over time, result in a lower level of serotonin activity in the brain through one of three mechanisms: the brain site that synthesizes serotonin (called the raphe nucleus) could reduce its secretory activity, a class of receptors on serotonin neurons could decrease in number, or another receptor could inhibit the release of this molecule. Under any one of these scenarios, the brains of those with the short allele would operate at a lower level of serotonin activity that, in turn, would be accompanied by increased excitability of the amygdala and other sites. The resulting brain state is likely to create a heightened feeling of arousal, vigilance, or tension. The specific consequences of this psychological state, however, depend on the person's life history, gender, culture, and, especially, their total genome.

Caucasian adults with the short allele who encountered serious trauma during childhood or the adult years are a little more vulnerable than most to a family 2 disorder. But the primary symptom could be depression, anxiety, posttraumatic stress disorder, panic attacks, or compulsive rituals. A majority develop no mental illness. Avshalom Caspi of Duke University and his colleagues at the University of Otago found that about 6 percent of a large number of New Zealand adults developed a persistently depressed mood.[19] However, the proportion of persistently depressed adults who combined the two short alleles (one from each parent) with a report of serious maltreatment was not much larger than the proportion who combined early maltreatment with two long alleles or with one short and one long allele. Joan Kaufman and her colleagues at Yale University, who used objective proof of removal from the home as evidence of childhood maltreatment rather than an adult's memory of childhood events, found that maltreatment alone predicted adult depression independent of the short allele.[20] And a team of German scientists discovered that the carriers of the short allele did not develop a depression unless they also experienced at least two major stressors during the adult years, along with childhood maltreatment. Only 1 percent of their German sample possessed all three properties. All of this evidence implies that the relation between a combination of the short allele and maltreatment, on the one hand, and adult depression, on the other, is not robust enough to be regarded as a principle that applies to all humans independent of their gender, class, or culture and the evidence for maltreatment.[21]

One reason for the uncertainty surrounding this issue is that possession of the short allele appears to render individuals susceptible to a vigilant tension that causes them to exaggerate the seriousness of events—say, childhood punishments—that a majority would regard as less important. Kenneth Kendler and his colleagues at Virginia Commonwealth University found that an inherited temperamental bias causes some adult twins to interpret a relatively innocuous event—say, an encounter with a friend that was not completely satisfying—as a very unpleasant experience.[22] Those who inherit a different temperament are more likely to minimize the seriousness of the same event. The former are at greater risk for a bout of anxiety or depression than the latter. Hence, a correlation between reports of stressful experiences during childhood and a later bout of anxiety or depression could be due to a temperament that favors both outcomes. Remember, from Chapter 5, the watchmaker and the man who rang the church bells who relied on each other to know when it was noon. Investigators should gather objective measures of childhood maltreatment as well as the child's psychological reaction to the trauma at the time it occurred in order to understand the relation among genes, childhood stressors, and later mental illness.

A completed suicide is one of the few family 2 symptoms that is more common among males than females (the sex ratio is 3 or 4 to 1). The reasons for this difference include the fact that men have easier access to guns, suicides require suppression of the fear associated with shooting or hanging oneself, and the sex-role standards in many cultures require males to deny any psychological weakness. Depressed males are reluctant to confess a problem to a friend or relative and, seeing no solution to their misery, commit suicide. Depressed females are more willing to tell a close friend or parent that they are thinking about suicide as a way of asking for help.

In 2011, about 1 million individuals across the world committed suicide (1 per 6,000) and about 15 million made a suicide attempt (1 per 400). Many more, perhaps 5 percent, thought about suicide. Although genetic vulnerabilities contribute to suicides, environmental and social conditions are always relevant. Suicides in the northern hemisphere peak during March and April, when the hours of daylight are increasing. It is not known whether this association is due to the suppression of melatonin or to the fact that depressed individuals become more conscious of their apathy when spring arrives and they see their friends becoming more joyous.

Adolescent suicides, which are on the rise in many countries, are more frequent among the economically disadvantaged. The increased level of economic inequality in China during the past decade has been accompanied by a suicide rate of 25 per 10,000, which is among the highest in the world. China's one-child policy—which resulted in parents' treating their only child, often a boy, as if he were a little emperor—represents one cause: the marked contrast between being pampered at home and the competitive, impersonal, and crowded conditions in Chinese colleges could contribute to the fact that one in five students think about suicide.[23] Although the overall prevalence of suicide in the United States is low (only 1 in 10,000), it is the second-highest cause of death among Americans between fifteen and thirty-four years of age.[24]

Adolescents who starve themselves are diagnosed as anorexic; those who engage in bouts of binge eating followed by vomiting are called bulimic. Almost 1 percent of Americans experienced at least one episode of anorexia during their lifetime. Close to one-half of adolescent anorexics recover; the remaining half develop symptoms of anxiety or depression as adults. The increased prevalence of anorexia over the past half-century is found mainly among middle-class adolescent and young-adult females living in economically developed societies that have a surfeit of food and celebrate a thin body.

Most anorexics are perfectionists with a strong need to be in control of all aspects of their lives because they want to avoid unpredictable and unwanted events. An inability to tolerate uncertainty over the immediate future is a characteristic common to many family 2 disorders. These individuals continually think about the possibility of unwanted surprises occurring during the next moments, days, or weeks and try to do something to prevent them. Because the slightest mistake or failure is an unwanted surprise, they are often incapable of deciding on an action, even one as innocent as purchasing a ballpoint pen, if they have any doubt about the correctness of their choice. They resemble bronze statues with a half-raised arm frozen in indecision.

Unexpected parental punishments for trivial childhood misbehaviors represent one way to create adolescents who are continually on-guard against any event for which they might not be prepared. Many anorexics had exceptionally strict parents who, by punishing trivial misbehaviors, created children who were always worried about an unwanted event they could not control. These are the youths who are at a special risk for anorexia. Once they feel that their control of events or ability to predict the future has been compromised, they decide to restrict their eating as one way to assure the self that a measure of control has been regained. One anorexic described how she felt when she began to starve herself: "I finally felt as though I was in control of my own welfare. It was strange but wonderful . . . a sort of power-ful feeling."[25]

Family 2 illnesses are more prevalent among adolescents and adults who were high-reactive infants. Readers will recall that high-reactive four-month-olds react to unexpected events with vigorous motor behavior and crying because of a brain chemistry and/or anatomy that created a hyper-excitable amygdala. These infants are biased toward becoming shy, timid children and adolescents with unreasonable worries that include sitting next to a stranger on a bus or visiting a new city. These are the adults who expect the worst when a weather report predicts a storm, the lights go out, or they hear a noise at midnight.

My colleague Carl Schwartz, a psychiatrist at Massachusetts General Hospital, discovered that high- and low-reactive infants possessed different biological features when they were eighteen years old. High-reactives had a thicker cortex in a small region within the ventromedial prefrontal cortex in the right hemisphere. This region is connected to the amygdala, to sites in the autonomic nervous system that create racing of the heart, and to neurons in a region called the central gray that would have generated the frequent arching of the back displayed by the high-reactive four-month-olds. Although the likely explanation of the thicker cortex is that high-reactives experienced more frequent bouts of anxiety throughout their first eighteen years, there is the slim possibility that the thicker cortex was present at birth.[26]

These high-reactive eighteen-year-olds showed two other biological signs of their temperament. First, they maintained large surges of blood flow to the amygdala across repeated presentations of unfamiliar pictures they could not have antici-pated, whereas most adolescents and adults show a decrease in blood flow to the continued presentation of unfamiliar pictures. Second, they displayed a larger surge of blood flow to the right amygdala the first time they saw a photo of an angry face they did not expect. These observations imply that high-reactives possess a neuro-chemistry that renders neuronal clusters in the amygdala hyper-excitable to unex-pected events. As a result, they treat experiences that a majority ignore or regard as improbable as sources of worry. More of the high- than low-reactive eighteen-year-olds told a clinician that they felt intense anxiety over a variety of innocent events, including taking a subway, being part of a crowd, or sitting next to a stranger on a bus. Some had also experienced a bout of depression during the past few years. The eighteen-year-old high-reactives with these symptoms were most likely to show the three biological features described above that separated high- from low-reactives. Although some low-reactive girls also reported a bout of anxiety or depression, these girls did not possess a thicker ventromedial cortex and failed to display the large surge of blood flow when they saw the angry face.

These facts imply that the current psychiatric categories of depression, social anxiety, and generalized anxiety disorder can result from varied temperaments and life histories. It is likely that the optimal therapy for anxiety or depression depends on the origin of the symptom. For example, depressed patients with high levels of activation of the right ventromedial prefrontal cortex were helped by therapy that suppressed neuronal activity in this region, whereas other depressed patients were not helped by the same treatment.[27]

McHugh's family 3 includes individuals whose biological vulnerabilities make it difficult to inhibit aggressive or sexual urges, sustain attention, resist temptations for drugs or alcohol, or feel empathic toward those in distress. Family 3 disorders are more common among males than females and are especially prevalent among men who grew up in disadvantaged families. About 10 percent of American children are diagnosed with one or more of the three most common family 3 disorders: ADHD, conduct disorder, and oppositional defiant disorder. All three are heterogeneous in their profile of symptoms and etiology.[28]

Family 3 children are only a little more likely than others to become criminals. Most restless, inattentive, defiant, or disobedient five-year-olds do not become chronically aggressive, asocial adolescents. Fewer than 15 percent of such children retain these behaviors through adolescence. The small proportion of American men (fewer than 2 percent) who admitted to at least two serious crimes (for example, arson, murder, or armed robbery) were likely to have abused drugs, fathered a child while an adolescent, and had a parent with a psychological problem. The men who committed less serious violations of the law (for example, shoplifting) were not at a higher risk for violent behaviors. Rolf Loeber and Dustin Pardini at the University of Pittsburgh discovered that children who met the criteria for nine of eleven risk factors (including a delinquent behavior before age ten, poor academic grades, and nine different indexes of economic disadvantage) were highly likely to commit a violent act as an adult.[29] Children who had fewer than four risk factors were unlikely to engage in any violence—another example of the tipping point principle.

The symptoms of family 3 patients often originate in compromised functioning of sites in the prefrontal cortex (especially the dorsolateral region and the anterior cingulate cortex) that contribute to the suppression of inappropriate actions. These sites are influenced by molecules and receptors that are different from those affecting the amygdala and the circuitry implicated in family 2 illnesses. Some children with ADHD have delayed pruning of the synapses in the frontal lobe. Others possess a less responsive sympathetic nervous system, often reflected in a smaller-than-normal rise in systolic blood pressure when they stand up. If clinicians measured this last biological trait in all children suspected of having ADHD, they might detect a special type of ADHD that responds best to a particular therapy.[30]

A low and variable heart rate, while sitting quietly, doing nothing, is a stable, inherited biological property reflecting the dominance of parasympathetic control of the heart that has modest correlations with a variety of behaviors. The brain profile accompanying parasympathetic control of the heart often generates bodily sensations that most people interpret as a mood of relaxation and low anxiety. The consequences of this brain-psychological state depend on the person's history and current circumstances. For example, boys with a low and variable heart rate living in crime-ridden disadvantaged neighborhoods might not feel afraid if and when they contemplated asocial behavior, whereas boys with a low and variable heart rate growing up in advantaged families and boasting a good school record are likely to exploit their relaxed mood to become leaders with peers.

Most of the low-reactive boys my colleagues and I studied had low and variable heart rates. But because they were raised in comfortable, affectionate families they were popular and seemed prepared to become courageous soldiers, successful CEOs, or charismatic political candidates should the proper conditions arise. One of these boys who was interviewed when he was fifteen years old told the interviewer that he was thinking of entering politics and, perhaps, seeking the presidency when he was older. Many adults who attempt difficult feats such as climbing Mt. Everest, swimming the English Channel, or sailing around the world alone were probably low-reactive infants.[31]

A small proportion of adolescents and adults fail to experience an obvious feeling of empathy for a victim they have harmed or intend to harm. These individuals do not activate the visceral schemata and thoughts they created when they were in pain. Although we do not yet understand the brain patterns that permit such an extreme callousness, one possible villain is an abnormality in the circuit that links the amygdala, the insula, and the ventromedial prefrontal cortex. A compromise in this circuit could render a person incapable of intense feelings, whether empathy or the states that are interpreted as shame, guilt, fear, or anxiety. The gradual loss of an empathic reaction following many acts of aggression toward others is a second possible reason for the development of a callous attitude. This state resembles the emotional numbing that builds up in soldiers who have killed many enemy combatants.

V. S. Ramachandran, a neuroscientist at the University of California, has described the rare individuals who think that a relative or close friend is an imposter.[32] The failure to recognize someone who previously had been a regular source of pleasant feelings could be due to abnormal functioning of the amygdala-insula-prefrontal circuit, which contributes to the subtle feeling, often unrecognized, that occurs upon encountering a familiar person. It is possible that a small proportion of callous criminals possess this abnormality.

Historical events that alter a society's moral values influence the decision to treat some of the behaviors of family 3 either as illnesses or as ethical flaws. Contemporary debates over how to classify deviant sexual behaviors reflect this dilemma. Is an adult who has an erotic interest in prepubescent children mentally ill, or is this person guilty of violating the community's ethical standard? Anthropologists and historians remind psychiatrists of the cultures that regard such sexual interests as perfectly normal.

David Veale of the Institute of Psychiatry at Kings College in Cambridge, England, described a thirty-three-year-old happily married woman who chose to have her labia and clitoris surgically removed because she regarded them as unattractive.[33] She was pleased with the results of the surgery and reported enjoying sexual relations with her husband. Despite no signs of mental disturbance in the conduct of her life, some psychiatrists insisted that her actions meant that she had to be mentally ill. It is worth noting that these psychiatrists would not have regarded her as ill if she had chosen to have cosmetic surgery on her face.

Many Americans born before 1920 regarded excessive drinking and fighting as character weaknesses, not mental disorders. Before chlorination of the water supply, most nineteenth-century Americans drank large amounts of beer and the annual consumption of alcohol was much larger than it is today. Disobedience and fighting among boys in nineteenth-century rural America were considered normative rather than a sign of mutated genes.

The committee composing DSM-5 for publication in 2013 will continue to include a diagnosis called narcissistic personality disorder for adults who are arrogant, feel entitled to admiration, and exploit or devalue others with little guilt. The antihero James Bond is an example from popular culture. Scott Lilenfeld of Emory University points out that these traits were present in many admired persons—for example, Theodore Roosevelt, George Patton, Douglas MacArthur, Winston Churchill, and a number of kings, queens, sultans, emperors, and ante-bellum plantation owners.[34] Surely psychiatrists do not want to defend a position declaring that selfishness and arrogance in an ordinary person with no accomplishments is an illness but the same behaviors in a successful adult are adaptive.

The media's criticism of the increased narcissism among the current generation of young Americans is motivated by the community's strong disapproval of adults who behave as if they are superior to others. This attitude reflects an ethical preference for a personality type in the twenty-first century that is more agreeable and willing to enter into egalitarian relationships with those who are less well-educated, less wealthy, or from a different ethnic group. At some point between 1960 and 1970, the hero typified by Rhett Butler was replaced with a hero resembling Forrest Gump. When I joined the Harvard faculty in 1964 I met many undergraduate men who, having enjoyed the privilege of an excellent education at a private high school, paraded the depth of their knowledge as a way to intimidate their less privileged classmates. This personality type had largely vanished by the 1970s because the ethics of the undergraduate body had changed.

The new DSM-5 manual plans to categorize gambling, or an inability to suppress a craving to gamble, as a mental illness, probably because of enhanced societal worry over the increased numbers of casinos and arcades and the ease of online betting. The claim that those who cannot inhibit the desire to play slot machines have a mental disorder, but adults who play the stock market to make larger amounts of money are not ill, reflects an ethical judgment. The men and women working for investment firms who rise each day before dawn to buy billions of dollars of credit default swaps are gambling. Many find this activity exciting, are addicted to checking their Blackberries every minute for market news, and experience the same dopamine surges that occur in those who cannot stay away from gambling arcades or Internet sites that allow gambling of smaller amounts. Yet few psychiatrists regard the employees of investment banks as mentally ill.

If gambling performed in the service of one's job is not a sign of a mental illness but gambling for excitement over the weekend is, psychiatrists may have to classify women who choose to be highly paid prostitutes in order to make money as mentally healthy but categorize women who enjoy the pleasure of changing sex partners frequently as mentally ill, as seventeenth-century physicians did when they invented the concept *nymphomania*. Surely, there is something wrong with this logic.[35]

A small number of officially defined mental illnesses are, in effect, ethical evaluations of what should count as normal. The decision by American psychiatrists to diagnose women who rarely had an orgasm during sex with a lover or husband as having a mental disorder did not emerge until the 1980s. Psychiatrists are getting dangerously close to composing their own tablet of ten commandments for the twenty-first century: thou shall have orgasms, be self-interested, and autonomous; thou shall not be too dependent, arrogant, worried, dour, guilty, sexually aroused by photos of naked children, or fond of gambling.

The penetration of ethical values into decisions about who is mentally ill troubles many, including Allen Frances, a distinguished psychiatrist at Duke University, who criticized this practice in the May 12, 2012, issue of the *New York Times* and in a chapter written for a professional audience. Psychiatrists have so overextended the definition of a disorder, it is likely that by 2030 one of every two adults over age sixty will have met the criteria for at least one mental illness during their lifetime. This conception of mental illness replaces the Greek view of madness as a rare and dangerous phenomenon with the common annoyances of colds, skin rashes, and tooth cavities.

The ability to measure the brains and genomes of criminals raises a serious ethical issue that earlier generations were able to avoid. A case described by David Rigoni and his colleagues at the University of Padua illustrates this enigma.[36] A twenty-four-year-old woman, J.F., smothered her newborn infant moments after it was born in her boyfriend's apartment. J.F. was judged legally sane, for she had normal reasoning, memory, and perceptual abilities. Measures of her brain, however, revealed less than the expected amount of gray matter in a site in the prefrontal cortex that is correlated with control of impulsive actions. But most adults with this particular brain feature do not commit murders, and most law-abiding adults older than age sixty have lost equivalent volumes of gray matter in this location. In addition, J.F. possessed several genes that, in some adults, are modestly associated with impulsivity. However, a majority of individuals with the same genes do not commit crimes. Thus, we must ask: Could J.F. have controlled the urge to kill her infant, or did her biology render her incapable of suppressing her murderous action?

I do not know the answer. But it is likely that defense attorneys will more regularly use measures of their clients' brains and genes to argue that even though they understood that their consciously chosen actions were morally wrong and illegal, their biology prohibited them from exercising the self-control needed to avoid committing a crime. Lisa Aspinwall of the University of Utah confirmed this intuition.[37] She presented a legal vignette of a man accused of a brutal murder to state trial court judges. One-half of the judges read the defense lawyer's argument, which did not include any information about the man's genome. The remaining judges read the same argument, except that it included an expert's testimony stating that the man had a gene that made him vulnerable to impulsive acts of violence. The latter judges recommended a lighter sentence than the first group with no genetic information, even though they knew little about genes or the predictive relations between genes and acts of murder.

Two observations are worth noting here. First, most adults with serious brain damage, far more serious than J.F.'s loss of gray matter, do not commit murders. Second, the vast majority of adults who commit murder when emotionally aroused do not have a known genetic or brain-related abnormality and never killed anyone in the past, despite being emotionally aroused on many occasions. These facts imply that such individuals, and perhaps J.F., were perfectly capable of controlling their homicidal actions.

The symptoms that define family 4 disorders resemble those of families 2 and 3, but these patients do not share the same biological vulnerabilities. Rather, their life history and current circumstances are the more important causes of symptoms. This claim does not mean that these patients possess no biological vulnerabilities, only that if they do they will not be the vulnerabilities that characterize the patients in families 2 and 3.

An addiction to watching pornographic films online provides an example of the effect of local conditions on symptom formation, inasmuch as this behavior became possible only during the past few decades. A majority of males in all societies are interested in and aroused by visual displays of naked women, especially if the women are engaged in sexual behaviors. Historical circumstances made access to such scenes so easy that many men became addicted to this form of arousal, just as the invention of the cigarette created nicotine addicts.

Membership in a less advantaged social class is the best predictor of a family 4 disorder in every society. Even in Scandinavia, where most residents have an adequate income and differences in income and education are small, youths from poorer families were at the highest risk for a mental illness. This robust fact is probably due to a combination of several conditions, including a compromised state of health that creates bodily feelings interpreted as anxiety or depression, dangerous neighborhoods, and, most important, chronic feelings of powerlessness, inadequacy, envy, or anger.

Adults who are ashamed of their impoverished or marginalized status are at risk for social anxiety disorder, those who feel guilty because they cannot support their family are at risk for depression, and those who are angry are vulnerable to committing asocial acts. On the other hand, youth who interpret their disadvantaged status as having minimal implications for their sense of virtue are likely to be protected from serious symptoms.

Listen to a poor, minority woman describing the corrosive state of impotence that chronic poverty can create: "Your fingers get slow, . . . your whole body slows down. You can't really do much, you try to put a good face on for the kids, but when they leave, you just keep still, keep the covers around you. Almost like you kind of fold into the floor."[38]

Close to 40 percent of working Americans in 2012 did not work the traditional nine-to-five schedule. The women in this group, many of whom belonged to a disadvantaged minority group, who had a young child and no relative to care for them, had to find a day care facility that was open twenty-four hours a day. It is not surprising that the working mothers who deposited their infant at a center at 1:00 A.M. or picked up a child at midnight were vulnerable to bouts of depression. There was a comparably large increase in mental illness in the 1870s following the arrival of large numbers of poor immigrants from Europe.[39]

Historical events that rendered gender roles fuzzier than they were a century earlier provide another reason for the currently high prevalence of family 4 symptoms of anxiety or depression among adolescent and adult males. Boys and men are continually concerned with their psychological potency and are vulnerable to a gnawing uncertainty when they are unsure of their status in the groups to which they belong. Many young men who feel vital while serving in the armed forces, where each person's rank is clear, become depressed or anxious after returning to civilian life to confront social contexts in which they are unsure of their status at home or in the workplace.

Men assumed the dominant role in the family in most cultures throughout most of human history. Husbands who had lower ranks in the community because they had less land, less education, or less wealth could reassure themselves of their potency by dominating their wives and children at home. This source of assurance began to erode during the last century after American women became empowered, youth became more autonomous, and more men began working in bureaucracies offering little autonomy and minimal information on their status. A melancholic mood, frequent drinking, abuse of wives, or, in some cases, abandonment of the family were reactions to the uncertainty generated by the ambiguous hierarchies that characterized daily life.

Writers accommodated to this historical change by celebrating gentler men who were able to assume an equal or passive role with women and accept the healing power of their love. The central figure in the popular 1984 film *Paris, Texas* was a melancholic man who drank heavily and was irrationally cruel to the young, beautiful wife he loved who left him and her son soon after giving birth to their child. He does not attain heroic status until the end of the film when, after a long search, he finds his former wife, unites her with the son she has not seen for ten years, and then drives away.

The historical events that brought an egalitarian, anti-elitist ethos to America, which has had many social advantages, exacted a cost on the adolescent and adult males who found it difficult to provide themselves with some sign of their potency. The hapless husband in the film *Chicago,* dismissed by his unfaithful wife as irrelevant, laments that he is a cellophane man because the people he meets "look right through me and never know I'm there." Willy Loman, the failed husband and father in Arthur Miller's 1949 play *Death of a Salesman,* confessed to his wife, "I'm not noticed."

The symptoms of families 2, 3, and 4 are accompanied by one of four feeling states: a tense vigilance that is interpreted as anxiety, an apathy interpreted as depression, a combination of vigilance and apathy that can be interpreted as anxiety or depression, or the absence of vigilance, apathy, and empathy that is often interpreted as infallibility. Each state, however, can lead to more than one symptom. The symptom that eventually develops depends on the person's genome, past history, and current setting.

McHugh did not propose a family for children or youths with a serious retardation in language, arithmetic skills, or reading ability, many of whom do not experience the intense anxiety or depression characteristic of families 2 or 4 or the impulsivity of family 3. Each of these compromises in cognitive ability has a variety of causes. Among the school-age children having difficulty learning to read, who are often diagnosed as dyslexic, some cannot process tones and vowels normally. Others are unable to read several lines of alphabetic letters rapidly. Still others possess an allele of a molecule that interferes with the ability to sustain attention for long periods of time.

However, most of these children share one interesting behavioral feature: they show frequent lapses in attentiveness. For example, normal children asked to hit a button as fast as they can every time they see a certain design on a screen respond at the same rapid speed trial after trial for several minutes. Children with one or more of these cognitive problems, however, are more variable. They react as rapidly as normal children on some trials but more slowly on others. This measure, called intra-subject variability, is a potential sign of a compromise in brain function.[40]

I remember asking dyslexic adolescents to reply "true" or "false" as quickly as possible to a lengthy series of questions that assumed the following form: "Asparagus is green," "Dogs are plants," or "Cookies are sweet." Their replies were as fast as those of normal children for five or six questions in a row and then, suddenly, they would take several seconds to reply to the next item, as if the circuit that maintains attention was interrupted. This variability in speed of response implies that they were able to sustain attention for short intervals, ranging from twenty to sixty seconds, but could not do so for several minutes.

Before we move on to the pressing issue of how to treat mental illness, it is important to appreciate two facts that bear on the varied genetic contributions to mental illness. First, the symptoms of youths or adults born to a mentally ill parent are usually different from those the parent displayed. This fact implies that the genes that contributed to the parent's symptoms do not specify a particular set of moods or actions in the offspring. Rather, the risk genes render a person vulnerable to a variety of psychological problems.[41]

The second fact has implications for those looking for a small number of risk genes for each illness. The ability to detect subtle differences in the sweetness of a liquid is an inherited trait. But the eleven genes that predict this sensory capacity explain only 13 percent of the variation in this talent. If, as is likely, the variation in the sensitivity to sweet tastes rests on fewer genes than those that contribute to most mental illnesses, scientists searching for a small number of alleles that they hope will account for a large amount of the variation in the risk for an illness will be frustrated.

This claim is supported by the fact that the genomes of European-Americans contain a large number of rare alleles not found in the genomes of African-Americans, and African-Americans have some rare alleles not present in those with a European pedigree. Hence, identical symptoms in whites and blacks could be due to different genes. We know this is true for the ability to live at a high altitude. Long-term residents of Tibet and the highlands of Bolivia rely on different genes to create a physiology that allows them to survive at the low oxygen levels at these high altitudes.

Investigators looking for the genes that place a person at risk for a mental illness face a daunting task. A team of scientists led by Jacob Tennessen at the University of Washington found many more rare alleles than had been expected.[42] (A rare allele is one that is present in less than 0.5 percent of the population.) Geneticists suspect that the dramatic increase in the size of the human population over the past three hundred years is one reason for the prevalence of rare alleles. This means that scientists will have to recruit much larger samples of patients, in some cases as many as ten thousand, in order to detect the particular genes that contribute to a specific symptom. One reason why past research failed to discover risk genes for a mental illness is that the number of patients studied was too small, usually less than two hundred, and a majority belonged to one ethnic group, usually white.

TREATING THE MENTALLY ILL

Drugs have become the most frequent form of therapy for children and adults diagnosed with any disorder. More than one in ten Americans in 2011 took some drug to alleviate a depressed mood. More serious is the fact that many American physicians, not just psychiatrists, are prescribing drugs previously restricted to family 1 patients to those with the less serious symptoms of insomnia, mild anxiety, apathy, or the restlessness and inattention characteristic of ADHD. Heavy reliance on drugs does have the advantage of removing some of the responsibility for an illness from patients and their families and placing it on the roll of the biological dice. Why add the burden of self-blame to those who are already unhappy?

Unfortunately, no drug affects only the symptoms of an illness. All drugs modulate neuronal activity in many brain sites, and some even alter the microanatomy of select sites. Drugs create abnormal brain states that change many psychological properties, including a muting of the frequency or intensity of a symptom. Some drugs given to schizophrenics, for example, eliminate their hallucinations and delusions because these chemicals slow all cognitive activity, often by enhancing the expression of genes whose molecular products suppress neuronal excitability across most of the brain. However, these drugs have little effect on the blunted emotion or compromises in reasoning that are characteristic of family 1 patients.

Most drugs, therefore, can be compared to a blow on the head, not unlike the cocktail of drugs used to treat cancers that kill both healthy and cancerous tissues. That is one reason why some healthy adults who volunteered to take one of the drugs prescribed for schizophrenics became seriously depressed. Indeed, close to 60 percent of first-episode schizophrenics given a drug for the first time stop taking the medicine after several months because they do not like the uncomfortable side effects.

Most drugs create bodily sensations that patients interpret as a sign of the medicine's effectiveness. For example, the drugs prescribed most often for socially anxious adults decrease the patient's usual heart rate. The patient might interpret the resulting sensation as a reduction in nervous tension and therefore as symptom improvement, even though the drug had no direct effect on the reason for the anxiety that is evoked in social situations. Healthy individuals without symptoms might impose a different interpretation on the same feeling. Healthy adults do not interpret the feeling following two hours of exercise as a sign that they are less depressed. Depressed patients, however, do impose that interpretation after exercise. Drugs dilute the intensity of apathetic moods in about three-fourths of depressed adults, at least initially, because the patients interpret their altered feelings as meaning that they are on their way to better mental health.

Alan Sroufe, a psychologist at the University of Minnesota, was blunt in his criticism of the widespread use of the drugs Ritalin and Adderall for children with ADHD in an essay in the *New York Times* on January 29, 2012. Sroufe's evidence, and the results of others, led him to conclude that there is no long-term benefit of either drug on the academic performances, peer relationships, or behavior problems of children diagnosed with ADHD, even though there is often an initial, temporary improvement in the capacity for sustained attention.

Robert Gibbons and his colleagues at the University of Chicago evaluated the differential effects of an antidepressant drug and a placebo during the first thirty days of treatment.[43] There was a precipitous drop in self-reported depression in both groups, and only a slight advantage for the drug over the placebo. About one-half of a group of Swedish patients suffering from social anxiety disorder reported improvement after taking either a selective serotonin reuptake inhibitor (SSRI) or a placebo. Moreover, the less anxious patients showed reduced activity in the amygdala whether they were on the drug or a placebo. This result suggests that if anxious patients expect a medicine to be helpful, their amygdala responds appropriately, as long as they think they are taking a medicine. Healthy adults who agreed to take an SSRI for four weeks showed no reduction in the stress hormone cortisol because, unlike patients, they had no expectation of better mental health.[44] Perhaps that is why the common practice of relying on the behaviors of rats or mice as a way to evaluate the efficacy of a drug for human symptoms has serious flaws. Mice do not have expectations of the consequences of being injected with a drug.

Joel Paris, a psychiatrist at McGill University, has written a wise summary of the advantages and disadvantages of drugs. The first of his six conclusions is optimistic. Some drugs help some patients, even if the long-term, benevolent effects are limited to those with specific genomes and/or life histories. For example, whereas depressed or anxious patients of European ancestry who possess the short allele of the serotonin transporter are unlikely to be helped by the drugs called SSRIs, depressed Koreans with the short allele are helped by these drugs. Koreans, like most Asians, are more likely than Europeans or Africans to possess the short allele. In short, the effectiveness of a drug often depends on the patient's total genome. These facts complicate matters, for they imply that psychiatrists must take the patient's ethnicity into account when prescribing drug therapy. One size does not fit all.

Paris's other conclusions are less optimistic. (See Figure 8.3.) All drugs are being overprescribed, scientists do not know why a drug is helpful when it alleviates symptoms, the pharmaceutical industry's statements about a drug's effectiveness cannot be trusted, psychotherapy is not being used as often as it should be with milder cases of anxiety or depression, and a patient's report of initial improvement after taking a drug is often no different from the improvement following exercise or a sugar pill placebo.[45]

Much of the public is unaware of the fact that over the past three decades scientists have not discovered a qualitatively new class of drug for a mental disorder that acts on the brain in a novel way. All the so-called new medicines for mental illness are slight variations on what was already known. Moreover, the reliance on drugs to treat mental symptoms is less than forty years old. No medicine that was both specific for and effective with any of the physical diseases that have plagued humans for thousands of years was discovered in an interval as short as four decades.

1. Some drugs are helpful with some symptoms.
2. Scientists do not understand why drugs help you when they do.
3. All drugs are overprescribed.
4. The claims of pharmaceutical companies are exaggerated.
5. Psychotherapy is not being used as often as it should.
6. Remission of some symptoms through use of a drug is often no better than the effects of a placebo.

FIGURE 8.3   Joel Paris's evaluation of efficacy of drugs for treating mental illness

Although drugs are easy to dispense, they have the disadvantage of placing patients in the role of passive recipients of substances they do not understand designed to alleviate symptoms that are equally mysterious. Psychotherapy, by contrast, forces the patient to be a more active partner in the curative process. Drugs are currently the therapy of choice because they are less expensive than psychotherapy and require less effort from both doctor and patient. If the illness were cancer of the pancreas, the expense and effort would not be major considerations.

Another disadvantage of drugs is that they deprive some patients of the therapeutic consequences of a period of temporary suffering. The psychiatrists and psychologists who believe that all psychic suffering is dysfunctional forget that humans try to extract meaning from their unhappiness. An adolescent girl who becomes depressed a week after the unexpected death of a mother to whom she felt ambivalent might interpret her dark mood as punishment for her failure to be a more loving daughter. Under these conditions, the depression could have therapeutic advantages. Some adolescents cut their skin in order to inflict a punishment for a private moral violation. Some young children who feel guilty about an undiscovered misdemeanor commit another prohibited act in front of a parent in order to receive a punishment that will alleviate their guilt.

Evaluations of the effectiveness of the many different forms of psychotherapy reveal that most therapies are equally effective with the symptoms of families 2, 3, or 4. Fans of Lewis Carroll's *Alice in Wonderland* will remember that the Dodo's reply, when asked who won the race, was that everybody won and, therefore, all should receive a prize. The reason for this equivalence is that patients who develop a trusting relationship with their therapist are likely to implement the therapist's advice and, as a result, feel better, independent of the specific therapy they are receiving.

That is why depressed patients who believe their mood is due to a chemical imbalance prefer a drug, whereas those who believe their depression is a consequence of stressors or an unloving parent prefer psychotherapy or a combination of psychotherapy and a medicine.

Florian Weck and his colleagues at the University of Frankfurt found that the probability of relapse among depressed patients treated with one popular form of psychotherapy bore no relation to the therapist's adherence to the rituals that define the therapy.[46] Rather, the quality of the patient's alliance with the therapist, and fewer prior bouts of depression, predicted the absence of relapse.

A patient's subjective evaluation of how he or she feels is the usual measure of a therapy's effectiveness. There are at least two problems with this criterion.

First, humans possess a natural bias to judge any action that requires effort and money as beneficial. Otherwise, they are vulnerable to judging themselves as naïve or, worse yet, stupid for having participated in a worthless enterprise. Second, patients who like their therapist do not want to disappoint the person who worked so hard to be of help. It is not surprising, therefore, that most patients say they feel better after a bout of therapy, even if more objective evaluations of the symptoms reveal little change.

Jerome Frank anticipated these facts more than fifty years ago when he suggested that in many cases, but obviously not all, patients improve in psychotherapy when three conditions are met: First, the patient and therapist agree on the cause of the patient's distress, whether or not their interpretation is correct. Second, the patient and therapist share the same belief about the best therapeutic regimen, whether or not this assumption is valid. And, finally, patients respect and like their therapist, assume that he or she sincerely cares about them, and, most important, believe that the therapeutic regimen will be effective. Increased secretion of the molecule dopamine is often accompanied by a feeling of greater vitality. Adults who believe their therapy will be helpful secrete dopamine, which lifts their spirits.[47]

The memoirs of patients who have been in therapy affirm Frank's insights, as does Bruce Wampold, a respected psychotherapist who told an audience at the 2011 annual convention of the American Psychological Association that the therapist's ability to establish a trusting relationship with the patient, rather than adherence to specific rituals, was the most important ingredient in remission. Freud agreed with this premise, for in a letter to Carl Jung he wrote: "The cure is effected by love." Freud meant that the patient tries to get better in order to repay the therapist for his or her concern and kindness. Discussions of the differential effectiveness of various forms of psychotherapy ignore the curative power inherent in the relationship between the patient and the person in the therapeutic role. A form of therapy cannot be compared to an appendectomy, in which the relationship between the surgeon and the patient is less relevant.

I add one more requirement to Frank's list. Faith in a therapy is enhanced when it is novel. One new form of therapy consists of a series of twelve weekly modules designed for patients' particular anxieties and delivered over the Internet. Although these clients never see a therapist and take no drugs, about one in four report a significant reduction in symptoms, compared with patients who did not take part in the program.

Denise Sloan and her colleagues at Boston University found that adults suffering from posttraumatic stress disorder following a motor-vehicle accident improved considerably after a regimen in which five times a week for six months they came to the therapist's office and spent thirty minutes writing out the details of the accident and their emotions.[48] The application of weak electric current to the scalp over intervals of several weeks is another novel therapy for depression. However, Colleen Loo and her colleagues from St. George Hospital in Australia found that this treatment was no more effective than a sham procedure in which the patient did not know that current was not being applied.[49] The most expensive new therapy for depression or obsessive-compulsive disorder involves implanting permanent electrodes in particular brain sites and giving patients the power to stimulate the sites briefly. It is too early to evaluate the long-term advantages of this method, which costs about $80,000.

If and when research reveals that one of these therapies, or any other novel therapy, is less effective than promised, or not effective with every patient, both therapist and patient will lose faith in the power of the regimen and the mutual commitment required for cure will be diluted. History reveals that this sequence dimmed earlier enthusiasms for genital stimulation, ice-cold baths, frontal lobotomy, sex hormones, and psychoanalysis. In time, it may also affect the current popularity of cognitive behavioral therapy for depression.

Indeed, several evaluations of cognitive behavioral therapy, compared with other forms of psychotherapy, have found that all therapies have roughly equivalent success rates when the therapist is experienced. It is probably not a coincidence that cognitive behavioral therapy, introduced in 1964, is close to five decades old. Faith in psychoanalytic therapy in the United States and Europe also began to wane about fifty years after its dissemination. And the first signs of a skeptical view of the specificity and long-term effectiveness of most drugs is emerging about fifty years after the manufacture of the first pills for a mental illness. It is likely that, by 2060, therapy over the Internet, writing down the details of a trauma, and application of a weak electric current will suffer a similar fate. I suspect that by 2100 most, if not all, currently popular therapies will be regarded as obsolescent. Clinicians who are still practicing them might lose their license, as would today's doctors if they adopted Galen's second-century therapeutic practice of treating an anxious woman by masturbating her to an orgasm.

Some scientists and clinicians are troubled by the fact that the advice a sizable proportion of American therapists give their patients is colored by ethically tinged values that are "simply dripping with moral evaluations."[50] One such value is the assumption that patients ought to award greater priority to their own desires than to the needs of their family, spouse, lover, or close friend. Research has not yet proven that this assumption is inherent in the human genome. It is certainly not the Dalai Lama's prescription for the optimal path to happiness. This ethical premise, however, does have adaptive advantages in the current economic and social structures of North American and European societies. These societies force many people to be more competitive, selfish, suspicious, and disloyal than they would like to be. This profile was not adaptive when small bands of hunter-gatherers were roaming the African savannah 100,000 years ago.

Many investigators trying to understand the causes of mental illnesses belong to one of two opposing armies that have been waging an ideological battle for centuries. The biological determinists temporarily defeat those who argue for the influence of life histories in specific cultural settings. But their victory is usually followed by the equally temporary advance of the other army, followed by their retreat. Biological explanations and cures are in ascendancy as of this writing, in 2012. The scientists and clinicians who belong to neither army hope that the two warring factions will sign a treaty that respects the integrity of both territories.

A satisfying and valid understanding of the causes of mental illnesses and the forms they assume requires inclusion of psychological processes described with a vocabulary that refers to feelings, emotions, beliefs, values, expectations, and interpretations of experience. An adolescent's feeling of shame generated by an identification with a father who is uneducated, unemployed, and alcoholic cannot be translated into sentences whose words refer only to the properties of genes, proteins, neurons, neurotransmitters, hormones, receptors, and circuits without losing a substantial amount of meaning. The neuroscientist's concept of anxiety, based on activation of a rat's amygdala in a setting that had been associated with an electric shock to the paws, does not come close to capturing the meaning Albert Camus had in mind when he wrote: "If I still feel a grain of anxiety, it is the thought of this unseizable moment slipping through my fingers like a ball of quicksilver."

CHAPTER NINE

New Certainties, Old Uncertainties

The scientific discoveries of the past century that illuminate our understanding of human nature would have brought full smiles to a host of philosophers, novelists, poets, and historians who recognized some of the themes in this narrative. But empirical research added important new details to the humanist's rough outline. We now have a richer appreciation of the biologically prepared biases of infants; recognize the developmental stages that are marked by the acquisition of a language, a moral sense, consciousness, and inferential talents; recognize that blends of temperaments and experiences create variation in personality and mental illness symptoms; and, hopefully, are ready to acknowledge that the display of a psychological property is often limited to specific settings. (See Figure 9.1 for a summary of the biological and psychological changes that occur over the first fifteen years of life.)

Despite many victories, a number of important problems that are amenable to inquiry or reconceptualization are being ignored. I consider four issues that deserve more attention than they are currently receiving. (See Figure 9.2.)

First, scientists studying psychological phenomena should replace their habit of linking one cause to one outcome with an examination of the relations between patterns of causal conditions and patterns of outcomes. A single condition (whether a

Summary of Psychological and Biological Changes over the First 15 Years		
Age	*Psychological Advances*	*Biological Changes*
8–12 weeks	Inhibition of brainstem reflexes; decrease in crying and endogenous smiles	• Synaptic contact between supplementary motor area and brainstem and between cingulate cortex and brainstem
	Establish circadian rhythm	• Myelination of the pyramidal tracts
		• Increased number of neurons in the suprachiasmatic nucleus of the hypothalamus
	Enhanced recognition memory	• Increase in melatonin synthesis
7–12 months	Enhanced working memory	• Growth of hippocampus • Enhanced growth of pyramidal neurons and interneurons in the prefrontal cortex
	Stranger and separation fear	• Increased number of spines in CA-3 region of the hippocampus
	Schematic concepts	• Myelination of the connections between the amygdala and cortex • Establishment of a 6 to 9 Hz alpha rhythm and 40-Hz gamma rhythm
12–24 months	Language	• Growth of pyramidal neurons and dendrites in layer 3 of prefrontal cortex
	Inference	• Enhanced linking of the two hemispheres
	Moral Sense	• Elongation of dendrites in Wernicke's area
	Self-awareness	• Increased GABA-ergic and acetylcholine activity in layer 3
2–8 years	Integration of past with present Increased reliance on semantic categories	• Brain attains 90% of its weight • Peak synaptic density in prefrontal cortex
	Detecting the relations between different categories	• Peak glucose uptake
		• Pruning
		• Peak density of GABA and glutamate receptors
		• Peak dopamine and norepinephrine receptors
		• Myelination of long cortical tracts
		• Increased coherence
		• Shift in blood flow from right to left hemisphere
		• Maximum dendritic differentiation in hippocampus
11–15 years	Deal with the hypothetical	• Rate of pruning slows
	Understand metaphor	• More efficient connectivity
	Certainty that all solutions have been examined	• Higher frequency of neuronal oscillations
	Detection of inconsistency among premises	

FIGURE 9.1 **The major psychological advances and the accompanying changes in the brain**

---

1. The issue of reliance on single causes and outcomes rather than patterns
2. The question of how the experiences associated with a person's social class affect mood and behavior?
3. The practice of relying on abstract words as basis for research
4. The question of how does any psychological phenomenon emerge from brain activity?

FIGURE 9.2   **Four current problems facing psychologists and psychiatrists**

gene, a secure attachment, premature birth, abuse, harsh socialization, or bullying) that ignores the child's gender, temperament, ethnicity, social class, and culture usually explains little of the variation in most psychological outcomes.

Prediction of the probability of suicide by an American adolescent is aided in a major way by knowing that the youth is a member of a disadvantaged social class, resides in a rural area of a western state, and made the suicidal attempt on a Monday during the spring or summer months. Psychologists who assume that being a victim of bullying increases the likelihood of aggressive behavior, depression, or social anxiety in the absence of other conditions are ignoring the contributions of the child's social class, ethnicity, gender, body size, school performance, and personality traits to the probability of being selected as a target for bullying, because the victims are not a random sample of all youths.

A team of Danish scientists found that the adolescents most likely to be bullied in each of thirty-five different countries came from poorer families but were attending schools that had many students from affluent families. High school youths from suburban Boston communities who reported being bullied were more likely to be deviant in some way; for example, they were gay, were small for their age, came from a poor family, or performed poorly on examinations. Hence, discovery of a relation between being bullied and a later trait is usually confounded with other properties that make a necessary contribution to the outcome. In the case of Mao Zedong, who was bullied by the wealthy boys at the school he attended because of his shabby clothes and peasant dialect, the experience of being a victim of derisive taunts increased his desire to become a person of importance who commanded respect. Adolescent boys from different homes and possessing different personalities might react to the same cruelty by deciding that they would never achieve the goals they wished to command. Investigators should also measure patterns of outcomes. Too often scientists measure a single variable—for example, the concentration of a molecule (cortisol or a sex hormone), answers to a questionnaire, a behavior (time looking at a stimulus or time to respond to a target), an autonomic response (blood pressure or heart rate), or a brain reaction (an event related potential or the BOLD signal discussed in Chapter 7). The problem with this strategy, however, is that each of these single measures is affected by more than one process and thus has an ambiguous meaning.

Adults who had initially seen many pictures of familiar objects, such as guitars and combs, were later shown three kinds of pictures: the same object in its original position, the same object at a different angle, and a totally new object. The fusiform area in the right hemisphere was activated by the familiar object presented at a different angle; the fusiform site in the left hemisphere was not. An investigator who examined only the evidence from the left hemisphere would arrive at the wrong conclusion regarding the brain's response to the change in perspective. Examining the evidence from both hemispheres protects the scientist from the error of claiming that the brain did or did not detect the change in the angle of presentation.

An event as simple as a continuous loud noise, usually experienced as annoying or stressful, activates a circuit of at least nine interconnected brain sites. Scientists cannot know the person's psychological state by measuring activity in only one location in this circuit. The act of reaching for a cup involves the simultaneous activation of a pattern of arm muscles by the spinal cord and cannot be explained by the activity of individual muscles.

Earlier I described a student who wanted to discover the features of sound that were most likely to alert newborn infants. Richard Kearsley recorded the behaviors of two-day-old infants in reaction to sounds that varied in frequency, loudness, and rise time. After spending several years gathering evidence and then analyzing the infants' level of alertness to each stimulus, he was disappointed to learn that no particular frequency, loudness, or rise time had a significant influence on the infants' behavior. When he came to me for advice, I suggested that he look for the patterns of frequency, loudness, and rise time that produced the most obvious alerting in a majority of the newborns. When he did so, he discovered one pattern that combined a specific frequency, loudness, and rise time that was maximally alerting. It is not a coincidence that that this sound bore the closest resemblance to the qualities of the human voice.

Investigators wishing to discover what infants know about an object or event should record looking time along with event-related potentials, eye movements, heart rate, or facial expressions. No single measure can reveal all that an infant knows about an event. Psychologists who study human memory have learned that the recall of a poem learned years earlier is not the most accurate index of how much information was preserved. That is why they also measure recognition of words from the poem and the ease of relearning the poem. Because scientists at the University of Lausanne measured both duration of body immobility and heart rate, they did not make the mistake of concluding that oxytocin reduced the intensity of a rat's fear. Although high levels of oxytocin resulted in a shorter duration of body immobility, implying less fear, this molecule had no effect on the animal's heart rate, implying no change in the level of fear.

Verbal reports, behaviors, and biological measures reveal different aspects of the invisible phenomena that psychologists wish to understand. Verbal descriptions imply that psychological traits, such as *extraverted* or *agreeable,* are displayed across different settings. Observations of behavior in natural contexts complement the verbal replies by revealing that traits such as extraversion or agreeableness are often displayed in select settings. The observations fine-tune the semantic concepts and allow the investigator to appreciate which contexts release the trait in question and which do not. I suspect that no more than 50 percent of a group of adults who describe themselves as extraverts on questionnaires would show the behavior that is expected of extraverts in a variety of settings. The other half belong to different categories.

Sadly, only a small proportion of psychologists study the effect of the context on the behaviors that define a trait, despite their acknowledgment that one of psychology's major goals is to predict behavior. Instead, the evidence gathered in the vast majority of investigations of human participants comes from verbal reports, a brain measure, or the speed of a simple motor response in a laboratory setting.

Neither questionnaire replies nor BOLD signals are adequate proxies for the behaviors that are displayed in the settings in which individuals live. Adding measures of behavior in settings that approximate natural contexts to the verbal reports and brain profiles is mandatory if psychologists want to keep the promises they have made to the public and to the agencies that support them.

The assumption that a single measure, whose power depends on it being part of a pattern, has some of the power possessed by the complete pattern is analogous to conferring aesthetic qualities to a single thread from a Gobelin tapestry. Georg von Bekesy, who was awarded a Nobel Prize in 1961 for discovering how sounds affect the sensory cells of the inner ear, told a younger colleague that significant discoveries require studying a phenomenon under as many different conditions and

with as many measures as possible in order to avoid a premature and incorrect conclusion. Although psychologists are familiar with the many discoveries in biology
that reveal more complexity than had been assumed, they continue to favor simple
cause-effect relations in which one condition—an insecure attachment, bullying,
childhood neglect, or a gene—can make a significant contribution to an outcome
that is measured with one procedure. This flight from complexity, which comes
naturally to the human mind, is not a recipe for progress.

A second phenomenon requiring a more satisfactory explanation is the fact that
the social class of rearing, which is correlated with the adult's class, is a powerful
predictor of many important outcomes in childhood and the adult years, whether
children grow up in a developed nation like the United States or a poor country like
Madagascar. The political attitudes, ethical positions, styles of social interaction,
feelings of agency, and health of individuals born to college-educated parents differ
from those of individuals born to parents who did not graduate high school. Yet scientists do not understand the processes that were responsible for these distinctive
collections of properties.

What are parents from different classes doing in the home? How do children
react to their parents' practices and personal traits? When does an identification
with one's class emerge, and how is it manifested? What conditions differentiate
the school environments of the poor and the affluent? Because we cannot answer
these and other questions, we are deprived of a persuasive explanation of the robust
relations between class of rearing and a host of outcomes that affect governmental expenditures for health care, prisons, and special education, as well as the person's quality of life. The failure to understand the reasons why class is so important
makes it difficult for experts to suggest strategies that might improve the lives of
millions of individuals across the world's societies.

Despite the obvious significance of this problem, I suspect that no social scientist
is currently writing a grant request that proposes to gather behavioral and biological
evidence—not just questionnaire data—on the temperaments, family experiences,
peer relationships, school experiences, and identifications of one thousand children
from different class and ethnic groups who will be studied from the early postnatal
months through the adolescent years. One reason is that such a project would probably cost several billion dollars.

Social scientists are reluctant to make requests for that much money because
they do not expect them to be approved. This timidity exacts a cost. The small-scale,

relatively inexpensive studies that are most often published in technical journals are unlikely to yield discoveries that have a half-life greater than ten years. The reliance on this strategy over the past few decades persuaded government agencies to award a smaller proportion of funds to social science research than they did sixty years ago. Social scientists might take note of the fact that physicists regularly request and receive large amounts of money to study a feature of the material universe. The United States spent more than $2 billion for the project that allowed the landing of a vehicle on Mars in August 2012.

The high cost of studying the psychological consequences of class membership is not the only reason why social scientists are reluctant to explore the actual experiences that accompany growing up in families belonging to divergent classes. Another reason stems from an unwillingness among many Americans to acknowledge the profound class differences in a society that values egalitarianism and equal opportunity. Perhaps investigators are a little apprehensive over discovering facts that would require faulting some parents for their practices and criticizing some teachers for indifference, especially if both groups belong to an ethnic minority. The dissemination of these findings might also raise the average citizen's consciousness—or, in some cases, guilt—over the serious health burdens that accompany a life of poverty and provoke a more vocal demand for allocating additional resources to the poor. This is politically dangerous territory.

A similar reluctance surrounded research on sexual behavior before the end of World War II. Frank Beach, who was my mentor when I was a graduate student at Yale in the 1950s, had been studying animal sexual behavior at the American Museum of Natural History in New York when he learned in the late 1940s that he was being considered for a distinguished professorial chair at Yale. Several members of the committee of Yale professors reviewing his credentials resisted his appointment because they felt it was unseemly for a Yale professor to study sex, even among animals. Fortunately, they were outvoted. Diluted, but similar, attitudes toward research on sexual behavior persist today. Neuroscientists interested in the brain sites that contribute to basic psychological systems usually condition a fear state in rats or mice, and less often condition a state of sexual arousal, despite their ability to do so and the evolutionary significance of sexual behavior.

A long-standing bias favoring the material causes of mental phenomena helps to explain an indifference to inventing novel ways to measure the psychological states created by rearing in an advantaged or disadvantaged class. Genes, brains, neurons, and molecules are material things with features that can be measured accurately and manipulated. The emotions that accompany class membership are invisible, non-material entities that emerge and disappear at unpredictable times and are more difficult to measure and manipulate.

The failure to develop more powerful methods to study psychological states prevents a deeper insight into the processes that mediate the relation between class of rearing and the child's command of skills and traits. Most research on this issue relies on the crude evidence that questionnaires or interviews provide. Social scientists have insufficient enthusiasm for spending many years developing a method that might uncover new phenomena or measure a theoretically important process. Physicists, chemists, and biologists regularly support and celebrate colleagues who are willing to devote many years to perfecting a new machine or procedure. Anthony Greenwald of the University of Washington notes that 80 percent of the Nobel Prizes in physics, chemistry, physiology, and medicine from 1991 to 2011 were given to scientists who invented a new method or improved on an older one.[1] The two scientists responsible for the development of the magnetic scanner, Paul Lauterbur and Sir Peter Mansfield, are examples.

I cannot think of many psychologists who worked for a decade or more trying to perfect a new, more accurate procedure to evaluate a person's identification with his or her social class, beliefs about the self, or conception of society. As a result, questionnaires remain, as they have for a hundred years, the primary source of information on these concepts. The technologies that psychologists often use—cameras, DVD players, and computers—were invented by engineers and natural scientists for other purposes.

Natural scientists are regularly attracted to the challenge of inventing a new technology because of the promise of discovering a novel phenomenon with an elegant new machine. As I wrote this sentence I was reminded of an afternoon almost fifty years ago when I was sitting with fourteen other social scientists at a long, polished table in an elegant room of a mansion given to the Massachusetts Institute of Technology for conferences. New machines that recorded sounds with great fidelity on reels of tape had just become available. The speaker, wearing a dark suit, vest, and a carefully trimmed van Dyke beard, wheeled in a large, expensive recorder, cleared his throat, and told his audience: "We will now hear a baby cry." He flicked on the recorder and that is what we heard. He stopped the recorder after about thirty seconds and said: "Now we will hear a second baby cry." When these cries terminated he announced that his presentation was complete, and he sat down. I was surprised that no one was laughing.

A third issue deserving closer scrutiny is the psychologist's continued attraction to abstract, semantic concepts that ignore the properties of the agent, the features of the setting, and the source of evidence. Natural scientists typically select a puzzling phenomenon as the primary reason for initiating research. Most eminent physicists during the 1920s agreed that accounting for the spectral lines emitted by an atom was a pressing problem deserving inquiry. The subsequent answers led to the body of equations called quantum mechanics. Crick and Watson chose the molecular structure of DNA as the puzzle to solve. They did not begin by assuming it was a double helix. Rather, they inferred that structure from Crick's metal models of the molecule and from Rosalind Franklin's photographs. Linus Pauling's incorrect assumption that DNA was a triple helix made it easier for Crick and Watson to arrive at the correct solution first.

Many psychologists, by contrast, prefer to prove the validity of intuitively attractive, abstract ideas, perhaps because philosophy is one of the discipline's parents. Philosophers typically analyze single words with a controversial meaning and generate a semantic argument that defends the utility, often temporary, of one particular meaning. Theory of mind, self-concept, well-being, impulsivity, stress, risk aversion, fear, intelligence, social cognition, cooperation, altruism, positive affect, and regulation are among the popular concepts that psychologists try to measure. Each term is indifferent to the specific agent to whom the property applies, the setting, and the fact that often only a single source of evidence is used to infer the property.

Most social scientists favor one of two research strategies. One group prefers to use a robust observation that is not yet understood as the reason for further inquiry—for example, discovering the biological properties and experiences of children who have great difficulty learning to read. The second, larger group prefers to begin with a semantic concept whose validity they want to prove. The psychologists wishing to demonstrate that infants understand causality, and use looking time as the only measure, provide an example. The psychologists who are attracted to the study of puzzles would have noted that infants vary in the duration of time they look at various events. Because this variation is not understood, they would have studied the conditions that produce long, medium, and short looking times. If the evidence they gathered required the conclusion that infants understand causality, they would have entertained that possibility—but only after the fact, not before they understood the factors modulating the amount of time infants of varied ages look at varied classes of events.

One problem trailing the strategy of beginning with intuitions about fruitful semantic concepts rather than puzzling phenomena is that the different schemata linked to a concept confer divergent meanings to the same term. For example, the term *anxiety* could evoke schemata of task failure, a parent's harsh criticisms, losing money, a social blunder, the disruption of a satisfying relationship, or the health of a parent. Each schema awards a different meaning to the word. Similar ambiguities apply to the concepts *stress, intelligence,* and *regulation.*

Many commentators have noted that humans are susceptible to believing that if a word is used frequently it probably names something that exists. The psychologists' frequent use of the word *regulate* invites the inference that this term must name a property that some humans display consistently across diverse settings. However, Eli Tsukayama and his colleagues at the University of Pennsylvania found that few adults regulate inappropriate, impulsive decisions across the domains of work, social relationships, sex, gambling, and investing money.[2] Most who admit to making impulsive decisions in one domain—say, eating too much at restaurants—are not impulsive when spending money or working. Tiger Woods effectively regulated impulsive decisions in most areas of his life but failed to activate that property when he was tempted by sexual desire.

It is misleading to argue, as a few psychologists do, that youths from poor, single-parent families living in urban neighborhoods with drug dealers, pimps, and rival gangs do not regulate their aggression as well as children from comfortable, affectionate, two-parent families living in safer small towns. The latter youths encounter far fewer occasions where they have to regulate inappropriate actions. A marble in a groove is not effectively regulating its perfectly straight motion.

A popular illustration in journal articles on the effects of stress on children features a box enclosing the term *adversity* and an arrow pointing to a second box enclosing the phrase *problems with self-regulation.* Two additional boxes, sitting on top of the first pair, enclose the terms *family environment* and *genetic background.* Arrows from each of the four boxes point to a fifth box enclosing a list of undesirable outcomes that accompany poor regulation. The intended message in this array of boxes is that any adversity can, under some family and genetic conditions, compromise a child's ability to control impulses and lead to a variety of maladaptive responses. The form of the adversity, the child's interpretation, the specific family practices, the genes, and the settings in which regulation is required are free to vary, allowing readers to insert in the boxes any adverse event, parental practice, gene, form of regulation, and outcome they wish. This permissiveness makes it close to impossible to disprove the claim that some adversities compromise some aspect of regulation in some children born with certain genomes and growing up in certain families.

The concept *victim of bullying* is another example. Herbert Marsh and his colleagues at the University of Western Sydney found that some Australian boys who physically bullied others became victims of bullying months later.[3] Psychologists do not have a category for youths who are both bullies and victims at different times during the same year. Some men who are bullied by their employer in the workplace bully their wives at home. The wives in turn bully their school-age sons, who bully timid boys at recess, who in turn bully their younger sisters. This sequence makes it difficult to decide who is a bully and who is a victim. The Chinese note that the moment the sun reaches the highest point in the sky, it is prepared to begin its descent.

I confess to being initially surprised and then saddened by reading a review essay, by two geneticists from North Carolina State University, titled "The Genetics of Aggression." The authors never defined *aggression* and simply assumed that readers understood what it meant. More seriously, these biologists declared, without adequate evidence, that one set of genes contributed to all forms of aggression— whether ants defending a nest, sharks attacking a human, snakes killing a mouse, mice biting an intruder, alpha baboons defending their status, or jealous spouses stabbing their mate for infidelity.

The related, equally abstract term *violence,* intended to apply to humans, fails to specify the class of person committing the violence, their motives, the form the violence assumed, or the contexts in which a violent action occurred. These four features assumed different combinations when one of Napoleon's troops killed a Russian soldier who was about to shoot him, a Nazi official ordered the gassing of innocent Jewish women, a new Ottoman sultan murdered his brothers and all the pregnant women in the harem of the recently deceased sultan, an estranged adolescent killed twelve classmates in a rampage, a bank robber murdered a teller, a white racist lynched an African-American, a Hutu man slaughtered a pregnant Tutsi woman, a Syrian soldier shelled a crowd protesting the regime's legitimacy, one gentleman shot another in a duel because the latter questioned his honor, and an unmarried adolescent girl drowned her newborn infant.

Steven Pinker's decision in *The Better Angels of Our Nature*[4] to pool different types of violent actions by agents who varied in gender, age, ethnicity, and motive into a single category called *violence* is analogous to grouping the olfactory signals of ants, dances of bees, songs of birds, croaks of frogs, grimaces of monkeys, screams of infants, lullabies by mothers, lectures by professors, and spam messages over the Internet into an omnibus category called *communication.*

The probability of a violent act is palpably higher for males compared with females across the life span. Males between seventeen and thirty years of age commit the vast majority of violent behaviors, in the past as well as today. Older men and children are unlikely to kill, rape, or torture anyone. Males between age seventeen and thirty represented a large proportion of the European population between 1200 and 1700 because more than 50 percent of children died before age five and more than 80 percent of adults died before age fifty. By contrast, males between seventeen and thirty make up less than 20 percent of today's European population. Hence, a scientist who bases the prevalence of violence on the ratio of the number of homicides over the total population would be likely to discover that the rate of violence decreased across the interval from 1200 to 2000 because the proportion of the total population that was male and between age seventeen and thirty had declined precipitously over those eight hundred years.

This statement is not intended to question the fact, noted by many scholars, that there has been a steady decline in deaths due to violence over the past eight centuries—a fact that seems secure rather than an artifact. However, I suspect that the decline might be less steep if the index of violence was the ratio of the number of violent acts, or deaths due to violence, divided by the total number of males between seventeen and thirty years of age, rather than divided by the total population. If, for example, the absolute number of violent acts committed by males between seventeen and thirty was the same in the fourteenth and twentieth centuries, the ratios based on the total population would indicate a decline in violence. Conclusions based on ratios are always tricky, however, because they can vary with the denominator that is selected. An estimate of the population density of the United States based on the ratio of the total population over the total land area of the country implies a low density. But a ratio whose denominator is the land area where two-thirds of Americans live implies a high density.

A personal experience taught me the advantages of resisting abstract concepts that have insufficient support from evidence. I was fond of the popular ideas of motive and conflict in 1957 when, as a twenty-eight-year-old psychologist at the Fels Research Institute in Ohio, I needed a battery of procedures to measure personality traits in young adults who had been studied since their early childhood. Many psychologists I respected believed that adults would reveal their motives and conflicts through their interpretations of ambiguous stimuli. A task that was popular at the time involved giving a person arrays of twenty-two small cardboard figures in postures that suggested anger, anxiety, sexuality, dependence, frailty, authority, or neutral traits. Each individual was asked to select groups of figures that he or she believed "went together." The assumption behind this instruction was that a person who grouped the figures suggestive of anger was preoccupied with the motive of hostility, whereas a person who selected figures suggestive of sexual motives was concerned with or conflicted over this desire.

After poring over the groupings the adults produced, I was disappointed to learn that the data were totally unrelated to the extensive, objective information available on their child and adult personalities. Frustrated, I tried to figure out what biases, if any, guided the groupings. One evening, after many weeks of study, a possible answer emerged. Some individuals based their groups on the physical features of the figures—say, all the figures that were standing up, lying down, or with their arms raised. Others grouped figures that formed a narrative; for example, the figure of a woman with her arm raised was grouped with the figure of a child on his knees. Fortunately, I recorded the time each person took to create each group. Those who based their groupings on physical features took longer than the others. Equally important, these adults were more cautious and compulsive as children and as adults than those who grouped figures in narrative relations. It appeared that the groupings did reveal a personality trait, but not the one I had predicted. This new interpretation of the evidence led to the invention of the concept of a reflective cognitive style, which I pursued for many years. This example illustrates the problem trailing the premature acceptance of an intuitively attractive word and assuming the validity of a procedure to measure the concept underlying it.

Young psychologists are expected to test the validity of a theoretical idea and are often criticized by their elders for gathering observations that are not guided by a well-argued prediction that enjoys legitimacy among investigators working in the same domain. This practice is odd because a large number of the most important discoveries in psychology were unanticipated by any hypothesis. Ivan Pavlov had no strong expectations about what he would find when he began his experiments on the conditioning of salivation in dogs. The scientists studying the man called H.M., who lost his hippocampus in an operation intended to relieve his epilepsy, were surprised to learn that H.M. had a satisfactory memory for many facts of his childhood but could not remember a sentence heard twenty seconds earlier.

Torsten Wiesel, who shared the 1981 Nobel Prize with David Hubel for discovering the receptivity of neurons in the visual cortex to particular contours, confessed to a reporter: "We started out with no hypothesis but just forged ahead to the best of our intuition." The discovery that led to the 2011 Nobel Prize in chemistry was equally unexpected. Daniel Shechtman's decision to cool a molten glob of aluminum and manganese quickly led to a totally new class of crystal that no scientist believed existed. The three biologists who won the 1995 Nobel Prize in Physiology had absolutely no idea what might happen when they fed male fruit flies chemicals that they hoped would cause mutations in the flies' sperm. They were surprised to find that the chemicals caused changes in a small number of genes that controlled the shape of the body axis. This fact has become one of the momentous discoveries of the past few decades. We need more playful curiosity in psychology laboratories and among the directors of the agencies awarding funds for the study of psychological phenomena.

Psychologists who prefer to design experiments that affirm the validity of big words, which the writer Helen Sword calls "zombie nouns," should descend from the high tower—from which objects on the ground below look the same—to the street level where their distinctive features are obvious.[5] The problem with concepts like *introversion, attend, remember, fearful, bold, positive affect, stress,* and *regulate* is that they fail to tell readers who, when, where, and what. Alecia Carter and her colleagues at Australian National University remind psychologists that the baboons who were exceedingly bold when presented with a stuffed version of a predator snake were not at all bold when the object was a novel food.[6] And a team of scientists led by Frank Albert found that the trait called *tameness,* when applied to the domesticated species of dogs, pigs, and rabbits, compared with their less tame forms in the wild, can be the product of different genes and brain physiologies in each domesticated species.[7] These examples illustrate why scientists must specify the context and the species when using adjectives like *bold* or *tame* to describe an animal or a human. Despite the reasonableness of this suggestion, one team used the words *cooperators* and *cheaters* to describe the activity of different kinds of yeast cells. A similar indifference to species and source of evidence is common among scientists who are fond of the concept *stress.* They assume that the state of rats who are restrained in a narrow tube or forced to swim in a tub of water resembles the state of adults who have lost a job, money, their home, or a loved one.

The mathematician Peter Woit described an occasion when the physicist Wolfgang Pauli became irritated with a young Werner Heisenberg because the latter insisted that he had come up with a unified theory of matter that was missing only a few technical details. The next day Pauli sent his friends a piece of paper containing a blank rectangle in the shape of a frame for a painting. Written below the frame was the sentence: "This is to show that I can paint like Titian. Only the technical details are missing."

There is a wooden bench close to the edge of a small pond in a nature preserve about a mile from my home where I walk regularly. A plaque on the back of the bench contains a quote by the late Paul Samuelson, a Nobel Laureate in economics: "A professor must have a theory as a dog must have fleas." That pithy statement has a complementary truth: "A professor must question her theory as her students and colleagues must question her."

A number of abstract psychological concepts remain popular because they satisfy the need for consistency among the investigator's semantic networks. The networks for the concepts *positive emotion* and *negative emotion* are an example. Joy is always classified as a positive emotion and guilt as a negative one. Hence, they should not occur together. Yet it is possible that some adolescents who experience joy upon learning that a disliked rival failed an examination might immediately experience guilt because feeling happy over another's misfortune violates their ethical code. The young Rousseau felt the positive emotion of sexual arousal when he was spanked by his governess, although the spanking evoked the unpleasant sensation of pain, which should have created a negative emotion. The continued use of the terms *positive* and *negative* to describe emotions or experiences allows investigators to avoid specifying whether these words refer to the brain states or feelings evoked by objectively pleasant or unpleasant events (food, sex, and money or pain, loss, and frustration) or to the subjective appraisals of those feelings in a particular context (a masochist being whipped). Authors who let readers decide on the meaning of *positive* and *negative* are protected from being wrong. Biologists would never use these evaluative adjectives to describe the states of organs or cells. That is, they would not write that a heart was in a negative state because colleagues want to know the objective state of the heart.

The problems trailing attempts to preserve semantic consistency are clearest for concepts related to the antonyms *good* and *bad*. Many popular terms for human qualities belong to semantic networks that have *good* and *bad* as nodes. This contrast includes a secure versus an insecure attachment, effective versus ineffective regulation, and a vulnerable versus a resilient personality. Investigators hold the implicit premise that all bad properties, as well as all good properties, should be positively correlated.

The contemporary Western mind prefers a symmetry in which good experiences are followed by good outcomes and bad experiences by bad ones. This

premise is falsified by the fact that many stressful events, classified as bad, motivate some children to acquire the coping defenses that lead to a good outcome
later. By contrast, many good experiences early in life are followed by undesirable
outcomes. One-year-old American girls with a secure attachment to the mother
are apt to become anxious adolescents if their mothers socialize their daughters
to be passive with boys, noncompetitive in school, and guilty over sexual feelings.
Most Americans born to college-educated parents between 1987 and 1992 were
the childhood recipients of the good family experiences of affection, gentle socialization, and consistent praise. But experts are describing this generation as narcissistic, which is a bad trait. Professional tennis players who avoid close attachments
to other players when on tour, which some psychologists would regard as a bad
trait, win more matches.

Psychologists should infer concepts from a diverse set of observations in different contexts and resist the temptation to posit correlations among concepts simply
because they are semantically consistent. Natural phenomena are under no obligation to honor a semantic consistency among all good outcomes or all bad ones. The
amygdala is activated by the unexpected sight of a tarantula as well as by a pile of
hundred-dollar bills under a log. Maple leaves are most beautiful the week before
they fall. Flamingos are least beautiful the moment they hatch.

About twelve years ago, while chatting with one of the world's most respected neuroscientists, I asked whether he believed that if he had complete knowledge of my
brain at that moment he would be able to predict whether I was about to crawl
under the table at which we were sitting. To my surprise, he said "yes." His reply
captures the fourth puzzle that this final chapter considers—namely, explaining
how any psychological phenomenon could emerge from a profile of brain activity.
A great many psychologists have decided that this problem has an obvious priority over other candidates because of the new technologies permitting study of the
brain and a long-standing preference for measuring material phenomena that can
be observed rather than psychological processes that cannot be seen under a microscope or inferred from patterns on an oscilloscope.

Very few scientists question the popular assumption that the brain is the foundation of all psychological phenomena. We have gained an initial understanding of the
bases for some aspects of visual, auditory, and olfactory perception as well as a few
motor actions. However, the brain bases for beliefs, feelings, emotions, intentions,

personality traits, complex actions, and consciousness, as well as the correlations between the development of the brain and the emergence of new cognitive talents, remain more mysterious.

Rarely does any brain measure predict a psychological outcome in 90 percent of research participants. This claim holds even for the perception of acute pain. Kay Brodersen and her colleagues at the University of Oxford found that about 60 percent of the time adult reports of pain to a stimulus were correlated with a pattern of brain activation.[8] Reports of a painful sensation in the remaining 40 percent of the trials were unrelated to a particular brain profile.

Similarly, a team of neuroscientists studying monkeys at the Max Planck Institute in Tubingen discovered that even when the outcome is an extremely well-defined, simple motor response indicating whether the animal recognized an object as familiar or unfamiliar, an appropriate brain measure could predict the monkey's behavior only about one-third of the time.

Despite the efforts of many brilliant investigators who have addressed this problem with new technologies over the past forty years (admittedly a short time), the veil separating patterns of brain activity from most psychological phenomena remains opaque. In *The Organisation of Mind,* Tim Shallice and Richard Cooper of the University of London wrote an extensive and fair summary of what is known about the relation of brain measures to perception, memory, consciousness, and thinking.[9] Although the book reflects the authors' belief that future scientists will discover more robust relations, Shallice and Cooper had to admit that every major conclusion wrested from nature as of 2011 was vulnerable to the criticism of one or more skeptics who could mount a reasonable, but different, explanation of the same evidence.

One reason for the persistent disagreements, which I noted earlier, is the habit of writing about abstract psychological processes without specifying agents, targets, and sources of evidence. The final chapter on thinking in Shallice and Cooper's book contains an illustration with boxes labeled *goal generation, working memory, monitoring system,* and *running of cognitive procedures.* These boxes fail to specify the age of the subjects, the goals being sought, the representations being remembered or monitored, or the cognitive procedures being run.

The brain circuit activated when adults attend to a salient figure in the foreground of a scene is not the circuit activated when they attend to the spatial relationships between the figure and the scene's background objects. The terms describing cognitive processes have to specify what these processes are working on. There is no single brain circuit corresponding to the abstract term *remember;* there probably is a circuit, however, that is the foundation of *remembering a sibling's birthday.*

Terrence Deacon in *Incomplete Nature* tries to remove some of the mystery surrounding the relation between brain and mind by resurrecting George Lewes's nineteenth-century concept of emergence.[10] Briefly, this idea means that although novel phenomena emerge from patterns of elementary components, the emergent phenomena obey special laws and require their own vocabulary. The mathematician Terence Tao reminds us that the laws governing an emergent system are typically independent of the laws governing the elements that are its foundation.

Charles Gilbert of Rockefeller University, who studies the reactions of neurons in the visual cortex to simple stimuli, notes that it is impossible to predict a neuron's response to a vertical line inside a square from the cell's response to the square or the vertical line presented alone.[11] Analogously, the anticipation of danger while walking in a dark alley at midnight, the intention to pick up a fork, and the emotion of sadness while listening to a Brahms piano sonata are emergent. No neural circuit possesses these psychological properties. As a viewer slowly approaches one of Claude Monet's paintings of a lily pond, there comes a moment when the coherent scene suddenly dissolves into many patches of color.

There are two ways to think about the functions of the neurons at a brain site. A fair number of neuroscientists would like to believe that the brain is modular, meaning that many sites have an exclusive function that is not shared by other sites. Advocates of a less popular view argue that each site has more than one function because most sites receive inputs from multiple sources, project to more than one neuronal cluster, and participate in more than one circuit. Broca's area, for example, is not restricted to processing only grammatically correct sentences. The amygdala is not limited to the acquisition of body immobility or a bodily startle to an event signaling danger. At least eleven sites are activated when the first rays of morning sunlight enter the eyes.

This perspective likens the functions of a brain site to those of a hand, which can grab a glass, hold an ice cream cone, carve a spearhead, deliver an infant, slap a mosquito, catch a ball, or caress a loved one but cannot smell a fire or taste chocolate. The brain sites that allowed eighteenth-century humans to hold a quill and write a message did not actualize those functions for close to 100,000 years. These circuits had other functions before written languages, paper, and writing instruments were

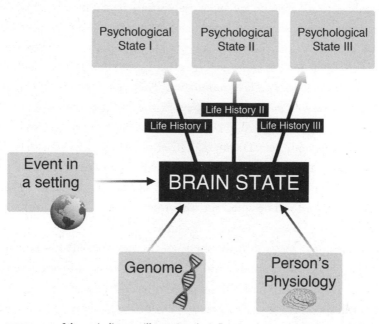

FIGURE 9.3   Schematic diagram illustrating the influence of a person's biology and life history on psychological outcomes

invented. Every cell in a person's body (except for ova and sperm) contains the same genes, but the chemistry of each cell in each kind of bodily tissue suppresses some genes and allows others to be expressed. Analogously, each distinctive setting, or task assignment, selects a particular pattern of brain activity and psychological outcome from an envelope of possibilities. The sight of a rattlesnake on a trail provokes a brain pattern and a psychological reaction unlike the brain pattern and reaction to the same snake in a glass cage at a zoo. Attending to the height of a spruce tree compared with attending to the tree's spatial relations to other trees, shrubs, and rocks in the immediate area evoke different brain profiles.

There is an inherent indeterminacy in the relation between a brain state and an emergent psychological state. The brain state at any one moment is a product of the person's genome, the physiology of brain and body, and the external event or thought that is ongoing. This brain state can be the origin of more than one psychological state because the person's life history and the nature of the context combine to select one psychological outcome from an envelope of possibilities. (See Figure 9.3.)

Despite this indeterminacy between brain and mind, some neuroscientists believe that one day there will be no need for psychological concepts and the words that describe neurons, circuits, and brain molecules will be sufficient. This is an odd position. When physicists have a complete understanding of the energies and particles that comprise matter, they will not be able to explain why a wooden wheel can roll. Each discipline invents some concepts that cannot be described with the vocabulary of the discipline that is its foundation. The chemist's concept of oxidation cannot be replaced with the language of physics, the biologist's concept of inclusive fitness cannot be described with the chemist's vocabulary, and the psychologist's concept of identification with a family pedigree cannot be described with biological terms. Put plainly, the language used to describe the brain does not have the terms needed to describe restless, inattentive children. Those who retain the hope that a biological vocabulary will be sufficient are, in the words of Marilynne Robinson, using a straight-edge ruler to measure a fractal world.[12]

One reason for the incommensurability of the two vocabularies is that many psychological phenomena are discrete, whereas most brain measures are continuous. The perception of a face, the semantic interpretation of a feeling, and the grasping of an object are yes or no events. They do or do not occur. However, the measures of brain activity that are the presumed foundations of these discrete events are continuous. The former include magnitudes of blood flow, magnitudes of waveforms in the electroencephalogram, and rates of discharge of neurons. A tornado provides an analogy for this phenomenon, inasmuch as it is the product of a series of continuous changes in the temperatures of the air masses in the upper and lower atmosphere. When these values exceed a tipping point, a tornado suddenly forms. Scientists do not yet know how to map the emergence of a tornado or a psychological event, such as the grasping of a glass, on the continuous conditions that are its origins. Some scientists might reply that psychological outcomes do vary continuously. Perceptions vary in *clarity*; thoughts vary in *logical consistency*; feelings vary in *intrusiveness*; actions vary in *force*. But none of these adjectives can be used to describe neurons or brain circuits.

The optimistic hope that a future vocabulary for the brain will eventually capture mental processes adequately is unlikely to be realized because a particular brain pattern can be the foundation for more than one psychological outcome. The setting and the person's life history select one outcome from an envelope of possibilities. Rather than assume that one brain pattern is the foundation of only one psychological event, investigators should realize it is likely that a particular perception, semantic network, feeling, or action can be the product of more than one brain state.

A blizzard provides an analogy. There is more than one arrangement of water and air molecules, temperatures, and wind velocities that can generate a blizzard that drops eight inches of snow over an area of 3,000 square miles. I borrow from the physicist Erwin Schrodinger a metaphor that likens a particular perception, feeling, or thought to the whitecap on a wave. The wave represents all the possible outcomes that could result from an envelope of brain profiles created by an event. The whitecap represents the one that actually occurs.

This nondeterministic, probabilistic conception of the relation between brain and mind frustrates the many neuroscientists who believe that one day they will discover deterministic relations between events in the brain and specific perceptions, memories, beliefs, and actions in animals and humans. Faith in the possibility of making certain predictions has always distinguished European from Chinese scholars. Kepler, Galileo, Descartes, Newton, and Einstein held, as a matter of faith, that all natural phenomena were potentially knowable and predictable. One of Einstein's most famous comments was that God does not play dice. Far Eastern scholars never entertained the notion that they might possess an understanding of nature so complete it would allow them to make perfect predictions.

The early advances in geometry by the Greeks and in mathematical formulations by seventeenth-century Europeans who wrote accurate descriptions of the orbits of the planets, combined with the belief in an omniscient Judeo-Christian God, are possible reasons for the current Western confidence in a material determinism. Mathematics promises and often delivers exact answers and certain conclusions. An all-knowing God who is a prime mover of all events can create any outcome He wishes. These two magisterial ideas were missing from the Chinese understanding of the world.

The main point is that each phase in the cascade from brain to perception to thought or feeling and finally to behavior has to be described with its own vocabulary. When scientists have a more coherent understanding of how a brain event contributes to a psychological one, they will need a psychological vocabulary for the latter. The debate boils down to the rules specifying the words, or mathematical statements, that are appropriate for different domains of nature. Physicists agree that *up* and *down* refer to the properties of different kinds of quarks. Geneticists concur that *crossing over* refers to genes exchanging locations within pairs of chromosomes. Neuroscientists, however, feel free to borrow the psychologist's vocabulary to describe brain activity. When investigators write that an activated amygdala is the foundation of fear or the prefrontal cortex integrates information, some readers interpret these sentences as implying that brain tissue can be fearful or able to integrate information. Rather, fear and the integration of information are emergent psychological properties of whole animals.

Natural scientists studying animal behavior have taken advantage of the fact that English allows a verb to be used with a variety of nouns and have written, for example, that a firefly larva is "bold," an adult mongoose "teaches," a mouse is "aggressive," a bear can "count," a baboon is "aloof," or a chimpanzee "is befriended." I noted earlier that some biologists extend human properties to yeast cells that presumably can "cooperate" or "cheat." These twenty-first century scientists are adopting Darwin's permissive frame of mind in *The Descent of Man,* compared with his more careful language in *The Origin of Species* written twelve years earlier. Darwin ascribed intelligence, misery, happiness, courage, love, grief, and ennui to dogs, monkeys, and apes. To one particular female baboon Darwin attributed "a capacious heart." The problem with this practice is that these terms were invented to refer to human acts that are usually accompanied by conscious awareness of a goal, an evaluation of its moral status, and/or an evaluation of the self by another. Because animals do not possess this trio of talents, it is misleading to use these words to describe animals.

Fortunately, these scientists are reluctant to suggest that a female monkey who mated with several males in an afternoon is "adulterous" or a lion who brutally kills a gazelle is "a callous psychopath." Accurate comprehension of the meaning of a word requires that it be part of a full sentence. The meaning of the word *aggressive* in the sentence "Some mice are aggressive toward an intruder," often based on the biting of an intruder, is not the meaning psychologists intend when they write "Some youths are aggressive with their peers," based on the fighting that sometimes occurs between rival gangs from different ethnic groups involving guns and knives. Hence, behavioral biologists should find other terms to describe animals' behavior.

Two German biologists note that surface similarity between a behavior observed in an animal and a human does not mean that the same neural or psychological mechanisms are involved.[13] The evolutionary events that allow a person to inform a friend about a new restaurant are not the ones that allow a honeybee who has returned from a flowering meadow to execute a waggle dance that informs other bees of the location of the blossoms. The biological bases for the social behavior of bees are unlikely to be the bases for human sociability.

Psychologists respect the meaning-boundaries of the words that behavioral biologists use. They do not borrow the term *predation* to describe the actions of a school bully or *territoriality* to describe a man who built a steel fence around his half-acre home. Biologists should reflect before applying to animals semantic concepts such as *nice, aloof,* or *loner* that are intended to apply to humans who possess ideas about ideal traits and theories about how others behave.

This issue is reminiscent of a disagreement between Alfred North Whitehead and Bertrand Russell. Whitehead insisted that, because an entity and its properties form an inseparable unit, a speaker cannot assign any property to any entity. Birds fly, flowers bloom, church bells ring, children talk, communities cohere, and nations conquer. One cannot ascribe the properties *fly, bloom, talk, cohere,* or *conquer* to church bells. That is why behavioral biologists should not assign the property *teach* to any animal other than a human. And neuroscientists should not write that a brain site regulates, computes, evaluates, or recognizes. These verbs can be used only in sentences in which an awake animal or human is the subject. The neurons in the motor cortex that make movements of the fingers possible do not caress the face of a beloved; only a conscious human can caress a face.[14]

Some lines in poems written originally in Farsi or Mandarin cannot be translated into English without losing important meaning. I remember my frustration when trying to explain to a Japanese colleague the meaning of the English word *alienated* in a sentence that described a mother who was alienated from her infant. The late Thomas Kuhn found a linguistic example that makes this point clear. The French use the word *doux* to refer to sweet tastes, soft touches, and bland-tasting soup. The English word *sweet* also refers to sweet tastes and soft touches and, in addition, to a victory on the athletic field and the middle strings of a tennis racquet—but it is never used to name bland-tasting soup. Hence, *doux* and *sweet* are not exact synonyms.

Analogously, the meaning of *fear* when it refers to activation of the amygdala to a tone that signals electric shock is not synonymous with the meaning an adolescent intends when she tells an interviewer that she fears rejection by the college she wants to attend. Neuroscientists should invent new words to describe patterns of brain sites responding to incentives. It is unlikely that a vocabulary consisting only of biological terms will be able to explain most psychological states.

Unfortunately, some biologists write as if psychological processes are not needed to explain why humans cooperate, imitate, and create cultures. The evolutionary biologist Mark Pagel in *Wired for Culture*[15] writes repeatedly that universal human properties (including those I have described in the present book) are hard-wired in our genes, although he provides no description of how this wiring is accomplished. Moreover, the biologist Eve Marder of Brandeis University points out that the behavioral outcomes of most so-called, hard-wired circuits depend on the local chemistry at the moment.[16] Change the chemistry and the outcome of the circuit is different. Seventy years ago, when the premises of learning theory were dominant, psychologists declared that the same universal properties were learned. These scholars, too, did not explain how this feat occurred.

Pagel wants to explain why humans established societies with distinctive languages and values, but he is reluctant to award psychological processes any explanatory power. He assumes that new genes made cultures possible and ignores the role of any mediating psychological processes. For example, if some members of a community are marginalized by the majority because of a physical feature, value, or practice, they might decide to leave the community to start a new one. Identifications with a family pedigree, also a product of mental processes, facilitate the establishment of distinctive cultures.

Rather than assume that cultures are a defining feature of our species under the control of genes that contribute to fitness, it remains possible that cultures might be by-products of the genes responsible for our large frontal lobe and the resulting abilities to infer the thoughts of others, possess a moral sense, be conscious of our traits, and identify with individuals with whom distinctive features are shared. The actualization of these psychological processes requires a host of experiences in a cascade that is more complicated than the one implied by Pagel's terse phrase *hardwired*. Indeed, because all psychological phenomena are products of brain states that genes made possible, every human property is hard-wired. On the other hand, since no gene guarantees the possession of a specific belief, emotion, value, or habit, nothing is hard-wired.

The biologist Roger Sperry appreciated the need to award autonomous influences to psychological processes. In his 1981 Nobel acceptance address he emphasized the ballet between the psychological processes that emerge from one pattern of brain activity, which, in turn, create a new brain pattern. Psychological events have the unusual property of being both the end product of one set of biological processes and the origin of a second set. That is why Sperry insisted that psychological phenomena follow special laws that must be described with their own vocabulary. The phrase *wired by our genes* has no place in this vocabulary. It is unlikely that scientists will discover the genes that led some humans to treat others as slaves and the presumably different genes that led other humans to abolish slavery.

The relative insensitivity of current methods for measuring brain activity is an important reason for the inability to account for psychological phenomena by examining the brain evidence alone. In Chapter 7, I noted that most psychological outcomes are the result of patterns of activity in a large number of interconnected sites. Because every neurotransmitter can activate more than one kind of receptor in more than one site, there cannot be a one-to-one relation between an event that evokes the release of a transmitter and the activation of only one neuronal cluster.

Changes in the BOLD signal derived from patterns of blood flow are the most popular measure of brain activity in humans. Unfortunately, the psychological meaning of this measurement remains controversial, for the many reasons detailed earlier. I was surprised, therefore, by a paper authored by a team of French scientists who suggested that the pattern of brain activity recorded in men lying alone in a scanner looking at sexually explicit, erotic pictures of unfamiliar women resembled the pattern that would occur in a man lying in a hotel bed gazing for the first time at the nude body of a woman he has been sexually attracted to for many months.

No machine, not even the electron microscope, reveals everything scientists need to know about the invisible phenomena responsible for the events we call the perceptible world. That is why Niels Bohr wrote that scientists cannot separate what they observe from the combination of the procedure, which can include a machine, and the evidence it generates. The observations and the entire experimental setup form a unitary whole.

Hence, there is no guarantee that the BOLD signals generated by individuals lying supine and motionless in the narrow tube of a scanner looking at a picture of a man with a gun would be the same if these individuals encountered the same event while walking to work in the morning. Conclusions about the brain that are based on measures gathered in a scanner cannot provide the only valid understanding of the relation between neuronal activity and all psychological outcomes. These data are valuable, but they represent only one source of information. Although astrophysicists learned a great deal about the cosmos from the optical telescope, they now recognize that this machine does not tell them all they need to know.

Each person's idiosyncratic properties prevent neuroscientists from arriving at a determinate relation between a brain profile and a particular psychological outcome in a large group of individuals. Thomas Pearce and Daniel Moran of Washington University were surprised that two adult monkeys subjected to identical training designed to teach them to reach around an obstacle to grasp an object adopted different strategies and displayed different brain patterns.[17]

Consider the cascade of brain activity among individuals shown a man's face with a fearful expression. The brain pattern evoked by the face, which I shall call brain state *E* for *event,* represents the initial response to the face. Stefan Bode of the University of Melbourne discovered that a person's private expectation of what he or she might see affects the subsequent brain activity in individuals with different expectations.[18]

Brain state E is imposed on each person's usual brain state, called U for *usual*, which is different for individuals with a high compared with a low heart rate.

Each person's symbolic associations to the face are accompanied by a third brain profile, called A for *associations*, which is imposed on the combination of brain states E and U. The brain pattern that scientists measure about six seconds after the face appears, called F for *final*, is a product of the combination of states E, U, and A. Because states E, U, and A vary across persons, it is impossible to treat the measured brain profile F as an accurate index of the thoughts or feelings generated by the face. For example, some individuals may interpret the face as reflecting fear, others may see surprise, and still others may be unsure as to the emotion being displayed. But all three are likely to show activation of the amygdala because they did not expect to see this kind of face. These three classes of individuals would activate different patterns of brain activity inasmuch as their psychological reactions to the face were dissimilar.

Despite these and other problems, scientists studying psychological processes are entitled to many moments of pride. Reflection on the concepts and explanations contained in the textbooks of 1912, only a hundred years ago, reveals the extraordinary progress that occurred in only a century. Humans have wondered why "like begets like" for at least 100,000 years, but preliminary answers did not emerge until the middle of the last century. Scientists have been studying human development systematically for less than 150 years. The elimination of bad ideas usually marks the first stage in every discipline. The ancient Greeks were certain that the air inspired when one breathes was the foundation of all mental and bodily activity. Only 75 years ago almost every psychologist was certain that a rejecting mother could create the symptoms of autism. No one holds that wild premise today. Psychologists have eliminated many other concepts that were held with conviction during the first half of the last century, including Pavlov's freedom reflex, Freud's oral stage, Neal Miller's belief that all rewards are reductions in stimulation, and B. F. Skinner's insistence that the principles of stimulus-response association could explain how children learn the vocabulary and grammar of a language.

The public finds the rationale for allocating government funds for research in biology persuasive because this work promises to discover ways to prolong life and improve health. The public is far less appreciative of the benevolent implications of the facts social scientists discover that allow the public to become aware of the flaws in popular beliefs. Research during the early decades of the last century stopped a growing eugenics movement by disproving the idea that the low IQ scores and smaller skull circumferences of uneducated European immigrants were due primarily to genes. Psychological research also led to rejection of Freud's strong statements regarding the consequences of early weaning from the breast and a toilet-training regimen begun too early. Studies of the flawed memories of those who witnessed a crime have saved innocent adults from a prison sentence. The research demonstrating that good quality day care does not harm infants alleviated the anxiety of millions of working mothers with young children in surrogate care. Parents who blamed themselves for an exceedingly timid child were relieved when they learned that some of these children were born with a temperament that favored extreme levels of fear in response to novelty. Still other evidence freed the mothers of autistic children from the guilt generated by physicians who had accused them of being cold and aloof with their infants. Psychological inquiry also led to serious questioning of the doctrine of infant determinism, illuminated the complexity of memory, and discovered that many of the cognitive changes of the first decade of life are dependent on brain maturation.

Social scientists have explained some puzzling phenomena, eliminated superstition, articulated concerns that were still inchoate among a majority, aided an appreciation of cultural variation, and prevented simplistic biological explanations of psychological phenomena from becoming popular. These gains are, I submit, as beneficial to the society as ten extra years of life or the opportunity to use a GPS signal or cell phone.

There are good reasons to be sanguine over the discoveries that future cohorts will make, as long as they acknowledge the joint influences of biology and interpreted experience, are sensitive to the constraints that contexts impose on the inferences taken from all observations, and examine relations between patterns of conditions and patterns of evidence. Philip Teitelbaum, a creative psychologist who studied the relation between brain function and behavior, wrote an essay in an issue of a journal that was devoted to celebrating his long, productive career.[19] Teitelbaum's five suggestions to young psychologists are worth citing: pick an important puzzle to probe, gather many different measurements, don't trust what a statistical analysis reveals unless your careful examination of the evidence agrees with it, read many old books, analyze evidence with a detective's care for detail, and be prepared for facts that require a new concept. If the present and future cohorts of psychologists follow this wise advice they are likely to solve some of the stubborn problems that six generations of psychologists struggled, unsuccessfully, to resolve. Perhaps they will even understand what a four-week-old feels when a smiling parent asks "How are you, pretty baby?" which genes and molecules create high- and low-reactive infants, and why some deprived children become depressed adults, some criminals, and others, reflecting on their past on the morning of their eightieth birthday, conclude with a smile that, on balance, they enjoyed wonderful lives.

NOTES

CHAPTER ONE

1. Herdt, G. H. (1987), *Guardians of the Flutes: Idioms of Masculinity,* New York: Columbia University Press.

2. Degler, C. (1980), *At Odds,* New York: Oxford University Press.

3. Rogoff, B. (2011), *Developing Destinies: A Mayan Midwife and Town,* New York: Oxford University Press.

4. Rothschild, E. (2001), *Economic Sentiments,* Cambridge, MA: Harvard University Press.

5. Lahat, A., Degnan, K. A., White, L. K., McDerrmott, J. M., Henderson, H. A., Lejuez, C. W., & Fox, N. A. (2012), Temperamental exuberance and executive function predict propensity for risk taking in childhood, *Development and Psychopathology,* 24, 847–856.

6. Meltzoff, A. N., & Moore, M. K. (1977), Imitations of facial and manual gestures by human neonates, *Science,* 198, 75–76.

7. Rentfrow, P. (2010), Statewide differences in personality, *American Psychologist,* 65, 548–558.

8. Kagan, J., Reznick, J. S., Davies, J., Smith, J., Sigal, H., & Miyake, K. (1986), Selective memory and belief, *International Journal of Behavioral Development,* 9, 205–218; Durbin, C. E., & Wilson, S. (2012), Convergent validity of and bias in maternal reports of child emotion, *Psychological Assessment,* 24, 647–660; Podsakoff, P. M., MacKenzie, S. B., & Podsakoff, N. P. (2012), Sources of method bias in social science research, in Fiske, S. T., Schacter, D. L., & Taylor, S. E., eds., *Annual Review of Psychology* (pp. 539–570), Palo Alto, CA: Annual Reviews.

9. Wang, Q. (2004), The emergence of cultural self-constructs: Autobiographical memory and self-description in European-American and Chinese children, *Developmental Psychology,* 40, 3–15; Cheung, F. M., van de Vijver, F. J. R., & Leong, F. T. L. (2011), Toward a new approach to the study of personality in culture, *American Psychologist,* 66, 593–603; Church, A. T., Alvarez, J. M., Mai, N. T. Q., French, B. F., et al. (2011), Are cross-cultural comparisons of personality profiles meaningful? *Journal of Personality and Social Psychology,* 101, 1068–1089.

10. Woolley, J. D. (2006), Verbal-behavioral dissociations in development, *Child Development,* 27, 1539–1553.

11. Smoller, J. (2012), *The Other Side of Normal,* New York: William Morrow.

12. Zimring, F. (2012), *The City That Became Safe,* New York: Oxford University Press.

13. Dodge, K. A. (2011), Context matters in child and family policy, *Child Development,* 82, 443–442.

14. Learmonth, A. E., Newcombe, N. S., & Huttenlocher, J. (2001), Toddlers' use of metric information and landmarks to reorient, *Journal of Experimental Child Psychology,* 80, 225–244; Azzi, J. C. B., Sirigu, A., & Duhamel, J. R. (2012), Modulation of value representation by social context in the primate orbitofrontal cortex, *Proceedings of the National Academy of Sciences,* 109, 2126–2131; Campbell, F. A., Pungello, E. P., Burchinal, M., Kainz, K., Pan, Y., Wasik, B. H., et al. (2012), Adult outcomes as a function of an early childhood educational program, *Developmental Psychology,* 48, 1033–1043.

15. Barrett, L. F., & Kensinger, E. A. (2010), Context is routinely encoded during emotion perception, *Psychological Science,* 21, 595–599.

16. Galison, P. (2012), Blacked-out spaces, *British Journal of the History of Science,* 45, 235–266.

17. Kuwabara, M., & Smith, L. B. (2012), Cross-cultural differences in cognitive development, *Journal of Experimental Child Psychology,* 113, 20–35.

18. Taleb, N. (2010), *The Black Swan,* New York: Random House.

19. Berlin. B., & Kay, P. (1969), *Basic Color Terms,* Berkeley: University of California Press.

20. Loreto, V., Mukherjee, A., & Tria, F. (2012), On the origin of the hierarchy of color names, *Proceedings of the National Academy of Sciences,* 109, 6819–6824.

CHAPTER TWO

1. Kagan, J., & Herschkowitz, N. (2005), *A Young Mind in A Growing Brain,* Mahwah, NJ: L. Erlbaum; Habas, P. A., Scott, J. A., Roosta, A., Rajagopian, V., et al. (2012), Early folding patterns and asymmetries of the normal human brain detected from in utero MRI, *Cerebral Cortex,* 22, 13–25.

2. Bauer, M., Glenn, T., Alda, M., Andreassen, O. A., Ardau, R., et al. (2012), Impact of sunlight on the age of onset of bipolar disorder, *Bipolar Disorder,* 14, 654–663.

3. Lombardo, M. V., Ashwin, E., Auyeung, B., Chakrabarti, B., Taylor, K., et al. (2012), Fetal testosterone influences sexually dimorphic gray matter in the human brain, *The Journal of Neuroscience,* 32, 674–680.

4. Alexander, G. M., & Saenz, J. (2012), Early androgens, activity levels and toy choices of children in the second year of life, *Hormones and Behavior,* 62, 500–504.

5. Knickmeyer, R. C., Woolson, S., Hamer, R. M., Konneker, P., & Gilmore, J. H. (2011), 2D:4D ratios in the first two years of life, *Hormones and Behavior,* 60, 251–263; Coates, J. M., & Herbert, J. (2008), Endogenous steroids and financial risk taking on a London trading floor, *Proceedings of the National Academy of Sciences,* 10, 6167–6172; Wong, E. M., Ormiston, M. E., & Haselhuhn, M. P. (2011), A face only an investor could love, *Psychological Science,* 22, 1478–1483; Schwerdtfeger, A., Heims, R., & Heer, J. (2010), Digit ratio (2D:4D) is associated with traffic violations for male frequent car drivers, *Accidental Analysis and Prevention,* 42, 269–274; Bailey, A. A., & Hurd, P. L. (2005),

Finger length ratio (2D:4D) correlates with physical aggression in men but not in women, *Biological Psychology,* 68, 215–222; Zheng, Z., & Cohn, M. J. (2011), Developmental basis of sexually dimorphic digit ratios, *Proceedings of the National Academy of Sciences,* 108, 16289–16294; Ferdenzi, C., Lemaitre, J. F., Leongomez, J. D., & Roberts, S. C. (2011), Digit ratio (2D:4D) predicts facial, but not voice or body odour, attractiveness in men, *Proceedings in the Biological Sciences,* in press; Giffin, N. A., Kennedy, R. M., Jones, M. E., & Barber, C. A. (2011), Varsity athletes have lower 2D:4D ratios than other university students, *Journal of Sports Science,* in press; Hiraishi, K., Sasaki, S., Shikishima, C., & Ando, J. (2012), The second to fourth digit ratio (2D:4D) in a Japanese twin sample. *Archives of Sexual Behavior,* in press; Chai, X. J., & Jacobs, L. F. (2012), Digit ratio predicts sense of direction in women, *PLoS One,* 7, no. 32816; McIntyre, M. H., Herrmann, E., Wobber, V., Halbwax, M., et al. (2009), Bonobos have a more human-like second- to fourth-finger length ratio (2D:4D) than chimpanzees, *Journal of Human Evolution,* 44, 1–5; Galis, F., Broek, C. M. A., Van Dongen, S., & Wijnaendts, L. C. D. (2010), Sexual dimorphism in the prenatal digit ratio (2D:4D), *Archives of Sexual Behavior,* 39, 57–62.

6. Burriss, R. P., Little, A. C., & Nelson, E. C. (2007), 2D:4D and sexually dimorphic facial characteristics. *Archives of Sexual Behavior,* 36, 377–384.

7. Beltz, A. M., Swanson, J. L., & Berenbaum, S. A. (2011), Gendered occupational interests, *Hormones and Behavior,* 60, 313–317; Pokrywka, L., Rachon, D., Suchecka-Rachon, K., & Bitel, L. (2005), The second to fourth digit ratio in elite and non-elite female athletes, *American Journal of Human Biology,* 17, 796–800; Lourenco, S. F., Addy, D., Huttenlocher, J., & Fabian, L. (2011), Early sex differences in weighting geometric cues, *Developmental Science,* 14, 1365–1378; Mukai, H., Hatanaka, Y., Mitsuhashi, K., Hojo, Y., et al. (2011), Automated analysis of spines from confocal laser microscopy images, *Cerebral Cortex,* 21, 2704–2711; Brain Development Cooperative Group (2012), Total and regional brain volumes in a population-based normative sample from 4 to 18 years, *Cerebral Cortex,* 22, 1–12; Balthazart, J. (2011), Minireview: Hormones and human sexual orientation, *Endocrinology,* 152, 2937–2947; Berenbaum, S. A., Bryk, L. L. K., & Beltz, A. M. (2012), Early androgen effects on spatial and mechanical abilities, *Behavioral Neuroscience,* 126, 86–96.

8. Entringer, S., Buss, C., Andersen, J., Chicz-De Met, A., & Wadhwa, P. D. (2011), Ecological momentary assessment of maternal cortisol profiles over a multiple-day period predicts the length of human gestation, *Psychosomatic Medicine,* 73, 469–474; Kinney, D. K., Miller, A. M., Crawley, D. J., Huang, E., & Gerber, E. (2008), Autism prevalence following prenatal exposure to hurricanes and tropical storms in Louisiana, *Journal of Autism and Developmental Disorders,* 38, 31–48; Christian, L. M. (2012), Psychoneuroimmunology in pregnancy, *Neuroscience and Biobehavioral Reviews,* 36, 350–361; Zhang, G. H., Chen, M. L., Liu, S. S., Zhan, Y. H., et al. (2011), Effects of mother's dietary exposure to Acesulfame-K in pregnancy or lactation on the adult offspring's sweet preference, *Chemical Senses,* 36, 763–770; Kane, A. D., Herrera, E. A., Hansell, J. A., & Giussani, D. A. (2012), Statin treatment depresses the fetal defence to acute hypoxia via increasing nitric oxide bioavailability, *Journal of Physiology,* in press; Ehrlich, S. F., Eskenazi, B., Hedderson, M. M., & Ferrara, A. (2012), Sex ratio variations among the offspring of women with diabetes in pregnancy, *Diabetes Medicine,* in press; Raznahan, A., Greenstein, D., Lee, N. R., Clasen, L. S., & Giedd, J. N. (2012), Prenatal growth in humans and postnatal brain

maturation into late adolescence, *Proceedings of the National Academy of Sciences*, 109, 11366–11371; Oberlander, T. F. (2012), Fetal serotonin signaling, *Journal of Adolescent Health*, 51, S9–S16.

9. Dancause, K. N., Laplante, D. P., Oremus, C., Fraser, S., Brunet, A., & King, S. (2011), Disaster-related prenatal maternal stress influences birth outcomes, *Early Human Development*, in press; King, S., Mancini-Marie, A., Brunet, A., Walker, E., Meaney, M., & Laplante, D. P. (2009), Prenatal maternal stress from a natural disaster predicts dermatoglyphic asymmetry in humans, *Development and Psychopathology*, 21, 343–353; Hines, M. (2011), Gender development and the human brain, *Annual Review of Neuroscience*, 34, 69–88; Morgan, C. P., & Bale, T. L. (2011), Early prenatal stress epigenetically programs dysmasculinization in second generation offspring via the paternal lineage, *Journal of Neuroscience*, 17, 11748–11755; de Rooij, S. R., Veenendaal, M. V., Raikkonen, K., & Roseboom, T. J. (2011), Personality and stress appraisal in adults prenatally exposed to the Dutch famine, *Early Human Development*, in press; Chapil, A., Laplante, P. D., Vaillancourt, C., & King, S. (2010), Prenatal stress and brain development, *Brain Research Reviews*, 65, 56–79; Mychasiuk, R., Schmold, N., Ilnytskyy, S., Kovalchuk, O., et al. (2012), Prenatal bystander stress alters brain, behavior, and the epigenome of developing rat offspring, *Developmental Neuroscience*, 33, 159–169; Forbes-Lorman, R. M., Rautio, J. J., Kurian, J. R., Auger, A. P., et al. (2012), Neonatal MeCP2 is important for the organization of sex differences in vasopressin expression, *Epigenetics*, 1, 230–238.

10. Sandman, C. A., Davis, E. P., Buss, C., & Glynn, L. N. (2011), Exposure to prenatal psychobiological stress exerts programming influences on the mother and her fetus, *Neuroendocrinology*, in press; DiPietro, J. A., Hilton, S. C., Hawkins, M., Costigan, K. A., & Pressman, E. K. (2002), Stress and affect influence fetal neurobehavioral development, *Developmental Psychology*, 38, 659–668; Favaro, A., Tenconi, E., Ceschin, L., Zanetti, T., Bosello, R., & Santonastaso, P. (2011), In utero exposure to virus infections and the risk of developing anorexia nervosa, *Psychological Medicine*, 41, 2193–2199; Halverson, C. F., & Victor, J. B. (1976), Minor physical anomalies and problem behavior in elementary school children, *Child Development*, 47, 281–285; Smith, S. E. P., Li, J., Garbett, K., Mirnics, K., & Patterson, P. H. (2007), Maternal immune activation alters fetal brain development through Interleukin-6, *The Journal of Neuroscience*, 27, 10695–10702; Lewis, M., & Kestler, L., eds. (2012), *Gender Differences in Prenatal Substance Exposure*, Washington, DC: American Psychological Association; Haberling, I. S., Badzakova-Trajkov, G., &Corballis, M. C. (2012), The corpus callosum in monozygotic twins concordant and discordant for handedness and language dominance, *Journal of Cognitive Neuroscience*, 24, 1971–1982.

11. Linn, S., Reznick, J. S., Kagan, J., & Hans, S. (1982), Salience of visual patterns of the human infant, *Developmental Psychology*, 18, 651–657; Roseberry, S., Richie, R., Hirsh-Pasek, K., Golinkoff, R. M., & Shipley, T. F. (2011), Babies catch a break, *Psychological Science*, 22, 1422–1424.

12. Mash, C., & Bornstein, M. H. (2012), 5-month-olds' categorization of novel objects, *Infancy*, 17, 179–197.

13. Reynolds, G. D., & Guy, M. V. V. (2012), Brain-behavior relations in infancy, *Developmental Neuropsychology*, 37, 210–225.

14. Wynn, K. (1992), Addition and subtraction by human infants, *Nature*, 358, 749–750.

15. Haith, M. M. (1980), *Rules That Babies Look By,* Hillsdale, NJ: Erlbaum; Watanabe, H., Homae, F., & Taga, G. (2012), Activation and deactivation in response to visual stimulation in the occipital cortex of 6-month-old infants, *Developmental Psychobiology,* 54, 1–15; Schwartz, M., & Day, R. H. (1979), Visual shape perception in early infancy, *Monographs of the Society for Research in Child Development,* 44, No. 7, 1–57; Hubel, D. H., & Wiesel, T. N. (1998), Early exploration of the visual cortex. *Neuron,* 20, 401–412.

16. Turati, C., & Simion, S. (2002), Newborns' recognition of changing and unchanging aspects of schematic faces, *Journal of Experimental Child Psychology,* 83, 239–261; Simion, F., Valenza, E., Macchi, C. W., Turati, C., & Umilta, C. (2002), Newborns' preference for up-down asymmetrical configurations, *Developmental Science,* 5, 427–434.

17. Woodhead, Z. V. J., Wise, R. J. S., Sereno, M., & Leech, R. (2011), Dissociation of sensitivity to spatial frequency in word and face preferential areas of the fusiform gyrus, *Cerebral Cortex,* 21, 2307–2312; Zatorre, R. J., & Belin, P. (2001), Spatial and temporal processing in human auditory cortex, *Cerebral Cortex,* 11, 946–953; Kumar, D., & Srinivasan, N. (2011), Emotion perception is mediated by spatial frequency content, *Emotion,* 11, 1144–1151; Bahrick, L. F., Gogate, L. J., & Ruiz, I. (2002), Attention and memory for faces and actions in infancy, *Child Development,* 73, 1629–1643; Amir, O., Biederman, I., & Hayworth, K. J. (2012), The neural basis for shape preferences, *Vision Research,* 51, 2198–2206.

18. Lorenz, K. (1981), *The Foundations of Ethology* (trans. Lorenz, K., & Kickert, R. W.), New York: Springer-Verlag.

19. Lloyd-Fox, S., Blasi. A., Everdell, N., Elwell, C. E., & Johnson, M. H. (2011), Selected cortical mapping of biological motion processing in young infants, *Journal of Cognitive Neuroscience,* 23, 2521–2532.

20. Rubenstein, A. J., Kalakanis, L., & Langlois, J. H. (1999), Infant preferences for attractive faces, *Developmental Psychology,* 35, 848–855; Cattaneo, Z., Fantino, M., Silvanto, J., Tinti, C., et al. (2010), Symmetry perception in the blind, *Acta Psychologica (Amst),* 134, 398–402.

21. Bremner, J. G. (2011), Four themes for twenty years of research on infant perception and cognition, *Infant Behavior and Development,* 20, 137–147; Pollen, D. A. (2011), On the emergence of primary visual perception, *Cerebral Cortex,* in press; Sugita, Y. (2009), Innate face processing, *Current Opinion in Neurobiology,* 19, 39–44; Rosa-Salva, O., Farroni, L., Vallortigara, G., & Johnson, M. H. (2011), The evolution of social orienting, *PLoS One,* 20, no. 18802; Meletti, S., Cantalupo, G., Benuzzi, F., Mai, R., et al. (2011), Fear and happiness in the eyes. *Neuropsychologia,* in press; Di Giorgio, E., Leo, I., Pascalis, O., & Simion, F. (2012), Is the face-perception system human specific at birth? *Developmental Psychology,* 48, 1083–1090.

22. Reeb-Sutherland, B. C., Feifer, W. P., Byrd, D., Hammock, E. A. D., Levitt, P., & Fox, N. A. (2011), One-month-old human infants learn about the social world while they sleep, *Developmental Science,* 14, 1134–1141; Vouloumanos, A., Hauser, M. D., Werker, J. F., & Martin, A. (2010), The tuning of human neonates' preference for speech, *Child Development,* 81, 517–527; Kearsley, R. B. (1973), The newborn's response to auditory stimulation, *Child Development,* 44, 582–590; Beauchemin, M., Gonzalez-Frankenberger, B., Tremblay, J., Vannasing, P., Martinez-Montes, E., et al. (2011), Mother and Stranger: An electrophysiological study of voice processing in newborns, *Life Sciences & Medicine,* 21, 1705–1711; Sato, H., Hirabayashi, Y., Tsubokura, H., Kanai, M. Ashida, T., et al.

(2012), Cerebral hemodynamics in newborn infants exposed to speech sounds, *Human Brain Mapping,* 33, 2092–2103.

23. Sansavini, A., Bertoncini, J., & Giovanelli, G. (1997), Newborns discriminate the rhythm of multisyllabic stressed words, *Developmental Psychology,* 33, 3–11; Zentner, M. R., & Kagan, J. (1998), Infants' perception of consonance and dissonance in music, *Infant Behavior and Development,* 21, 483–492; Chiandetti, C., & Vallortigara, G. (2011), Chicks like consonant music, *Psychological Science,* in press; Sugimoto, T., Kobayashi, H., Nobuyoshi, N., Kiriyama, Y., et al. (2010), Preference for consonant music over dissonant music by an infant chimpanzee, *Primates,* 51, 7–12.

24. Bremner, J. G., Slater, A. M., Johnson, S. P., Mason, U. C., Spring, J., & Bremner, M. E. (2011), Two- to eight-month-old infants' perception of dynamic auditory visual spatial colocation, *Child Development,* 82, 1210–1223; He, C., Hotson, L., & Trainor, L. J. (2009), Development of infant mismatch responses to auditory pattern changes between 2 and 4 months old, *European Journal of Neuroscience,* 29, 861–867; Huberle, E., & Karnath, H. O. (2011), The role of temporo-parietal junction (TPJ) in global Gestalt perception, *Brain Structure and Function,* in press; Lebedeva, G. C., & Kuhl, P. K. (2010), Sing that tune, *Infant Behavior and Development,* 33, 419–430.

25. Blass, E. M., & Cant, C. A. (2001), The ontogeny of face recognition, *Developmental Psychology,* 37, 762–774; Gilmore, J. H., Shi, F., Woolson, S. L., Knickmeyer, R. C., et al. (2012), Longitudinal development of cortical and subcortical gray matter from birth to 2 years, *Cerebral Cortex,* 22, 2478–2485.

26. Delauney-el, A. M., Allan, M., Soussignan, R., Patris, B., Marlier, L., & Schaal, B. (2010), Long-lasting memory for an odor acquired on the mother's breast, *Developmental Science,* 13, 849–863; Nishitani, S., Miyamura, T., Tagawa, M., Sumi, M., Takase, R., Doi, H., Moriuchi, H., & Shinohara, K. (2009), The calming effect of a maternal breast milk odor on the human newborn infant, *Neuroscience Research,* 63, 66–71.

27. Kuhl, P. K. (1991), Human adults and human infants show a perceptual magnet effect for the prototypes of speech categories; monkeys do not, *Perception and Psychophysics,* 50, 93–107; Kuhl, P. K. (1993), Innate predispositions and the effects of experience on speech perception, in Boysson-Bardies, B. D., Schoen, S. D., Jusczyk, P. W., McNeilage, P., & Norton, J., eds., *Developmental Neurocognition* (pp. 259–274), Dordrecht, The Netherlands: Kluwer.

28. Rivera-Gaxiola, M., Garcia-Sierra, A., Lara-Ayala, L., Cadena, S., Jackson-Maldonado, D., & Kuhl, P. K. (2012), Event-related potentials to an English/Spanish syllabic contrast in Mexican 10–13-month-old infants, *ISRN Neurology,* Epub, February 29.

29. Best, C. T. (1995), Learning to perceive the sound patterns of English, in Rovee-Collier, C., & Lipsitt, L. P., eds., *Advances in Infancy Research,* Vol. 9 (pp. 217–234), Norwood, NJ: Ablex; Rivera-Gaxiola, M., Garcia-Sierra, A., Lara-Ayala, L., Cadena, C., Jackson-Maldonado, D., & Kuhl, P. K. (2012), Event-related potentials to an English-Spanish syllabic contrast in Mexican 10–13- month-old infants, *ISRN Neurology,* Epub, February 29; Werker, J. F., Yeung, H. H. & Yoshida, K. A. (2012), How do infants become experts at native-speech perception? *Current Directions in Psychological Science,* 21, 221–226.

30. Mandler, J. M., & McDonough, L. (1998), On developing a knowledge base in infancy, *Developmental Psychology,* 34, 1274–1288; Scott, L. S. (2011), Mechanisms underlying the emergence of object representations during infancy, *Journal of Cognitive Neuroscience,* 23, 2935–2944; Cuevas. K., Bell, M. A., Marcovitch, S., & Calkins, S. D. (2012),

Electroencephalogram and heart rate measures of working memory at 5 and 10 months of age, *Developmental Psychology*, 48, 907–917.

31. Short, S. J., Elison, J. T., Goldman, B. D., Styner, M., Gu, H., et al. (2012), Associations between white matter microstructure and infants' working memory, *NeuroImage*, 16, 156–166.

32. Cuevas, K., & Bell, M. A. (2011), EEG and ECG from 5 to 10 months of age, *International Journal of Psychophysiology*, 80, 119–128; Fox, N., Kagan, J., & Weiskopf, S. (1979), The growth of memory during infancy, *Genetic Psychology Monographs*, 99, 91–130; Zentner, M., & Eerola, T. (2010), Rhythmic engagement with music in infancy, *Proceedings of the National Academy of Sciences*, 107, 5768–5773; Heurer, E., & Bachevalier, J. (2011), Neonatal hippocampal lesions in rhesus macaques alter the monitoring, but not the maintenance, of information in working memory, *Behavioral Neuroscience*, 125, 859–870; Sanchez, C. E., Richards, J. E., & Almli, C. R. (2012), Neurodevelopmental MRI brain templates for children from 2 weeks to 4 years of age, *Developmental Psychobiology*, 54, 77–91.

33. Kagan, J. (1976), Emergent themes in human development, *American Scientist*, 64, 186–196; Super, C. M., Guldan, G. S., Ahmed, N., & Zeitlin, M. (2012), The emergence of separation protest is robust under conditions of severe developmental stress in rural Bangladesh, *Infant Behavior and Development*, 35, 393–396.

34. Gibson, E. J., & Walk, R. D. (1960), The visual cliff, *Scientific American*, 202, 64–71; Ueno, M., Uchiyama, I., Campos, J., Dahl, J. J., & Anderson, D. (2012), The organization of wariness of heights in experienced crawlers, *Infancy*, 17, 376–392.

35. Ariansen, J. L., Heien, M. L., Hermans, A., Phillips, P. E., Hernadi, I., et al. (2012), Monitoring extracellular pH, oxygen, and dopamine during reward delivery in the striatum of primates, *Frontiers in Behavioral Neuroscience*, 6, Epub, July 5.

36. Gottfried, A. W., Rose, S. A., & Bridger, W. H. (1977), Cross-modal transfer in human infants, *Child Development*, 48, 118–123.

37. Keen, R. E., & Berthier, N. E. (2004), Continuities and discontinuities in infants' representations of objects and events, *Advances in Child Development and Behavior*, 32, 243–279.

38. Peterson, C., Warren, K. L., & Short, M. M. (2011), Infantile amnesia across the years, *Child Development*, 82, 1092–1105.

39. Singh, L., Liederman, J., Mierzejewski, R., & Barnes, J. (2011), Rapid recognition of native phoneme contrasts after disuse, *Developmental Science*, 14, 949–959.

40. Callaghan, T., Moll, H., Rakoczy, H., Warneka, F., Liszkowski, U., Behne, T., & Tomasello, M. (2011), Early social cognition in three cultural contexts, *Monographs of the Society for Research in Child Development*, 76, 1–123; Benenson, J. F., Tennyson, R., & Wrangham, R. W. (2011), Male more than female infants imitate propulsive motion, *Cognition*, in press.

41. Seehagen, S., & Herbert, J. S. (2012), Selective imitation in 6-month-olds, *Infant Behavior and Development*, 35, 509–512.

42. Posner, M. I., Attentional networks and consciousness, *Frontiers in Psychology*, 64, Epub, March 12.

43. Spelke, E. S., & Kinzler, K. D. (2007), Core knowledge, *Developmental Science*, 10, 89–96; Carey, S. (2009), *The Origin of Concepts*, New York: Oxford University Press.

44. Feigenson, L. (2005), The concept of number, *Cognition*, 95, 627–648.

45. Mix, K. S., Levine, S. C., & Huttenlocher, J. (1997), Numerical abstraction in infants: Another look, *Developmental Psychology*, 33, 423–428; Zosh, J. M., Halberda, J., & Feigenson, L. (2011), Memory for multiple visual ensembles in infancy, *Journal of Experimental Psychology: General*, 140, 141–158; Hyde, D. C., & Spelke, E. S. (2011), Neural signatures of number processing in human infants, *Developmental Science*, 14, 360–371; Hyde, D. C., & Spelke, E. S. (2012), Spatiotemporal dynamics of processing nonsymbolic number, *Human Brain Mapping*, 33, 2189–2203; Dakin, S. C., Tibber, M. S., Greenwood, J. A., Kingdom, F. A. A., & Morgan, M. J. (2011), A common visual metric for approximate number and density, *Proceedings of the National Academy of Sciences*, 108, 19552–19557.

46. Brez, C. C., Colombo, J., & Cohen, L. (2012), Infants' integration of featural and numerical information, *Infant Behavior and Development*, 35, 705–710.

47. Izard, V., Sann, C., Spelke, E. S., & Streri, A. (2009), Newborn infants perceive abstract numbers, *Proceedings of the National Academy of Sciences*, 106, 10382–10385; Houde, O., Pineau, A., Leroux, G., Poirel, N., Perchey, G., et al. (2011), Functional magnetic resonance imaging study of Piaget's conservation of number task in preschool and school-age children, *Journal of Experimental Child Psychology*, 110, 332–346; Barner, D., Lui, T., & Zapf, J. (2012), Is two a plural marker in early child language? *Developmental Psychology*, 48, 10–17; Cohen-Kadosh, R., Bahrami, B., Walsh, V., Butterworth, B., Popescu, T., & Price, C. J. (2011), Specialization in the human brain: The case of numbers, *Frontiers in Human Neuroscience*, 5, in press; Holloway, I. D., & Ansari, D. (2010), Developmental specialization in the right intraparietal sulcus for the abstract representation of numerical magnitude, *Journal of Cognitive Neuroscience*, 22, 2627–2637; Prado, J., Mutreja, R., Chang, H., Mehta, R., et al. (2011), Distinct representations of subtraction and multiplication in the neural systems for numerosity and language, *Human Brain Mapping*, 32, 1932–1947; Halberda, J., Ly, R., Wilmer, J. B., Naiman, D. Q., & Germaine, L. (2012), Number sense across the life span as revealed by a massive Internet-based sample, *Proceedings of the National Academy of Sciences*, 109, 1116–11120.

48. Harvey, D. Y., & Burgund, E. D. (2012), Neural adaptation across viewpoint and exemplar in fusiform cortex, *Brain and Cognition*, 80, 33–44.

49. Schleidt, W., Shalter, M. D., & Moura-Meto, H. (2011), The hawk-goose story, *Journal of Comparative Psychology*, 125, 121–133.

50. Hane, A. A., Fox, N. A., Henderson, H. A., & Marshall, P. J. (2008), Behavioral reactivity and approach-withdrawal bias in infancy, *Developmental Psychology*, 34, 1491–1496; Fox, N. A., Henderson, H. A., Rubin, K. H., Calkins, S. D., & Schmidt, L. A. (2001), Continuity and discontinuity of behavioral inhibition and exuberance, *Child Development*, 72, 1–21; Kagan, J., Snidman, N., & Arcus, D. (1998), Childhood derivatives of high and low reactivity in infancy, *Child Development*, 69, 1483–1490; Pfeifer, M., Goldsmith, H. H., Davidson, R. J., & Rickman, M. (2002), Continuity and change in inhibited and uninhibited children, *Child Development*, 73, 1474–1485; Bell, R. Q., Weller, G. M., & Waldrop, M. F. (1971), Newborn and preschooler, *Monographs of the Society for Research in Child Development*, 36, 1–142; Suomi, S J. (2011), Risk, resilience, and gene-environment interplay in primates, *Journal of the Canadian Academy of Child and Adolescent Psychiatry*, 20, 289–297; Bliss-Moreau, E., Bauman, M. D., & Amaral, D. G. (2011), Neonatal amygdala lesions result in globally blunted affect in adult rhesus macaques, *Behavioral Neuroscience*, 125, 848–858; Hawken, P. A. R., Fiol, C., & Blanche, D. (2012), Genetic differences in temperament determine whether lavender oil alleviates or exacerbates anxiety in sheep, *Physiology and Behavior*, 105, 1117–1123; Kagan, J. (1994), *Galen's Prophecy*, New York: Basic Books;

Moehler, E., Kagan, J., Brunner, R., Wiebel, A., et al. (2006), Association of behavioral inhibition with hair pigmentation in a European sample, *Biological Psychology,* 72, 344–346.

CHAPTER THREE

1. Aldridge, K. (2011), Patterns of differences in brain morphology in humans as compared to extant apes, *Journal of Human Evolution,* 60, 94–105.

2. McCune, L. (1995), A normative study of representational play at the transition to language, *Developmental Psychology,* 31, 198–206; Ungerer, J. A., & Sigman, M. (1984), The relation of play and sensorimotor behavior to language in the second year, *Child Development,* 55, 1448–1455; Monaghan, P., Christiansen, M. H., & Fitneva, S. V. (2011), The arbitrariness of the sign, *Journal of Experimental Psychology: General,* 140, 325–347.

3. Lewkowicz, D. J., & Hansen-Tilt, A. M. (2012), Infants deploy selective attention to the mouth of a talking face when learning speech, *Proceedings of the National Academy of Sciences,* 109, 1431–1436.

4. Kuhl, P. K. (2011), Early language learning and literacy, *Mind, Brain and Education,* 5, 128–142.

5. Kuhl, P. K. (2000), A new view of language acquisition, *Proceedings of the National Academy of Sciences,* 97, 11850–11857; Kuhl, P. K., Stevens, E., Takayashi, A., Deguchi, T., et al. (2006), Infants show a facilitation effect for native language phonetic perception between 6 and 12 months, *Developmental Science,* 9, F13–F21; Lieven, E., & Stoll, S. (2010), Language, in Bornstein, M. H., ed., *Handbook of Cultural Developmental Science* (pp. 143–160), New York: Psychology Press; Mani, N., Mills, D. L., & Plunkett, K. (2012), Vowels in early words, *Developmental Science,* 15, 2–11.

6. Pinker, S., & Jackendoff, R. (2005), The faculty of language, *Cognition,* 95, 201–235.

7. Cochet, H., Jover, M., & Vauclair, J. (2011), Hand preference for pointing gestures and bimanual manipulation around the vocabulary spurt period, *Journal of Experimental Child Psychology,* 110, 393–407; Gao, W., Zhu, H., Giovanello, K. S., Smith, J. K., Shen, D., Gilmore, J. H., & Lin, W. (2009), Evidence on the emergence of the brain's default network from 2-week-old to 2-year-old healthy pediatric subjects, *Proceedings of the National Academy of Sciences,* 106, 6790–6795; Friederici, A. D. (2011), The brain basis of language processing: From structure to function, *Physiological Reviews,* 91, 1357–1392; Camoes-Costa, V., Erjavec, M., & Horne, P. J. (2011), Comprehension and production of body part labels in 2- to 3-year-old children, *British Journal of Developmental Psychology,* 29, 552–571; Jacquet, A. Y., Esseily, R., Rider, D., & Fagard, J. (2012), Handedness for grasping objects and declarative pointing, *Developmental Psychobiology,* 54, 36–46; Bergelson, E., & Swingley, D. (2012), At 6–9 months, human infants know the meanings of many common nouns, *Proceedings of the National Academy of Sciences,* 109, 3253–3258; Tincoff, R., & Jusczyk, P. W. (2012), Six-month-olds comprehend words that refer to parts of the body, *Infancy,* 17, 432–444; Parise, E., & Csibra, G. (2012), Electrophysiological evidence for the understanding of maternal speech by 9-month-old infants, *Psychological Science,* 23, 728–733.

8. Tardif, T., Fletcher, P., Liang, W., Zhang, Z., Kaciroti, N., & Marchman, V. A. (2008), Babys' first ten words, *Developmental Psychology,* 44, 929–938; Clerget, E., Poncin, W., Fadiga, L., & Olivier, E. (2012), Role of Broca's area in implicit motor skill learning, *Journal of Cognitive Neuroscience,* 24, 80–92; Vargha-Khadem, F., Carr, L. J., Isaacs, E., Brett, E., et al. (1997), Onset of speech after left hemispherectomy in a nine-year-old boy, *Brain,* 120, 159–182; Thatcher, R. W., North, D. M., & Biver, C. J. (2008), Development of cortical

connections as measured by EEG coherence and phase delays, *Human Brain Mapping,* 29, 1400–1415.

9. Mayor, J., & Plunkett, K. (2011), A statistical estimate of infant and toddler vocabulary size from CDI analysis, *Developmental Science,* 14, 769–785; Whitehouse, A. J., Robinson, M., & Zubrick, S. R. (2011), Late talking and the risk for psychological problems during childhood and adolescence, *Pediatrics,* 128, 324–332; Mervis, C. B., & Johnson, K. E. (1991), The acquisition of the plural noun phase, *Developmental Psychology,* 27, 222–235; Zambrana, I. M., Ystrom, E., & Pons, F. (2012), Impact of gender, maternal education, and birth order on the development of language comprehension, *Journal of Developmental and Behavioral Pediatrics,* in press.

10. Maurer, D., Pathman, T., & Mondloch, C. J. (2006), The shape of boubas, *Developmental Science,* 9, 316–322; Nielsen, A., & Rendell, D. (2011), The sound of round, *Canadian Journal of Experimental Psychology,* 65–124; Mondloch, C. J., & Maurer, D. (2004), Do small white balls squeak? *Cognitive, Affective, & Behavioral Neuroscience,* 4, 133–136.

11. Fausey, C. M., & Boroditsky, L. (2010), Subtle linguistic cues influence perceived blame and financial liability, *Psychonomic Bulletin and Review,* 17, 644–650.

12. Taylor, C., & Franklin, A. (2012), The relationship between color-object associations and color preference, *Psychonomic Bulletin and Review,* 19, 190–197.

13. Cvencek, D., Greenwald, A. G., & Meltzoff, A. N. (2011), Measuring implicit attitudes of four-year-olds: The preschool implicit association test, *Journal of Experimental Child Psychology,* 109, 187–200; Hill, S. E., & Flom, R. (2007), 18- and 24-month-olds' discrimination of gender-consistent and inconsistent activities, *Infant Behavior and Development,* 30, 168–173; Kuhn, D., Nash, S. C., & Brucken, L. (1978), Sex role concepts of two- and three-year-olds, *Child Development,* 49, 445–451.

14. Frisell, T., Pawitan, Y., Langstrom, N., & Lichenstein, P. (2012), Heritability, assortative mating and gender differences in violent crime, *Behavior Genetics,* in press.

15. Rowe, D. L., Jacobson, K. C., & van den Oord, E. J. C. G. (1999), Genetic and environmental influences on vocabulary IQ, *Child Development,* 1151–1162.

16. Kersten, A. W., & Smith, L. B. (2002), Attention to novel objects during verb learning, *Child Development,* 73, 93–109; Cheri, C. Y., Tardif, T., Chen, J., Pulverman, R. B., Zhu, L., & Meng, X. (2011), English- and Chinese-learning infants map novel labels to objects and actions differently, *Developmental Psychology,* 47, 1459–1471; Tomasello, M., Call, J., & Gluckman, A. (1997), Comprehension of novel communicative signs by apes and human children, *Child Development,* 68, 1067–1080; Moll, H., & Tomasello, M. (2004), 12- and 18-month-old infants follow gaze to spaces behind barriers, *Developmental Science,* 7, F1–F5; Grasse, G., & Tomasello, M. (2012), Two-year-old children differentiate test questions from genuine questions, *Journal of Child Language,* 39, 192–204; Hare, B. (2011), From hominoid to hominid—Mind: What changed and why? *Annual Review of Anthropology,* 40, 293–309.

17. Kagan, J. (1981), *The Second Year,* Cambridge, MA: Harvard University Press; Senju, A., Southgate, V., Snape, C., Leonard, M., & Csibra, G. (2011), Do 18-month-olds really attribute mental states to others? A critical test, *Psychological Science,* 22, 878–880; Warneken, F., & Tomasello, M. (2009), The roots of human altruism, *British Journal of Psychology,* 100, 455–471; Yamamoto, S., Humie, T., & Tanaka, M. (2012), Chimpanzees' flexible targeted helping based on an understanding of conspecifics' goals, *Proceedings of the National Academy of Sciences,* in press; Warneken, F., Hare, B., Melis, A. P., Hanus, D., & Tomasello, M. (2007), Spontaneous altruism by chimpanzees and young children,

PLoS Biology, 5, no. 184; Dean, L. G., Kendal, R. L., Schapiro, B., & Laland, K. N. (2012), Identification of the social and cognitive processes underlying human cumulative culture, *Science,* 335, 1114–1118.

18. Zahn-Waxler, C., Robinson, J. L., & Emde, R. N. (1992), The development of empathy in twins, *Developmental Psychology,* 28, 1038–1047.

19. Melis, A. P., Altrichter, K., & Tomasello, M. (2012), Allocation of resources to collaborators and free-riders in 3-year-olds, *Journal of Experimental Child Psychology,* in press.

20. Rossano, F., Rakoczy, H., & Tomasello, M. (2011), Young children's understanding of violations of property rights, *Cognition,* in press.

21. Sloane, S., Baillargeon, R., & Premack, D. (2012), Do infants have a sense of fairness? *Psychological Science,* 23, 196–204.

22. Kagan, J. (2009), *The Three Cultures,* New York: Cambridge University Press.

23. Allman, J. M., Tetreault, N. A., Hakeem, A. Y., & Park, S. (2011), Von economo neurons in apes and humans, *American Journal of Human Biology,* 23, 5–21; Damasio, A. (2011), *Self Comes to Mind: Constructing the Conscious Brain,* New York: Pantheon; Owen, A. M., Coleman, M. R., Boly, M., Davis, M. H., Laureys, S., & Pickard, J. D. (2006), Detecting awareness in the vegetative state, *Science,* 313, 1402; Gazzaniga, M. (2011), Interview with Michael Gazzaniga, *Annals of the New York Academy of Sciences,* 1224, 1–8.

24. Lewis, M., & Ramsay, D. (2004), Development of self-recognition, personal pronoun use, and pretend play during the 2nd year, *Child Development,* 75, 1821–1831; Bertenthal, B. I., & Fischer, K. W. (1978), Development of self-recognition in the infant, *Developmental Psychology,* 14, 44–50; Kartner, J., Keller, H., Chaudry, N., & Yovsi, R. D. (2012), The development of mirror self-recognition in different sociocultural contexts, *Monographs of the Society for Research in Child Development,* 77, 1–86.

25. Kagan, J. (1981), *The Second Year,* Cambridge, MA: Harvard University Press.

26. Kaneko, T., & Tomonaga, M. (2012), Relative contributions of goal representation and kinematic information to self-monitoring by chimpanzees and humans, *Cognition,* 125, 168–178.

27. Damasio, A. (1994), *Descartes' Error,* New York: G. P. Putnam.

28. Dobzhansky, T. (1973), Ethics and values in biological and cultural evolution, *Zygon,* 8, 261–281.

CHAPTER FOUR

1. Hagenaars, M. A., Stins, J. F., & Roelofs, K. (2012), Aversive life events enhance human freezing responses, *Journal of Experimental Psychology,* 141, 98–105.

2. Dana Jr., R. H. (1840), *Two Years Before the Mast,* New York: Harpers; Lansford, J. E., Bornstein, M. H., Dodge, K. A., Skinner, A. T., Putnick, D. L., et al. (2011), Attributions and attitudes of mothers and fathers in the United States, *Parenting,* 11, 199–213; Huttenlocher, J., Vasilyeva, M., Waterfall, H. R., Vevea, J. L., & Hedges, L. V. (2007), The varieties of speech to young children, *Developmental Psychology,* 43, 1062–1083; Tulkin, S. R., & Kagan, J. (1972), Mother-child interaction in the first year of life, *Child Development,* 43, 31–41; Minton, C., Kagan, J., & Levine, J. (1971), Maternal control and obedience in the two-year-old, *Child Development,* 42, 1873–1892; Stone, L. (1977), *The Family, Sex, and Marriage,* New York: Harper & Row; Lorber, M. F., & Egeland, B. (2011), Parenting and infant difficulty, *Child Development,* 82, 2006–2020; Georgas, J., Berry, J. W., van de Vijver, F. J. R., Kagitcibasi, C., & Poortinga, Y. H. (2006), eds., *Families Across Cultures,*

New York: Cambridge University Press; Kraus, M. W., Piff, P. K., Mendoza-Denton, R., Rheinschmidt, M. L., & Keltner, D. (2012), Social class, solipsism, and contextualism, *Psychological Review,* 119, 546–572.

3. Duyme, M. (1988), School success and social class, *Developmental Psychology,* 24, 203–206; Rowe, D. C., Jacobson, K. C., & van den Oord, E. J. C. G. (1999), Genetic and environmental influences on vocabulary IQ: Parental education level as moderator, *Child Development,* 70, 1151–1162; Tucker-Drob, E. M. (2012), Preschools reduce early academic achievement gaps, *Psychological Science,* 23, 310–319; Rumberger, R. W. (2011), *Dropping Out,* Cambridge, MA: Harvard University Press.

4. Roopnarine, J. L., Fouts, H. N., Lamb, M. E., & Lewis-Elligan, T. Y. (2005), Mothers' and fathers' behaviors toward their 3- to 4-month-old infants in lower-, middle-, and upper socioeconomic African-American families, *Developmental Psychology,* 41, 723–732; Fernald, L. C. H., Weber, A., Galasso, E., & Raitsifandrihamanana, L. (2011), Socioeconomic gradients in child development in a very low income population: evidence from Madagascar, *Developmental Science,* in press.

5. Henry, P. J. (2009), Low-status compensation: A theory for understanding the role of status in cultures of honor, *Journal of Personality and Social Psychology,* 97, 451–466; Miller, G. E., Chen, E., & Parker, K. J. (2011), Psychological stress in childhood and susceptibility to the chronic diseases of aging, *Psychological Bulletin,* 137, 959–997; Miller, G. E., Lachman, M. E., Chen, E., Gruenewald, T. L., et al. (2011), Pathways to resilience, *Psychological Science,* 22, 1591–1599; Patterson, P. H. (2011), *Infectious Behavior,* Cambridge, MA: MIT Press; Tung, J., Barreiro, L. B., Johnson, Z. P., Hansen, K. D., et al. (2012), Social environment is associated with gene regulatory variation in the rhesus macaque immune system, *Proceedings of the National Academy of Sciences,* April 16, in press; Cohen, S., Janicki-Deverts, D., Doyle, W. J., Miller, G. E., et al. (2012), Chronic stress, glucocorticoid receptor resistance, inflammation, and disease risk, *Proceedings of the National Academy of Sciences,* 109, 5995–5999; Sampson, R. J. (2012), *Great American City,* Chicago: University of Chicago Press; Blair, C., & Raver, C. C. (2012), Child development in the context of adversity, *American Psychologist,* 67, 309–318; Borghol, N., Suderman, M., McArdle, W., Racine, A., Hallett, M., et al. (2012), Associations with early-life socio-economic position in adult DNA methylation, *International Journal of Epidemiology,* 41, 62–74; Cavigelli, S. A., & Chaudry, H. S. (2012), Social status, glucocorticoids, immune function, and health, *Hormones and Behavior,* in press.

6. Updike, J. (1989), *Self-Consciousness: Memoirs,* New York: Knopf; MacDonald, M. P. (1999), *All Souls,* Boston, MA: Beacon Press; Shutts, K., Kinzler, K. D., Tredoux, C., & Spelke, E. S. (2011), Race preferences in children: Insights from South Africa, *Developmental Science,* 14, 1283–1291; Welten, S. C., Zeelenberg, M., & Breugelmans, S. M. (2012), Vicarious shame, *Cognition and Emotion,* in press; Vachon-Presseau, E., Roy, M., Martel, M. O., Albouy, G., Chen, J., Budell, L., et al. (2012), Neural processing of sensory and emotional-communicative information associated with the perception of vicarious pain, *NeuroImage,* in press; Sagiv, L., Toccas, S., & Hazan, O. (2012), Identification with groups, *Journal of Personality,* 80, 345–374; Murray, M. S., Neal-Barnett, A., Demmings, J. L., & Stadulis, R. E. (2012), The acting white accusation, racial identity, and anxiety in African-American adolescents, *Journal of Anxiety Disorders,* 26, 526–531.

7. Nozick, R. (1981), *Philosophical Explanations,* Cambridge, MA: Harvard University Press, p. vii.

8. Kermode, F. (1995), *Not Entitled,* New York: Farrar, Straus & Giroux.

9. Hobsbawm, E. (2002), *Interesting Times*, London: Allen Lane.

10. Grieshaber, K. (2011), Associated Press, May 15.

11. Piff, P. K., Martinez, A. G., & Keltner, D. (2012), Me against we, *Cognition and Emotion*, 26, 634–649.

12. Stellar, J. E., Manzo, V. M., Kraus, M. W., & Keltner, D. (2012), Class and compassion, *Emotion*, 12, 449–459.

13. Ferguson, N., & Gordon, M. (2007), Intragroup variability among Northern Irish Catholics and Protestants, *Journal of Social Psychology*, 147, 317–319.

14. Fuligni, A. J., Witkow, M., & Garcia, C. (2005), Ethnic identity and the academic adjustment of adolescents from Mexican, Chinese, and European backgrounds, *Developmental Psychology*, 41, 799–811; Kazin, A. (2011), *Alfred Kazin's Journals*, in Cook, R. M., ed., New Haven, CT: Yale University Press; Fuller-Rowell, T. E., & Doan, S. N. (2010), A safer course of academic success across ethnic groups, *Child Development*, 81, 1696–1713.

15. Pollock, L. A. (1983), *Forgotten Children*, New York: Cambridge University Press.

16. Erikson, E. H. (1963), *Childhood and Society*, New York: Norton.

17. Bowlby, J. (1969), *Attachment and Loss*, New York: Basic Books.

18. Kagan, J., Kearsley, R. B., & Zelazo, P. R. (1978), *Infancy: Its Place in Human Development*, Cambridge, MA: Harvard University Press; Rabin, A. I., & Beit-Hallahmi, B. (1982), *Twenty Years Later: Kibbutz Children Grown Up*, New York: Springer; Doyle, N. (2011), "The highest pleasure of which woman's nature is capable": Breast feeding and the sentimental maternal ideal in America, 1750–1860, *Journal of American History*, 97, 958–973; Tan, K. L. (2009), Bed sharing among mother-infant pairs in Klang district, Peninsular Malaysia and the relationship to breast-feeding, *Journal of Developmental and Behavioral Pediatrics*, 30, 420–425.

19. Ainsworth, M. D. S., Blehar, M. C., Waters, E., & Wall, S. (1978), *Patterns of Attachment*, Hillsdale, NJ: Erlbaum; Cicchetti, D., Rogosch, F. A., & Toth, S. C. (2011), The effect of child maltreatment and polymorphisms of the serotonin transporter and dopamine D4 receptor genes on infant attachment and intervention efficacy, *Development and Psychopathology*, 23, 357–362.

20. Burgess, K. B., Marshall, P. J., Rubin, K. H., & Nathan Fox, N. A. (2003), Infant attachment and temperament as predictors of subsequent externalizing problems and cardiac physiology, *Journal of Child Psychology and Psychiatry*, 44, 819–831.

21. Takahashi, K. (1986), Examining the Strange Situation procedure with Japanese mothers and 12-month-old infants, *Developmental Psychology*, 22, 265–270; Sagi, A., Van IJzendoorn, M. H., & Koren-Karie (1991), Primary appraisal of the Strange Situation, *Developmental Psychology*, 27, 587–596.

22. Blehar, M. C., Lieberman, A. F., & Ainsworth, M. D. S. (1977), Early face-to-face interaction and its relation to later infant-mother attachment, *Child Development*, 48, 182–194; Vaughn, B. E., Lefever, G. D., Seifer, R., & Barglow, P. (1989), Attachment behavior, attachment security, and temperament during infancy, *Child Development*, 60, 728–737; Crockenberg, S. B. M. (1981), Infant irritability, mother responsiveness, and social support influences on the security of infant-mother attachment, *Child Development*, 52, 857–865.

23. Vaughn, B., Egeland, B., Sroufe, L. A., & Waters, E. (1979), Individual differences in infant-mother attachment at twelve and eighteen months, *Child Development*, 59, 971–975; van den Boom, D. C., & Hoeksma, J. B. (1994), The effect of infant irritability on mother-infant interaction: A growth curve analysis, *Developmental Psychology*, 30, 581–590; Crognola, C. R., Tambelli, R., Spinelli, M., Gazzotti, S., Caprin, C., & Albizzati,

P. (2011), Attachment patterns and emotion responsivity to strangers in the second year, *Infant Behavior and Development,* 34, 136–151; Isabella, R. A., Belsky, J., & von Eye, A. (1989), Origins of infant-mother attachment: An examination of interactional synchrony during the infant's first year, *Developmental Psychology,* 25, 12–21; Kochanska, G. (2001), Emotional development in children with different attachment histories: The first three years, *Child Development,* 72, 474–490; Seifer, R., Schiller, M., Sameroff, A. J., Resnick, S., & Riordan, K. (1996), Attachment, maternal sensitivity, and infant development during the first year of life, *Developmental Psychology,* 32, 12–25; Nelson, C. A., Furtado, E. A., Fox, N. A., & Zeanah, C. H. (2009), The deprived human brain, *American Scientist,* 97, 222–229.

24. Fearon, R. M. P., & Belsky, J. (2004), Attachment and attention: protection in relation to gender and cumulative social-contextual adversity, *Child Development,* 75, 1677–1693; Sylva, K., Stein, A., Leach, P., Barnes, J., Malmberg, L. E. (2011), Effects of early child care on cognition, language, and task-related behaviors at 18 months: An English study, *British Journal of Developmental Psychology,* 29, 18–45; Jaffee, S. R., Van Hulle, C., & Rodgers, J. L. (2011), Effects of non-maternal care in the first 3 years on children's academic skills and behavioral functioning in childhood and early adolescence, *Child Development,* 82, 1076–1091; NICHD Early Child Care Research Network (1998), Early child care and self-control, compliance, and problem behavior at 24 and 36 months, *Child Development,* 69, 1145–1170; NICHD Early Child Care Research Network (1997), The effects of infant child care on infant-mother attachment security, *Child Development,* 68, 860–879; Fearon, R. D., Bakermans-Kranenburg, M. J., van IJzendoorn, M. H., Lapsley, A. M., & Roisman, G. I. (2010), The significance of insecure attachment and disorganization in the development of children's externalizing behavior, *Child Development,* 81, 435–456; Haltigan, J. D., Lambert, B. L., Seifer, R., Elkas, N. V., et al. (2012), Security of attachment and quality of mother-toddler social interaction in a high-risk sample, *Infant Behavior and Development,* 35, 83–93.

25. Sroufe, L. A., Caffino, B., & Carlson, E. A. (2010), Conceptualizing the role of early experience, *Developmental Review,* 30, 36–51; Goldberg, W. A., Prause, J., Lucas-Thompson, R., & Himsel, A. (2008), Maternal employment and children's achievement in context, *Psychological Bulletin,* 134, 77–108; Sroufe, L. A., Egeland, B., Carlson, E. A., & Collins, W. A. (2005), *The Development of the Person,* New York: Guilford; Raby, K. L., Cicchetti, D., Carlson, E. A., Cutuli, J. J., Englund, M. M., & Egeland, B. (2012), Genetic and caregiving-based contributions to infant attachment, *Psychological Science,* in press.

26. Feldman, R., Gordon, I., & Zagoory-Sharon, O. (2011), Maternal and paternal plasma, salivary, and urinary oxytocin in parent-infant synchrony, *Developmental Science,* 14, 752–761; Izard, C. E., Haynes, O. M., Chisholm, G., & Baak, K. (1991), Emotional determinants of infant-mother attachment, *Child Development,* 62, 906–917; Luijk, M. P. C. M., Tharner, A., Bakermans-Kranenburg, M. J., van IJzendoorn, M. H., et al. (2011), The association between parenting and attachment security is moderated by a polymorphism in the mineralocorticoid receptor gene, *Biological Psychology,* 88, 37–40.

27. Bowlby, J. (1969), *Attachment and Loss,* New York: Basic Books.

28. van der Horst, F. C. T. (2011), *John Bowlby—From Psychoanalysis to Ethology,* Malden, MA: Wiley-Blackwell; Fox, N. (1977), Attachment of kibbutz infants to mother and metatelet, *Child Development,* 48, 1228–1239.

29. Snow, M. E., Jacklin, C. N., & Maccoby, E. E. (1981), Birth order differences in peer sociability at 33 months, *Child Development,* 52, 589–595.

30. Kolak, N. M., & Vallins, B. C. (2011), Sibling jealousy in early childhood, *Infant Behavior and Development,* 20, 213–226; Abel, E. L., & Kruger, M. L. (2007), Performance of older versus younger brothers, *Perceptual and Motor Skills,* 105, 1117–1118.

31. Sulloway, F. J. (1996), *Born to Rebel,* New York: Pantheon.

32. Menesini, E., Canedeca, M., & Nocentini, A. (2010), Bullying among siblings, *British Journal of Developmental Psychology,* 28, 921–939; Ziv, I., & Hermel, O. (2011), Birth order effects on the separation process in young adults, *American Journal of Psychology,* 124, 261–273; Hudson, V. M. (1990), Birth order of world leaders, *Political Psychology,* 11, 583–601; Newman, J., & Taylor, A. (1994), Family training for political leadership, *Political Psychology,* 15, 435–442; Steinberg, B. S. (2001), The making of female presidents and prime ministers, *Political Psychology,* 22, 89–111.

33. Sulloway, F. J. (1996), *Born to Rebel,* New York: Pantheon.

34. Harriss, L., & Hawton, K. (2011), Deliberate self-harm in rural and urban regions: A comparative study of prevalence and patient characteristics, *Social Science and Medicine,* 73, 274–281; Donath, C., Grassel, E., Baier, D., Pfeiffer, C., et al. (2011), Alcohol consumption and binge drinking in adolescents, *BMC Public Health,* 11, 84–88; Harriss, L., & Hawton, K. (2011), Deliberate self-harm in rural and urban regions, *Social Science and Medicine,* 73, 274–281; Garcia-Retamero, R., Muller, S. M., & Lopez-Zafra, E. (2011), The malleability of gender stereotypes, *Journal of Social Psychology,* 151, 635–656; Chiu, M. S. (2012), The internal/external frame of reference model, big fish–little pond effect, and combined model for mathematics and science, *Journal of Educational Psychology,* 104, 87–107.

35. Kuwabara, M., & Smith, L. B. (2012), Cross-cultural differences in cognitive development, *Journal of Experimental Child Psychology,* 113, 20–35.

36. Chen, X., Hastings, P. D., Rubin, K. H., Chen, H., Cen, G., & Stewart, S. L. (1998), Child rearing attitudes and behavior inhibition in Chinese and Canadian toddlers, *Developmental Psychology,* 34, 677–686; Murray, J., Irving, B., Farrington, D., Colman, I., & Bloxsom, C. A. (2010), Very early predictors of conduct problems and crime, *Journal of Child Psychology and Psychiatry,* 51, 1198–1207; Collishaw, S., Maughan, B., Natarajan, L., & Pickles, A. (2010), Trends in adolescent emotional problems in England, *Journal of Child Psychology and Psychiatry,* 51, 885–894.

37. Jacobsson, G., Tysklind, F., & Werbart, A. (2011), Young adults talk about their problems, *Scandinavian Journal of Psychology,* 52, 282–289.

38. Hong, K. (2008), Is this maltreatment? unpublished thesis for Doctor of Education, Harvard Graduate School of Education, Cambridge, MA; Noll, J. G., Haralson, K. J., Butler, E. M., & Shenk, C. E. (2011), Childhood maltreatment, psychological disregulation, and risky sexual behaviors in female adolescents, *Journal of Pediatric Psychology,* 36, 742–752; Trickett, P. K., Noll, J. G., & Putnam, F. L. (2011), The impact of sexual abuse on female development, *Development and Psychopathology,* 23, 453–476; Kumsta, R., Stevens, S., Brookes, K., Schlotz, W., Castle, J., et al. (2010), 5HTT genotype moderates the influence of early institutional deprivation on emotional problems in adolescence, *Journal of Child Psychology and Psychiatry,* 51, 755–762; Scott, K. M., McLaughlin, K. A., Smith, D. A. R., & Ellis, D. M. (2012), Childhood maltreatment and DSM-IV adult mental disorders, *The British Journal of Psychiatry,* 200, 469–475.

39. Nelson, C. A., Zeanah, C. H., Fox, N. A., Marshall, P. J., Smyke, A. T., & Guthrie, D. (2007), Cognitive recovery in socially deprived young children, *Science,* 318, 1937–1940.

40. Tottenham, N., Hare, T. A., Quinn, B. T., McCarry, T. W., Nurse, M., et al. (2010), Prolonged institutional rearing is associated with atypically large amygdala volume and

difficulties in emotional regulation, *Developmental Science,* 13, 46–61; Kreppner, J. M., Rutter, M., Beckett, C., Castle, J., Colvert, E., et al. (2007), Normality and impairment following profound early institutional deprivation, *Developmental Psychology,* 43, 931–946; Rutter, M., O'Connor, T. G., & the English and Romanian adoptees study team (2004), Are there biological programming effects for psychological development? Findings from a study of Romanian adoptees, *Developmental Psychology,* 40, 81–94; Beckett, C., Maughan, B., Rutter, M., Castle, J., Colbert, E., Groothues, C., et al. (2006), Do the effects of early severe deprivation on cognition persist into early adolescence? Findings from the English and Romanian adoptee study, *Child Development,* 77, 696–711; Rutter, M., Sonuga-Barke, E. J., Beckett, C., Castle, J., et al. (2010), Deprivation-specific psychological patterns, *Monographs of the Society for Research in Child Development,* 75, 1–229.

41. McCall, R. B., van IJzendoorn, M. H., Juffer, F., Groark, C. J., & Groza, V. K. (2011), Children without permanent parents: Research, practice, and policy, *Monographs of the Society for Research in Child Development,* 76, 1–281.

42. Masten, A. S., & Narayan, A. J. (2012), Child development in the context of disaster, war, and terrorism, in Fiske, S. T., Schacter, D. L., & Taylor, S. E., eds., *Annual Review of Psychology,* Vol. 63 (pp. 227–258), Palo Alto, CA: Annual Reviews.

43. Horvitz, H. R. (2003), Nobel lecture: Worms, life and death, *Bioscience Reports,* 23, 239–303.

44. Joseph, S. (2011), *What Doesn't Kill Us: The New Psychology of Posttraumatic Growth,* New York: Basic Books.

CHAPTER FIVE

1. Bernfeld, S. (1929), *The Psychology of the Infant,* New York: Brentanos, pp. 138, 213.

2. Fenton, J. C. (1925), *The Practical Side of Babyhood,* Boston: Houghton Mifflin, pp. 293–294.

3. Yu, H., Majewska, A. K., & Sur, M. (2011), Rapid experience-dependent plasticity of synapse function and structure in ferret visual cortex, *Proceedings of the National Academy of Sciences,* 108, 21235–21240.

4. Grant, P. R., & Grant, B. (2008), *How Species Multiplied: The Radiation of Darwin's Finches,* Princeton: Princeton University Press.

5. Letzring, T. D., Wells, S. M., & Funder, D. C. (2006), Information and quality affect the realistic accuracy of personality judgment, *Journal of Personality and Social Psychology,* 91, 111–123; Macedo, A., Marques, M., Boss, S., Maia, B. R., Periera, T., et al. (2011), Mother's personality and infant temperament, *Infant Behavior and Development,* 34, 552–568; Samuel, D. B., Hopwood, C. J., Ansell, E. B., Morey, L. C., Sanislow, C. A., et al. (2011), Comparing the temporal stability of self report and interview assessed personality disorder, *Journal of Abnormal Psychology,* 120, 670–680; Hay, D. F., Mundy, L., Roberts, S., Carta, R., Waters, C. S., et al. (2011), Known risk factors for violence predict 12-month-old infants' aggressiveness with peers, *Psychological Science,* 22, 1205–1211; Marini, V. A., & Kurtz, J. E. (2011), Birth order differences in normal personality traits, *Personality and Individual Differences,* 51, 910–914; Loughman, S., Kuppens, P., Allik, J., Balazs, K., et al. (2011), Economic inequality is linked to biased self-perception, *Psychological Science,* 22, 1254–1258; Yarrow, M. R., Campbell, J. D., & Burton, R. V. (1970), Recollections of childhood, *Monographs of the Society for Research in Child Development,* 35, 1–83.

6. Kwan, V. S., Wojcik, S. P., Miron-Shatz, T., Votruba, A. M., & Olivola, C. Y. (2012), Effects of symptom presentation order on perceived disease risk, *Psychological Science,* 23, 381–385.

7. Kagan, J., & Snidman, N. (2004), *The Long Shadow of Temperament,* Cambridge, MA: Harvard University Press; Kagan, J., Snidman, N., Kahn, V., & Towsley, S. (2007), The preservation of two infant temperaments into adolescence, *Monographs of the Society for Research in Child Development,* 72, 1–75; Schwartz, C. E., Kunwar, P. S., Greve, D. N., Kagan, J., Snidman, N. C., & Bloch, R. B. (2011), A phenotype of early infancy predicts reactivity of the amygdala in male adults, *Molecular Psychiatry,* in press; Schwartz, C. E., Kunwar, P. S., Greve, D. N., Moran, D. N., Viner, J. C., et al. (2010), Structural differences in adult orbital and ventromedial prefrontal cortex predicted by infant temperament at four months of age, *Archives of General Psychiatry,* 67, 1–7; Lyons, D. M., Afarian, H., Schatzberg, A. F., Sawyer-Glover, A., & Mosely, M. E. (2002), Experience dependent asymmetric variation in monkeys in prefrontal morphology, *Behavioral Brain Research,* 136, 51–59; Young, L., Bechara, A., Tranel, D., Damasio, H., Hauser, M., & Damasio, A. (2010), Damage to ventromedial prefrontal cortex impairs judgment of harmful intent, *Neuron,* 65, 1–7; Grabenhorst, F., & Rolls, E. T. (2011), Value, pleasure and choice in the ventral prefrontal cortex, *Trends in Cognitive Science,* 15, 56–67; Mendez, M. F. (2010), The unique predisposition to criminal violations in frontotemporal dementia, *Journal of American Academy of Psychiatry and Law,* 38, 318–323; Groen-Blokhuis, M. M., Middeldorp, C. M., van Beijsterveldt, C. E. M., & Boomsma, D. I. (2011), Crying without a cause and being easily upset in two-year-olds, *Twin Research and Human Genetics,* 14, 393–400; Terasawa, Y., Fukushima, H., & Umeda, S. (2011), How does interoceptive awareness interact with the subjective experience of emotion? *Human Brain Mapping,* in press; Sroufe, L. A., Egeland, B., Carlson, E. A., & Collins, W. A. (2005), *The Development of the Person,* New York: Guilford.

8. Fontaine, N. M. G., McCrory, E. J. P., Boivin, M., Moffitt, T. E., & Viding, E. (2011), Predictors and outcomes of joint trajectories of callous-unemotional traits and current problems in childhood, *Journal of Abnormal Psychology,* 120, 730–742; Henry, B., Caspi, A., Moffitt, T. E., & Silva, P. A. (1996), Temperament and familial predictors of violent and nonviolent criminal convictions: Age 3 to age 18, *Developmental Psychology,* 32, 614–623; Segal, N. L. (2012), *Born Together—Reared Apart,* Cambridge, MA: Harvard University Press; Asendorpf, J. B., Denissen, J., Harrist, A. W., Zaia, A. F., Bates, J. E., Dodge, K. A., & Pettit, G. S. (1997), Subtypes of social withdrawal in early childhood, *Child Development,* 68, 278–294; Broidy, L. M., Nagin, D. S., Tremblay, R. E., Bates, J. E., Brame, B., et al. (2003), Developmental trajectories of childhood disruptive behaviors and adolescent delinquency, *Developmental Psychology,* 39, 222–245; Kubzansky, L. D., Martin, L. T., & Buka, S. L. (2004), Early manifestations of personality and adult emotional functioning, *Emotion,* 4, 364–377; Tarullo, A. R., Mliner, S., & Gunnar, M. R. (2011), Inhibition and exuberance in preschool classrooms, *Developmental Psychology,* 47, 1374–1388; Chapman, B. P., & Goldberg, L. R. (2011), Replicability and 40 year predictive power of childhood ARC types, *Journal of Personality and Social Psychology,* 101, 593–606; Caspi, A., & Bem, D. J. (1990), Personality continuity and change across the life course, in Pervin, L. A., ed., *Handbook of Personality* (pp. 549–575), New York: Guilford Press; Glenn, A. L., Raine, A., Venables, P. H., & Mednick, S. A. (2007), Early

temperamental and psychophysiological precursors of adult psychopathic personality, *Journal of Abnormal Psychology*, 116, 508–518; Feng, X., Shaw, D. S., & Silk, J. S. (2008), Developmental trajectories of anxiety symptoms among boys across early and middle childhood, *Journal of Abnormal Psychology*, 117, 32–47; Dannlowski, U., Stuhrmann, A., Beutelmann, V., Zwanger, P., et al. (2011), Limbic scars, *Biological Psychiatry*, in press.

9. Newman, D. L., Caspi, A., Moffitt, T. E., & Silva, P. A. (1997), Antecedents of adult interpersonal functioning, *Developmental Psychology*, 33, 206–217; Roberts, B. W., & DelVecchio, W. F. (2000), The rank-order consistency of personality traits from childhood to old age, *Psychological Bulletin*, 126, 3–25.

10. Friedman, N. D., Miyake, A., Robinson, J. L., & Hewitt, J. K. (2011), Developmental trajectories in toddlers' self-restraint predict individual differences in executive functions 14 years later, *Developmental Psychology*, 47, 1410–1430; Lanciano, T., & Curci, A. (2012), Type or dimension? A taxometric investigation of flashbulb memories, *Memory*, 20, 177–188.

11. Schiff, M., Duyme, M., Dumaret, A., Stewart, J., Tomkiewicz, S., & Feingold, J. (1978), Intellectual status of working-class children adopted early into upper-middle-class families, *Science*, 200, 1503–1504.

12. Skoe, E., & Kraus, N. (2012), A little goes a long way, *Journal of Neuroscience*, 32, 11507–11510.

13. Panhume, V. B. (2011), Sensitive periods in human development, *Cortex*, 47, 1126–1137.

14. Povinelli, D. J., Landry, A. M., Theall, L. A., Clark, B. R., & Castille, C. M. (1999), Development of young children's understanding that the recent past is causally bound to the present, *Developmental Psychology*, 35, 1426–1439; Bernard, S., Mercier, A., & Clement, F. (2011), The power of well-connected arguments, *Journal of Experimental Child Psychology*, 111, 128–135; Flavell, J. H., Green, F. L., & Flavell, E. R. (1995), Young children's knowledge about thinking, *Monographs of the Society for Research in Child Development*, 60, 1–113.

15. Ceci, S. J., Loftus, E. F., Leichtman, M. D., & Bruck, M. (1994), The possible role of source misattributions in the creation of false beliefs among preschoolers, *International Journal of Clinical and Experimental Hypnosis*, 42, 304–320.

16. Kagan, J. (1981), *The Second Year*, Cambridge, MA: Harvard University Press; Frick, A., & Newcombe, N. S. (2012), Getting the big picture, *Cognitive Development*, 27, 270–282.

17. Houde, O., Pineau, A., Leroux, G., Poirel, N., Perchey, G., et al. (2011), Functional magnetic resonance imaging study of Piaget's conservation-of-number task in preschool and school-age children, *Journal of Experimental Child Psychology*, 110, 332–346.

18. Piaget, J. (1952), *The Origins of Intelligence*, New York: International Universities Press.

19. Friedman, W. J. (1991), The development of children's memory for the time of past events, *Child Development*, 62, 639–655.

20. Pillemer, D. B. (1998), What is remembered about early childhood events? *Clinical Psychology Review*, 18, 895–917; St. Jacques, P. L., Conway, M. A., & Cabeza, R. (2011), Gender differences in autobiographical memory for everyday events, *Memory*, 19, 723–732.

21. Badger, J. R., & Shapiro, L. R. (2012), Evidence of a transition from perceptual to category induction in 3- to 9-year-old children, *Journal of Experimental Child Psychology,* 113, 131–146.

22. Holmes, K. J., & Wolff, P. (2012), Does categorical perception in the left hemisphere depend on language? *Journal of Experimental Psychology: General,* 141, 439–443.

23. Simcock, G., & Hayne, H. (2002), Breaking the barrier? Children fail to translate their preverbal memories into language, *Psychological Science,* 13, 225–231; Herrmann, P. A., Medin, D. L., & Waxman, S. R. (2011), When humans become animals, *Cognition,* 122, 74–79; Moncrieff, D. W. (2011), Dichotic listening in children, *Brain and Cognition,* 76, 316–322; Okamoto, M., Wada, Y., Yamaguchi, Y., Kimura, A., et al. (2009), Influences of food-name labels on perceived tastes, *Chemical Senses,* 34, 187–194; Endress, A. D., & Potter, M. C. (2012), Early conceptual and linguistic processes operate in independent channels, *Psychological Science,* 23, 235–245.

24. Flemming, T. M., & Kennedy, E. H. (2011), Chimpanzee (Pan troglodytes) relational matching, *Journal of Comparative Psychology,* 125, 207–215; Tribushina, E. (2012), Adjective semantics, world knowledge and visual context, *Journal of Psycholinguistics Research,* in press.

25. Gur, R. C., Richard, J., Calkins, M. E., Chiavacci, R., Hansen, J. A., et al. (2012), Age group and sex differences in performance on a computerized neurocognitive battery in children age 8–21, *Neuropsychology,* 26, 251–265.

26. Kogan, N., Connor, K., Gross, A., & Fava, D. (1980), Understanding visual metaphor, *Monographs of the Society for Research in Child Development,* 45, 1–78.

27. Petanjek, Z., Judas, M., Simic, G., Rasin, M. R., Uylings, H. B. M., Rakic, P., & Kostovic, I. (2011), Extraordinary neoteny of synactic spines in the human prefrontal cortex, *Proceedings of the National Academy of Sciences,* 108, 13281–13286; Ostby, Y., Tamnes, C. K., Fjell, A. M., & Walhoud, K. B. (2011), Morphometry and connectivity of the fronto-parietal verbal working memory network in development, *Neuropsychologia,* 49, 3854–3861; Shaw, P., Kabani, N. J., Lerch, J. P., Eckstrand, K., et al. (2008), Neurodevelopmental trajectories of the human cerebral cortex, *The Journal of Neuroscience,* 28, 3586–359; Hertig, M. M., Maxwell, E. C., Irvine, C., & Nagel, B. J. (2012), The impact of sex, puberty, and hormones on white matter microstructure in adolescents, *Cerebral Cortex,* 22, 1979–1992.

28. Kagan, J., Lapidus, D. R., & Moore, M. (1978), Infant antecedents of cognitive functioning, *Child Development,* 49, 1005–1023.

CHAPTER SIX

1. Posada, R., & Wainryb, C. (2008), Moral development in a violent society, *Child Development,* 79, 882–898; Goodwin, G. P., & Darley, J. M. (2012), Why are some moral beliefs perceived to be more objective than others? *Journal of Experimental Social Psychology,* 48, 250–256.

2. Hupka, R. B., Lenton, A. P., & Hutchison, K. A. (1999), Universal developmental emotion categories and natural language, *Journal of Personality and Social Psychology,* 77, 247–278.

3. Rutherford, M. B. (2004), Authority and autonomy: Moral choice in twentieth-century commencement speeches, *Sociological Forum,* 19, 583–609.

4. Kohlberg, L. (1981), *The Philosophy of Moral Development,* Vol. 1, New York: Harper & Row.

5. Schwartz, S. H., Cieciuch, J., Vecchione, M., Davidov, E., Fischer, R., et al. (2012), Refining the theory of basic individual values, *Journal of Personality and Social Psychology,* 103, 663–688.

6. Bersoff, D. M., & Miller, J. G. (1993), Culture, context, and the development of moral accountability judgments, *Developmental Psychology,* 29, 664–676; Fu, G., Xu, F., Cameron, C. A., & Heyman, G., & Lee, K. (2007), Cross-cultural differences in children's choices, categorizations, and evaluations of truths and lies, *Developmental Psychology,* 43, 278–293; Fu, G., Brunet, M. K., Yin, L., Xiaopan, D., Heyman, G. D., Cameron, C. A., & Lee, K. (2010), Chinese children's moral evaluation of lies and truths—Roles of context in parental individualism-collectivism tendencies, *Infant and Child Development,* 18, 498–515; Haidt, J., & Joseph, C. (2007), The moral mind, in Carruthers, T., Laurence, S., & Stich, S., eds., *The Innate Mind,* Vol. 3 (pp. 367–391), New York: Oxford University Press; Hardy, S. A., Walker, L. J., Olsen, J. A., Skalski, J. E., & Basinger, J. C. (2011), Adolescent naturalistic conceptions of moral maturity, *Social Development,* 20, 562–586; Parfit, D. (2012), *On What Matters,* New York: Oxford University Press.

7. Lewis, M., Stanger, C., & Sullivan, M. W. (1989), Deception in three-year-olds, *Developmental Psychology,* 25, 439–443.

8. Vaish, A., Carpenter, M., & Tomasello, M. (2011), Young children's responses to guilt displays, *Developmental Psychology,* 47, 1248–1262; Kline, M. (1980), *Mathematics,* New York: Oxford University Press, p. 134.

9. Sereny, G. (1999), *Cries Unheard: The Story of Mary Bell,* London: MacMillan; Escobedo, J. R., & Adolphs, R. (2010), Becoming a better person: Temporal remoteness biases autobiographical memories for moral events, *Emotion,* 10, 511–518.

10. Moller, S. J., & Tenenbaum, H. R. (2011), Danish majority children's reasoning about exclusion based on gender and ethnicity, *Child Development,* 82, 520–532; Graham, S., Doubleday, C., & Guarino, P. A. (1984), The development of relations between perceived controllability and the emotions of pity, anger, and guilt, *Child Development,* 55, 561–565.

11. Kuhn, D., Nash, S. C., & Brucken, L. (1978), Sexual concepts of 2- and 3-year-olds, *Child Development,* 49, 445–451; Jadva, V., Hines, M., & Golombok, S. (2010), Infants' preferences for toys, colors, and shapes, *Archives of Sexual Behavior,* 39, 1261–1273; Wondergen, T. R., & Friedlmeier, M. (2012), Gender and ethnic differences in smiling, *Sex Roles,* 67, 403–411.

12. Gilmore, D. G. (1990), *Manhood in the Making,* New Haven, CT: Yale University Press.

13. Stott, R. (2009), *Male Milieus in Nineteenth-Century America,* Baltimore: Johns Hopkins University Press.

14. Kimmel, M. S. (2012), *Manhood in America,* New York: Oxford University Press.

15. Hardy, S. A., Walker, L. J., Olsen, J. A., Skaliski, J. E., & Basinger, J. C. (2011), Adolescent naturalistic conceptions of moral maturity, *Social Development,* 20, 562–586; Wuest, J., Malcolm, J., & Merritt-Glan, M. (2010), Daughters' obligation to care in the context of past abuse, *Health Care for Women International,* 31, 1047–1067; Delacroix, E. (1951), *The Journal of Eugene Delacroix,* ed., Wellington, H., London: Phaidon.

16. Churchland, P. S. (2011), *Brain Trust,* Princeton: Princeton University Press.

17. Kazin, A. (2011), *Journals,* ed. Cook, R. M., New Haven, CT: Yale University Press.

18. Boehm, C. (2012), *Moral Origins,* New York: Basic Books.

19. Zeng, J., Konopka, G., Hunt, B. G., Preuss, T. M., Geschwind, D., & Yi, S. V. (2012), Divergent whole-genome methylation maps of human and chimpanzee brains reveal epigenetic basis of human regulatory evolution, *American Journal of Human Genetics,* 91, 455–465.

20. Riedl, K., Jensen, K., Call, J., & Tomasello, M. (2012), No third-party punishment in chimpanzees, *Proceedings of the National Academy of Sciences,* 109, 14824–14829.

21. Wilson, E. O. (2012), *The Social Conquest of Earth,* London: Liveright.

22. Song, M. J., Smetana, J. G., & Kim, S. Y. (1987), Korean children's conceptions of moral and conventional transgressions, *Developmental Psychology,* 23, 577–582; Harris, B. (1977), Developmental differences in the attribution of responsibility, *Developmental Psychology,* 13, 257–265.

23. Kojima, H. (1989), Family life and child development in early modern Japan, *Presented at the Tenth Biennial Meeting of the International Society for the Study of Behavioral Development,* Jydaskala, Finland, July; Nachman, S. R. (1984), Shame and moral aggression on a Melanesian atoll, *Journal of Psychoanalytic Anthropology,* 7, 336–365.

24. Barash, D. P. (1979), *Whisperings Within,* London.

25. Aksan, N., & Kochanska, G. (2005), Conscience in childhood, *Developmental Psychology,* 41, 506–516; Loke, I. C., Heyman, G. D., Forgie, J., McCarthy, A., & Lee, K. (2011), Children's moral evaluations of reporting the transgressions of peers, *Developmental Psychology,* 47, 1757–1762; Smetana, J. G., Rote, W. M., Jambon, M., Tasopoulos-Chan, M., Villalobos, M., & Comer, J. (2012), Developmental changes and individual differences in young children's moral judgments, *Child Development,* 83, 683–696.

26. Smetana, J. G. (1981), Preschool children's conceptions of moral and social rules, *Child Development,* 52, 1333–1336; Harkness, S., Edwards, C. P., & Super, C. (1981), Social roles and moral reasoning, *Developmental Psychology,* 17, 595–603; Sakharov, A. (1990), *Memoirs,* New York: Alfred Knopf.

27. Long. S., Mollen, D., & Smith, N. (2012), College women's attitudes toward sex workers, *Sex Roles,* 66, 117–127.

28. Eisenstadt, S. N. (1996), *Japanese Civilization,* Chicago: University of Chicago Press; Airenti, G., & Angeleri, R. (2011), Situation-sensitive use of insincerity, *British Journal of Developmental Psychology,* 29, 765–782.

29. Sandel, M. (2012), *What Money Can't Buy,* New York: Farrar, Straus & Giroux.

30. De Millo, R. (2011), *Abelard to Apple,* Cambridge, MA: MIT Press.

31. Callahan, D. (2003), *What Price Better Health? Hazards of the Research Imperative,* Berkeley: University of California Press.

32. Walker, L. J., & Pitts, R. C. (1998), Naturalistic conceptions of moral maturity, *Developmental Psychology,* 34, 403–419.

33. Kloep, M., & Hendry, L. B. (2010), Letting go or holding on? *British Journal of Developmental Psychology,* 28, 817–834; Rachman, S. (2010), Betrayal: A psychological analysis, *Behaviour Research and Therapy,* 48, 304–311; Way, N. (2011), *Deep Secrets,* Cambridge, MA: Harvard University Press.

34. Eiseley, L. (1971), *The Night Country,* New York: Scribner's.

35. Guterl, F. (2012), *The Fate of the Species,* London: Bloomsbury.

36. Fang, F. C., Steen, R. G., & Casadevall, A. (2012), Misconduct accounts for the majority of retracted scientific publications, *Proceedings of the National Academy of Sciences,* 109, 17028–17033.

37. McDade, T. W. (2012), Early environments and the ecology of inflammation, *Proceedings of the National Academy of Sciences,* 109, Suppl. 2: 17281–17288.

CHAPTER SEVEN

1. Rolls, E. (2012), *Neuroculture: On the Implications of Brain Science,* New York: Oxford University Press.

2. Churchland, P. S., & Winkielman, P. (2012), Modulating social behavior with oxytocin, *Hormones and Behavior,* 61, 392–399.

3. Herzmann, G., Young, B., Bird, C. W., & Curran, T. (2012), Oxytocin can impair memory for social and non-social visual objects, *Brain Research,* in press; Lischke, A., Gamer, M., Berger, C., Grossmann, A., et al. (2012), Oxytocin increases amygdala reactivity to threatening scenes in females, *Psychoneuroendocrinology,* in press; Fischer-Shofty, M., Levkovitz, Y., & Shamay-Tsoory, S. G. (2012), Oxytocin facilitates accurate perception of competition in men and kinship in women, *Social Cognitive and Affective Neurosciences,* in press; Cardoso, C., Ellenbogen, M., & Linnen, A. M. (2012), Acute intranasal oxytocin improves positive self-perceptions of personality, *Psychopharmacology,* 220, 741–749; Bartz, J., Simeon, D., Hamilton, H., Kim, S., et al. (2012), Oxytocin can hinder trust and cooperation in borderline personality disorder, *Social Cognitive and Affective Neuroscience,* 6, 556–563; MacDonald, E., Dadds, M. R., Brennan, J. L., Wallman, S. K., Levy, F., & Cauchi, A. J. (2011), A review of safety, side effects, and subjective reactions to intranasal oxytocin in human research, *Psychoneuroendocrinology,* 36, 1114–1126; Wittfoth-Schardt, D., Grunding, J., Wittfoth, M., Lanfermann, H., Heinrich, M., Domes, G., et. al. (2012), Oxytocin modulates neural reactivity to children's faces as a function of social salience, *Neuropsychopharmacology,* 37, 1799–1807.

4. Darwin, C. (1872), *The Expression of the Emotions in Man and Animals,* London: John Murray; Barrett, L. F. (2011), Was Darwin wrong about emotional expressions? *Current Directions in Psychological Science,* 20, 400–406; Shariff, A. F., & Tracy, J. L. (2011), What are emotional expressions for? *Current Directions in Psychological Science,* 20, 395–399; Ekman, P. (1992), An argument for basic emotions, *Cognition and Emotion,* 6, 169–200; Barrett, L. F. (2012), Emotions are real, *Emotion,* 12, 413–429.

5. Basile, B., Bassi, A., Calcagnini, G., Strano, S., Caltagirone, C., et al. (2012), Direct stimulation of the autonomic nervous system modulates activity of the brain at rest and when engaged in a cognitive task, *Human Brain Mapping,* in press.

6. Tateuchi, T., Itoh, K., & Nakada, T. (2012), Neural mechanisms underlying the orienting response to subject's own name, *Psychophysiology,* 49, 786–791.

7. Bruneau, E. G., & Saxe, R. (2010), Attitudes towards the outgroup are predicted by activity in the precuneus in Arabs and Israelis, *NeuroImage,* 52, 1704–1711.

8. Wagner, U., N'Diaye, K., Ethofer, T., & Vuilleimier, P. (2011), Guilt-specific processing in the prefrontal cortex, *Cerebral Cortex,* 21, 2461–2470; de Jong, P. J., van Overveld, M., & Peters, M. L. (2011), Sympathetic and parasympathetic responses to a core disgust video clip as a function of disgust propensity and sensitivity, *Biological Psychology,* 88, 174–179; Langner, R., Kellerman, T., Boers, F., Sturm, W., et al. (2011), Modality-specific perceptual expectations selectively modulate baseline activity in auditory, somatosensory, and visual cortices, *Cerebral Cortex,* 21, 2850–2862; Klucken, T., Schweckendiek,

J., Koppe, G., Merz, J. C., et al. (2011), Neural correlates of disgust and fear conditioned responses, *Neuroscience,* in press.

9. Kuhn, S., & Gallinat, J. (2012), The neural correlates of subjective pleasantness, *NeuroImage,* 61, 289–294.

10. Pamuk, O. (2006), The beauty of landscape resides in its melancholy, *World Literature Today,* 80, 42–43.

11. Soto, J. A., Levenson, R W., & Ebling, R. (2005), Cultures of moderation and expression, *Emotion,* 5, 154–165; Briggs, J. (1970), *Never in Anger,* Cambridge, MA: Harvard University Press; Bauer, P., Stennes, L., & Haight, J. (2003), Representation of the inner self, *Memory,* 11, 27–42; Schwerdrfeger, A. (2004), Predicting autonomic activity to public speaking, *International Journal of Psychophysiology,* 52, 217–224; Heider, K. (2011), *The Cultural Context of Emotion,* New York: Palgrave Macmillan; Tenenbaum, H. R., Ford, S., & Alkhedairy, B. (2011), Telling stories, *British Journal of Developmental Psychology,* 29, 707–721; Fischer, A. H., Rodriguez, H., Masquera, P. M., van Vianen, A., & Manstead, A. S. R. (2004), Gender and culture differences in emotion, *Emotion,* 4, 87–94; Fessler, D. M. T. (1999), Toward an understanding of the universality of second order emotions, in Hinton, A. L., ed., *Biocultural Approaches to the Emotions* (pp. 75–116), New York: Cambridge University Press; Fogel, A. R., Midgley, K. J., Delaney-Busch, N., & Holcomb, P. J. F. (2012), Processing emotion and taboo in a native vs. a second language, paper presented at the fifty-second annual meeting of the Society for Psychophysiological Research, New Orleans, LA, September 19–23, Poster 1-96; Smith, M., Hubbard, J. A., & Laurenceau, J. D. (2011), Profiles of anger control in second grade children, *Journal of Experimental Child Psychology,* 110, 213–226; Wilkins, R., & Gareis, E. (2006), Emotion expression and the locution "I love you," *International Journal of Intercultural Relations,* 30, 51–75; Steiner, A. R. W., & Coan, J. A. (2011), Prefrontal asymmetry predicts affect, but not beliefs about affect, *Biological Psychology,* 88, 65–71; Hirst, W., Phelps, E. A., Buckner, R. L., Budson, A. E., et al. (2009), Long-term memory for the terrorist attack of September 11, *Journal of Experimental Psychology,* 138, 161–176.

12. Camras, L. A., Meng, C., Ujiie, T., Dharamsi, S., Miyake, K., et al. (2002), Observing emotion in infants, *Emotion,* 2, 179–193.

13. Heller, A. S., Greischar, L. L., Honor, A., Anderle, M. J., & Davidson, R. J. (2011), Simultaneous acquisition of corrugator electromyography and functional magnetic imaging, *NeuroImage,* 58, 930–934.

14. Cacioppo, J. T., & Gardner, W. L. (1999), Emotion, in Spence, T., Darley, J. M., & Foss, D. J., eds., *Annual Review of Psychology,* Vol. 50 (pp. 191–214), Palo Alto, CA: Annual Reviews.

15. Rozin, P., Fallon, A., & Augustoni-Ziskind, M. L. (1985), The child's conception of food: The development of contamination sensitivity to disgusting substances, *Developmental Psychology,* 21, 1075–1079.

CHAPTER EIGHT

1. Kessler, R. C., Avenevoli, S., Costello, J., Georgiades, K., et al. (2012), Prevalence, persistence, and sociodemographic correlates of DSM-IV disorders in the National Comorbidity Survey Replication Adolescent Supplement, *Archives of General Psychiatry,* 69, 372–380.

2. Le Brocque, R. M., Hendrikz, J., & Kenardy, J. A. (2011), The course of post-traumatic stress in children, *Journal of Pediatric Psychology,* 35, 637–645; Wang, J., Iannotti, R. J., Luk,

J. W., & Nansel, T. R. (2011), Co-occurrence of victimization from five subtypes of bullying, *Journal of Pediatric Psychology,* 35, 1103–1112; Melhem, N. M., Porta, G., Shamseddeen, W., Payne, M. W., & Brent, D. A. (2011), Grief in children and adolescents bereaved by sudden parental death, *Archives of Journal of Psychiatry,* 68, 911–919; Kendler, K. S., Eaves, L. J., Loken, E. K., Pedersen, N. L., et al. (2011), The impact of environmental experiences on symptoms of anxiety and depression across the life span, *Psychological Science,* 22, 1343–1352.

3. Beckett, S. (1958), *Endgame,* New York: Grove Press.

4. Kaess, M., Hille, M., Parzer, P., Maser-Gluth, C., et al. (2011), Alterations in the neuroendrocrinological stress response to acute psychosocial stress in adolescents engaged in nonsuicidal self-injury, *Neuroendocrinology,* in press.

5. Leboyer, M., Soreca, I., Scott, J., Frye, M., Henry, C., Tamouza, R., & Kupfer, D. J. (2012), Can bipolar disease be viewed as a multi-system inflammatory disease? *Journal of Affective Disorders,* 141, 1–10.

6. Kessler, R. C., Avenevoli, S., Costello, J., Georgiades, K., et al. (2012), Prevalence, persistence, and sociodemographic correlates of DSM-IV disorders in the National Comorbidity Survey Replication Adolescent Supplement, *Archives of General Psychiatry,* 69, 372–380.

7. Schuster, D. (2011), *Neurasthenia Nation,* New Brunswick, NJ: Rutgers University Press.

8. McHugh, P. R. (2008), *Try to Remember,* Washington, DC: Dana Press; Rutter, M. (2011), Research review: Child psychiatric diagnosis and classification, *Journal of Child Psychology and Psychiatry,* 52, 647–660; Diamantopoulou, S., Verhulst, F. C., & van der Ende (2011), Gender differences in the development and adult outcome of co-occurring depression and delinquency in adolescence, *Journal of Abnormal Psychology,* 120, 644–655; Monroe, S. M., & Harkness, K. L. (2011), Recurrences in major depression, *Psychological Review,* 118, 655–674.

9. Lacey, N. (2010), American imprisonment in comparative perspective, *Daedalus,* summer issue, 102–114; Western, B., & Pettit, B. (2010), Incarceration and social inequality, *Daedalus,* summer issue, 8–19; Herrenkohl, T. I., Kosterman, R., Mason, W. A., Hawkins, J. D., McCarthy, C. A., & McCauley, E. (2010), Effects of childhood conduct problems and family adversity on health, health behaviors, and service use in early childhood, *Development and Psychopathology,* 22, 655–665; Martin, M. T. T., Conger, R. D., Schofield, T. J., Dogan, S. T., Widaman, K. F., et al. (2010), Evaluation of the interactionist model of socioeconomic status and problem behavior, *Development and Psychopathology,* 22, 695–713.

10. Troy, A. S., Wilhelm, F. H., Shallacross, A. J., & Mauss, I. B. (2010), Seeing the silver lining, *Emotion,* 10, 783–795; Kar, N., Mohapatra, P. K., Nayak, K. C., Pattanaik, P., Swain, S. P., & Kar, H. C. (2007), Post-traumatic stress disorder in children and adolescents one year after a super-cyclone in Orissa, India, *BMC Psychiatry,* 7, 8–14; Marx, B. P., Foley, K. M., Feinstein, B. A., Wolf, E. J., Kaloupek, D. G., & Keane, T. M. (2010), Combat-related guilt mediates the relations between exposure to combat-related abusive violence and psychiatric diagnoses, *Depression and Anxiety,* 10, 1–7; Kroneman, M., Verheij, R., Tacken, M., & van der Zee, J. (2010), Urban-rural health differences, *Health Place,* 16, 893–902.

11. Feiring, C., Taska, L., & Lewis, M. (2002), Adjustment following sexual abuse, *Developmental Psychology*, 38, 78–92.

12. Vickery, K. (2010), Widen the psychiatric gaze, *Transcultural Psychiatry*, 47, 263–391; Johansen, J. P., Tarpley, J. W., Le Doux, J. E., & Blair, H. T. (2010), Neural substrates for expectation-modulated fear learning in the amygdala and periaqueductal gray, *Nature Neuroscience*, 13, 979–986; Pillemer, D. B. (1998), *Momentous Events, Vivid Memories*, Cambridge, MA: Harvard University Press.

13. Greenwood, T. A., Lazzeroni, L. C., Murray, S. S., Cadenhead, K. S., et al. (2011), Analysis of 94 candidate genes and 12 endophenotypes for schizophrenia from the consortium on the genetics of schizophrenia, *American Journal of Psychiatry*, 168, 930–946; Hallmayer, J., Cleveland, S., Torres, A., Phillips, J., Cohen, B., et al. (2011), Genetic heritability and shared environmental factors among twin pairs with autism, *Archives of General Psychiatry*, in press; Benros, M. E., Nielson, P. R., Nordentoft, M., Eaton, W. W., et al. (2011), Autoimmune diseases and severe infections as risk factors for schizophrenia, *American Journal of Psychiatry*, 168, 1303–1310; Clarke, M. C., Tanskannen, A., Huttunen, M., Leon, D. A., et al. (2011), Increased risk of schizophrenia from additive interaction between infant motor developmental delay and obstetric complications, *American Journal of Psychiatry*, 168, 1295–1302; Butler, T. C., Benayoun, M., Wallace, E., van Dranglen, W., et al. (2012), Evolutionary constraints on visual cortex architecture from the dynamics of hallucinations, *Proceedings of the National Academy of Sciences*, 109, 606–609; Lieberman, J. A., Stroup, T. S., & Perkins, D. O. (2012), eds., *Schizophrenia*, Washington, DC: American Psychiatric Association; Cole, V. T., Apud, J. A., Weinberger, D. R., & Dickinson, D. (2012), Using latent class growth analysis to form trajectories of premorbid adjustment in schizophrenia, *Journal of Abnormal Psychology*, 121, 388–395; Boshes, R. A., Manschrek, T. C., & Konigsberg, W. (2012), Genetics of the schizophrenias, *Harvard Review of Psychiatry*, 20, 119–129.

14. Ting, J. T., Peca, J., & Feng, G. (2012), Functional consequences of mutations in postsynaptic scaffolding proteins and relevance to psychiatric disorders, *Annual Review of Neuroscience*, 35, 49–71.

15. Barglow, P., & Murphy, T. (2011), An early Greek portrayal of a mad mind, *American Journal of Psychiatry*, 168, 893; Kyaga, S., Lichenstein, P., & Boman, M. (2011), Creativity and mental disorder, *The British Journal of Psychiatry*, 199, 373–379.

16. Levy, D., Ronemos, M., Yamrom, B., Lee, Y., Leotta, A., et al. (2011), Rare de novo and transmitted copy-number variations in autistic spectrum, *Neuron*, 70, 886–897; Paul, R., Fuerst, Y., Ramsay, G., Chawarska, K., & Klin, A. (2011), Out of the mouths of babes, *Journal of Child Psychology and Psychiatry*, 52, 588–598; Hallmayer, J., Cleveland, S., Torres, A., Phillips, J., et al. (2011), Genetic heritability and shared environmental factors among twin pairs with autism, *Archives of General Psychiatry*, 68, 1095–1102; Kaiser, M. D., Hudac, C. M., Shultz, S., Lee, S. M., et al. (2010), Neural signatures of autism, *Proceedings of the National Academy of Sciences*, 107, 21223–21228; Nordahl, C. W., Schulz, R., Yang, X., Buonocore, M. H., et al. (2012), Increased rate of amygdala growth in children aged 2 to 4 years with autism spectrum disorders, *Archives of General Psychiatry*, 69, 53–61; Teitelbaum, O., Benton, T., Shah, P. K., Prince, A., et al. (2004), Eshkol-Wachman movement notation in diagnosis, *Proceedings of the National Academy of Sciences*, 101, 11909–11914.

17. Tsai, L. Y. (2012), Sensitivity and specificity: DSM-IV versus DSM-5 criteria for autism spectrum disorder, *American Journal of Psychiatry,* 169, 1009–1111.

18. Lamers, F., Burstein, M., He, J. P., Avenevoli, S., Angst, J., & Merikangas, K. R. (2012), Structure of major depressive disorder in adolescents and adults in the US general population, *British Journal of Psychiatry,* 201, 143–150.

19. Uher, R., Caspi, A., Houts, R., Sugden, K., Williams, B., et al. (2011), Serotonin transporter gene moderates childhood maltreatments's effects on persistent but not single-episode depression, *Journal of Affective Disorders,* 135, 56–65.

20. Kaufman, J., Yang, B. Z., Douglas-Palumberi, H., Houshyar, S., Lipschitz, D., et al. (2004), Social supports and serotonin transporter gene moderate depression in maltreated children, *Proceedings of the National Academy of Sciences,* 101, 17316–17321.

21. Lyons, D. M., Yang, C., Sawyer-Glover, A. M., Moseley, M. E., & Schatzberg, A. F. (2001), Early life stress and inherited variation in monkey hippocampal volume, *Archives of General Psychiatry,* 58, 1145–1151; Nordquist, N., & Oreland, L. (2010), Serotonin, genetic variability, behavior, and psychiatric disorders—A review, *Uppsala Journal of Medical Science,* 115, 2–10; Zink, C. F., Stein, J. L., Kemp, L., Hakima, S., & Meyer-Lindeberg, A. (2010), Vasopressin modulates medial prefrontal cortex—Amygdala circuitry during emotion processing in humans, *Journal of Neuroscience,* 30, 7017–7022; Grool, A. M., van der Graaf, Y., Mali, W. P. T. M., Witkamp, T. D., et al. (2011), Location and progression of cerebral small-vessel disease and atrophy, and depressive symptom profiles, *Psychological Medicine,* in press; Uher, R., Caspi, A., Houts, R., Sugden, K., et al. (2011), Serotonin transporter gene modulates childhood maltreatment's effects on persistent but not single episode depression, *Journal of Affective Disorders,* 135, 56–65; Meis, L. A., Erbes, C. R., Kaler, M. E., Arbis, P. A., et al. (2011), The structure of PTSD among two cohorts of returning soldiers, *Journal of Abnormal Psychology,* 120, 807–818; Scott, K. M., Smith, D. A. R., & Ellis, P. M. (2012), A population study of childhood maltreatment and asthma diagnosis, *Psychosomatic Medicine,* 74, 817–823.

22. Torgersen, S., Myers, J., Reichborn-Kjennerud, T., Roysamb, E., Kubarych, T. S., & Kendler, K. (2012), The heritability of cluster B personality disorders assessed both by personal interview and questionnaire, *Journal of Personality Disorders,* in press.

23. Zhao, J., Yang, X., Xiao, R., Zhang, X., Aguilera, D., & Zhao, J. (2012), Belief system, meaningfulness, and psychopathology associated with suicidality among Chinese college students, *BMC Public Health,* in press.

24. Joiner, T. (2010), *Myths About Suicide,* Cambridge, MA: Harvard University Press; Kukkei, A., Rotsiki, V., Arapaki, A., & Richardson, C. (2011), Adolescents' self-reported suicide attempts, *The Journal of Child Psychology and Psychiatry,* in press; Thompson, A. H., Deuva, C. S., & Phare, S. (2011), The suicidal process, *Social Psychiatry and Psychiatric Epidemiology,* in press; Cleary, A. (2011), Suicidal action, emotional expression, and the defense of masculinities, *Social Science and Medicine,* in press; Sarma, K., & Kola, S. (2010), The socio-demographic profile of hanging suicides in Ireland from 1980 to 2005, *Journal of Forensic and Legal Medicine,* 17, 374–377; Tidemaim, D., Runeson, B., Waern, M., Frisell, T., et al. (2011), Familial clustering of suicide risk, *Psychological Medicine,* in press; Kasen, S., Wickramaratne, P., Gameroff, M. J., & Weissman, M. M. (2011), Religiosity and resilience in persons at high risk for major depression, *Psychological Medicine,* in press; Abela, J. R. Z., Stolow, D., Mineka, S., Yao. S., et al. (2011), Cognitive vulnerability

to depressive symptoms in adolescents in urban or rural China, *Journal of Abnormal Psychology,* 120, 765–778.

25. Swanson, S. A., Crow, S. J., Le Grange, D., Swendsen, J., & Merikangas, K. R. (2011), Prevalence and correlates of eating disorders in adolescents, *Archives of General Psychiatry,* 68, 714–723; Mehler, P. S., & Andersen, A. E. (2010), *Eating Disorders,* 2nd ed., Baltimore: Johns Hopkins University Press; Stryer, S. B. (2009), *Anorexia,* Santa Barbara, CA: Greenwood Press.

26. Myers-Schulz, B., & Koenigs, M. (2011), Functional anatomy of ventromedial prefrontal cortex, *Molecular Psychiatry,* in press; Ray, R. D., & Zald, D. H. (2012), Anatomical insights into the interaction of emotion and cognition in the prefrontal cortex, *Neuroscience and Biobehavioral Reviews,* 36, 479–501; Schwartz, C. E., Kunwar, P. S., Greve, D. N., Moran, L. R., Viner, J. C., et al. (2010), Structural differences in adult orbital and ventromedial prefrontal cortex predicted by infant temperament at 5 months of age, *Archives of General Psychiatry,* 67, 78–84; Schwartz, C. E., Kunwar, P. S., Greve, D. N., Kagan, J., et al. (2012), A phenotype of early infancy predicts reactivity of the amygdala in male adult, *Molecular Psychiatry,* 17, 1042–1050; Boes, A. D., Grafft, A. H., Joshi, C., Chuang, N. A., et al. (2011), Behavioral effects of congenital ventromedial prefrontal cortex malformation, *BMC Neurology,* 11, 151; Chen, C. H., Gutierrez, E. D., Thompson, W., Panizzon, M. S., et al. (2012), Hierarchical genetic organization of human cortical surface area, *Science,* 335, 1634–1636; Amemori, K., & Graybiel, A. M. (2012), Localized microstimulation of primate pregenual cingulated cortex induces negative decision-making, *Nature Neuroscience,* 15, 776–785; Hudson, J. L., Dodd, H. F., Lyneham, H. J., & Bovopoulos, N. (2011), Temperament and family environment in the development of anxiety disorder, *Journal of the American Academy of Child and Adolescent Psychiatry,* 50, 1255–1264; Dyson, M. W., Klein, D. N., Olino, T. M., Dougherty, L. R., & Durbin, C. E. (2011), Social and non-social behavioral inhibition in preschool-age children, *Child Psychiatry and Human Development,* 42, 390–405; Monosov, I. E., & Hikosaka, O. (2012), Regionally distinct processing of rewards and punishments by the primate ventromedial prefrontal cortex, *The Journal of Neuroscience,* 32, 10318–10330.

27. Diekhof, E. K., Geier, K., Falkai, P., & Gruber, O. (2011), Fear is only as deep as the mind allows, *NeuroImage,* 58, 275–285; van Kesteren, M. T. R., Ruiter, D. J., Fernandez, G., & Henson, R. N. (2012), How schema and novelty augment memory formation, *Trends in Neuroscience,* in press; Young, C. B., Wu, S. S., & Menon, V. (2012), The neurodevelopmental basis of math anxiety, *Psychological Science,* 23, 492–501.

28. Baillargeon, R. H., Sward, G. D., Keenan, K., & Cao, G. (2011), Opposition-defiance in the second year of life, *Infancy,* 16, 418–434; Skeem, J. L., Polaschek, D. L. L., Patrick, C. J., & Lilienfeld, S. O. (2011), Psychopathic personality, *Psychological Science in the Public Interest,* 12, 95–162; Breslau, J., Saito, N., Tancredi, D. J., Nock, M., & Gilmore, S. E. (2012), Classes of conduct disorder symptoms and their life course correlates in a U. S. national sample, *Psychological Medicine,* in press; Fair, D. E., Bathula, D., Nikolas, M. A., & Nigg, J. T. (2012), Distinct neuropsychological subgroups in typically developing youth inform heterogeneity in children with ADHD, *Proceedings of the National Academy of Sciences,* 109, 6769–6774.

29. Loeber, R., & Pardini, D. (2008), Neurobiology and the development of violence, *Philosophical Transactions of the Royal Society of London, B Social Sciences,* 363, 2491–2503.

30. Fergusson, D. M., Boden, J. M., & Harwood, L. J. (2010), Classification of behavior disorders in adolescence, *Journal of Abnormal Psychology*, 119, 699–712; Galera, C., Cote, S. M., Bouvard, M. P., Pingault, J. B., et al. (2011), Early risk factors for hyperactivity-impulsivity and inattention from 17 months to 8 years, *Archives of General Psychiatry*, 68, 1261–1275; Casavant, V., Chae, C., Sherwani, A., & Perlmutter, L. C. (2012), Subclinical orthostatic pulse pressure confirms mothers' ratings of ADHD in preschoolers, *Psychophysiology*, 49, 708–712; Fair, D. A., Bathula, D., Nikolas, M. A., & Nigg, J. T. (2012), Distinct neuropsychological subgroups in typically developing youth inform heterogeneity in children with ADHD, *Proceedings of the National Academy of Sciences*, 109, 6769–6774; Koenigs, M. (2012), The role of prefrontal cortex in psychopathy, *Review of Neuroscience*, 23, 253–262.

31. De Bries-Bouw, M., Popma, A., Vermeiren, R., Doreleijers, T. A. H., et al. (2011), The predictive value of low heart rate and heart rate variability during stress for reoffending in delinquent male adolescents, *Psychophysiology*, 48, 1596–1603.

32. Ramachandran, V. S. (1998), Consciousness and body image, *Philosophical Transactions of the Royal Society of London, B Biological Sciences*, 353, 1851–1859.

33. Veale, D., & Daniels, J. (2011), Cosmetic clitoridectomy in a 33-year-old woman, *Archives of Sexual Behavior*, 41, 9831–9834.

34. Lilenfeld, S. O., Waldman, I. D., Landfield, K., Watts, A. L., Rubenzer, S., et al. (2012), Fearless dominance and the U.S. presidency, *Journal of Personality and Social Psychology*, 103, 489–505.

35. Volkow, N. D., Wang, G. J., Newcom, J. H., Kollins, S. H., et al. (2011), Motivation deficit in ADHD is associated with dysfunction of the dopamine reward pathway, *Molecular Psychiatry*, 16, 1147–1154; Forrest, D., & McHale, I. G. (2011), Gambling and problem gambling among young adolescents in Great Britain, *Journal of Gambling Studies*, in press; Nikolaidis, A., & Gray, J. R. (2010), ADHD and the DRD4 exon III 7-repeat polymorphism, *Social, Cognitive and Affective Neuroscience*, 5, 189–193; Shumay, E., Chen, J., Fowler, J. S., & Volkow, N. D. (2011), Genotype and ancestry modulate brain's DAT availability in healthy humans, *PLoS One*, 6, no. 22754; Fiorillo, C. D. (2011), Transient activation of midbrain dopamine neurons by reward risk, *Neuroscience*, 197, 162–171; Langley, K., Heron, J., O'Donovan, M. C., Owen, M. J., & Thapor, A. (2010), Genotype link with extreme antisocial behavior, *Archives of General Psychiatry*, 67, 1317–1323.

36. Rigoni, D., Pellegrini, S., Matriotti, V., Cozza, A., Mechelli, A., et al. (2010), How neuroscience and behavioral genetics improve psychiatric assessment, *Frontiers in Behavioral Neuroscience*, 4, 160–166.

37. Aspinwall, L. G., Brown, T. R., & Tabery, J. (2012), The double-edged sword, *Science*, 337, 846–849.

38. Goffman, A., personal communication, June 2012.

39. Karevold, E., Roysamb, E., Ystrom, E., & Mathiesen, K. S. (2009), Predictors and pathways from infancy to symptoms of anxiety and depression in early adolescence, *Developmental Psychology*, 45, 1051–1060; Poongothai, S., Pradeepa, R., Ganesan, A., & Mohan, V. (2009), Prevalence of depression in a large urban South Indian population— The Chennai urban rural epidemiology study (CURES-70), *PLoS One*, 4, no. 7185; Velthorst, E., Nieman, D. H., Veling, W., Klaassen, R. M., et al. (2011), Ethnicity and baseline symptomatology in patients with an at risk mental state for psychosis, *Psychological Medicine*, in press; Hammen, C., Hazel, N. A., Brennan, P. A., & Najman, J. (2011), Intergenerational transmission and continuity of stress and depression, *Psychological Medicine*,

in press; Shanahan, L., Copeland, W. E., Costello, E. J., & Angold, A. (2011), Child-, adolescent-, and young-adult-onset depressions, *Psychological Medicine*, 41, 2265–2274; Tambs, K., Kendler, K. S., Reichborn-Kjennerud, T., Aggen, S. H., et al. (2011), Genetic and environmental contributions to the relationship between education and anxiety disorders, *Acta Psychiatrica Scandinavia*, in press; Tyrer, P., Cooper, S., Crawford, M., Dupont, S., et al. (2011), Prevalence of health anxiety problems in medical clinics, *Journal of Psychosomatic Research*, 71, 392–394; Slopen, N., Fitzmaurice, G. M., Williams, D. R., & Gilman, S. E. (2012), Common patterns of violence experiences and depression and anxiety among adolescents, *Social Psychiatry and Psychiatric Epidemiology*, in press; Goldston, D. B., Molock, S. D., Whitbeck, L. B., Murakami, J. L., et al. (2008), Cultural considerations in adolescent suicide prevention and treatment, *American Psychologist*, 63, 14–31; Werner, E., & Smith, R. S. (1982), *Vulnerable but Invisible*, New York: McGraw-Hill; Pickett, K. E., & Wilkinson, R. G. (2010), Inequality: An underacknowledged source of mental illness and disorder, *British Journal of Psychiatry*, 197, 426–428; Wicks, S., Hjern, A., & Dalman, C. (2010), Social risk or genetic liability for psychosis? *American Journal of Psychiatry*, 167, 1240–1246; Simm, R. W., & Nath, L. E. (2004), Gender and emotion, *American Journal of Sociology*, 109, 1137–1176; Langton, E. G., Collishaw, S., Goodman, R., Pickles, A., & Maughan, B. (2011), An emerging income differential for adolescent emotional problems, *Journal of Child Psychology and Psychiatry*, 52, 1081–1088; Kosidou, K., Dalman, C., Lundberg, M., Hallqvist, J., Isacsson, G., & Magnusson, C. (2011), Socioeconomic status and risk of psychological distress and depression in the Stockholm public health cohort, *Journal of Affective Disorders*, 134, 160–167; Reinholdt-Dunne, M. L., Esbjorn, B. H., Hoyer, M., Dahl, S., et al. (2011), Emotional difficulties in seventh grade children in Denmark, *Scandinavian Journal of Psychology*, 52, 433–439; Pih, K. K., De La Rosa, M., Rugh, D., & Mao, K. (2011), Different strokes for different gangs? *Sociological Perspectives*, 51, 473–494; Rios, R., & Zautra, A. J. (2011), Socioeconomic disparities in pain, *Health Psychology*, 30, 58–66.

40. van Bokhoven, H. (2011), Genetic and epigenetic networks in intellectual disabilities, *Annual Review of Genetics*, 45, in press; Marinelli, C. V., Angelelli, P., Di Filippo, G., & Zoccolotti, P. (2011), Is developmental dyslexia modality specific? *Neuropsychologia*, in press; Leppanen, P. H., Hamalainen, J. A., Guttorm, T. K., Eklund, K. M., et al. (2012), Infant brain responses associated with reading-related skills before school and at school age, *Neurophysiology Clinics*, 42, 35–41; Svensson., I., Nilsson, S., Wahlstrom, J., Jemas, M. M., et al. (2011), Familial dyslexia in a large Swedish family, *Behavior Genetics*, 41, 443–449.

41. Dean, K., Stevens, H., Mortensen, T. B., Murray, R. M., et al. (2010), Full spectrum of psychiatric outcomes among offspring with parental history of mental disorder, *Archives of General Psychiatry*, 67, 822–827.

42. Tennessen, J. A., Bigham, A. W., O'Connor, T. D., Fu, W., Kenny, E. E., et al. (2012), Evolution and functional impact of rare coding variation from deep sequencing of human exomes, *Science*, 337, 64–69.

43. Gibbons, R. D., Hur, K., Brown, C. H., Davis, J. M., & Mann, J. J. (2012), Benefits from antidepressants, *Archives of General Psychiatry*, 69, 572–579.

44. Paris, J. (2010), *The Use and Misuse of Psychiatric Drugs*, Oxford, England: Wiley-Blackwell; Walsh, R. (2011), Lifestyle and mental health, *American Psychologist*, 66, 579–592; van Holstein, M., Aarts, E., van der Schaff, M. E., Geurts, D. E. M., et al., Human cognitive flexibility depends on dopamine D2 receptor signaling, *Psychopharmacology*,

218, 567–578; Noble, L. (2011), *Medicinal Cannibalism in Early Modern English Literature and Culture,* New York: Palgrave Macmillan; Sugg, R. (2011), *Mummies, Cannibals and Vampires,* London, England: Routledge; Myung, W., Lim, S. W., Kim, S., Chung, J. W., et al. (2012), Serotonin transporter genotype and function in relation to antidepressant response in Koreans, *Psychopharmacology,* in press; Faria, V., Appel, L., Ahs, F., Linnman, C., Pissiota, A., et al. (2012), Amygdala subregions tied to SSRI and placebo response in patients with social anxiety disorder, *Neuropsychopharmacology,* 37, 2222–2232.

45. Paris, J. (2010), *The Use and Misuse of Psychiatric Drugs,* Oxford, England: Wiley-Blackwell.

46. Ginzburg, D. M., Bohn, C., Hofling, V., Weck, F., Clark, D. M., & Stangier, U. (2012), Treatment specific competence predicts outcome in cognitive therapy for social anxiety disorder, *Behaviour Research and Therapy,* 50, 747–752.

47. Frank, J. D. (1961), *Persuasion and Healing: A Comparative Study of Psychotherapy,* 1st ed., Baltimore: Johns Hopkins University Press.

48. Sloan, D. M., Marx, B. P., Bovin, M. J., Feinstein, B. A., & Gallagher, M. W. (2012), Written exposure as an intervention for PTSD, *Behaviour Research and Therapy,* 50, 627– 635.

49. Martin, D. M., Alonzo, A., Ho, K. A., Player, M., Mitchell, P. B., Sachdev, P., & Loo, C. K. (2012), Continuation transcranial direct current stimulation for the prevention of relapse in major depression, *Journal of Affective Disorders,* in press.

50. Throop, E. A. (2009), *Psychotherapy, American Culture, and Social Policy,* New York: Palgrave MacMillan, p. 29; Mirsalimi, H. (2010), Perspectives of an Iranian psychologist practicing in America, *Psychotherapy Series Research Practice,* 47, 151–161.

CHAPTER NINE

1. Greenwald, A. G. (2012), There is nothing so theoretical as a good method, *Perspectives on Psychological Science,* 7, 99–108.

2. Tsukayama, E., Toomey, S. L., Faith, M. S., & Duckworth, A. L. (2010), Self-control as a protective factor against overweight status in the transition from childhood to adolescence, *Archives of Pediatric and Adolescent Medicine,* 164, 631–635.

3. Marsh, H. W., & Hau, K. T. (2003), Big-fish-little-pond effect on academic self-concept, *American Psychologist,* 58, 364–376.

4. Pinker, S. (2011), *The Better Angels of Our Nature: Why Violence Has Declined,* New York: Viking.

5. Sword, H. (2012), *Stylish Academic Writing,* Cambridge, MA: Harvard University Press.

6. Carter, A. J., & Feeney, W. E. (2012), Taking a comparative approach, *PLoS One,* 7, no. 2440.

7. Albert, F. W., Somel, M., Carneiro, N., Aximu-Petri, A., Halbwax, M., et al. (2012), A comparison of brain gene expression levels in domesticated and wild animals, *PLoS Genetics,* 8, no. 1002962.

8. Brodersen, K. H., Wiech, K., Lomakina, E. I., Lin, C. S., Buhmann, J. M., et al. (2012), Decoding the perception of pain from fMRI using multivariate pattern analysis, *NeuroImage,* 63, 1162–1170.

9. Shallice, T., & Cooper, R. (2011), *The Organisation of Mind,* New York: Oxford University Press.

10. Deacon, T. (2012), *Incomplete Nature,* New York: W. W. Norton.

11. McManus, J. N., Li, W., & Gilbert, C. D. (2011), Adaptive shape processing in primary visual cortex, *Proceedings of the National Academy of Sciences,* 108, 9739–9746.

12. Robinson, M. (2011), *Absence of Mind,* New Haven: Yale University Press.

13. Menzel, R., & Fischer, J., eds. (2012), *Animal Thinking,* Cambridge, MA: MIT Press.

14. Caria, A., de Falco, S., Venuti, P., Lee, S., et al. (2012), Species-specific responses to human infant faces in the premotor cortex, *NeuroImage,* in press.

15. Pagel, M. (2012), *Wired for Culture,* New York: W. W. Norton.

16. Marder, E. (2012), Neuromodulation of neuronal circuits, *Neuron,* 76, 1–11.

17. Pearce, T. M., & Moran, D. W. (2012), Strategy-dependent encoding of planned arm movements in the dorsal premotor cortex, *Science,* 337, 984–988.

18. Bode, S., Bogler, C., Soon, C. S., & Haynes, J. D. (2012), The neural encoding of guesses in the human brain, *NeuroImage,* 59, 1924–1931.

19. Teitelbaum, P. (2012), Some useful insights for graduate students beginning their research in physiological psychology, *Behavior and Brain Research,* 231, 234–249.

INDEX

Index